Pearson New International Edition

The Art and Science of Leadership
Afsaneh Nahavandi
Sixth Edition

BPP Professional Education
32-34 Colmore Circus
Birmingham B4 6BN
Phone: 0121 345 9843

Pearson Education Limited
Edinburgh Gate
Harlow
Essex CM20 2JE
England and Associated Companies throughout the world

Visit us on the World Wide Web at: www.pearsoned.co.uk

© Pearson Education Limited 2014

ISBN 10: 1-292-02074-1
ISBN 13: 978-1-292-02074-7

British Library Cataloguing-in-Publication Data
A catalogue record for this book is available from the British Library

Printed in the United States of America

Table of Contents

1. Definition and Significance of Leadership
Afsaneh Nahavandi
1

2. The Global and Cultural Contexts
Afsaneh Nahavandi
29

3. Early Theories: The Foundations of Modern Leadership
Afsaneh Nahavandi
63

4. New Models of Leadership: Neocharisma, Inspiration, and the Relationship Followers
Afsaneh Nahavandi
103

5. Individual Differences and Traits
Afsaneh Nahavandi
137

6. Power
Afsaneh Nahavandi
181

7. Other Leadership Perspectives: Upper Echelon and Leadership of Nonprofits
Afsaneh Nahavandi
217

8. Participative Management and Leading Teams
Afsaneh Nahavandi
251

9. Leading Change
Afsaneh Nahavandi
283

Index
313

Definition and Significance of Leadership

From Chapter 1 of *The Art and Science of Leadership*, 6/e. Afsaneh Nahavandi. Copyright © 2012 by Pearson Education. Published by Prentice Hall. All rights reserved.

1

Definition and Significance of Leadership

*An army of sheep led by a lion would defeat an army
of lions led by a sheep.*

—ARAB PROVERB

After studying this chapter, you will be able to:

- Define leadership and leadership effectiveness.
- Explain why people need leadership.
- Discuss the major obstacles to effective leadership.
- Compare and contrast leadership and management.
- List the roles and functions of leaders and managers.
- Summarize the debate over the role and impact of leadership in organizations.

Who is a leader? When are leaders effective? These age-old questions appear simple, but their answers have kept philosophers, social scientists, scholars from many disciplines, and business practitioners busy for many years. It is easy to define bad leadership. Defining and understanding effective leadership, however, is more complex. This chapter defines leadership and its many aspects, roles, and functions and explores the impact of leaders on people and organizations.

EFFECTIVE LEADERSHIP

We recognize effective leaders when we work with them or observe them. However, leadership is a complex process, and there are many different definitions of leadership and leadership effectiveness.

What Is Leadership? Who Is a Leader?

Dictionaries define *leading* as "guiding and directing on a course" and as "serving as a channel." A leader is someone with commanding authority or influence. Researchers, for their part, have developed many working definitions of leadership. Although these definitions share several elements, they each consider different aspects of leadership. Some define leadership as an integral part of the group process (Green, 2002; Krech and Crutchfield, 1948). Others define it primarily as an influence process (Bass, 1960; Cartwright, 1965; Katz and Kahn, 1966). Still others see leadership as the initiation of structure (Homans, 1950) and the instrument of goal achievement. Several even consider leaders to be servants of their followers (Greenleaf, 1998). Despite the differences, the various definitions of leadership share three common elements:

- First, leadership is a *group phenomenon*; there can be no leaders without followers. As such, leadership always involves interpersonal influence or persuasion.
- Second, leadership is *goal directed* and *action oriented*; leaders play an active role in groups and organizations. They use influence to guide others through a certain course of action or toward the achievement of certain goals.
- Third, the presence of leaders assumes some form of *hierarchy within a group*. In some cases, the hierarchy is formal and well defined, with the leader at the top; in other cases, it is informal and flexible.

Combining these three elements, we can define a leader as any person who influences individuals and groups within an organization, helps them establish goals, and guides them toward achievement of those goals, thereby allowing them to be effective. This broad and general definition includes those who have formal leadership titles and many who do not. Wendy Kopp, CEO and founder of Teach for America, considers teaching successfully to be leadership (George and Kopp, 2007). For Cinta Putra, CEO of 3n (National Notification Network), having passion is key to leadership (Bisoux, 2008). Lorraine Monroe, executive director of the School Leadership Academy in New York City, a nonprofit organization she founded in 1997, is surprised at the number of leaders who lack the basic leadership skills. She states, "The job of a good leader is to articulate a vision that others are inspired to follow" (Canabou and Overholt, 2001: 98). For the CEO of the Container Store, "leadership and communication are the same thing. Communication is leadership" (Bryant 2010). In all these examples, the leader moves followers to action and helps them achieve goals, but each focuses on a different element that constitutes leadership.

> A leader is a person who influences individuals and groups within an organization, helps them establish goals, and guides them toward achievement of those goals, thereby allowing them to be effective.

What Is Effectiveness? When Is a Leader Effective?

What does it mean to be an effective leader? As is the case with the definition of leadership, effectiveness can be defined in various ways. Some researchers, such as Fred Fiedler, creator of the Contingency Model, define leadership effectiveness in terms of group performance. According to this view, leaders are effective when their group performs well. Other models—for example, Robert House's Path-Goal Theory, consider follower satisfaction as a primary factor in determining leadership effectiveness; leaders are effective when their followers are satisfied. Still others, namely researchers working on the transformational and visionary leadership models, define effectiveness as the successful implementation of large-scale change in an organization.

The definitions of leadership effectiveness are as diverse as the definitions of organizational effectiveness. The choice of a certain definition depends mostly on the point of view of the person trying to determine effectiveness and on the constituents who are being considered. For cardiologist Stephen Oesterle, senior vice president for medicine and technology at Medtronic, one the world's biggest manufacturer of medical devices and pacemakers, restoring lives is both a personal and an organizational goal (Tuggle, 2007). Barbara Waugh, a 1960s civil rights and antidiscrimination activist and once personnel director and worldwide change manager of Hewlett-Packard Laboratories (often known as the "World's Best Industrial Research Laboratory"—WBIRL), defines effectiveness as finding a story that is worth living: "You decide what you want your life to be about and go after it" (Marshall, 2009: 3). The mayor of Denver, Colorado, John Hickenlooper, focuses on an inclusive style, cooperation, aligning people's self-interest, and getting buy-in from the people who are affected by his decisions (Goldsmith, 2008). For Father Francis Kline (1948–2006), the abbot of Mepkin monastery outside Charleston, South Carolina, divine service, helping the community, and being self-sufficient are the indicators of effectiveness (Salter, 2000a). At Chick-fil-A, the U.S. chicken fast-food chain, effectiveness is defined as a satisfied customer, which can only be achieved by providing "attentive, sincere, memorable service" (McGregor, 2004a: 83).

Clearly, no one way best defines what it means to be an effective leader. Fred Luthans (1989) proposes an interesting twist on the concept of leadership effectiveness by distinguishing between effective and successful managers. According to Luthans, effective managers are those with satisfied and productive employees, whereas successful managers are those who are promoted quickly. After studying a group of managers, Luthans suggests that successful managers and effective managers engage in different types of activities. Whereas effective managers spend their time communicating with subordinates, managing conflict, and training, developing, and motivating employees, the primary focus of successful managers is not on employees. Instead, they concentrate on networking activities such as interacting with outsiders, socializing, and politicking.

The internal and external activities that effective and successful managers undertake are important to allowing leaders to achieve their goals. Luthans, however, finds that only 10 percent of the managers in his study are effective *and* successful. The results of his study present some grave implications for how we might measure our leaders' effectiveness and reward them. To encourage and reward performance, organizations need to reward the leadership activities that will lead to effectiveness rather than those that lead to quick promotion. If an organization cannot achieve balance, it quickly might find itself with a flashy but incompetent leaders who reached the top primarily through networking rather than through taking care of their employees and achieving goals. Barbara Waugh, mentioned earlier, considers the focus on what she call the "vocal visionary" at the expense of the "quiet implementer" one of the reasons many organizations do not achieve their full potential (Marshall, 2009). Joe Torre, the famed Los Angeles Dodgers baseball coach believes that solid quiet and steady managers who do not brag are the one who get things done (Hollon, 2009).

Ideally, any definition of leadership effectiveness should consider all the different roles and functions that a leader performs. Few organizations, however, perform such a thorough analysis, and they often fall back on simplistic measures. For example, stockholders and financial analysts consider the CEO of a company to be effective if company stock prices keep increasing, regardless of how satisfied the company's employees are. Politicians are effective if the polls indicate their popularity is high and if they are reelected. A football coach is effective when his team is winning. Students' scores on standardized tests determine a school principal's effectiveness. In all cases, the factors that make the leader effective are highly complex and multifaceted.

Consider the challenge faced by the executives of the *New York Times*, one of the world's most respected newspapers. In 2002, the paper won a record seven Pulitzer prizes, a clear measure of success. A year later, however, the same executive editor team that had led the company in that success was forced to step down because of plagiarism scandals (Bennis, 2003). The executive team's hierarchical structure, autocratic leadership style, and an organizational culture that focused on winning and hustling were partly blamed for the scandals (McGregor, 2005a). By one measure, the *Times* was highly effective; by another, it failed a basic tenet of the journalistic profession. Politics further provide examples of the complexity of defining leadership effectiveness. Consider former U.S. President Clinton, who, despite being tried and impeached in the U.S. Senate, maintained his popularity at the polls in 1998 and 1999; many voters continued to consider him effective. Hugo Chavez, the president of Venezuela, continues his hold on power and on many of his followers' hearts. He is adored by his supporters, who point to his social programs for the poor, and loathed by his detractors, who point to his dictatorial style (Profile, 2009). Similarly, President Evo Morales of Bolivia, who was recently reelected with a 63 percent majority, has been credited with revolutionary changes to help the country's indigenous populations (Bajak, 2009). However, his opponents worry about the disregard for human rights and the growing power of the central government (Bajak, 2009). Whether any of these leaders is considered effective or not depends on one's perspective. General Motors' recent troubles further illustrate the need for a broad definition of effectiveness. Bob Lutz, the vice chairman of the company, believes that one of GM's failures was that it focused too much on internal effectiveness and not enough on the customer, suggesting that both internal and external perspectives are essential to being an effective leader and organization (Amos, 2010).

The common thread in all these examples of effectiveness is the focus on outcome. To judge their effectiveness, we look at the results of what leaders accomplish. Process issues, such as employee satisfaction, are important but are rarely the primary indicator of effectiveness. Nancy McKintry, CEO of Wolters Kluwer, an information services company states, "At the end of the day, no matter how much somebody respects your intellect or your capabilities or how much they like you, in the end it is all about results in the business context" (Bryant, 2009c). The executive editorial team at the *New York Times* delivered the awards despite creating a difficult and sometimes hostile culture. Voters in the United States liked President Clinton because the economy flourished under his administration. Hugo Chavez survives challenges because he can point to specific accomplishments. Evo Morales highlights the gains indigenous people have made.

> Overall, leaders are effective when their followers achieve their goals, can function well together, and can adapt to changing demands from external forces.

One way to take a broad view of effectiveness is to consider leaders effective when their group is successful in maintaining internal stability and external adaptability while achieving goals. Overall, leaders are effective when their followers achieve their goals, can function well together, and can adapt to changing demands from external forces. The definition of leadership effectiveness, therefore, contains three elements:

1. *Goal achievement*, which includes meeting financial goals, producing quality products or services, addressing the needs of customers, and so forth
2. *Smooth internal processes*, including group cohesion, follower satisfaction, and efficient operations
3. *External adaptability*, which refers to a group's ability to change and evolve successfully

LEADING CHANGE

The Container Store

Chances are that if you have engaged in a home or office organization project, you have heard of the Container Store. The company offers creative, practical, and innovative solutions to a multitude of storage problems and has established a track record of success, having grown 15 to 20 percent a year since 1978 (Containing Culture, 2007). But organizing and storing things is not the only thing the company is known for. It has been consistently ranked one the best companies to work for by *Fortune* magazine, most recently in 2009. The company considers its employees its greatest asset, and having a unique culture and treating its employees well are other areas in which it claims leadership (Container Store Web site, 2010). "It's based on communication and understanding that you're part of something larger than just moving that box. . . . You're part of a very special company that is helping customers" is how Amy Carovillano, the company's vice president of logistics, describes the culture (Drickhamer, 2005: 16). Kip Tindell, cofounder of the company, states, "At the Container Store we are fond of saying communication is leadership—they are the same thing" (Bryant, 2010).

Tindell says, "We talk about getting the customer to dance . . . every time she goes into the closet . . . because the product has been designed and sold to her so carefully" (Birchall, 2006). Achieving this level of service takes a dedicated and, the company believes, happy group of employees that the company carefully recruits (often mostly through its existing employees) and trains. Whereas in comparable companies, the average salesperson gets about 8 hours of training during the first year on the job, it is not unusual for Container Store salespeople to get over 200 hours of training before a new store opens (Birchall, 2006). In addition to a family-friendly work environment, the company covers close to 70 percent of its employees' health-care insurance costs, pays 50 to 100 percent higher wages than its competitors' pay, and provides flexible shifts to accommodate its employees' work–life balance.

The investment in employees has paid off. The Container Store has an annual turnover of about 10 percent, compared with 90 percent for most retail stores. Its founders, Kip Tindell and Garrett Boone, believe that the unique culture and the success of the company are inseparable. Their belief is so strong that when they were looking for investors, Boone stated, "Anyone who does not embrace our culture would be a lousy investor. Everything that we do is built on culture. How in the world would we otherwise have been able to create an environment where people love to come to work?" (Containing Culture, 2007: 24).

Sources: Birchall, J., 2006. "Training improves shelf life," *Financial Times*, March 8. http://search.ft.com/ftArticle?queryText=Kip+Tindell&y=0&aje=true&x=0&id=060307009431 (accessed July 8, 2007); Bryant, A. 2010. "The Container Store," *The New York Times,* March 12, http://www.nytimes.com/2010/03/14/business/14corners.html (accessed May 13, 2010); Containing Culture. 2007. *Chain Store Age* (April): 23–24; Duff, M., 2006. "Container Store Web site," http://www.containerstore.com/careers/cultureAndBenefits.html (accessed January 4, 2010). "New president named at Container Store," *DSN Retailing Today*, January 23: 3, 21; Drickhammer, D., 2005. "The Container Store: Thinking outside the box," *Material Handling Management*, June: 16, 18.

Why Do We Need Leaders?

Leadership is a universal phenomenon across cultures. Why is leadership necessary? Why do people accept to be led? What problems does leadership address? What needs does it fulfill? Although these can be philosophical and even spiritual questions about the human condition, discussions that are beyond the scope of this book, there are more practical and maybe simpler reasons why we need leaders. These reasons closely fall in line with the functions and roles that leaders play and are related to the need or desire to be in collectives. Overall, we need leaders:

- **To keep groups orderly and focused.** Human beings have formed groups and societies for close to 50,000 years. Whether the formation of groups itself is an instinct or whether it is based on the need to accomplish complex tasks too difficult for individuals to undertake, the existence of groups requires some form of organization and hierarchy. Whereas individual group members may have common goals, they also have individual needs and aspirations. Leaders are needed to pull the individuals together, organize, and coordinate their efforts.
- **To accomplish tasks.** Groups allow us to accomplish tasks that individuals alone could not undertake or complete. Leaders are needed to facilitate that accomplishment, to provide goals and directions and coordinate activities. They are the instrument of goal achievement.
- **To make sense of the world.** Groups and their leaders provide individuals with a perceptual check. Leaders help us make sense of the world, establish social reality, and assign meaning to events and situations that may be ambiguous.
- **To be romantic ideals.** Finally, as some researchers have suggested (e.g., Meindl and Ehrlick, 1987), leadership is needed to fulfill our desire for mythical or romantic figures who represent us and symbolize our own and our culture's ideals and accomplishments.

With all its benefits, the need for leadership presents a sizeable challenge. The presence of leaders necessarily and unavoidably creates hierarchy and inequality in groups and with it the potential for abuse. Even though some consider any unequal relationship inherently wrong and suggest that leadership should only be used to describe egalitarian, participative, and willing relationships between leaders and followers (Hicks cited in Wren, 2006), such a view would limit who would be considered a leader. We often follow people we agree with most, but not necessarily all the time. We are willing to tolerate some degree of inequality in exchange for the security of groups and the ability to reach our individual and collective goals. Culture greatly affects how much people tolerate inequality. Managing the inequality inherent in leader–follower relationships and the use of proper power by leaders are essential components of leadership.

OBSTACLES TO EFFECTIVE LEADERSHIP

In any setting, being an effective leader is a challenging task. Even with a clear definition of leadership and what makes a leader effective, being effective is not easy. Meanwhile, organizations pay a heavy price for ineffective, incompetent, or unethical leadership (Bedeian and Armenakis, 1998; Kellerman, 2004). The keys to becoming an effective leader are knowledge, experience, practice, and learning from one's mistakes. Unfortunately, many organizations do not provide an environment in which leaders can practice new skills, try out new behaviors, and observe their impact. In most cases, the price for making mistakes is so high that new leaders and managers opt for routine actions.

Without such practice and without failure, it is difficult for leaders to learn how to be effective. The experience of failure, in some cases, may be a defining moment in the development of a leader (George, 2009). The question is, therefore, what are the obstacles to becoming an effective leader? Aside from different levels of skills and aptitudes that might prevent a leader from being effective, several other obstacles to effective leadership exist:

- First, organizations face considerable *uncertainty* that creates pressure for quick responses and solutions. External forces, such as voters and investors, demand immediate attention. In an atmosphere of crisis, there is no time or patience for learning. Ironically, implementing new methods of leadership, if they are allowed, would make dealing with complexity and uncertainty easier in the long run. Therefore, a vicious cycle that allows no time for the learning that would help current crises continues. The lack of learning and experimentation in turn causes the continuation of the crises, which makes the time needed to learn and practice innovative behaviors unavailable.
- Second, organizations are often *rigid and unforgiving*. In their push for short-term and immediate performance, they do not allow any room for mistakes and experimentation. A few organizations, such as Virgin Group Ltd., 3M, and Apple Computers that encourage taking risks and making mistakes, are the exception. The rigidity and rewards systems of many institutions discourage such endeavors.
- Third, organizations fall back on *old ideas* about what effective leadership is and, therefore, rely on *simplistic solutions* that do not fit new and complex problems. The use of simple ideas, such as those proposed in many popular books, provides only temporary solutions.
- Fourth, over time, all organizations develop a particular *culture* that strongly influences how things are done and what is considered acceptable behavior. As leaders try to implement new ideas and experiment with new methods, they may face resistance generated by the established culture. For example, as Ford Motor company struggles for survival, its new leaders face what many consider the company's dysfunctional culture (Kiley, 2007).
- Finally, another factor that can pose an obstacle to effective leadership is the difficulty involved in understanding and applying the findings of *academic research*. In the laudable search for precision and scientific rigor, academic researchers sometimes do not clarify the application of their research, making the research inaccessible to practitioners.

The complex and never-ending learning process of becoming an effective leader requires experimentation and organizational support. The inaccessibility of academic research to many practitioners and the short-term orientation of the organizations in which most managers operate provide challenging obstacles to effective leadership. Except for the few individuals who are talented and learn quickly and easily or those rare leaders who have the luxury of time, these obstacles are not easily surmounted. Organizations that allow their leaders at all levels to make mistakes, learn, and develop new skills are training effective leaders.

LEADERSHIP AND MANAGEMENT

What is the difference between a leader and a manager? Are the two basically the same, or are there sharp distinctions between them? These questions have been at the forefront of the discussion of leadership for many years. Carol Hymowitz, a writer with *The Wall Street Journal*, considers herself lucky to have worked for two bosses who were "leaders more than managers" (Hymowitz, 1998: B1). She believes leaders inspire their followers to take risks. Carol Bartz, chief executive at Autodesk, suggests that managers "know how to write business plans, while leaders get companies—and people—to change" (Hymowitz, 1998: B1). Brad Anderson, the CEO of Best Buy, who retired in 2009, is an example of how leaders may be different from

TABLE 1 Managers and Leaders

Managers	Leaders
Focus on the present	Focus on the future
Maintain status quo and stability	Create change
Implement policies and procedures	Initiate goals and strategies
Maintain existing structure	Create a culture based on shared values
Remain aloof to maintain objectivity	Establish an emotional link with followers
Use position power	Use personal power

managers. He states, "My primary job as a leader is to provide the right sort of emotional support or relief" (McGregor, 2005b). Table 1 presents the major distinctions between managers and leaders. Whereas leaders have long-term and future-oriented perspectives and provide a vision for their followers that looks beyond their immediate surroundings, managers take short-term perspectives and focus on routine issues within their own immediate departments or groups. Zaleznik (1990) further suggests that leaders, but not managers, are charismatic and can create a sense of excitement and purpose in their followers. Kotter (1990) takes a historical perspective in the debate and proposes that leadership is an age-old concept, but the concept of management developed in the past 100 years as a result of the complex organizations created after the Industrial Revolution. A manager's role is to bring order and consistency through planning, budgeting, and controlling. Leadership, on the other hand, is aimed at producing movement and change (Kotter, 1990, 1996).

The debates suggest that for those who draw a distinction between leaders and managers, leaders demonstrate attributes that allow them to energize their followers, whereas managers simply take care of the mundane and routine details. Both are necessary for organizations to function, and one cannot replace the other. By considering the issue of effectiveness, many of the arguments regarding the differences between leadership and management can be clarified. For example are managers who motivate their followers and whose departments achieve all their goals simply effective managers, or are they leaders as well? Being an effective manager often involves performing many of the functions that are attributed to leaders with or without some degree of charisma. The distinctions drawn between leadership and management may be more related to effectiveness than to the difference between the two concepts. An effective manager of people provides a mission and sense of purpose with future-oriented goals, initiates goals and actions, and builds a sense of shared values that allows followers to be focused and motivated, all actions that are attributed to leaders. Therefore, effective managers can often be considered leaders. Management professor Henry Mintzberg further suggests that good leaders must manage their team and organizations as well. By focusing too much on leadership, at the expense of management, much of the hard work needed to make organizations effective may be left unattended. He states: "Being an engaged leader means you must be reflective while staying in the fray-the hectic, fragmented, never-ending world of managing" (Mintzberg, 2009).

Thus, any manager who guides a group toward goal accomplishment can be considered a leader, and any good leader must perform many management functions. Much of the distinction between management and leadership comes from the fact that the title *leader* assumes competence. Consequently, an effective and successful manager can be considered a leader, but a less-competent manager is not a leader. Overall, the debate over the difference between the two concepts does not add much to our understanding of what constitutes good leadership or good management and how to achieve these goals. It does, however, point to the need felt by many people and organizations for effective, competent, and visionary leadership/management. This book does not dwell on the distinction between the two concepts and uses the terms interchangeably.

ROLES AND FUNCTIONS OF LEADERS

Although leaders in different organizations and different cultures perform dissimilar functions and play unique roles, researchers have identified a number of managerial roles and functions that cut across most settings.

Managerial Roles

To be effective, leaders perform a number of roles. The roles are sets of expected behaviors ascribed to them by virtue of their leadership position. Along with the basic managerial functions of planning, organizing, staffing, directing, and controlling, leaders are ascribed a number of strategic and external roles. Furthermore, one of the major functions of leaders is to provide their group or organization with a sense of vision and mission. For example, department managers need to plan and organize their department's activities and assign various people to perform tasks. They also monitor their employees' performance and correct employees' actions when needed. Aside from these internal functions, managers negotiate with their boss and other department managers for resources and coordinate decisions and activities with them. Additionally, many department managers must participate in strategic planning and the development of their organization's mission beyond the immediate focus on their own department or team.

One of the most cited taxonomies of managerial activities is proposed by Henry Mintzberg (1973), who added the 10 executive roles of figurehead, leader, liaison, monitor, disseminator, spokesperson, entrepreneur, disturbance handler, resource allocator, and negotiator to an already long list of what leaders do. Mintzberg's research further suggests that few, if any, managers perform these roles in an organized, compartmentalized, and coherent fashion. Instead, a typical manager's days are characterized by a wide variety of tasks, frequent interruptions, and little time to think or to connect with their subordinates. Mintzberg's findings are an integral part of many definitions of leadership and management. The roles he defines are typically considered the major roles and functions of leaders.

Interestingly, research suggests that male and female managers may perform their roles differently. In her book, *The Female Advantage: Women's Way of Leadership*, Sally Helgesen (1995) questions many myths about the universality of management behaviors. Through case studies of five female executives, Helgesen faithfully replicated the methodology used 20 years earlier by Mintzberg in his study of seven male managers. Mintzberg had found that his managers often worked at an unrelenting pace, with many interruptions and few non–work-related activities. The men felt that their identity was tied directly to their job and often reported feeling isolated, with no time to reflect, plan, and share information with others. They also reported having a complex network of colleagues outside work and preferring face-to-face interaction to all other means of communication.

Helgesen's findings of female managers matched Mintzberg's only in the last two categories. Her female managers also were part of a complex network and preferred face-to-face communication. The other findings, however, were surprisingly different. The women reported working at a calm, steady pace with frequent breaks. They did not consider unscheduled events to be interruptions; they instead viewed them as a normal part of their work. All of them reported working at a number of non–work-related activities. They each cultivated multifaceted identities and, therefore, did not feel isolated. They found themselves with time to read and reflect on the big picture. Additionally, the female executives scheduled time to share information with their colleagues and subordinates.

The gender differences found between the two studies can be attributed partly to the 20-year time difference. However, Helgesen's suggestions about a different female leadership style, which she calls "the web," are supported by a number of other research and anecdotal studies. Helgesen's web is compared to a circle with the manager in the center and interconnected to all other parts of the department or organization. This view differs sharply from the traditional pyramid structure common in many organizations.

Functions of the Leader: Creation and Maintenance of an Organizational Culture

One of the major functions of leaders is the creation and development of a culture and climate for their group or organization (Nahavandi and Malekzadeh, 1993a; Schein, 2004). Leaders, particularly founders, leave an almost-indelible mark on the assumptions that are passed down from one generation to the next. In fact, organizations often come to mirror their founders' personalities. Consider, for example, how Starbucks, the worldwide provider of gourmet coffee, reflects the dreams and fears of its founder, Howard Schultz. The company is known for its generous benefit package and its focus on taking care of its employees. Schultz often repeats the story of his father losing his job after breaking his leg and the devastating and long-

> Leaders, particularly founders, leave an almost-indelible mark on the assumptions that are passed down from one generation to the next. In fact, organizations often come to mirror their founders' personalities.

lasting effect this event had on him and his family (George, 2007). As is the case in many other organizations, the founder's style, or in the case of Starbucks, the founder's family history, has an impact on the culture of an organization.

If the founder is workaholic and control oriented, the organization is likely to push for fast-paced decision making and be centralized. If the founder is participative and team oriented, the organization will be decentralized and open. Norm Brodsky, a veteran entrepreneur who created several businesses, realized how much his hard-driving personality affected the culture of his company. He also realized that his wife and partner's more caring style was having a positive impact on employees, so he worked on softening his own style and supporting her initiatives (Brodsky, 2006). The leader's passion often translates into the mission or one of the primary goals of the organization, as is the case of Howard Schultz for Starbucks. Similarly, David Neeleman's passion for customers and high-quality service (see Leadership in Action at the end of this chapter) has shaped all of JetBlue's operations. The leaders make most, if not all, of the decisions regarding the various factors that will shape the culture (Figure 1).

Leaders are role models for other organizational members. They establish and grant the status symbols that are the main artifacts of organizational culture. Followers take their cues from the leaders on what behaviors are and are not acceptable. For example, Stephen Oesterle of Medtronics leads by example. As a marathon runner, he promotes a healthy lifestyle and its role in restoring lives, which is the mission of his company (Tuggle, 2007). Another example is Tyler Winkler, the senior vice president of sales and business development for Secure Works, who is obsessed with improving sales numbers. One of his first statements to his employees was, "Make your numbers in three months or you're out" (Cummings, 2004). He measures everything, observes employees

FIGURE 1 Leader's Functions in Shaping Organizational Culture

closely, and provides detailed feedback and training, all to improve sales. His methods became the norm in the organization and created a legion of loyal employees.

Recent research about the importance of empathy in leadership suggests another function for leaders, related to cultural factors. Researchers argue that a key function of leaders is to manage the emotions of group members (Humphrey, 2002). Even though attention to internal process issues, such as the emotional state of followers, has always been considered a factor in leadership, it is increasingly seen not as a peripheral task, but rather as one of the main functions. This function is particularly critical to maintaining followers' positive outlook in uncertain and ambiguous situations. Followers observe their leaders' emotional reactions and take their cue from them to determine appropriate reactions (Pescosolido, 2002). Kellett and colleagues (2002) suggest that the increasing use of teams, rapid globalization, and the growing challenge to retain valued employees all make the consideration of employee emotions and feelings a factor in effectiveness. An unlikely example of the emotion management role of leaders is Bob Ladouceur, the La Salle, California, prep high-school football coach considered one of the greatest, with a 51-game winning streak between 1992 and 2003 (Abend, 2008). The coach focuses on shaping the lives of his students, rather than simply winning. His players are not generally considered to be the most talented or the strongest. Ladouceur, however, gets extraordinary performance from them through hard training and character building. He states, "If a team has no soul, you're just wasting your time" (Wallace, 2003: 100–104). He wants his players to get in touch with their emotions and develop "love" for their teammates. For Ladouceur, managing these emotions is the key to his teams' winning streaks.

Another behavior that leaders need to model is accepting responsibility for one's actions. With the power and status conferred to leaders comes the obligation of accepting responsibility for their own decisions and the organization's impact on others. The willingness to accept such responsibility often is lacking in many U.S. corporations, where finger-pointing consumes more energy than acknowledging and correcting mistakes. A leader's demeanor can set the tone for others in the organization to either accept or shirk responsibility for their actions and decisions.

Other means through which the leader shapes culture are by decisions regarding the reward system (Kerr and Slocum, 1987) and by controlling decision standards. In one organization, rewards (financial and nonfinancial) go to only the highest contributors to the bottom line. In another, accomplishments such as contribution to cultural diversity or the degree of social responsibility are also valued and rewarded. Additionally, leaders are in charge of selecting other leaders and managers for the organization. Those selected are likely to fit the existing leader's ideal model and, therefore, fit the culture. Other influential members of the organization provide leaders with yet another opportunity to shape the culture. Many firms, for example, establish a nominating committee of the board of directors. In such committees, top managers nominate and select their successors. Therefore, they not only control the current culture but also exert a strong influence on the future of their organization. To select his successor before he left in 2001, General Electric's (GE) Jack Welch carefully observed, interacted with, and interviewed many of the company's executives. He sought feedback from top company leaders, and after selecting Jeff Immelt, Welch orchestrated the transition of power. This carefully orchestrated succession ensured that the new leader, although bringing about some new ideas, fit the existing culture of the organization (J. Useem, 2001). A similar careful process took place at Procter and Gamble in 2009.

The power of the leader to make decisions for the organization about its structure and strategy is another effective means of shaping culture. By determining the hierarchy, span of control, reporting relationship, and degree of formalization and specialization, the leader molds culture. A highly decentralized and organic structure is likely to be the result of an open and participative culture, whereas a highly centralized structure will go hand in hand with a mechanistic/bureaucratic culture. The structure of an organization limits or encourages interaction and by doing so affects, as well as is affected by, the assumptions shared by members of the organization. Similarly, the strategy selected by the leader or the top management team will be determined by, as well as help shape, the culture of the organization. Therefore, a leader who adopts a proactive growth strategy that requires innovation and risk taking will have to create a culture different from a leader who selects a strategy of retrenchment.

Applying What You Learn
Leadership Basics

Leadership is a complex process that is a journey rather than a destination. All effective leaders continue to grow and improve, learning from each situation they face and from their mistakes. Here are some basic points that we will revisit throughout the book:

- *Find your passion:* We can be at our best when we lead others into something for which we have passion.
- *Learn about yourself:* Self-awareness of your values, strengths, and weaknesses is an essential starting point for leaders.
- *Experiment with new behaviors and situations:* Learning and growth occur when we are exposed to new situations that challenge us; seek them out.
- *Get comfortable with failure:* All leaders fail; good leaders learn from their mistakes

and consider them learning opportunities. Mistakes are more likely to happen when you are placed in new challenging situations that provide you with opportunities to learn.

- *Pay attention to your environment:* Understanding all the elements of a leadership situation, and particularly followers, is essential to effectiveness. Ask questions, listen carefully, and observe intently so that you can understand the people and the situations around you.
- *Don't take yourself too seriously:* A good sense of humor and keeping a perspective on priorities will help you. You are not as good as your most fervent supporters believe and not as flawed as your reticent detractors think, so lighten up!

Definition and Significance of Leadership

DOES LEADERSHIP MAKE A DIFFERENCE?

Open any newspaper or periodical, and you will find the profile of a political, community, or business leader or a lengthy article about how an organization is likely to be greatly affected by its new leadership. Company stocks fluctuate because of changes in leadership. For example, while the board of directors of American Express was debating the fate of CEO Robinson (he was eventually replaced), the company's stock price plummeted a steep 13 percent in four days. Similarly, a new leader can influence a firm's credit rating by affecting the confidence of the financial community in this person. While Xerox weathered considerable financial and leadership problems in 2000 and 2001, the selection of Anne Mulcahy, a company veteran, as CEO helped ease stakeholders' concerns. A city or nation might feel a sense of revival and optimism or considerable concern when a new leader comes to power, as was the case in the 2008 United States with the election of Barak Obama. We believe that leadership matters. Researchers have found that when asked who is responsible for a group's or an organization's success and performance, people are more likely to attribute the success to the leader than to other factors. This tendency occurs even when available data indicate that attributing success to the leader alone is not warranted.

Despite this common belief, considerable debate among leadership scholars addresses whether leadership actually affects organizations. There are two key questions:

- To what extent, if at all, does the leadership affect various organizational elements and organizational performance?
- What are the situations where leadership has more impact?

Arguments against the Impact of Leadership

Affirmation that leaders are not important has been made by many throughout history. Leo Tolstoy suggested that leaders are simply slaves of history; their presence and actions are irrelevant and determined by the inevitable course of events. Karl Marx made similar assertions about the power of history and irrelevance of leaders. Modern researchers suggest that environmental, social, industrial, and economic conditions, just to name a few factors, determine organizational direction and performance to a much higher degree than does leadership. Furthermore, some researchers consider leadership to be a simple symbol or myth rather than an objective factor in organizations (Meindl and Ehrlick, 1987). The research about the lack of impact of leadership asserts that organizations are driven by powerful factors other than their management (Brown, 1982; Cyert and March, 1963; Hannan and Freeman, 1977; Salancik and Pfeffer, 1977a). External factors, along with organizational elements such as structure and strategy, are assumed to limit the leader's decision-making options, further reducing the leader's discretion. The support for this approach comes primarily from two areas:

- First, a group of researchers studied the impact of leadership succession in organizations. Results from studies in the private and public sectors support the notion that the change of leadership does not affect organizational performance strongly. For example, Salancik and Pfeffer (1977a), in a study of the performance of mayors, found that leadership accounted for only 7 to 15 percent of changes in city budgets. Similarly, Lieberson and O'Connor (1972) found that whereas leadership has minimal effects on the performance of large corporations (accounting for only 7 to 14 percent of the performance), company size and economic factors show considerable links to firm performance.
- Second, support for the lack-of-importance hypothesis is found in an area of research that focuses on the extent of managerial discretion (Finkelstein and Hambrick, 1996; Hambrick and Finkelstein, 1987). Although the goal of the research is not to show the insignificance

14

TABLE 2	Arguments Regarding the Impact of Leadership
Leadership Is Insignificant	**Leadership Has an Impact**
• Outside environmental factors affect organizations more than leadership. • Internal structure and strategy determine the course an organization takes. • Leadership accounts for only 7 to 15 percent of financial performance. • Leaders have little discretion to really make an impact. • Leadership is a romantic myth rather than a real organizational factor.	• Leadership is one of the many important factors. • Leadership is key in providing vision and direction. • Leadership can account for up to 44 percent of a firm's profitability. • Leadership is critical in orchestrating change. • Leadership's impact is moderated by situational factors.

of leadership, some of the results show that CEOs have limited discretion in their choices and activities. The lack of managerial discretion in decision making further reinforces the notion that external environmental elements and internal organizational elements have more impact than does leadership.

Overall, the early evidence from the leadership succession research together with some of the managerial discretion findings hint at two conclusions. First, leaders have minimal impact on organizations. Second, even when leaders do make decisions that affect organizations, their decisions are determined by environmental and organizational factors and are, therefore, not a reflection of the leader's preferences or style. Based on these findings, researchers concluded that the effect of leaders, although interesting, is not objective and actual, but rather reflects a romantic notion of the role and impact of leaders. Table 2 summarizes the arguments regarding the impact of leadership.

Arguments for the Impact of Leadership

Along with popular belief, many research findings dispute the position that leadership is insignificant. For example, in reevaluating Lieberson and O'Connor's 1972 study, Weiner and Mahoney (1981) find that a change in leadership accounts for 44 percent of the profitability of the firms studied. Other researchers (Day and Lord, 1988; Thomas, 1988) indicate that the early results were not as strong as originally believed, and recent studies suggest that leadership can have an impact by looking at the disruption that can come from changes in leadership (Ballinger and Schoorman, 2007) and find a strong effect of CEOs on company performance (Mackey, 2008). Additionally, studies of school systems show that the principal is the most important factor in the climate of a school and the success of students (Allen, 1981). Still other studies find that the leadership is critical to orchestrating and organizing all the complex elements necessary to change an organization (Burke, Richley, and DeAngelis, 1985).

Reconciling the Differences

The debates about the impact of leadership make valuable contributions to our understanding of leadership. First, it is important to recognize that leadership is one of many factors that influence the performance of a group or an organization. Second, the leader's contribution, although not always tangible, is significant in providing a vision and direction for followers and in integrating their activities. Third, the key is to identify situations in which the leader's power and discretion over the group and the organization are limited. Finally, the potential lack of impact

Definition and Significance of Leadership

of leaders in some situations further emphasizes the importance of followers in the success of leadership and the need to understand organizations as broad systems. After years of debate, the popular view that leaders affect organizations continues to receive research support (Hambrick, 2007), as the focus shifts from whether a leader has an impact to understanding a leader's impact and its consequences.

CHANGES IN ORGANIZATIONS AND IN EXPECTATIONS OF LEADERS

To some, a leader is someone who takes charge and jumps in to make decisions whenever the situation requires. This view is particularly dominant in traditional organizations with a clear hierarchy in which employees and managers carry out narrowly defined responsibilities. To others, a leader is a facilitator who simply channels the group's desires. The extent to which a leader is attributed power and knowledge varies by culture. In cultures in which power is highly differentiated, such as in Mexico, managers are expected to provide all the answers and solutions to work problems and control the activities of their employees. Although the U.S. mainstream culture is not as authority oriented as some other cultures, a large number of our leadership theories are implicitly or explicitly based on the assumptions that leaders have to take charge and provide others with instructions. For example, the initiation-of-structure concept provides that effective leadership involves giving direction, assigning tasks to followers, and setting deadlines. These activities are considered an inherent part of an effective leader's behaviors. Similarly, the widely used concept of motivation to manage (Miner and Smith, 1982) includes desire for power and control over others as an essential component.

New Roles for Leaders

With the constant need for innovation, intense global competition, changing demographics, and reliance on teams, organizations and their hierarchies are changing drastically. As a result, many of the traditional leadership functions and roles are changing as well. Figure 2 presents

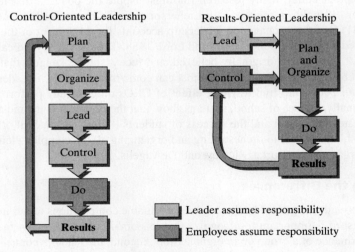

FIGURE 2 Control- versus Results-Oriented Leadership

16

the traditional model and the new model for the role of leaders in organizations. The changing environment for organizations has forced us to reconsider our expectations and requirements for leadership. Effective leaders of diverse and global teams are not necessarily in control of the group. They might need facilitation and participation skills much more than initiation-of-structure skills. For example, employees in traditional organizations are responsible only for production; the planning, leading, and controlling functions, as well as the responsibility for results, fall on the manager (see Figure 2). An increasing number of organizations, however, are shifting the activities and responsibilities typically associated with managers to employees. Managers are expected to provide the vision, get the needed resources to employees, act as support persons, and get out of employees' way. The employees, in turn, learn about the strategic and financial issues related to their job, plan their own activities, set production goals, and take responsibility for their results.

Many executives have adopted new management techniques to help them with the challenges inherent in the new roles for leaders. Teresa Taylor, the chief operating officer of Qwest, believes that her most important role as a leader is to listen to followers and get their feedback (Bryant, 2009a). When Rick Sapio was the CEO of the 37-employee New York City Mutual.com, a mutual fund advisory company, he knew that his business was high pressure with little time to stay in touch with his employees (Buchanan, 2001). Recognizing the importance of involving employees, however, Sapio created "Hassles," an electronic mailbox through which employees could express their concerns and ideas with a guarantee from the CEO that they will be addressed within a week. For those who preferred to see the boss in person, Sapio scheduled 1 hour each week in a conference room (rather than his office, which seemed inaccessible) where anyone could drop in to give him input. Jeffrey Immelt, CEO of General Electric, has made learning and getting to hear everybody's ideas one of his priorities. His predecessor, Jack Welch, notes that a great leader needs to "get under the skin of every person who works for the company" (Hammonds, 2004: 32). The Hay Group, a Philadelphia-based management consulting firm, conducted a study that identified elements of an effective corporate culture. They found that "in the most admired companies, the key priorities were teamwork, customer focus, fair treatment of employees, initiative, and innovation" (Kahn, 1998: 218). Companies such as Procter & Gamble, Whole Foods, Toyota, and Best Buy practice being egalitarian and cooperative. Their priorities are fast decision making, training, and innovation.

The new leadership styles are not limited to business organizations; they can also be seen in government and other not-for-profit organizations. Harry Baxter, chairman and CEO of Baxter Healthcare in Deerfield, Illinois, likes to focus on doing the right thing instead of being right. He suggests, "I have very few definitive answers, but I have a lot of opinions" (Kraemer, 2003: 16). Philip Diehl, former director of the U.S. Mint, and his leadership team transformed the stodgy government bureaucracy into an efficient and customer-centered organization by asking questions, listening to stakeholders, creating a sense of urgency in employees, and involving them in the change (Muio, 1999). These changes also occur in local, state, and federal government agencies. For example, Ron Sims, who was recognized in 2006 as one of the most innovative public officials, is known for always looking for common ground while operating from a clear set of principles (Walters, 2006). Ron Sims is also known for leading by example. When he talked about county employees adopting a healthier lifestyle, he started eating better and biking and lost 40 pounds (Walters, 2006).

These leaders leave their top-floor offices to keep in touch with the members of their organizations. Given the rapid pace of change and complexity of the environment in which many organizations operate, cultivating extensive sources of information and involving many people in the decision-making process are essential.

FIGURE 3 Factors Fueling Changes in Organizations and Their Leadership

Factors Fueling Changes

A number of external and internal organizational factors are driving the changes in our organizations and in the role of leaders and managers (Figure 3). First, political changes worldwide are leading to more openness and democracy. These political changes shape and are shaped by images of what is considered to be appropriate leadership. With the fall of the Soviet Union at the end of the twentieth century, the world has seen a spread in democratic principles aimed at power sharing. In the United States, the public continues to expect transparency in both the private and the public sectors. Politicians are forced to reveal much of their past and justify to the public many, if not all, of their decisions. Communities increasingly demand participation in the decisions regarding their schools, health-care systems, and environment.

Second, with the worldwide economic downturn, increasing global and local competition, and complex and fast-changing technologies, numerous organizations struggle for survival and to justify their existence. Many are forced to reconsider how they provide goods and services to their customers and to the public and to reevaluate the assumptions they held as basic truths. For example, Bill Ford, Jr., who served as CEO of Ford for five years (Kiley, 2007), not only is an environmentalist who agreed to speak at a Greenpeace conference but also attended union contract negotiations wearing union buttons stating that he hates the "us versus them" mentality. He stayed close to employees, regularly ate at Ford's cafeteria, and was interested in joining the employee hockey league (Truby, 2003).

The global competition associated with consumer demands for improved quality in products and services intensifies the need for flexibility and creativity on the part of organizations. The fierce international competition and perceptions of global competitors' management practices push everyone to look for new solutions. Poor management and lack of leadership often are blamed for the problems facing many organizations. Whether it is through restructuring in the private sector or through reinventing government in the public arena, our old institutions seek new vitality. Many are redefining and reengineering themselves, drastically altering the way managers lead and employees do their jobs. These practices demand new leadership roles and procedures.

Definition and Significance of Leadership

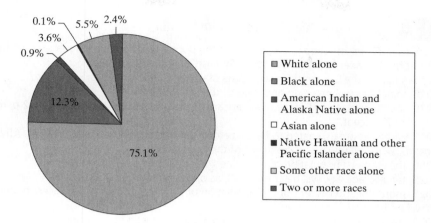

Hispanic or Latino is not considered a racial factor in the U.S. Census and therefore not included in this chart; 12.5% of the U.S. population is considered Hispanic or Latina

FIGURE 4 Diversity in the U.S. Population *Source:* U.S. Census Bureau. Census 2000 at http://www.census.gov/prod/2001pubs/c2br01-1.pdf

Another key factor fueling changes in leadership is the demographic changes in the United States and many other countries (Figure 4). These demographic changes lead to increased diversity in the various groups and organizations; their leaders must consider this diversity when making decisions. In some cases, the diversity is related to age; in others, it is related to gender, ethnic, or cultural background. Many countries include similar or even greater cultural diversity. For example, Malaysia's population is highly diverse and consists of Malays, Chinese, Indians, Arabs, Sinhalese, Eurasians, and Europeans, with the Muslim, Buddhist, Daoist, Hindu, Christian, Sikh, and Shamanistic religions all practiced (*World Fact Book: Malaysia*, 2010). Although the majority of Singapore's population of more than 4 million is Chinese, it also includes Malays, Indians, and Eurasians. As a result, the country has four official languages: English, Malay, Mandarin, and Tamil (*World Fact Book: Singapore*, 2010). Table 3 highlights some of the ethnic and demographic changes and trends in the United States.

The increasing number of women in the workforce is another factor that has an impact on leadership. Although women currently hold only 10 percent of the executive positions in the United States, they make up over 46.5 percent of the general workforce and are projected to grow to 47 percent by 2016. Furthermore, a clear majority of women are part of the labor force (Quick Stats, 2008). Women further make up 51 percent of the managerial and professional ranks (Quick Stats, 2008). Similar trends exist all over the world. For example, women make up almost 47 percent of the labor force and 36 percent of managerial positions in Canada (Tallarico and Gillis, 2007). Scandinavian countries are leading the way with the number of women in top management and leadership positions in the executive offices and boardrooms. In Sweden, women hold 23 percent of the board seats (Amble, 2006). As a result, the old ways that were designed for a gender and ethnically homogeneous population do not always work with employees and customers from varied backgrounds and cultures. Much of the burden for devising and implementing the needed changes falls on the leadership of our organizations. The demand to listen to and address the needs of nonhomogeneous groups requires skills that go beyond controlling and monitoring.

TABLE 3	U.S. Demographic Highlights and Trends

- In 2000, over 37 million people (13 percent of the population) spoke a language other than English at home—over half of those speak Spanish.
- More than half of the U.S. workforce consists of women and minorities.
- By 2016, minorities will make up one-third of the U.S. population.
- By 2025, the percentage of European Americans in the population will drop from 72 percent in 2000 to 62 percent.
- By 2025, Hispanics are estimated to be 21 percent of the population, outnumbering African Americans, who will make up 13 percent of the population.
- By 2050, the Hispanic population of the United States will grow to 30.25 percent.
- By 2025, the *average* age will be close to 40, as opposed to under 35 in 2000.
- By 2025, more than 50 percent of the population of Hawaii, California, New Mexico, and Texas will be from a minority group.
- By 2050, the average U.S. resident will be from a non-European background.
- By 2050, only about 60 percent of the entrants into the labor force will be white, with half that number being women.

Source: U.S. Census Bureau, Census 2000: www.census.gov/population

Other demographic trends in the United States include what is called the population hourglass, with the largest percentage of the population being older baby boomers (born between the late 1940s and the 1960s) at the top, and the millennial generation (born after the mid-1980s) at the bottom, with the generation Xers (born between the 1970s and 1980s) pinched in the middle (Zolli, 2006). The shape of the hourglass suggests that many organizational leaders are managing employees from generations other than their own and therefore must take cultural and generational factors into account. Additionally, employees attain increased levels of education today, and the younger generation enters the workplace with expectations of participation and autonomy. They expect fast promotions, challenging learning opportunities, training, and work–life balance. The increase in service jobs at the expense of traditional manufacturing jobs further puts employees in direct contact with customers and, therefore, requires changes in how we manage and train employees. This increase in service jobs also means that employees must use judgment and make many quick decisions that previously were reserved for management.

Because of the pressures for change, many organizations find themselves rewriting their policies to address the needs of a diverse community and consumer base. Ted Childs, IBM's president of global workforce diversity, who has been described as the most effective diversity executive on the planet (Malveaux, 2005) states, "You're going to have to sell to people who are different from you, and buy from people who are different from you, and manage people who are different from you. . . . This is how we do business. If it's not your destination, you should get off the plane now" (Swan, 2000: 260). He views getting people to respect those who are different from them as the biggest challenge in managing diversity.

Barriers to Change

Despite the factors that fuel the need for change, few organizations and individuals have adopted new models for leadership painlessly. In part because of perceived financial pressures and attempts to find a quick way out of them, organizations turn to tough autocratic leaders whose goals are clearly not employee motivation and loyalty. For example, John Grundhofer, nick-named "Jack the Ripper," specialized in implementing massive layoffs and found his skills in high demand. Similarly, Al Dunlap, with nicknames such as "Ming the Merciless" and "Chainsaw Al," for a long time moved successfully from the top position of one organization to another before being fired from Sunbeam Corporation in 1998. For many years, the financial community applauded him for his drastic cost-cutting strategies that involved widespread lay-offs. Bill George, the highly respected former CEO of Medtronic, states that this focus on short-term and quick results cannot create the motivation necessary for the innovation and superior service that are essential to leadership and organizational effectiveness (George, 2003).

Another obstacle to implementing new models of leadership is that even though teams are fairly common in lower and middle levels of organizations, top management still remains a one-person show. The hierarchical structure of many organizations makes change difficult. Old cultures resist change. Few organizations truly reward enterprising employees and managers for crossing the traditional hierarchical barriers. Instead, most organizations continue to reward their leaders for tried-and-true approaches or sometimes for nonperformance- and nonproductivity-related behav-iors, despite the lack of success (Luthans, 1989). Marcus Buckingham, a researcher at the Gallup Organization, has studied global leadership practice for 15 years. According to Buckingham, "The corporate world is appallingly bad at capitalizing on the strengths of its people" (LaBarre, 2001: 90). Gallup's extensive surveys show that employee engagement can have a considerable positive impact on an organization's performance. Recent surveys of employees in the United States by the Conference Board indicates the lowest level of overall satisfaction with jobs, at 45 percent (Conference Board, 2010). Other research indicates that job satisfaction is lower in larger compa-nies with more bureaucracy, lower autonomy, and low responsibility (*Wall Street Journal*, 2006). Few organizations take full advantage of their employees' input. Tom Peters, the well-known man-agement consultant, suggests that while business leaders focus on strategy, they often "skip over the incredibly boring part called people," thereby failing to take advantage of one of the most important aspects of their organization (Reingold, 2003: 94). In addition, changing the established behaviors of managers is very difficult. John Kotter, Harvard Business School professor and noted authority on change, suggests, "The central issue is never strategy, structure, culture, or systems. The core of the matter is always about changing the behavior of people" (Deutschman, 2005).

In addition, although they might spend a great deal of time working in teams, employees are still rewarded for individual performance. In other words, our reward structures fail to keep up with our attempts to increase cooperation among employees and managers. Furthermore, many employees are not willing or able to accept their new roles as partners and decision mak-ers, even when such roles are offered to them. Their training and previous experiences make them balk at taking on what they might consider to be their leader's job. Even when organiza-tions encourage change, many leaders find giving up control difficult. Many receive training in the benefits of empowerment, teams, and softer images of leadership, but they simply continue to repeat what seemingly worked in the past, engaging in what researcher Pfeffer calls substituting memory for thinking (1998). With all that training on how to be in charge and in control, allow-ing employees to do more might appear to be a personal failure. Either because of years of tradi-tional training or because of personality characteristics that make them more comfortable with control and hierarchy, managers' styles often create an obstacle to implementing necessary changes. Research about children's images of leadership indicates that the belief that leaders need to be in control develops early in life. Children, particularly boys, continue to perceive a sex-typed schema of leaders: leaders are supposed to have male characteristics, including domi-nance and aggression (Ayman-Nolley, Ayman, and Becker, 1993).

Summary and Conclusions

A leader is any person who influences individuals and groups within an organization, helps them in the establishment of goals, and guides them toward achievement of those goals, thereby allowing them to be effective. Leaders are needed because they create order and organization in groups, allowing them to achieve their goals; they help people make sense of the world and can serve as ideal and romantic symbols for their followers. To be effective, leaders must help the organization maintain internal health and external adaptability. Despite the apparent simplicity of the definitions of leadership and effectiveness, both are difficult concepts to implement.

Various studies propose separate definitions for leadership and management. The activities performed by leaders, however, are similar to those typically considered the domain of effective managers. Although some view the roles of leaders and managers as being different, effective, and competent managers are often also leaders within their groups and organizations. In addition to performing the traditional managerial roles and duties, leaders also play a special role in the creation of a culture for their organizations. They can affect culture by making direct decisions regarding reward systems and hiring of other managers and employees and also by being role models for others in the organization. The role of leaders is changing with our shifting expectations and global and organizational pressures. Leaders find themselves providing more vision and direction rather than command and control. While new roles take hold slowly, political, economic, demographic, and social changes drive the need for change. However, leaders find use of traditional models, lack of involvement of followers, and falling back on old practices hard obstacles to overcome.

Review and Discussion Questions

1. What are the essential components of the definition of leadership?
2. What are the essential components of the definition of leadership effectiveness?
3. Why do we need leaders?
4. Provide one example each of an effective leader and a successful leader. Consider how they differ and what you can learn from each.
5. What are the obstacles to effective leadership?
6. Based on your knowledge of the field of management and your personal definition of leadership, how are management and leadership similar or different? How can the differences be reconciled?

How do these differences add to our understanding of leadership?
7. What are the ways in which leaders influence the creation of culture in their organizations?
8. What are the basic assumptions guiding the "insignificant leadership" concept? What is your position on this issue? Document your arguments.
9. What are the elements of the emerging leadership styles? What are the factors that support such styles?
10. What obstacles do new leadership styles face in traditional organizations? How can obstacles to new models be overcome?

Leadership Challenge: Moving to Leadership

You have been a member of a cohesive and productive department for the past three years. Your department manager has accepted a job in another organization, and you have been moved into her position. You are not one of most senior members, but you have the most education, have been volunteering for many training programs, and have been an outstanding individual contributor. Over the past three years, you have developed close relationships with several of your department members who are around your age. You often go out to lunch together, have drinks after work, and get together on weekends. There are also a couple of "old-timers" who were very helpful in training you when you first came in. They have much more experience than you, but little education. Although you get along with them, you feel a bit awkward about being promoted to be their boss.

1. What are the challenges you are likely to face as the new leader?
2. What are some actions you should take to help smooth the transition?
3. What are some things you should avoid?

Exercise 1: What Is Leadership?

This exercise is designed to help you develop a personal definition of leadership and clarify your assumptions and expectations about leadership and effectiveness.

1. **Describe your ideal leader**
   Individually list five desirable and five, undesirable characteristics of your ideal leader.

Desirable	Undesirable
1.	1.
2.	2.
3.	3.
4.	4.
5.	5.

2. **Develop group definition:** In groups of four or five discuss your list and your reasons and draw up a common definition.

3. **Present and defend definition:** Each group will make a 5-minute presentation of its definition.

4. **Common themes**
   a. What are the common themes?

   b. Which views of leadership are presented?

   c. What are the assumptions about the role of the leader?

Exercise 2: Images of Leadership

One way you can clarify your assumptions about leadership is to use images to describe your ideal leader. Through the use of such images, you can understand your views of the role of leaders in organizations and your expectations of leaders. These images are your personal theories of leadership. For example, viewing leaders as facilitators presents a considerably different image from viewing them as parents.

1. **Select your image:** List the characteristics of that image

2. **Share and clarify:** In groups of three or four, share your leadership image and discuss its implications for your own leadership style

3. **Class discussion**

   Groups will share two of their individual members' images of leadership. Discuss implications of various images for the following aspects:
   1. A person's leadership style

   2. Impact on organizational culture and structure

   3. Compatibility with current or past leaders

   4. Potential shortcomings of each image

Exercise 3: Understanding the Leadership Context

This exercise is designed to highlight the importance and role of the context in the leadership process.

1. **Individual/group work**

   Select a leader and identify the contextual factors that affect his/her leadership. Consider various elements that may be relevant, such as the following:

   a. Long-term historical, political, and economic factors or forces

   b. Current contemporary forces, including social values, changes, and cultural factors

   c. The immediate context, including organizational characteristics, the task, and followers

2. **Discussion**

   How do all these factors affect the leader? Do they hinder or help the leader achieve his/her goals?

LEADERSHIP IN ACTION

David Neeleman Reinvents Airlines

David Neeleman has become a legend in the airline industry. In 1984, he cofounded Morris Air and sold it to Southwest Airlines. In 2000, he launched the highly successful JetBlue Airways, and he is now engaged in a new venture as CEO of the new Brazilian domestic airline Azul (blue in Portuguese) founded in 2008. His vision for what an airline should be and his leadership style set him apart from most other leaders in the industry. His vision for JetBlue was to make flying fun again and: "above all else, JetBlue Airways is dedicated to bringing humanity back to air travel" (JetBlue Airways Customer Bill of Rights, 2007). "As long as we can delight our customers, there's plenty of business for us" (BW Online, 2003), states David Neeleman. For many years at JetBlue, Neeleman, successfully navigated turbulent times with a no-layoffs strategy and expansion plans that targeted routes that other airlines dropped. Neeleman was outsted in 2007 after the airline was caught in a wave of negative publicity after it kept passengers in planes on the tarmac for seven hours during a storm. Neeleman provided a very public and sincere apology (posted on the Web at http://www.jetblue.com/about/ourcompany/apology/index.html), and JetBlue instituted a much publicized Passenger Bill of Rights to ensure that its much-valued customers continue to remain loyal.

JetBlue has daily flights to more than 50 destinations in the United States and Central America. Continuing to rely on the principles of its founder, the airline emphasizes teamwork and quick decisions and implementation. Top executives and managers consistently interact with employees and customers to listen and get feedback from them to keep addressing their concerns (Salter, 2004), a practice Neeleman has also instituted at Azul (Mount, 2008). The attention to employees and customers has earned JetBlue high ratings and its former CEO awards for being a visionary (www.jetblueairways.com). Programs such as generous profit sharing, excellent benefits, open communication, and extensive training all get the right employees in the company and retain them.

At JetBlue as well as with Azul, Neeleman not only provides the vision, but also knows to listen to people who, on occasion, veto his decisions. Neeleman takes it in stride and says, "I'm being totally deferential and patient. . . . It's because I think the situation demands it. I have to trust the instincts of the people around me" (Judge, 2001: 131). At Azul, he has a similar approach having started a "hearts and minds" campaign to get feedback from potential customers even before the airline started operations (Schmall, 2008). Neeleman believes that "If you treat people well, the company's philosophy goes, they'll treat the customer well." The senior vice president of operations at JetBlue echoed the focus on people: "There is no 'they' here. It's 'we' and 'us'" (Salter, 2004). "We select the best people, but we do extensive training to make sure they understand what is expected of them. . . . Our leadership are held to a very high standard as to how they treat the other crew members," says Neeleman, regarding JetBlue's commitment to its employees (Ford, 2004: 141).

Azul is made of much of the same mold as JetBlue: simple reservations systems, low prices, more leg room, online Internet, and a TV in every seat (Scanlon, 2008). Neeleman is obsessive about staying in touch with both customers and employees. He stops by the call center at Azul regularly, talks to the trainees, and reminds his executives to talk to customers and those closest to them because "we think we know what happens. But they really know" (Mount, 2008). He strongly believes that "it is the people that make it happen" (Ford, 2004: 140). Neeleman's leadership style and magic seems to be continuing to work. Azul is growing fast, with 11,000 passengers when it started up to 45,000 in January of 2009 (Brazil's Azul, 2009), and is flying 70 percent full, which close to 20 percent better than Brazil's biggest airline (Moura, 2009).

In the couple of years it has been in operations, Azul has doubled doubled its revenues.

Questions

1. What are the key elements of JetBlue and Azul's culture?
2. What role does the leader play in the development and maintenance of the culture?

Sources: JetBlue Airways Customer Bill of Rights. 2007. http://www.jetblue.com/p/about/ourcompany/promise/Bill_Of_Rights.pdf (accessed June 16, 2007); BW Online. 2003. "David Neeleman, JetBlue." http://www.businessweek.com:/print/magazine/content/03_39/b3851620.htm?mz (accessed September 16, 2004); Judge, P., 2001. "How will your company adapt?" *Fast Company*, 54; Ford. 2004. "David Neeleman, CEO of JetBlue Airways, on people + strategy = growth," *Academy of Management Executive* 18, no. 2: 139–143; Salter, C., 2004a. "And now the hard part," *Fast Company* 82. http://pf.fastcompany.com/magazine/82/jetblue.html (accessed October 1, 2004); Brazil's Azul airlines to expand this year. 2008. http://www.usatoday.com/travel/flights/2009-02-11-azul-expansion_N.htm (accessed on January 7, 2010); Moura, F. 2009. Neeleman expects profit as Brazil's Azul Air flies 70 percent full. http://www.bloomberg.com/apps/news?pid=20601086&sid=aJl8vaK49DMQ (accessed January 7, 2010); Schmall, E. 2008. Next for David Neeleman: Jet Brazil, http://www.forbes.com/2008/03/27/neeleman-jetblue-airlines-biz-cz_es_0327neeleman.html (accessed January 7, 2010); Mount, I. 2009. JetBlue founder's revenge: A new airline. http://www.fortunesmallbusiness.com/2009/03/19/smallbusiness/jetblue_founder_flies_again.fsb/index.htm (accessed January 7, 2010); Scanlon. J. 2008. Braving Brazil's "airline graveyard." http://www.businessweek.com/innovate/content/may2008/id2008056_561046.htm (accessed January 7, 2010).

The Global
and Cultural Contexts

"Verité en-deçà des Pyrénées, erreur au–delà."
(There are truths on this side of the Pyrenees which are falsehoods
on the other.)

—BLAISE PASCAL

After studying this chapter, you will be able to:

- Understand the role culture can play in leadership.
- Describe the three levels of culture.
- Discuss the models of national culture.
- Identify the impact of gender on leadership.
- Address how organizations and leader can develop a cultural mindset.

Leadership is a social and an interpersonal process. As is the case with any such process, the impact of culture is undeniable. Different cultures define leadership differently and consider different types of leaders effective. A leader who is considered effective in Singapore might seem too authoritarian in Sweden. The charisma of an Egyptian political leader is likely to be lost on the French or the Japanese. The exuberant Brazilian leader will appear unnecessarily emotional to German employees. In addition, gender and other cultural differences among groups affect how leaders behave and how their followers perceive them. Understanding leadership, therefore, requires an understanding of the cultural context in which it takes place.

DEFINITION AND LEVELS OF CULTURE

Culture gives each group its uniqueness and differentiates one group from the other. Our culture strongly influences us; it determines how we think, what we consider right and wrong, and influences what and who we value, what we pay attention to, and how we behave. Culture affects values and beliefs and influences leadership and interpersonal styles.

Definition and Characteristics

Culture consists of the commonly held values within a group of people. It is a set of norms, customs, values, and assumptions that guides the behavior of a particular group of people. It includes the lifestyle of a group and the collective programming of the group members. Culture is shared by members of a group, it has permanence, and it is passed down from one generation to another. Group members learn about their culture through their parents and family, schools, and other social institutions and consciously and unconsciously transfer it to the young and new members. Culture affects how people view the world and how they think and, therefore, shapes behavior. Although culture has some permanence, it is also dynamic and changes over time as members adapt to new events and their environment.

> Culture affects how people view the world and how they think and, therefore, shapes behavior. Although culture has some permanence, it is also dynamic and changes over time as members adapt to new events and their environment.

Levels of Culture

Culture exists at three levels (Figure 1). The first is national culture, defined as a set of values and beliefs shared by people within a nation. Second, in addition to an overall national culture, different ethnic and other cultural groups that live within a nation might share a culture. Gender, religious, and racial differences, for example, fit into this second level of culture differences. Although these groups share national cultural values, they also develop their unique cultural traits. Some countries, such as the United States, Canada, and Indonesia, include many such subcultures. Different cultural, ethnic, and religious groups are part of the overall culture of these

FIGURE 1 The Three Levels of Culture

coountries, which leads to considerable cultural diversity. Diversity refers to the variety of human structures, beliefs systems, and strategies for adapting to situations that exist within different groups. It is typically used to refer to the variety in the second level of culture and includes such factors as race, ethnicity, language, religion, or any characteristic that may differentiate one group from another and give it a unique identity and beliefs. For example, some cultures' belief in a potential of a savior contributes to the rise of charismatic leadership. Similarly, cultural differences based on gender influence our expectations of leaders and whom we consider to be an effective leader. In particular, widely held gender stereotypes affect our views of leadership and create significant differences in power and authority between men and women (Eagly and Carli, 2004). Many traditional male traits, such as aggression and independence, often are associated with leaders, whereas traditional female traits of submissiveness and cooperation are not.

The third level of culture is organizational culture—the set of values, norms, and beliefs shared by members of an organization. Given time, all organizations develop a unique culture or character whereby employees share common values and beliefs about work-related issues. These organizational values often include deeply held beliefs about leadership (Schein, 2004). In many cases, leaders, and particularly founders, are instrumental in creating and encouraging the culture. The much-talked-about bank Goldman Sachs is known as a highly competitive organization. One of the company's chief accountants, Sarah Smith, says, "It's a 24/7 culture. When you're needed, you're here. And if you're needed and you're not answering your phone, you won't be needed very long" (Alridge, 2009). Another former employee describes the culture as "completely money-obsessed. I was like a donkey driven forward by the biggest, juiciest carrot I could imagine. Money is the way you define your success" (Alridge, 2009). Similarly, the example of the leadership team at the New York Times shows the power of organizational culture (McGregor, 2005a). Linda Greenhouse, one of the paper's senior reporters, states, "There is an endemic cultural issue at the *Times* . . . which is a top-down hierarchical structure" (Bennis, 2003). Other editors at the *Times* were reputed to focus relentlessly on the job at the expense of their employees' needs and personal life. Abe Rosenthal, who stepped in after the leadership team resigned in 2003, told one reporter, "If you are married, you don't belong in journalism!" (Bennis, 2003). Still other accounts of the culture at the *Times* indicate that leaders played favorites rather than focusing on performance (Cotts, 2003).

Another very unique organizational culture that focuses on employee concerns and needs is that of the Atlanta-based consulting firm North Highland, which employs 250. The company prides itself on providing consultants who live where their clients are (North Highland—Working here, 2010). The company established a "no-fly zone" when CEO David Peterson grew tired of being constantly on the road and missing out on his family life; so he created a company to serve local clients (Canabou, 2001). Peterson considers 50 miles to be the maximum distance people should have to travel for work. His company allows employees to balance their work life and home life and provides its clients with consultants who are part of their community. Richard Tuck, cofounder and CEO of Lander International, a company based in El Cerrito, California, similarly encourages his employees to spend less time at work (Fromartz, 2000). When Jon Westberg, the company's executive recruiter, hit a performance slump and sought Tuck's advice, Tuck suggested that "maybe he was spending too much time at work that he needed to devote more time to his art" (Fromartz, 2000). Tuck wants his employees to have outside hobbies and commitments. He hates rules. As a result, the company's culture is loose, with an emphasis on "anything goes." Office manager Helen Winters notes, "I kept waiting for policies to be firmed up, but he just wouldn't do it" (126). Compare Lander's culture with that of Goldman's or the

New York Times. These different organizational cultures have different models of leadership effectiveness. At North Highland, work–life balance is key to effectiveness; at Lander's, the leader is supportive and almost spiritual; at the *Times* and Goldman's, the leader pushes for performance and outcomes.

Because national culture addresses many different aspects of life, it exerts a strong and pervasive influence on people's behavior in everyday activities and in organizations. The influence of organizational culture is, generally, limited to work-related values and behaviors. However, national culture strongly influences organizational culture. French companies, for instance, share some characteristics that make them different from companies in other countries. For example, when compared with their Swedish counterparts, they are more hierarchical and status oriented.

All three levels of culture shape our views and expectations of our leaders. Whereas people in the United States do not expect leaders to be infallible, in many other cultures, leaders' admission of mistakes would be intolerable and a deadly blow to their authority and ability to lead. For example, several U.S. presidents—most recently President Clinton—when faced with no other option, recognized their mistakes openly and professed to have learned from them. Many in the United States expected President Bush to admit mistakes in the war against Iraq, although no apologies have been forthcoming. Such admissions rarely happen in other countries, and if they do, they are interpreted as signs of weakness. Former President Vincente Fox of Mexico steadfastly refused to admit any error or to change course in the handling of his country's economy. He categorically stated, "I believe there are no mistakes" (Government in Mexico, 2001: 35). When, in 1998, Indonesian president Suharto apparently admitted mistakes that contributed to his country's economic crisis, he was seen as weak. Indonesians did not forgive him, and he eventually resigned.

Each country and region in the world develops a particular organizational and management style based largely on its national culture. This style is called the *national organizational heritage* (Bartlett and Ghoshal, 1989, 1992). Although differences distinguish one organization from another and one manager from another, research indicates that national heritage is noticeable and distinct.

MODELS OF NATIONAL CULTURE

Because understanding and handling cultural differences effectively are key to organizational effectiveness in increasingly global organizations, researchers have developed several models for understanding national cultures. This section reviews four models with direct application to organizations and understanding leadership.

Hall's High-Context and Low-Context Cultural Framework

One of the simplest models for understanding culture, Edward Hall's model, divides communication styles within cultures into two groups: high context and low context (Hall, 1976). In Hall's model, context refers to the environment and the information that provide the background for interaction and communication. Leaders from high-context cultures rely heavily on the context, including nonverbal cues and situational factors, to communicate with others and understand the world around them. They use personal relationships to establish communication. Leaders from low-context cultures focus on explicit, specific verbal and written messages to understand people and situations (Munter, 1993).

For example, Japan, Saudi Arabia, Greece, Italy, Vietnam, Korea, and China are all high-context cultures, where subtle body posture, tone of voice, detailed rituals, and a person's title

The Global and Cultural Contexts

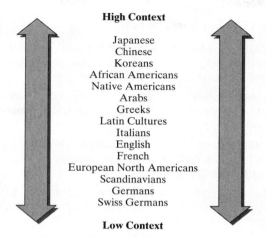

High Context

Japanese
Chinese
Koreans
African Americans
Native Americans
Arabs
Greeks
Latin Cultures
Italians
English
French
European North Americans
Scandinavians
Germans
Swiss Germans

Low Context

FIGURE 2 High- and Low-Context Cultures

and status convey strong messages that determine their behavior and others' reactions to them (Figure 2). In these cultures, communication does not always need to be explicit and specific, and trust is viewed as more important than written communication or legal contracts. In contrast, in low-context cultures, such as Germany, Scandinavia, Switzerland, the United States, Great Britain, and Canada, people pay attention to the verbal message. What is said or written is more important than nonverbal messages or the situation. People are, therefore, specific and clear in their communication with others.

> Leaders from high-context cultures rely heavily on the context, including nonverbal cues and situational factors, to communicate with others and understand the world around them. They use personal relationships to establish communication. Leaders from low-context cultures focus on explicit, specific verbal and written messages to understand people and situations.

The difference between high and low context can explain many cross-cultural communication problems that leaders face when they interact with those of a culture different from their own. The low-context European and North American leaders might get frustrated working with followers from high-context Asian or Middle Eastern cultures because whereas low-context leaders focus on specific instructions, the high-context followers aim at developing relationships. Similarly, high-context leaders might be offended by their low-context followers' directness, which they may interpret as rudeness, lack of respect, and a challenge to their authority.

Hofstede's Five Cultural Dimensions

Researcher Geert Hofstede developed one of the often-cited classifications of culture, known as Hofstede's dimensions (Hofstede, 1992, 2001; Hofstede and Hofstede, 2005). He originally conducted more than 100,000 surveys of IBM employees in 40 countries, supplemented by another series of surveys that led to the development of Confucian dynamism (Hofstede, 1996). He used the results to develop five basic cultural dimensions along which cultures differ: individualism, power distance, uncertainty avoidance, masculinity, and time orientation (Table 1). According to Hofstede, the combination of these five dimensions lends each national culture its distinctiveness and unique character.

> Hofstede developed five basic cultural dimensions along which cultures differ: individualism, power distance, uncertainty avoidance, masculinity, and time orientation. The combination of these five dimensions lends each national culture its distinctiveness and unique character.

TABLE 1	Hofstede's Five Cultural Dimensions
Individualism	The extent to which individuals or a closely knit social structure, such as the extended family, is the basis for social systems. Individualism leads to reliance on self and focus on individual achievement.
Power distance	The extent to which people accept unequal distribution of power. In higher power-distance cultures, there is a wider gap between the powerful and the powerless.
Uncertainty avoidance	The extent to which the culture tolerates ambiguity and uncertainty. High uncertainty avoidance leads to low tolerance for uncertainty and a search for absolute truths.
Masculinity	The extent to which assertiveness and independence from others is valued. High masculinity leads to high sex-role differentiation, focus on independence, ambition, and material goods.
Time orientation	The extent to which people focus on past, present, or future. Present orientation leads to a focus on short-term performance.

For example, when compared with 40 other nations, the United States is highest in individualism (closely followed by Australia), is below average on power distance and uncertainty avoidance, is above average on masculinity, and has a moderate to short-term time orientation. These scores indicate that the United States is a somewhat egalitarian culture in which uncertainty and ambiguity are well tolerated; a high value is placed on individual achievements, assertiveness, performance, and independence; sex roles are relatively well defined; and organizations look for quick results with a focus on the present. Japan, on the other hand, tends to be considerably lower in individualism than the United States, higher in power distance, masculinity (one of the highest scores), and uncertainty avoidance, and with a long-term orientation. These rankings are consistent with the popular image of Japan as a country in which social structures, such as family and organizations are important, their power and obedience to them tend to be absolute, risk and uncertainty are averted, gender roles are highly differentiated, and high value is placed on achievement.

Harry Triandis, a cross-cultural psychologist, expanded on some of Hofstede's cultural dimensions by introducing the concepts of tight and loose, and vertical and horizontal cultures. Triandis (2004) suggests that uncertainty avoidance can be better understood by further classifying cultures into either tight or loose categories. In tight cultures, such as Japan, members follow rules, norms, and standards closely. Behaviors are, therefore, closely regulated; those who do not abide by the rules are criticized, isolated, or even ostracized, depending on the severity of the offense. Loose cultures, such as Thailand, show much tolerance for behaviors that are considered acceptable, and although rules exist, violating them is often overlooked. Triandis (2004) places the United States in the moderate tight–loose category and suggests that the U.S. culture has moved toward becoming looser and more tolerant over the past 50 years.

Triandis further refined the concept of individualism/collectivism by arguing that there are different types of collectivist and individualist cultures (1995). He proposes that by adding the concept of vertical and horizontal, we can gain a much richer understanding of cultural values (Table 2). Vertical cultures focus on hierarchy; horizontal cultures emphasize equality (Triandis et al., 2001). For example, although Sweden and the United States are both individualist cultures, the Swedes are horizontal individualists (HV) and see individuals as unique but equal to others. In the United States, which is more vertical individualist (VI), the individual is

TABLE 2	Vertical and Horizontal Dimensions of Individualism and Collectivism	
	Vertical (Emphasis on Hierarchy)	**Horizontal (Emphasis on Equality)**
Individualistic	Focus on the individual where each person is considered unique and superior to others, often based on accomplishments and performance, or material wealth. Example: United States	Although the focus is on each individual being unique, individuals are considered equal to others without a strong hierarchy. Example: Sweden
Collectivistic	Strong group feeling with clear rank and status differentiation among group members; members feel obligation to obey authority and sacrifice self for good of the group if needed. Example: Japan	All group members are considered equal; the group has little hierarchy, and there is strong focus on democratic and egalitarian processes. Example: Israel

Source: Based on Triandis et al., 2001.

viewed not only as unique, but also superior to others. Similarly, in a horizontal collectivistic (HC) culture, such as Israel, all members of the group are seen as equal. In vertical collectivistic cultures (VC) such as Japan and Korea, authority is important and individuals must sacrifice themselves for the good of the group. The horizontal–vertical dimension, because it affects views of hierarchy and equality, is likely to affect leadership.

Hofstede's cultural values model along with the concepts proposed by Triandis provide a strong basis for explaining cultural differences. The model continues to be used as the basis for research on cross-cultural differences as well as for training leaders to work across cultures. Other researchers have provided additional means of understanding culture.

Trompenaars' Dimensions of Culture

Trompenaars and Hampden-Turner provide a complex model that helps leaders understand national culture and its effect on organizational and corporate cultures (Trompenaars and Hampden-Turner, 1998, 2004). They developed a model initially based on 15,000 people surveyed in organizations in 47 cultures and further tested it by adding data from more than 60,000 people. The model suggests that although understanding national culture requires many different dimensions, cross-cultural organizational cultures can be classified more efficiently based on two dimensions (Trompenaars and Hampden-Turner, 1998): egalitarian-hierarchical and orientation to the person or the task. When combined, they yield four general cross-cultural organizational cultures: incubator, guided missile, family, and Eiffel Tower (Figure 3). The four general types combine national and organizational cultures. The leader's role in each type differs, as do methods of employee motivation and evaluation.

Incubator cultures are egalitarian and focus on taking care of individual needs. Examples of incubator cultures can be found in many start-up, high-technology firms in the United States and Great Britain (Trompenaars, 1998). In these typically individualist cultures, professionals are given considerable latitude to do their jobs. Leaders in such organizations emerge from the group rather than being assigned. Therefore, leadership is based on competence and expertise, and the leader's responsibility is to provide resources, manage conflict, and remove obstacles.

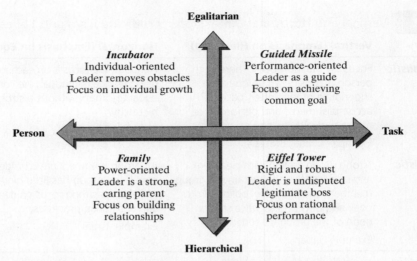

FIGURE 3   Trompenaar's Cross-Cultural Organizational Cultures

The *guided missile* is also an egalitarian culture, but the focus is on task completion rather than individual needs. As a result, the organizational culture is impersonal and, as indicated by its name, directed toward accomplishing the job. Trompenaars uses the U.S. National Aeronautics and Space Administration (NASA) as an example of the guided missile. In NASA and other guided-missile organizations, leadership is based on expertise, and follower participation is expected. People work in teams of professionals who have equal status, with performance being the primary criterion for effectiveness.

The *family* and *Eiffel Tower* cultures both are hierarchical. Whereas the Eiffel Tower is focused on the task, the family takes care of individuals. As its name indicates, the family culture functions like a traditional family. The leader's role is that of a powerful father figure, who is responsible for the welfare of all members. Trompenaars suggests that family organizational cultures are found in Greece, Italy, Singapore, South Korea, and Japan. The Eiffel Tower is hierarchical and task focused. Consistent with the name—the Eiffel Tower—many French organizations have such a culture, characterized by a steep, stable, and rigid organization. The focus is on performance through order and obedience of legal and legitimate authority. The leader is the undisputed head of the organization and has full responsibility for all that occurs.

Trompenaars' added dimensions and focus on culture in organizations provides a rich model for understanding culture. The most recent approach to explaining cultural differences will be presented next.

Global Leadership and Organizational Behavior Effectiveness Research

One of the most exciting and extensive research projects about cross-cultural differences and leadership was conducted by a group of researchers in 62 countries (House et al., 2004). Despite recent debates about the methodology used by researchers of Global Leadership and Organizational Behavior Effectiveness research (GLOBE; Graen, 2006; House et al., 2006), the model is comprehensive and highly useful in understanding leadership and culture. GLOBE examines culture using nine dimensions, predicting their impact on leadership and organizational processes (House et al., 2002; Table 3). Although some of the dimensions proposed by the

TABLE 3	Globe Dimensions	
Dimension	**Description**	**Country Rankings**
Power distance	The degree to which power is distributed equally	High—Russia, Spain, Thailand Moderate—England, U.S., Brazil Low—Denmark, Israel, Costa Rica
Uncertainty avoidance	The extent to which a culture relies on social norms and rules to reduce unpredictability (high score indicates high tolerance for uncertainty)	High—Denmark, Germany, Sweden Moderate—Israel, U.S., Mexico Low—Russia, Greece, Venezuela
Humane orientation	The degree to which a culture values fairness, generosity, caring and kindness	High—Indonesia, Egypt, Philippines Moderate—Hong Kong, Sweden, U.S. Low—Germany, Singapore, France
Collectivism I (institutional)	The degree to which a culture values and practices collective action and collective distribution of resources	High—Denmark, Singapore, Japan Moderate—U.S., Egypt, Indonesia Low—Greece, Germany, Italy
Collectivism II (in-group)	The degree to which individuals express pride and cohesion in their family or organizations	High—Egypt, China, Iran Moderate—Japan, Israel, Italy Low—Denmark, Finland, Sweden
Assertiveness	The degree to which individuals are assertive, direct, and confrontational	High—U.S., Germany Moderate—France, Philippines Low—Sweden, Japan, Kuwait
Gender egalitarianism	The extent of gender differentiation (high score indicates more differentiation)	High—South Korea, Egypt, India Moderate—Italy, The Netherlands Low—Sweden, Poland
Future orientation	The extent to which a culture invests in the future rather than in the present or past	High—Denmark, Singapore Moderate—Australia, India Low—Russia, Italy
Performance orientation	The degree to which a culture values and encourages performance and excellence	High—U.S., Taiwan, Singapore Moderate—Sweden, England, Japan Low—Russia, Venezuela, Italy

Sources: Based on House et al., 2004, 2002; Javidan and House, 2001.

GLOBE researchers are similar to those presented by Hofstede and Trompenaars and his colleagues, others are unique and refine our understanding of culture. As with previous research, GLOBE assumes that culture affects what leaders do and how organizations are structured and managed. Based on their findings, the United States is among the highest in assertiveness and performance orientation and falls in the middle in all the other dimensions (Javidan and House, 2001). Spaniards and Germans are the most assertive and direct, whereas Germans also avoid uncertainty and are the lowest in valuing generosity and caring. Austrians and the Swiss, like Germans, require clear communication and will rely on rules and procedures to determine their behaviors. Russians and Italians invest the least in the future and are least likely to focus on performance and excellence. Furthermore, like the Greeks, Russians do not require much structure and can tolerate uncertainty to a greater extent than some Germanic Europeans. Although they differ in gender egalitarianism, the Swedes and Japanese are among the least assertive and direct. In countries with high power distance, such as Thailand and Russia, communication is often directed one way, from the leader to followers, with little expectation of feedback. Finally, in cultures that value kindness and generosity, such as the Philippines or Egypt, leaders are likely to avoid conflict and act in a caring but paternalistic manner (Javidan and House, 2001).

GLOBE identifies several categories of leader behavior that are either universally desirable or undesirable or whose desirability is contingent on the culture (House et al., 2004). For example, charismatic/value-based leadership is generally desirable across most cultures. Similarly, team-based leadership is believed to contribute to outstanding leadership in many cultures. Although participative leadership is seen, generally, as positive, its effectiveness depends on the culture. Autonomous leaders are desirable in some cultures but not in all, and being self-protective is seen as impeding effective leadership in most cultures. Even some behaviors that are somewhat universal reflect cultural differences. For example, Americans and the British highly value charisma whereas Middle Easterners place less importance on this behavior from their leader. Nordic cultures are less favorable toward self-protective leadership behaviors whereas Southern Asians accept it more readily (House et al., 2004).

GLOBE assumes that culture affects what leaders do and how organizations are structured and managed. Based on their findings, the United States is among the highest in assertiveness and performance orientation and falls in the middle in all the other dimensions.

The models of culture presented in this section provide different ways of understanding national and organizational culture. Each model is not only useful but can also be misapplied if used to stereotype national or organizational cultures. Whereas Hall and Hofstede focus primarily on national culture, Trompenaars provides a model that combines national and organizational cultural and has a strong practitioner focus. GLOBE has one of the most comprehensive models available with a strong focus on leadership characteristics across cultures. All four are used throughout the book to provide a cross-cultural perspective on leadership.

Applying What You Learn
Using Culture to Be Effective

Culture at all levels can have a powerful impact on both leaders and followers. The following are some things to keep in mind to manage culture effectively:

- Be aware and conscious of your own culture and its various components. What are your values? How important are they to you? What are the conflicts you experience?
- Understand the culture of your organization. Is cooperation or competition valued? How formal is the environment? How much is performance valued? How about citizenship? What is rewarded?
- Be clear about any areas of agreement and disagreement between your culture and value system and that of your organization.

- Build on the agreements; they are likely to provide you with opportunities to shine. For example, if you value competition and high performance and so does the organization, you are likely to feel right at home.
- Carefully evaluate the disagreements. For example, you value competition and individual achievements, whereas the organization is highly team oriented. Can you adapt? Can you change the organization? A high degree of ongoing conflict among primary values is likely to lead to frustration and dissatisfaction.

GROUP CULTURE: GENDER AND DIVERSITY

Whereas national culture impacts us at a macro level, another strong cultural influence on individual behavior is group culture, which may consist of a number of primary factors such as gender, ethnicity, and age and other secondary factors such as income, education, and membership in various groups (Figure 4). The primary dimensions of diversity are the visible and stable aspects of a person. Factors that are considered secondary are more dynamic. Group culture can affect people in two important ways. First, people's leadership style may vary based on their group membership, as some evidence regarding gender differences suggests. Second, membership in those groups affects how others view the person and therefore how they may react to leadership from that person. For example, some research suggests that "being White" is still associated with being an effective leader (Rosette, Leonardelli, and Philips, 2008). Overall, the leadership of organizations continues to be primarily male and white in the case of Western countries. Few women and minorities head public, nonprofit, and business organizations, and few are members of company boards of directors, despite the many years of diversity policies and training and calls for inclusion of diverse populations in organizations (McCool, 2008). We will consider gender differences in leadership and review the causes and solutions to unequal treatment based on group membership.

Gender and Leadership

Leaders such as Francis Hesselbein, chief executive of the Girl Scouts; Nancy Bador, former executive director of Ford Motor Company; and Barbara Grogan, founder of Western Industrial Contractors and chair of the Volunteer Board of America, use an inclusive management style that they consider a female style of leadership. They shun the hierarchical structures for flat webs in which they are at the center rather than at the top. This structure, and their position within it, allows them to be accessible and informed. Whereas top-down and bottom-up information in a traditional hierarchy is filtered and altered as it travels, leaders at the center of the web gain direct access to all others in the organization, and their employees have access to them. As a result, the web structure prevents managers from feeling isolated and out of touch with the needs of their

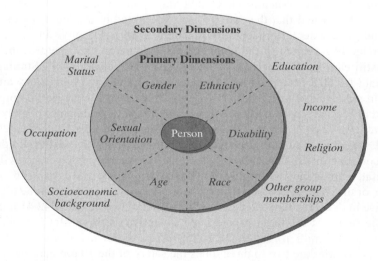

FIGURE 4 Dimensions of Group Cultures and Diversity

subordinates and their organization. Carol Smith, Senior VP of Elle Group, a media company, strongly believes that women are better managers, "In my experience, female bosses tend to be better managers, better advisers, mentors, rational thinkers. Men love to hear themselves talk." She further believes that men are better at letting things roll off their back while women rethink and replay events (Bryant, 2009p). Meg Whitman, who was CEO of eBay until 2008 and rated by *Fortune* as one of the most powerful woman in business in 2005, is known for her unconventional, noncommand, and control use of power. She believes that having power means that you must be willing to not have any (Sellers, 2004). Gerry Laybourne, former CEO of Oxygen Media, the executive who built the top-rated children's television network Nickelodeon while she was at Viacom, considers competition to be "nonfemale." When she found out that *Fortune* magazine was ranking women in business, she declared, "That's a nonfemale thing to do. Ranking is the opposite of what women are all about" (Sellers, 1998: 80). She contends women lead and manage differently and are better than men at making connections among ideas and building partnerships and joint ventures (Sellers, 2009a).

Many other successful female business leaders, however, do not see their leadership styles as drastically different from that of their male counterparts. Cherri Musser, chief information officer at EDS and formerly at GM, recommends, "You don't focus on being female—you focus on getting the job done. If you draw too much attention to your gender, you're not a member of the team" (Overholt, 2001: 66). Darla Moore, chief executive officer of the investment company Rainwater, Inc., and the first woman to have a business school named after her, argues that women's worse sin is to think, "'You should be a nice girl. You ought to fit in. You should find a female mentor.' What a colossal waste of time" (Sellers, 1998: 92). She contends, "There are only glass ceilings and closed doors for those who allow such impediments" (Darla Moore Speech, 2007).

Whether women and men lead differently or not, there are differences between them in terms of the presence and power each group has in organizations around the world.

Current State of Women in Organizations

There is no question that women in the United States, and in most other countries, have unequal access to power and that they are poorly represented in the higher levels of business, nonprofit, and governmental organizations (Horan, 2009). Although in the United States, women make up 49.5 percent of the labor force as compared to 35 percent in 1970 (Evans, 2009), they still earn only 80 percent of men's salary (Catalyst, 2009). Similarly, although women account for 50.8 percent of management and professional ranks, they are not as well represented in top levels of organizations. Women hold only 15.2 percent of corporate officer positions and only 3 percent of CEO positions in *Fortune* 500 companies (Catalyst, 2009). As of 2008, there were only 12 female CEOs in the *Fortune* 500 in the United States (one is featured in the Leadership in Action case at the end of this chapter). It is estimated that if the current trends continue, by 2016 maybe 6 percent of top leadership positions will be held by women (Helfat, Harris, and Wolfson, 2006). The salary gap between men and women is further evidence of the challenges women face. The compensation package of the highest-paid female executive in the United States in 2008 (Safra Catz of Oracle with $42.41 million) was 38 percent of the salary of the highest-paid male executive (Aubrey McClendon, Chesapeake Energy Corp., $112.5 million). All of the 10 highest-paid executives in United States in 2008 were men; their salaries are two to three times the salary of the 10 top-earning women executives (Highest paid CEOs, 2009). The wage gap is less pronounced at lower-level managerial levels and other jobs, around 70 percent by most accounts; however, it is still indicative of the challenges women face.

Even though in some cases, state, local, and national governments have many female and minority leaders, the situation is not considerably better. In 2009, out of 533 members of the U.S. House of Representatives, 76 were female, 41 were Black, 28 Hispanic, 8 Asian, and only one Native American (Manning, 2009). In the U.S. Senate, only 17 out of 100 senators were female; 1 Black; 2 Asians; and 1 Hispanic (Manning, 2009). Only 6 out of the 21 members of President Obama's cabinet in 2009 were women, with 20 women ever having held ministerial positions in the United States, while the United States has yet to elect a female head-of-state. Women in Scandinavian countries have achieved higher-level positions, but the percentage of women in power is roughly the same and generally not substantially better in most other Western nations (IWDC, 2007).

The trend is similar in other areas such as education, where although women make up a large majority of teachers and students of educational leadership; the actual leadership is predominantly and consistently male. Research over an 80-year period indicates that the number of women serving in superintendent positions has decreased since 1910 from 9.38 percent to only 4.6 percent in 1990 (Dana and Bourisaw, 2006). An even more disturbing fact is that even when women are in leadership positions, they have less decision-making power, less authority, and less access to the highly responsible and challenging assignments than their male counterparts (Smith, 2002). Another alarming development for women is that despite consistent gains in achieving equality with men in the workplace, a series of surveys conducted since 1972 indicate that overall, women are unhappier than they were previously, and they get less happy as they age, a finding that is reversed for men (Buckingham, 2009). The primary explanation provided is that women feel rushed and stressed much more than before and more than men, and that they feel drained rather than fulfilled. All the progress that women have made was assumed to make them happier; it has not.

Causes of Gender Differences in Leadership

What factors explain the lesser roles women play in the leadership of organizations? Researchers have proposed several reasons to explain those differences (for a review see Eagly and Carli, 2004; Table 4).

TABLE 4	Potential Causes of Poor Representation of Women in Leadership

- Gender differences in leadership style
- Balancing work and home
- Women are less committed to their work and career
- Women have less experience in organizations
- Women quit their jobs more often
- Women are less educated
- Blatant and subtle discrimination
- Persistent gender stereotypes
- Glass ceiling
- Cultural factors

GENDER DIFFERENCES IN STYLE AND EFFECTIVENESS Researchers have identified gender differences in several areas related to leadership such as interests (Su, Rounds, and Armstrong, 2009), communication styles (e.g., Tannen, 1993), and negotiation styles and effectiveness (e.g., Amanatullah and Morris, 2010). There is also much anecdotal evidence, such as those presented earlier in this chapter, that men and women differ in their leadership and management styles. We intuitively believe that there are clear gender differences in leadership. However, it is not clear whether these differences benefit or disadvantage female leaders.

Researchers have found some, although not overwhelming, gender differences in leadership. Eagly and Johnson's meta-analysis (1990) found that women tend to show more people-oriented and democratic styles, whereas men were more likely to be task focused and autocratic. The results, however, were more pronounced in laboratory rather than organizational settings. Interestingly, the most consistent gender difference in leadership relates to change- and future-oriented leadership style, often referred to as *transformational leadership*. Transformational leadership focuses on establishing an emotional connection with followers and inspiring them toward implementing change. A review by Eagly and her colleagues (2003) suggests that female leaders are more transformational, show more individualized attention to their followers, and are more supportive of them than male leaders.

Given the presence of some gender differences, the question is: Do these differences handicap women, preventing them from being effective and reaching leadership positions, thus providing an explanation for the presence of fewer female leaders? Much of the focus of current leadership practice is on styles that are more stereotypically female rather than male. Management guru Tom Peters believes that the success of the new economy depends on the collaborative style that women leaders use instead of the command and control style that male leaders have traditionally used (Reingold, 2003). Among practitioners, characteristics typically associated with the female leadership style are increasingly considered necessary, regardless of gender (M. Useem, 2001). The research on transformational leadership further supports the notion that transformational leadership is an effective style. Based on these assertions and research results, one would expect that organizations would seek more female leaders, that more women would be in leadership positions, and that they would be more effective than their male counterparts. That not being the case, gender differences in leadership style do not provide a clear explanation for the lesser role women play in the leadership of organizations.

WOMEN FACE CHALLENGES AT BALANCING FAMILY AND WORK "The greatest challenge has been balancing all the demand of being a women, a parent, a wife, a sister, a daughter, a friend *and* a CEO" states Cinta Putra, CEO of National Notification Network (Bisoux, 2008, p. 16). This belief is echoed by many women who still have a greater share of the household and child-rearing responsibilities than men do and continue to be challenged at balancing their work and personal life. Sheryl Sandberg, COO of Facebook, ranked one of the top 40 businesspeople under the age of 40 by *Fortune* in 2009, believes that the disequilibrium in household responsibilities is a basic reason for women's lack of progress (Seller, 2009b). Although there have been some changes over the past few years, research indicates that women still continue to carry most of the burden for child-care and household work (Bianchi, 2000), and that mothers are less employed than other women, whereas fathers work more than other men (Kaufman and Uhlenberg, 2000). However, although there is no clear evidence that parenthood reduces women's commitment to their work and career or that women do not seek leadership positions because they worry about the demands of such positions (Eagly and Carli, 2004), such beliefs continue to hamper women's progress in the workplace. Sandberg finds that many of the young women she targets for challenging positions take themselves out of the running because they think having a family, which is in their future plans, will not allow them to continue working as hard, so they slow down too early (Sandberg, 2009). Women are not alone in this belief. Research suggests that bosses' perception of potential conflict between family and work may affect their decision to promote women (Hoobler, Wayne, and Lemmon, 2009). In this case, as in some others, perception appears to play a bigger role than reality.

WOMEN ARE NOT WELL PREPARED AND NOT AS COMMITTED AS MEN   Another potential explanation for the differential presence and role of women in leadership is that women are generally not as well prepared as men to take on leadership roles because of their lower education. They have less work experience and are less interested in investing their time and resources in reaching top levels of organizations than men. Even though one can always find anecdotal evidence of women being unprepared for and less interested in leadership, demographic information and research do not support this explanation. First, women have been fully engaged in organizations for over 40 years. They have occupied close to 50 percent of supervisory and managerial ranks for many years now. There are many fully qualified women ready and able to move up the ranks of our organizations. Second, women are earning 59 percent of the undergraduate college degrees, 61 percent of the master's degrees (Buckingham, 2009), and 51 percent of MBAs. Women are therefore committed to education and are bypassing men in overall numbers.

Another factor that is often mentioned is that working mothers in particular are not able to devote as much time to their careers and are more likely to quit their jobs, thereby hindering their progress. Recent research indicates that although more professional women than men do take a break from work when they start a family (16 percent for women vs. 2 percent for men; Search for Women, 2006), over 90 percent of them try to get back in after about two years (Hewlett, 2007), further contradicting the idea that women have less commitment to their careers than men. Some women executives have even suggested that motherhood provides women with skills that can be helpful in taking on organizational leadership roles (Grzelakowski, 2005). Gerry Laybourne, founder of Oxygen states, "You learn about customer service from your 2-year-old (they are more demanding than any customer can be). You also learn patience, management skills, diversionary tactics, and 5-year planning" (*Startup Nation*, 2005).

DISCRIMINATION   Another explanation for fewer female leaders is discrimination. Discrimination would suggest that women, and members of other nondominant groups, are placed at a disadvantage not based on their abilities or actions, but based on other non–job-related factors. Women and minorities face a glass ceiling—invisible barriers and obstacles that prevent them from moving to the highest levels of organizations (Arfken, Bellar, and Helms, 2004). Some have suggested that men are fast-tracked to leadership position through a "glass elevator" (Maune, 1999), and a recent review suggests the presence of a "glass cliff," whereby successful women are appointed to precarious leadership positions with little chance of success, thereby exposing them to yet another form of discrimination (Ryan and Haslam, 2007). The common theme in all these situations is the presence of invisible barriers that discriminate against women and minorities based on their group membership and prevent them from achieving their full potential.

Sexual harassment, which is considered workplace discrimination, is another barrier for women. A survey done in New Zealand suggests that one in three women reported being sexually harassed (New Zealand Human Rights Commission, 2007). According to the U.S. Equal Employment Opportunity Commission (EEOC) 2009 report, of the 12,696 sexual harassment complaints filed in 2009, only 16 percent were from males (EEOC, 2009). Surveys indicate that women are almost three times as likely as men to report that they are victims of discrimination (Wilson, 2006). Other more subtle forms of discrimination include the fact that although they are in midmanagement positions, women and minorities are often not mentored by the right people at the right time, a factor that is critical to success in any organization. Men are also made team leaders more often than women are (46 vs. 34 percent), they get more budgetary authority (44 vs. 31 percent), and they have increased responsibilities (89 vs. 83 percent; Search for women, 2006). Furthermore, women and minorities are often not exposed to the type of positions or experiences that are essential to achieving high-level leadership. For example, women and minorities may not be encouraged to take on international assignments or kept in staff rather than line positions and therefore may lack essential operational experience. Finally, subtle social and organizational culture factors, such as going to lunch with the "right" group, playing sports, being members of certain clubs, and exclusion from informal socializing and the "good old boys" network, can contribute to the lack of proportional representation of women and minorities in leadership ranks.

> Discrimination would suggest that women, and members of other nondominant groups, are placed at a disadvantage not based on their abilities or actions, but based on other non–job-related factors.

PERSISTENT STEREOTYPES Cases from organizations and academic research consistently suggest that women are still subject to negative stereotypes. They are caught in the double bind of having to fulfill two contradictory roles and expectations: those of being a woman and those of being a leader (Eagly and Karau, 2002). Gender stereotypes that equate leadership with being male persist (de Pillis et. al., 2008), and conventional gender stereotypes help men (Judge and Livingston, 2008). In many traditional settings, being a leader requires forceful behaviors that are more masculine (e.g., being proactive and decisive) than feminine (being kind and not appearing too competent). Women who are masculine, however, are often not liked and not considered effective (Powell, Butterfield, and Parent, 2002). Men particularly expect women to act in ways that are stereotypically feminine and evaluate them poorly when they show the more masculine characteristics typically associated with leadership. In some cases, evidence suggests that women do not support other women in getting leadership positions (Dana and Barisaw, 2006). Further, women who actively seek leadership and show a desire to direct others are not well accepted (Carli, 1999). These stereotypes and contradictory expectations limit the range of behaviors women are "allowed" to use when leading others, further hampering their ability to be effective. Becoming an effective leader requires considerable practice and experimentation. If they want to be easily accepted, women leaders are restricted to a set of feminine behaviors characterized by interpersonal warmth as their primary, if not only, means of influence (Carli, 2001). Because of existing stereotypes, women, and in many cases minorities, are not able to fully practice to perfect their craft. Generally, stereotypes of women and minorities not being as competent or able to handle challenging leadership situations as men still persist, making blatant or subtle discrimination a continuing problem.

Real or perceived gender differences and continued used of stereotypes and discrimination all combine to prevent women from achieving their potential in organizations. Much research has been devoted to changing these situations, and organizations implement a variety of programs to ensure that women and minorities are well represented in their leadership ranks.

LEADING CHANGE

Deloitte Supports All Its Employees

Deloitte, one of the Big Four accounting firms with global reach, has 4,500 partners and other top executives. Ninety two percent of them are white (Crockett, 2009), despite many years of efforts to build diversity in the company. This statistic is on CEO Barry Salzberg's mind. He is focused on making his company a more diverse place and on opening doors for the talent that Deloitte needs to recruit and retain to succeed. One of the steps the company has taken is to recruit from community colleges rather than only from top-notch universities, a practice that is typical for large global companies. Salzberg states: "Targeting these schools offers us a unique opportunity to reach another distinct population of diverse top talent" (Crockett, 2009). In addition, Deloitte has implemented an innovative program call Mass Career Customization, which provides every employee, not just women and minorities, the opportunity to develop their own unique path. The program grew out of a women's initiative within the company but now applies to all employees. "Mass career customization provides a framework in which every employee, in conjunction with his or her manager, can tailor his or her respective career path within Deloitte over time" (Deloitte, 2010). The program allows employees to create a better fit between their life and career and provides multiple paths to the top of the organization, thereby addressing one of the primary challenges that women face in balancing work and life.

Deloitte's efforts have not gone unnoticed. The company was named by *Business Week* as the number one company for starting a career (Gerdes and Lavelle, 2009) and got high marks in the Shriver Report, a report that describes the status of women in the United States, as a model employer (Shriver Report, 2009). The report gives Deloitte high marks for being "an excellent example of an employer that has taken an aggressive leadership position in protean career approaches, providing career-life integration programs that allow both the organization and its workforce—women and men—to reach their goals" (Deloitte—Shriver Report, 2009). Cathy Benko, vice chairman and chief talent officer at Deloitte, believes that "through our own journey to retain and advance women, we know that what is good for women is good for all our people" (Model employer, 2009).

Sources: Crockett, R. O. 2009. Deloitte's diversity push. *Business Week*, October 2, http://www.businessweek.com/managing/content/oct2009/ca2009102_173180.htm (accessed January 18, 2010). Deloitte. 2010. http://careers.deloitte.com/united-states/students/culture_benefits.aspx?CountryContentID=13709 (accessed January 18, 2010). Deloitte—Shriver Report. 2009. Deloitte recognized for its strategies to adapt to the evolving workforce. http://www.deloitte.com/view/en_US/us/press/Press-Releases/press-release/5e6c7475aa455210VgnVCM200000bb42f00aRCRD.htm (accessed January 18, 2010). Gerdes, L. and L. Lavelle. Best place to launch a career 2009. *Business Week*. http://bwnt.businessweek.com/interactive_reports/career_launch_2009/ (accessed January 18, 2010). Model employer. 2009. http://www.deloitte.com/view/en_US/us/About/Womens-Initiative/article/c7aa98bbcf084210VgnVCM100000ba42f00aRCRD.htm (accessed January 18, 2010). Shriver Report: A woman's nation changes everything. 2009. http://awomansnation.com (accessed January 18, 2010).

DEVELOPING A CULTURAL MINDSET

More often than not, obstacles that women and minority face are not immediately apparent, are often not illegal, and are unwritten and unofficial policy. They are part of the organizational culture and are therefore difficult to identify and even more difficult to change. Although there are some differences, all members of nondominant groups face similar challenges. Some social factors, such as more even distribution of work at home and increased higher education, will provide a push in the right direction. The changing views of leadership and the need for leaders with strong interpersonal skills, a trait that is more *stereotypically feminine* than masculine, will also help in making leadership in organizations more accessible to women.

From an organizational point of view, aside from the fairness issue, developing talented leaders, regardless of their culture, race, and gender, is essential. The fundamental solution to addressing the challenges that women and minorities face is to make organizational climates hospitable to diverse groups with diverse needs (Solomon, 2010; Valerio, 2009). Organizations must cultivate a way of thinking where culture is taken into consideration in deliberations, decisions, and behaviors. Such an approach is beyond acquiring simple skills and competencies; it starts with and requires a new way of thinking: a cultural mindset. Although it is close to impossible for anyone to acquire in-depth knowledge about all the cultures he or she might encounter, it is possible to have a cultural mindset that allows one to understand cultural differences and their impact on behavior and to take that knowledge into consideration when interacting with and leading others. Such a cultural mindset engenders an awareness of and openness to culture and how it affects our own and others' thinking and behavior. It involves both how one thinks and how one acts. Attention to culture is essential because, as we discussed earlier, culture is stable and hard to change, it influences behavior, and organizations are facing highly diverse constituents. A cultural mindset allows for a multicultural approach, which aims at inclusiveness, social justice, affirmation, mutual respect, and harmony in a pluralistic world (Fowers and Davidov, 2006). Rather than being viewed as an issue of quotas and percentages, diversity and multiculturalism refer to building a culture of openness and inclusiveness. The benefits of building a multicultural organization with a cultural mindset go beyond women and other minority groups; they extend to all employees. A Gallup survey suggests that organizations where diversity is valued have the most satisfied employees and better retention (Wilson, 2006).

> Organizations must cultivate a way of thinking where culture is taken into consideration in deliberations, decisions, and behaviors. Such an approach is beyond acquiring simple skills and competencies; it starts with and requires a new way of thinking: a cultural mindset. Although it is close to impossible for anyone to acquire in-depth knowledge about all the cultures he or she might encounter, it is possible to have a cultural mindset that allows one to understand cultural differences and their impact on behavior and to take that knowledge into consideration when interacting with and leading others.

Organizational leaders play a critical role in encouraging a cultural mindset in organizations. Leaders demonstrate through their words and actions the value of maintaining a multicultural organization where discrimination is not tolerated and where cultural differences are fully considered as part of all decision making (Figure 5). Ed Zander, former CEO of Motorola, states, "Business and diversity are one and the same. Business means diversity, and diversity means business" (Winters, 2007: 7). Zander focuses on the three themes of ethics, quality, and diversity in all his meetings. Similarly, Barry Salzberg, CEO of Deloitte (see Leading Change box) is focused on increasing the diversity in his organization. The Gallup survey linking diversity to satisfaction further indicates that organizational leaders' commitment to diversity is linked to overall employee satisfaction (Wilson, 2006). Leaders influence the culture and organizational processes that determine how decisions are made, how others behave, and what is accepted and tolerated and what is not. The leader not only is a powerful decision maker, but also exercises considerable influence through formal and informal communication, role modeling, and other powerful means. The message the leader sends through words and actions about the role of women and minorities and the importance of multiculturalism in an organization is one of the most important factors.

Changing the culture of an organization to address discriminatory practices, behaviors, and symbols is another powerful tool. Changing culture is one of the most difficult and lengthy

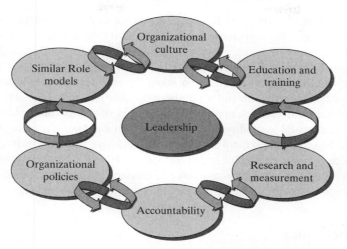

FIGURE 5 Factors in Becoming a Multicultural Organization

processes any organization can undertake. Without a cultural change toward addressing informal discriminatory practices and attitudes, however, other improvements are not likely to be as effective. The presence of diverse role models throughout an organization is another part of the solution to providing leadership opportunities for women and minorities. By having diverse people in leadership positions, an organization "walks the talk" and can demonstrate its commitment to diversity. Toyota U.S.A. has a "diversity champion" program it started in the late 1990s. Outstanding employees with leadership skills are nominated by their colleagues to receive intensive diversity management training and return to their work units with a "champion" badge and a mission to help implement changes to make the workplace more inclusive and emphasize commonalities (Wiscombe, 2007a). Another step toward changing culture is providing support groups for various diverse groups. The Chubb group, one of the largest insurance companies in the United States, has put in place networks for various employees. The company supports employee networks for working parents and young people, as well as more traditional diverse groups such as gays and lesbians, people with disabilities, Latinos, and women (Solomon, 2010). Donna Griffin, the company's diversity officer, believes these groups provide a positive image for the organization, help attract diverse talent, and affect the bottom line positively. She states: "We had a specific program that was geared toward our Asian-American agents and we utilized resources from our Asian business network in order to make that happen" (Solomon, 2010).

Training and education can help people become aware of their biases, understand their own and others' cultural point of view, and better accept differences. When the consulting firm of Bain & Company transfers its consultants from one part of the world to another, it not only provides them with information about living in the new country, but also arms them with cultural knowledge specific to the country to allow them to function more effectively (Holland, 2007). Other companies such as Procter & Gamble (P&G) value and encourage the development of cultural knowledge in their employees and leaders. Because their employees are as likely to work with someone from their own culture as with someone from a different culture, P&G immerses its employees in international assignments (Schoeff, 2007).

The case of Deloitte in the Leading Change feature is an example of how organizations need to change their existing policies and implement creative new systems to support the development of their employees. Many organizational policies such as those on family leave can hinder people's chances of advancement. Similarly, traditional performance evaluation criteria, which emphasize the stereotypical male and Western characteristics associated with leaders as the basis for success, may undermine the ability of people who have other diverse characteristics and skills to rise to leadership positions. Finally, successful change requires careful measurement and monitoring. Organizations must have baseline information about the hard facts about the actual numbers of women and minorities in leadership and about the softer data related to satisfaction, attitudes, and the less-visible obstacles that may be in place. Keeping track of changes and holding decision makers accountable are essential to solidifying any improvement that may take place. For example, another indicator of Toyota's commitment to a diverse and inclusive workforce is its quick action after one of its top executives was accused of sexual harassment. Not only did the executive leave his position, but the company also created a task force to enhance training of its executives and put in place better procedures for responding to allegations and complaints (Wiscombe, 2007b).

Summary and Conclusions

Culture can affect whom we consider to be an effective leader. Several models have been proposed to increase our understanding of culture and how it may affect behavior. Hall's cultural context focuses on the communication context. People from high-context cultures rely on the environment, nonverbal cues, situational factors, and subtle signals to communicate with others. Those from low-context cultures focus on specific written or oral messages. Hofstede's cultural values suggest that culture can be understood using the five dimensions of power distance, uncertainty avoidance, individualism, masculinity, and time orientation. Additionally, whether a culture is tight, with many rules and regulations, or loose, with fewer prescriptions for behavior, further affects how people behave. Trompenaars further refines our understanding of culture by considering nine dimensions and providing models for cross-cultural organizational cultures. The most recent and most comprehensive model for culture has been proposed by researchers in the Global Leadership and Organizational Behavior Effectiveness (GLOBE) model.

In addition to national culture, group culture, particularly as it relates to gender and minorities, plays a role in the leadership of organizations. Although women have active roles in organizations in the West and many other parts of the world, clearly they do not have access to the same power and leadership roles as men do. Gender differences, less desire to lead, and particularly enduring stereotypes and discrimination have been proposed as the primary reasons for the presence of fewer women in leadership positions. Creating multicultural organizations where a cultural mindset operates and where differences are valued and individuals are encouraged to thrive is the key to increasing the presence of women and minorities in organizations. Leadership plays a central role in bringing about the cultural and organizational changes necessary to achieve that goal.

Review and Discussion Questions

1. What are the four models of culture, and how do they affect leadership?
2. How are the different models of culture similar? What unique contributions does each model make?
3. How would the definitions of leaders and effectiveness differ based on the different cultural values presented by Hofstede, Trompenaars, and the GLOBE findings?
4. How does group membership affect leaders and leadership?
5. Name some of the gender differences in leaderships.
6. What are the causes of discrimination against women and minorities in organizations?
7. How can organizations develop a cultural mindset and become more multicultural?

Leadership Challenge: Juggling Cultures

Culture, gender, and leadership are closely related. In most cultures, even Western cultures, leadership is associated with males. This association is even stronger in many Arab Muslim countries, where women typically play a limited role in public and business life.

As a leader of an organization, you face the choice of selecting the leader of a negotiation team to draft a new deal with a potential Saudi Arabian client. By far, your best, most experienced, and most skilled negotiator is one of your female executives. She has,

for many years, successfully negotiated deals within the United States and in several other countries. Her second in command is a promising but relatively young male executive who still needs to develop his skills and experience.

1. Whom do you send to Saudi Arabia as head of your team?
2. What cultural factors do you need to consider?
3. What are the implications of your decision for your business and the message you send as a leader?

49

Exercise 1: Proverbs as a Window to Leadership

What do these proverbs tell us about the culture? What implications do they have for leadership in that culture?

United States (mainstream)

Proverb	Implications for Leadership
Actions speak louder than words.	
Strike while the iron is hot.	
Time is money.	
God helps those who help themselves.	

From Other Cultures

Proverb	Implications for Leadership
One does not make the wind, but is blown by it (Asian cultures).	
Order is half of life (Germany).	
When spider webs unite, they can tie up a lion (Ethiopia).	
We are all like well buckets, one goes up and the other comes down (Mexico).	
Sometimes you ride the horse; sometimes you carry the saddle (Iran).	
We will be known forever by the tracks we leave (Native American—Dakota).	
One finger cannot lift a pebble (Hopi).	
Force, no matter how concealed, begets resistance (Lakota).	

EXERCISE 2: Narian Bridges

The following exercise is a cross-cultural role-play designed to allow you to experience the challenges and opportunities of interacting with people from different cultures. The setting is the fictional country of Nari. You will be asked to play the role of either an American or a Narian. Read the exercise carefully; your instructor will provide you with further information.

Background

Nari is a Middle Eastern country with an old history and a rich cultural heritage. Through judicious excavation of a number of minerals, the country has obtained considerable wealth, and the stable political and social climate has attracted many foreign investors. As a result, Nari launched a careful and well-planned development campaign in the past 20 years that allowed the country's economy to become the strongest in the region. The per capita income is the highest in the region with a literacy rate greater than 80 percent for the population under 30 (which comprises 53 percent of the population).

The political system is an authoritarian monarchy. The powers of the elected parliament are limited to its consultative role to the king. This political system has been in place for more than 1,000 years, and the current dynasty began its reign 400 years ago. As compared with many of its unstable neighbors, Nari has enjoyed a calm political climate. The Western press, however, is highly critical of the lack of democracy and the authoritarian nature of the government. The king has unceremoniously dismissed the charges as cultural colonialism and emphasizes the need to preserve the Narian culture while welcoming the West's and the East's help in economic development.

The culture is warm and welcoming of outsiders. The Narian focus on politeness and kindness is easily extended to foreigners, although Narians do not accept criticism of their culture as well and do not tolerate debate about the topic, particularly with outsiders. Many younger Narians seek higher education in other parts of the world, but most return eagerly to their country. The extended family remains the core of society, with the father being the unquestioned head. Narians take pride in their family and maintain considerable commitment to it. They demonstrate a similar commitment to the organizations to which they belong; employees take pride in the accomplishments of their organizations. Although some rumblings can be heard about opening up the political systems and allowing for more democratic participation, the authority of the family, of the community, and of the monarch are rarely, if ever, questioned. Narians often mention the importance of individual sacrifice, social order, and stability and express dismay, with a smile, at how Westerners can get anything done when they behave in such unruly ways. They also contrast the inherent trust in their society, where a handshake and a person's word are as good as gold, with other countries' legalistic systems that require extensive contracts to get anything done.

Narian leaders hold total and absolute power. Although not viewed as having power derived from divine rights, leaders are assumed to be infallible. Narian leaders are confident in their complete knowledge of all that they come to face. They do not ask questions and do not seek advice, even from equals. Often autocratic, the Narian leader, however, is expected to take care of loyal followers under any circumstance. As followers owe unquestioning obedience, leaders owe them total devotion. The leaders are fully responsible for all that happens to their followers, in all aspects of their life. They are expected to help and guide them and come to their rescue when needed. Leaders are expected to be caring and fair. Their primary duty is to look out for their followers.

In return, Narian followers are expected to be loyal, obedient, dutiful, and subservient. They accept their leader's orders willingly and wholeheartedly; all Narians are taught from the youngest age that leaders are infallible and that the proper functioning of the social order hinges on obedience and loyalty to leaders and elders and on their fulfilling their responsibility as followers. Dissent and conflict are rarely expressed in the open. People value politeness and civility and go out of their way to be kind. When mistakes are made, regardless of where the fault lies, all individuals work on correcting it without assigning blame. If the leader makes a mistake, an event rarely, if ever, brought out in the open, one of the followers openly accepts the blame to protect the leader's face and the social harmony. The person accepting that responsibility is eventually rewarded for the demonstration of loyalty.

The Global and Cultural Contexts

The role of women in Narian society remains puzzling to Western observers. For more than 30 years, women have had practically equal rights with men. They can vote, conduct any kind of business transactions, take advantage of educational opportunities, file for divorce, obtain custody of their children, work in any organization, and so forth. The literacy rate for women is equal to that of men, and although fewer of them pursue higher education, it appears that most women who are interested in working outside the home find easy employment in the booming Narian economy. The society, however, remains highly patriarchal in its traditions.

Role-Play Situation

A U.S. engineering and construction company has won its first major governmental contract for constructing two bridges in Nari. With general terms agreed on, the company is working closely with several U.S.-educated Narian engineers employed at the Narian Ministry of Urban Development (UD) to draft precise plans and timetables. The minister of UD, Mr. Dafti, is a well-respected civil engineer, educated in Austria in the 1950s. In addition to Narian, he speaks fluent German, English, and French. He played instrumental roles in the development of his country. Although a consummate politician and negotiator and an expert on his country's resources and economic situation, he has not practiced his engineering skills for many years.

Mr. Dafti has decided on the general location and structure of the two bridges to be built. One of the locations and designs contains serious flaws. His more junior Narian associates appear to be aware of the potential problems and have hinted at the difficulties and challenges in building in that location, but have not clearly voiced their concerns to the U.S. contractors, who find the design requirements unworkable.

The role-play is a meeting with Mr. Dafti, his Narian associates, and representatives of the U.S. engineering firm. The U.S. head engineer requested the meeting, and the request was granted quickly. The U.S. team is eager to start the project. The Narians also are ready to engage in the new business venture.

Please wait for further instructions.

Exercise 3: Leadership and Gender

This exercise is designed to explore the relationship between gender roles and leadership. Your instructor will assign you to one of three groups and ask you to develop a list of characteristics of a particular leader. Each group will present its list to the class. Discussion will focus on the similarities and differences between gender roles and leadership.

Now, list eight to ten characteristics associated with _____ (wait for your instructor's direction). You can use specific personality traits or behavioral descriptions.

1.

2.

3.

4.

5.

6.

7.

8.

9.

10.

Exercise 4: Is This Sexual Harassment?

For each of the following scenarios, state whether you believe sexual harassment has taken place. Explain your reasoning.

1. A teacher stipulates that your grade (or participation on a team, in a play, etc.) will be based on whether you submit to a relationship.

    Is it harassment?

    Why?

2. Mary and Todd dated for a while. Mary broke off their relationship and no longer wants to date Todd and has told him so. Todd, however, continually behaves as if they are still dating. He phones her for dates. In the halls at the university, he comes up and puts his arms around her shoulders.

    Is it harassment?

    Why?

3. During a discussion at work regarding gay rights, Ricardo strongly defended the right of gays to have partner benefits at work and be able to form a civil union. He got very emotional when talking about the sadness he observed when one of his friends was not allowed to visit his partner of many years on his deathbed in the hospital because they were not legally related. Since that day, his coworkers have been making comments such as "Mama's boy," "You're such a girl," "Are you going to cry now?" and insinuating that he is gay. Ricardo is heterosexual.

    Is it harassment?

    Why?

4. Tara Washington has been Peter Jacobs's assistant for over five years, and they have had an excellent working relationship. Tara just found out that her father has terminal cancer, and one day recently at the office, she broke down and started crying. Peter came up to her and gave her hug.

Is it harassment?

Why?

5. Julie and Antonio started working at the office a few days apart. They are both recent college graduates. They immediately hit it off and soon started dating. Their supervisor talked to both of them and warned them not to let their relationship interfere with their work or affect others in the workplace. They both said that they understood the potential problems and made a commitment to keep things professional. After a couple of months, Antonio broke off the relationship. Julie was heartbroken. Both were very uncomfortable working with each other. After a few weeks, Julie talked to her supervisor about Antonio avoiding her and her belief that this may constitute sexual harassment.

Is it harassment?

Why?

6. Nadine is a very attractive young employee in a government office. She has developed a warm, friendly, and professional relationship with her colleagues, many of whom are males. They often joke and laugh with her, and she receives many compliments from them regarding her looks.

Is it harassment?

Why?

7. Nicholas is a recent immigrant from Greece who is working in a high-technology firm in Massachusetts. He really enjoys his job and likes his colleagues. They often go out to lunch and for drinks after work and play sports on weekends. Nicholas is shocked when he finds out that one of his colleagues has accused him of sexual harassment for inappropriate physical contact.

Is it harassment?

Why?

8. Kim is a realtor who specializes in selling homes from large developers. She shows a lot of property in construction sites and has a very successful track record. Recently, she has become very uncomfortable with rude and suggestive comments from the construction workers at one of the sites, so much so that she is avoiding showing property in that location. She complained to her office manager about the problem, but she was told that they cannot really control the construction workers because they do not work for the same company.

Is it harassment?

Why?

9. Gary has taken one of his company's biggest clients to dinner. The client is considering expanding her business with Gary's company. During dinner, she very clearly comes on to Gary who politely refuses her advances. The client brushes him off and says she will try again. The next day, Gary tells his supervisor about the incident and how uncomfortable he felt. His supervisor informs him that the client has specifically asked for Gary to stay on the case and has indicated that she looks forward to expanding her business with the company.

Is it harassment?

Why?

Self-Assessment 1: What Is Your Primary Cultural Background?

Identify the culture that you consider to be your primary cultural background (recognizing that you may be from multiple backgrounds).

1. What do you think makes that culture unique?

2. What are some of its key teachings about what is important? What is right?

3. How did you learn these?

4. How much do you agree with them? Why or why not?

5. How often do you share these cultural elements with others?

6. How much of your behavior do you think is influenced by that culture?

Please wait for further instructions.

Self-Assessement 2: Exploring Views of Women

Briefly describe the cultural views and expectations of women in your family and your culture. What are your personal views of the role of women in:

Relationships

Family

Business/work

Community

How would those views facilitate or present obstacles for women in the workplace?

Self-Assessment 3: Do You Have a Cultural Mindset?

For each of the following items, please use the scale below to indicate your answer.

1	2	3	4
Strongly Disagree	Disagree	Agree	Strongly Agree

Item	Response			
1. I know a lot about my own culture.	1	2	3	4
2. I don't think much about how my culture impacts me.	1	2	3	4
3. I can tell how my cultural background influences how I think and what I do.	1	2	3	4
4. I enjoy asking people about their culture.	1	2	3	4
5. I seek out various cultural experiences any chance I can (e.g., food, travel, festivals, music).	1	2	3	4
6. I know a lot about how cultural differences affect the thinking and behavior of those I work with.	1	2	3	4
7. I like sharing my culture and its customs and beliefs with those who don't know it.	1	2	3	4
8. I often include culture as one of the factors I consider when I think about solving problems either in my personal or professional life.	1	2	3	4
9. I am comfortable with people who are from different cultures.	1	2	3	4
10. When people around me speak a different language, it often makes me uncomfortable.	1	2	3	4
11. I think people are the same deep down, no matter where they are from.	1	2	3	4
12. Although I am from _____ (state your country), I often think of myself as a citizen of the world.	1	2	3	4

Scoring: Reverse the scoring for items 2, 10, and 11 (1 = 4; 2 = 3; 3 = 2; 4 = 1). Then, add up your scores for items all of the questions.

Total: _____

The range of scores is 12 to 48. A score in the upper third (48 to 35) indicates strong cultural mindfulness. A score in the bottom third (23 to 12) shows little awareness of culture. Review each of your responses and the material about "Cultural Mindset" at the end of the chapter to identify areas for strength and weakness.

LEADERSHIP IN ACTION

Indra Nooyi: The Indian-Born CEO of Pepsi Sets New Standards

Being one of only two women CEOs of a *Fortune* 100 company is no small accomplishment. Indra Nooyi, known for having a keen business sense and an irreverent personal style, is perfect for the job. Whereas female CEOs continue to be relatively rare, female CEOs of color are even rarer (Andrea Jung of Avon is the other one). Born and educated in South India before attending Yale University for her graduate degree, Nooyi joined PepsiCo in 1994, having worked for Motorola and the Boston Consulting Group. She became chief financial officer of PepsiCo in 2001 and its first female CEO in 2006. She is credited for guiding the company through major restructuring, divesting its restaurants, and refocusing on its beverage and other food businesses with the successful multibillion dollar mergers with Tropicana and Quaker Oats (Kavilanz, 2006).

"Brilliant," "supertalented," and able to think several steps ahead of everyone else are just some of the terms people use to describe her. The former company president Enrico states, "Indra can drive as deep and hard as anyone I've ever met, but she can do it with a sense of heart and fun" (Brady, 2007). On many dimensions, Nooyi does not fit the stereotype of the CEO of one of the world's largest companies. A former member of an all-girl rock band, non-Western, and female, she has overcome a complex set of barriers to reach the highest level of corporate leadership. She, however, is comfortable enough with herself to walk around the office barefoot, sing in the hallways—she is a karaoke fan—and go to a formal job interview with the button-down U.S. consulting firm, the Boston Consulting Group, and to PepsiCo board meetings wearing a traditional Indian sari. She believes that being genuine is a key to her success and likes to blend her cultural roots with her corporate image.

Nooyi's sharp wit and irreverence were most evident when she delivered the business school graduation speech at Columbia University in 2005 and compared the world with five major continents (with her apologies to Australia and Antarctica) to a hand, making the United States the middle finger for its strength, its most prominent position, and its ability to both help and offend (for a complete text of the speech, see Graduation Remarks, 2005). Although she had to clarify her statements and apologize for having offended some people, she also made a compelling case for global cooperation and diversity. She stated, "The five fingers are not the same . . . and yet the fingers work in harmony without us even thinking about them individually. . . . Our fingers—as different as they are—coexist to create a critically important whole" (Graduation Remarks, 2005). She further urged graduates to take an active part in developing cultural awareness and sensitivity, creating harmony and cooperation and developing bonds between countries: "My point is that it's not enough just to understand that the other fingers coexist. We've got to consciously and actively ensure that every one of them stands tall together, or that they bend together as needed" (Graduation Remarks, 2005).

Many celebrate Nooyi's leadership at Pepsi as a victory for diversity. PepsiCo, however, has been at the forefront of promoting diversity, with actress Joan Crawford, widow of the company's president, replacing her husband on the board of directors in 1959 and Brenda Barnes heading the North American divisions for many years (before leaving in 1989 with a much publicized statement that she wanted to spend more time with her family). In the 1940s, the company was one of the first to create an all-black sales team to market to African-American consumers (Cole, 2006). Nooyi's predecessor, Steven Reinemund, is recognized as a champion of diversity, who stated, "I often refer to our diversity and inclusion as a marathon. . . . The challenge comes in creating an environment in which every associate—regardless of ethnicity, sexual orientation, gender or physical ability—feels valued and want to be part of our growth" (Ortiz, 2006). Nooyi is sending a very strong message about what she calls "talent sustainability." She states: "By valuing our employees, we are ensuring that PepsiCo is the kind of company where talented people of all backgrounds want to work. . . . We foster an inclusive workplace by increasing female and minority representation in management ranks, creating rewarding opportunities for people with disabilities and recognizing our employees for their contributions" (Letter from Indra Nooyi, 2010).

Even before becoming CEO, while taking care of the CFO and other duties, Nooyi created programs to help women network, learn from successful role models, and develop skills to manage their careers better. She also sponsored events to showcase and promote the company's diversity and inclusiveness. She readily acknowl-

edges the challenges she has faced: "Being a women, immigrant, and person of color made it thrice as difficulty." She states, "So therefore, the only way out, was to work twice as hard as your male counterparts" (Indra Nooyi takes over Pepsi HQ, 2006). Her formula for success is relatively simple; she suggests that success comes from five "Cs": competence, confidence, communication skills, having a moral compass and integrity, and being the conscience for the organization (Indra Nooyi's 5-C formula, 2006). She continues to practice what she preaches. She admits at being consumed with PepsiCo; the company is her passion. Answering e-mails at 4 AM and being the last one to leave the office are typical behaviors for Nooyi, who balances a family and being CEO of a *Fortune* 100 company (Indra Nooyi's 5-C, 2006). And by most accounts, she does it all brilliantly.

Questions

1. What are the elements of Nooyi's leadership?
2. What role does diversity play?

Sources: Brady, D., 2007. "Indra Nooyi: Keeping cool in hot water," *Business Week*, June 11: 49; Cole, Y., 2008. "PepsiCo's diversity legacy," *Diversity Inc*. March 28. http://www.diversityinc.com/public/1627.cfm (accessed August 8, 2007); Kavilanz, P. B., 2006. "PepsiCo names first woman CEO," *CNN Money.com*, August 14. http://money.cnn.com/2006/08/14/news/companies/pepsico_ceo/ (accessed August 6, 2007); Graduation Remarks. 2005. *Business Week*, May 20. http://www.businessweek.com/bwdaily/dnflash/may2005/nf20050520_9852.htm (accessed August 6, 2007); Indra Nooyi's 5-C formula for global success. 2006. *The Times of India,* August 16. http://timesofindia.indiatimes.com/articleshow/1898674.cms (accessed August 6, 2007); Indra Nooyi takes over Pepsi HQ.2006. *India Times,* August 15. http://economictimes.indiatimes.com/articleshow/1893960.cms (accessed August 7, 2007); Ortiz, P., 2006. "Historic change: Indra Nooyi to be CEO of PepsiCo," *Diversity Inc.,* May. http://www.diversityinc.com/public/637.cfm (accessed August 8, 2007). "Letter from Indra Nooyi. 2010". Pepsico. (accessed January 18, 2010); Sellers, P. 2009. Indra Nooyi is the Queen of pop. *CNNmoney*, September 10. http://money.cnn.com/2009/09/09/news/companies/pepsico_indra_nooyi_ceo.fortune/index.htm (accessed May 13, 2010).

Early Theories
The Foundations of Modern Leadership

From Chapter 3 of *The Art and Science of Leadership*, 6/e. Afsaneh Nahavandi. Copyright © 2012 by Pearson Education. Published by Prentice Hall. All rights reserved.

Early Theories
The Foundations of Modern Leadership

The people who get on in this world are the people who get up and look for circumstances they want, and, if they can't find them, make them.

—GEORGE BERNARD SHAW

A pretzel-shaped world needs a pretzel-shaped theory.

—FRED FIEDLER

After studying this chapter, you will be able to:

- Identify the three major eras in the study of leadership and their contributions to modern leadership.
- Explain the methods, results, shortcomings, and contributions of the trait and behavior approaches to leadership and identify their impact on current approaches.
- Present the principles of a contingency approach to leadership
- Discuss the most significant early theories of leadership and their implications for current theory and practice of leadership.

The roots of the modern study of leadership can be traced to the Western Industrial Revolution that took place at the end of the nineteenth century. Although many scholars throughout history focused on leadership, the modern approach to leadership brings scientific rigor to the search for answers. Social and political scientists and management scholars tried, sometimes more successfully than other times, to measure leadership through a variety of means. This chapter reviews the history of modern leadership theory and research and outlines the early theories that are the foundations of modern leadership.

A HISTORY OF MODERN LEADERSHIP THEORY: THREE ERAS

During the Industrial Revolution, the study of leadership, much like research in other aspects of organizations, became more rigorous. Instead of relying on intuition and a description of common practices, researchers used scientific methods to understand and predict leadership effectiveness by identifying and measuring leadership characteristics. The history of the modern scientific approach to leadership can be divided into three general eras or approaches: the trait era, the behavior era, and the contingency era. Each era has made distinct contributions to our understanding of leadership and continues to influence our thinking about the process.

The Trait Era: Late 1800s to Mid-1940s

The belief that leaders are born rather than made dominated much of the late nineteenth century and the early part of the twentieth century. Thomas Carlyle's book *Heroes and Hero Worship* (1907), William James's writings (1880) about the great men of history, and Galton's study (1869) of the role of heredity were part of an era that can be characterized by a strong belief that innate qualities shape human personality and behavior. Consequently, it was commonly believed that leaders, by virtue of their birth, were endowed with special qualities that allowed them to lead others. These special characteristics were presumed to push them toward leadership, regardless of the context. The historical context and social structures of the period further reinforced such beliefs by providing limited opportunities for common people to become social, political, and industrial leaders. The belief in the power of personality and other innate characteristics strongly influenced leadership researchers and sent them on a massive hunt for leadership traits made possible by the advent of personality and individual characteristics testing such as IQ in the early twentieth century. The major assumption guiding hundreds of studies about leadership traits was that if certain traits distinguish between leaders and followers, then existing political, industrial, and religious leaders should possess them (for a thorough review of the literature, see Bass, 1990a). Based on this assumption, researchers identified and observed existing leaders and followers and collected detailed demographic and personality information about them.

More than 40 years of study provided little evidence to justify the assertion that leaders are born and that leadership can be explained through one or more traits. Some traits do emerge as important. For instance, much evidence indicates that, on average, leaders are more sociable, more aggressive, and more lively than other group members. In addition, leaders generally are original and popular and have a sense of humor. Which of the traits are most relevant, however, seems to depend on the requirements of the situation? In other words, being social, aggressive, lively, original, and popular or having any other combination of traits does not guarantee that a person will become a leader, let alone an effective one.

> More than 40 years of study provided little evidence to justify the assertion that leaders are born and that leadership can be explained through either one or a collection of traits. Some traits do emerge as important. Which of the traits are most relevant, however, seems to depend on the requirements of the situation.

Because of weak and inconsistent findings, the commonly shared belief among many researchers in the late 1930s and early 1940s was that although traits play a role in determining leadership ability and effectiveness, their role is minimal and that leadership should be viewed as a group phenomenon that cannot be studied outside a given situation (Ackerson, 1942; Bird, 1940; Jenkins, 1947; Newstetter, Feldstein, and Newcomb, 1938; Stogdill, 1948). More recent studies in the 1960s and 1970s reinforced these findings by showing that factors such as intelligence (Bray and Grant, 1966) or assertiveness (Rychlak, 1963) are related to leadership effectiveness, but they alone cannot account for much of a leader's effectiveness.

Recent views of the role of traits and other individual characteristics, such as skills, refined our understanding of the role of individual characteristics in leadership (for an example and review, see Mumford et al., 2000a, b). Current interest in emotional intelligence has also yielded new research on the leader's individual characteristics (e.g., Humphrey, 2002). The leader's personality, by limiting the leader's behavioral range or by making it more or less difficult to learn certain behaviors or undertake some actions, plays a key role in his or her effectiveness. However, it is by no means the only or even the dominant factor in effective leadership.

The Behavior Era: Mid-1940s to Early 1970s

Because the trait approach did not yield the expected results and as the need for identifying and training leaders came to the forefront during World War II, researchers turned to behaviors, rather than traits, as the source of leader effectiveness. The move to observable behaviors was triggered in part by the dominance of behaviorist theories during this period, particularly in the United States and Great Britain. Instead of identifying *who would be an effective leader*, the behavior approach emphasizes *what an effective leader does*. Focusing on behaviors provides several advantages over a trait approach:

- Behaviors can be observed more objectively than traits.
- Behaviors can be measured more precisely and more accurately than traits.
- As opposed to traits, which are either innate or develop early in life, behaviors can be taught.

These factors provided a clear benefit to the military and various other organizations with a practical interest in leadership. Instead of identifying leaders who had particular personality traits, they could focus on training people to perform effective leadership behaviors. The early work of Lewin and his associates (Lewin and Lippit, 1938; Lewin, Lippit, and White, 1939) concerning democratic, autocratic, and laissez-faire leadership laid the foundation for the behavior approach to leadership. Democratic leaders were defined as those who consult their followers and allow them to participate in decision making, autocratic leaders as those who make decisions alone, and laissez-faire leaders as those who provide no direction and do not become involved with their followers. Although the three types of leadership style were clearly defined, the research failed to establish which style would be most effective or which situational factors would lead to the use of one or another style. Furthermore, each of the styles had different effects on subordinates. For example, laissez-faire leadership, which involved providing information but little guidance or evaluation, led to frustrated and disorganized groups that, in turn, produced low-quality work. On the other hand, autocratic leadership caused followers to become submissive, whereas groups led by democratic leaders were relaxed and became cohesive.

Armed with the results of Lewin's work and other studies, different groups of researchers set out to identify leader behaviors (e.g., Hemphill and Coons, 1957). Among the best-known behavioral approaches to leadership are the Ohio State Leadership Studies. A number of researchers developed a list of almost 2,000 leadership behaviors (Hemphill and Coons, 1957). After subsequent analyses (Fleishman, 1953; Halpin and Winer, 1957), a condensed list yielded several central leadership behaviors. Among them, task- and relationship-related behaviors were established as primary leadership behaviors. The Ohio State studies led to the development of the Leader Behavior Description Questionnaire (LBDQ), which continues to be used today.

Although the Ohio State research, along with other studies (e.g., Bowers and Seashore, 1966), identified a number of leader behaviors, the links between those behaviors and leadership effectiveness were not clearly established. After many years of research, it is still not obvious which behaviors are most effective. It is consistently agreed, though, that considerate, supportive, people-oriented behaviors are associated with follower's satisfaction, loyalty, and trust, whereas structuring behaviors are more closely related to job performance (for a recent review, see Judge, Piccolo, and Ilies, 2004). Evidence, although somewhat weak, shows that effective leadership requires both consideration and structuring behaviors (Fleishman and Harris, 1962; House and Filley, 1971). These findings, however, have failed to receive overwhelming support. Furthermore, the leadership dimensions of initiation of structure and consideration do not describe leader's behavior adequately for cultures other than the United States that might be less individualistic and hold up different ideals of leadership (Ayman and Chemers, 1983; Chemers, 1969; Misumi and Peterson, 1985).

Similar to the trait approach, the behavior approach to leadership, by concentrating only on behaviors and disregarding powerful situational elements, provides a simplistic view of a highly complex process and, therefore, fails to provide a thorough understanding of the leadership phenomenon. However, the two general categories of task and relationship behaviors are well established as the primary leadership behaviors. Researchers and practitioners continue to discuss what leaders do in these general terms. William Green, CEO of Accenture, tells his employees that three things matter in leadership: competence, confidence, and caring (Bryant, 2009). The first and the third clearly fall into the task and relationship categories.

The Contingency Era: Early 1960s to Present

Even before the behavior approach's lack of success in explaining and predicting leadership effectiveness became evident, a number of researchers were calling for a more comprehensive approach to understanding leadership (Stogdill, 1948). Specifically, researchers recommended that situational factors, such as the task and type of work group, be taken into consideration. However, it was not until the 1960s that this recommendation was applied. In the 1960s, spearheaded by Fred Fiedler, whose Contingency Model of leadership is discussed later in this chapter, leadership research moved from simplistic models based solely on the leader to more complex models that take a contingency point of view. Other models such as the Path-Goal Theory and the Normative Decision Model, also presented in this chapter, soon followed. The primary assumption of the contingency view is that the personality, style, or behavior of effective leaders depends on the requirements of the situation in which the leaders find themselves. Additionally, this approach suggests the following:

- There is no one best way to lead.
- The situation and the various relevant contextual factors determine which style or behavior is most effective.
- People can learn to become good leaders.
- Leadership makes a difference in the effectiveness of groups and organizations.
- Personal and situational characteristics affect leadership effectiveness.

Although the contingency approach to leadership continues to be well accepted, the most recent approach to leadership focuses on the relationship between leaders and followers and on various aspects of charismatic and visionary leadership. Some researchers have labeled this approach the neo-charismatic school (Antonakis, Cianciolo, and Sternberg, 2004).

EARLY THEORIES

An effective leader must know how to use available resources and build a relationship with follower to achieve goals (Chemers, 1993). The early leadership theories of leadership addressed these two challenges in a variety of ways.

Fiedler's Contingency Model

Fred Fiedler was the first researcher to propose a contingency view of leadership. His Contingency Model is the oldest and most highly researched contingency approach to leadership (Fiedler, 1967). Fiedler's basic premise is that leadership effectiveness is a function of the match between the leader's style and the leadership situation. If the leader's style matches the situation, the leader will be effective; otherwise, the leader will not be effective. Fiedler considers how the leader uses available resources to make the group effective.

Leadership effectiveness is a function of the match between the leader's style and the leadership situation. If the leader's style matches the situation, the leader will be effective; otherwise, the leader will not be effective.

LEADER STYLE To determine a leader's style, Fiedler uses the least-preferred coworker (LPC) scale, a measure that determines what motivation the leader has: task motivation or relationship motivation. Fiedler's research shows that people's perceptions and descriptions of their least-preferred coworker provide insight into their basic goals and priorities toward either accomplishing a task or maintaining relationships (see Self-Assessment 1). According to Fiedler, people with low LPC scores—those who give a low rating to their least-preferred coworker (describing the person as incompetent, cold, untrustworthy, and quarrelsome)—are task motivated. They draw their self-esteem mostly from accomplishing their task well (Chemers and Skrzypek, 1972; Fiedler, 1967; Fiedler and Chemers, 1984; Rice, 1978a, b). When the task-motivated leaders or their groups fail, they tend to be harsh in judging their subordinates and are often highly punitive (Rice, 1978a, b). When the task is going well, however, the task-motivated leader is comfortable with details and with monitoring routine events (Fiedler and Chemers, 1984; Table 1).

People who have high LPC scores rate their least-preferred coworker relatively positively (describing that person as loyal, sincere, warm, and accepting); they are relationship motivated and draw their self-esteem from having good relationships with others. For them, the least-preferred coworker is often someone who has been disloyal and unsupportive rather than incompetent (Rice, 1978a, b). Relationship-motivated persons are easily bored with details (Fiedler, 1978; Fiedler and Chemers, 1984) and focus on social interactions (Rice, 1978a, b;

TABLE 1 Differences Between Task- and Relationship-Motivated Individuals	
Task-Motivated (Low LPC)	**Relationship-Motivated (High LPC)**
• Draws self-esteem from completion of task	• Draws self-esteem from interpersonal relationships
• Focuses on the task first	• Focuses on people first
• Can be harsh with failing employees	• Likes to please others
• Considers competence of coworkers to be key trait	• Considers loyalty of coworkers to be key trait
• Enjoys details	• Gets bored with details

see Table 1). The task-motivated person's focus on tasks and the relationship-motivated person's concern for relationships are most obvious in times of crisis when the person is under pressure.

A comparison between Hilary Clinton and Barrack Obama illustrates the differences between task- and relationship-oriented leaders. During the presidential campaign, H. Clinton very clearly stated that she considers the role of the president not only to provide vision, but also to control and direct the federal bureaucracy (O'Toole, 2008). Obama on the other hand, announced that he believes the president's role to be to provide vision and inspiration while delegating the responsibility of managing agencies (O'Toole, 2008). Although Obama's leadership style also fits that charismatic leaders, his broader focus and less attention to detail indicate a relationship-oriented style. Other leaders demonstrate both styles. Brady W. Dougan—the new 50-year-old CEO of Credit Suisse Group, a major global bank, and its youngest CEO to date—is detailed oriented and task motivated (Anderson, 2007). He gets to work around 5 AM and is known to work out twice a day while he trains for marathons. He recently spent two months practicing to dance with a Broadway star during a charity event (Anderson, 2007). Marissa Peterson, former executive vice president of worldwide operations of Sun Microsystems, is also task motivated. Her strength is in clearly outlining what role every one of her 2,000-strong staff plays. Her focus is on "developing the strategy for achieving my operation's goals and then laying out that vision for my team" (Overholt, 2002: 125). Peterson sticks to a strict routine in managing her daily and weekly activities. Contrast these task-motivated leaders with Mort Meyerson, chairman and CEO of 2M Companies of Perot Systems, a computer firm based in Dallas, Texas, and Darlene Ryan, founder and CEO of PharmaFab, a pharmaceuticals manufacturer, also located in Texas. Meyerson believes, "To win in today's brave new world of business, you must be more in-tune with your people and customers. . . . You must re-examine if you are creating an environment for your people to succeed and what that means. You must ask yourself: Am I really accessible? Am I really listening?" (Mort Meyerson, 2010). Darlene Ryan takes a similar approach. She runs her company like a family; she encourages dissent, delegates, and is a consensus builder. She is a great listener and is able to take her time when facing tough decisions (Black, 2004).

Individuals who fall in the middle of the scale have been labeled socio-independent. They tend to be less concerned with other people's opinions and may not actively seek leadership roles. Depending on how close their score is to the high or the low end of the scale, they might belong to either the task-motivated or relationship-motivated group (Fiedler and Chemers, 1984). Some research suggests that middle LPCs may be more effective than either high or low LPCs across all situations (Kennedy, 1982). A potential middle LPC is Colin Powell. Even though he has been in many leadership positions, he has shied away from the presidency, and he has proven himself an outstanding follower to several presidents.

Despite some problems with the validity of the LPC scale, it has received strong support from researchers and practitioners and has even translated well to other cultures for use in leadership research and training (Ayman and Chemers, 1983, 1991). A key premise of the LPC concept is that because it is an indicator of primary motivation, leadership style is stable. Leaders, then, cannot simply change their style to match the situation.

SITUATIONAL CONTROL Because effectiveness depends on a match between the person and the situation, Fiedler uses three factors to describe a leadership situation. In order of importance, they are (1) the relationship between the leader and the followers, (2) the amount of structure of the task, and (3) the position power of the leader. The three elements combine to define the amount of control the leader has over the situation (see Self-Assessment 2).

According to Fiedler, the most important element of any leadership situation is the quality of the relationship and the cohesion between the leader and the followers and among the followers (Fiedler, 1978). Good leader–member relations (LMR) mean that the group is cohesive and supportive, providing leaders with a high degree of control to implement what they want. When the group is divided or has little respect or support for the leader, the leader's control is low.

Task structure (TS) is the second element of a leadership situation. It refers to the degree of clarity of a task. A highly structured task has clear goals and procedures, few paths to the correct solution, and one or few correct solutions and can be evaluated easily (Fiedler and Chemers, 1974). The degree of task structure affects the leader's control. Whereas the leader has considerable control when doing a structured task, an unstructured task provides little sense of control. One factor that moderates task structure is the leader's experience level (Fiedler and Chemers, 1984). On the one hand, if leaders have experience with a task, they will perceive the task as more structured. On the other hand, not having experience will make any task appear to be unstructured. The third and least influential element of the leadership situation is the leader's position power (PP), which refers to the leader's formal power and influence over subordinates to hire, fire, reward, or punish. The leader with a high amount of formal power feels more in control than one who has little power.

The combination of LMR, TS, and PP yields the amount of situational control (Sit Con) the leader has over the situation. At one end of the continuum, good leader–member relations, a highly structured task, and high position power provide the leader with high control over the situation where the leader's influence is well accepted. In the middle of the continuum are situations in which either the leader and the followers do not get along or the task is unstructured. In such situations, the leader does not have full control over the situation, and the leadership environment is more difficult. At the other end of the situational control continuum, the leader–member relations are poor, the task is unstructured, and the leader has little power. Such a situation is chaotic and unlikely to continue for a long period of time in an organization. Clearly, this crisis environment does not provide the leader with a sense of control or any ease of leadership (see Self-Assessment 2 for Sit Con).

PREDICTIONS OF THE CONTINGENCY MODEL   At the core of the Contingency Model is the concept of match. If the leader's style matches the situation, the group will be effective. Because Fiedler suggests that the leader's style is constant, a leader's effectiveness changes as the situation changes. The Contingency Model predicts that low-LPC, task-motivated leaders will be effective in high- and low-situational control, whereas high-LPC, relationship-motivated leaders will be effective in moderate-situational control. Figure 1 presents the predictions of the model.

In high-control situations (left side of the graph in Figure 1), task-motivated, low-LPC leaders feel at ease. The leader's basic source of self-esteem—getting the task done—is not threatened, so the leader can relax, take care of details, and help the followers perform. The same high-control situation leads to a different effect on relationship-motivated, high-LPC leaders. They are likely to be bored and feel either that there is nothing to do or that nobody needs them. Because the group is cohesive and the task is clear, the leader is needed mainly to get the group the resources it needs, take care of details, and remove obstacles—all activities that are not appealing to high LPCs, who might, therefore, start being overly controlling and interfere with the group's performance to demonstrate that they are needed (Chemers, 1997; Fiedler and Garcia, 1987a). See Table 2 for a summary of the leaders' behaviors in each situation.

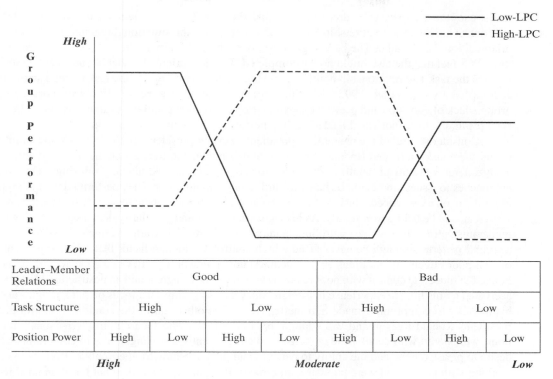

FIGURE 1 Fiedler's Contingency Model

Moderate-situational control (the middle of graph in Figure 1) stems from lack of cohesiveness or lack of task structure. In either case, the situation is ambiguous or uncertain, and task completion is in jeopardy. The relationship-motivated, high-LPC leader's skills at interpersonal relationships and participation are well suited for the situation. This type of leader seeks out followers' participation and focuses on resolving task and relationship conflicts. The high-LPC

TABLE 2 Leader Style and Behaviors in Different Levels of Sit Con			
	High Sit Con	**Moderate Sit Con**	**Low Sit Con**
Task-motivated (low-LPC) leader	Confident; considerate and supportive; removes obstacles and stays out of the way	Tense; task-focused; over-bearing and overly controlling; insists on getting things done	Directive; task-focused; serious; little concern for others
Relationship-motivated (high-LPC) leader	Bored; aloof and self-centered; somewhat autocratic; can interfere with group	Considerate; open to ideas and suggestions; concerned with resolving conflicts	Tense and nervous; hurt by group's conflict; indecisive

Sources: Partially based on F. E. Fiedler, *A Theory of Leadership Effectiveness* (New York: McGraw-Hill, 1967); F. E. Fiedler and M. M. Chemers, *Leadership and Effective Management* (Glenview, IL: Scott-Foresman, 1974); and F. E. Fiedler and M. M. Chemers, *Improving Leadership Effectiveness: The Leader Match Concept*, 2nd ed. (New York: John Wiley, 1984).

leader uses the group as a resource to accomplish the task. The same elements that make moderate control attractive to relationship-motivated leaders make the situation threatening to the task-oriented, low-LPC leader. The lack of group support, the ambiguity of the task, or both make the low LPCs feel that the task might not be completed. The task-oriented leader becomes autocratic, ignores the task and relationship conflicts, and tries to simply complete the task to get a sense of accomplishment (Fiedler, 1993). The inappropriate use of resources is likely to worsen the group's lack of cohesion and prevent the exploration of creative solutions to an unstructured task. As a result, the task-motivated leader's group performs poorly in moderate control.

Consider several of the recent U.S. presidents. Former presidents Richard Nixon and Jimmy Carter were task-motivated leaders. Both were highly intelligent, focused on the task, and able to analyze large amounts of detail. Both needed to stay in control, held uncompromising views and approaches to issues, and could be harsh toward failing subordinates. They performed well in high control. Nixon experienced considerable success in foreign policy, where he was respected, the task was clear, and he held power tightly. As his legitimate power and popularity decreased—leading to moderate control—he became controlling, punitive, and ineffective. Carter's effectiveness followed a similar pattern, although he never faced a high-control situation, a factor that might explain his overall poor effectiveness ratings as president. Almost immediately after being elected, he found himself in moderate control with poor relations with the U.S. Congress and an unstructured task exacerbated by his limited experience in foreign policy. His single-minded focus on human rights and his inability to compromise made him ineffective. At the other end of the continuum are former presidents Ronald Reagan and Bill Clinton, both high LPCs who focused on interpersonal relations, were bored with details, and demonstrated an apparently unending ability to compromise, a desire to please others, and the ability to perform and put on a show for their public. Both enjoyed working with people and were popular with crowds. Reagan was well liked but faced an unstructured task with moderate power. Clinton faced a novel and unstructured situation but continued to enjoy unprecedented support of the electorate. Both these relationship-motivated presidents were in moderate control where, by many accounts, they performed well.

As a situation becomes chaotic and reaches a crisis point with no group cohesion, no task structure, and no strong position power (the right side of the graph in Figure 1), the task-motivated, low-LPC leaders' need to complete the task pushes them to take over and make autocratic decisions without much concern for followers. As a result, although performance is not high and followers might not be satisfied, groups with a low-LPC leader get some work done. For the relationship-motivated, high-LPC leader, the low Sit Con environment is a nightmare. The group's lack of cohesion is further fueled by its inability to perform the task and makes efforts at reconciliation close to impossible. The high-LPC leader's efforts to gain support from the group, therefore, fall on deaf ears. In an attempt to protect their self-esteem, high-LPC leaders withdraw, leaving their group to fend for itself and causing low performance. The data for the socio-independent leaders are less clear. Fiedler (1978) suggests that they generally perform better in high-control situations, although more research is needed to predict and explain their performance.

EVALUATION AND APPLICATION   Although a large number of studies have supported the Contingency Model over the past 40 years, several researchers have voiced strong criticisms regarding the meaning and validity of the LPC scale (Schriesheim and Kerr, 1974), the predictive value of the model (Schriesheim, Tepper, and Tetrault, 1994; Vecchio, 1983), and the lack of research about the middle-LPC leaders (Kennedy, 1982). Forty years of research have addressed the majority, although not all, of the concerns. As a result, the Contingency Model continues to emerge as one of the most reliable and predictive models of leadership, with a number of research studies

Applying What You Learn

Putting the Contingency Model to Work

Fiedler's contingency model suggests that instead of focusing on changing their style, leaders should learn to understand and manage the situations in which they lead. Chances are however that most of the leadership training programs you may attend will focus on changing the leaders' style to adapt to different situations. Here's how you can take advantage of those training programs while following the contingency model's recommendations:

• Remember that learning will take place when you challenge yourself to undertake and master behaviors that do not come easily and therefore may be outside your comfort zone or primary motivation area.

• Regardless of your style, you can always learn new behaviors and expand your current range.

• All training, by design or default, will expose you to many new leadership situations. Take the opportunity to practice analyzing them to ascertain situational control.

• Do not expect miracles or even quick changes. Increasing your effectiveness as a leader is a long journey.

and meta-analyses supporting the hypotheses of the model (see Ayman, Chemers, and Fiedler, 1995; Chemers, 1997; Peters, Hartke, and Pohlmann, 1985; Strube and Garcia, 1981).

Importantly, a person's LPC is not the only or the strongest determinant of a leader's actions and beliefs. Although the focus has been on the description of stereotypical task-motivated and relationship-motivated leaders, a person's behavior is determined by many other internal and external factors. It would, therefore, be inappropriate to carry the task or relationship orientation considerably beyond its use in the Contingency Model. It is a reliable predictor of leadership effectiveness within the model, but not necessarily beyond it.

The Contingency Model has several practical implications for managers:

• Leaders must understand their style and the situation to predict how effective they will be.
• Leaders should focus on changing the situation to match their style instead of trying to change how they act.
• A good relationship with followers is important to a leader's ability to lead, and it can compensate for lack of power.
• Leaders can compensate for ambiguity of a task by getting training and experience.

Fiedler's focus on changing the situation rather than the leader is unique among leadership theories. Interestingly, Marcus Buckingham, a well-known leadership consultant, has recently suggested that leaders should focus on developing their strengths rather than trying to compensate for their weaknesses (Buckingham, 2005), advice that is consistent with Fiedler's approach. Other leaders also recognize the importance of the context. Drew Gilpin Faust, president of Harvard University says, "I think the most important leadership lessons I've learned have to do with understanding the context in which you are leading" (Bryant, 2009p). As opposed to Fiedler, the Normative Decision Model considered next, along with many other leadership models, assumes that the leader can change styles depending on the situation.

The Normative Decision Model

Should a leader make decisions alone or involve followers? What factors can help a leader determine how to make decisions? Consider the case of Junki Yoshida, the Japanese-born, 58-year-old martial artist and founder and owner of Yoshida Group enterprises. In 2005, he was voted one of the 100 most respected Japanese in the world by the Japanese edition of *Newsweek* magazine. His company includes Mr. Yoshida Original Gourmet sauces and marinades and is comprised of 18 highly diverse companies that include Jones Golf bags, OIA Global Logistics, and a graphic design company (Yoshida Group, 2007). When he starts a new venture, Yoshida plays an active role in every aspect and stays close to every decision. Once the business takes off, however, he delegates to carefully selected specialists and lets them make many of the decisions. The way he makes decisions about his businesses changes as each business matures (Brant, 2004). The Normative Decision Model (also referred to as the Vroom–Yetton model), developed by researchers Victor Vroom, Philip Yetton, and Arthur Jago, addresses such situations and prescribes when the leader needs to involve followers in decision making (Vroom and Jago, 1988, 2007; Vroom and Yetton, 1973). It is called *normative* because it recommends that leaders adopt certain styles based on the prescriptions of the model. Like Fiedler, Vroom and his associates recommend matching the leader and the situational requirements. They, however, differ on several points. The Normative Decision Model is limited to decision making rather than general leadership, and it assumes that leaders can adopt different decision-making styles as needed.

> The Normative Decision Model recommends that leaders adjust their decision style depending on the degree to which the quality of the decision is important and the likelihood that employees will accept the decision.

The model relies on two well-established group dynamic principles: first are the research findings that groups are wasteful and inefficient, and second, that participation in decision making leads to commitment. The model recommends that leaders adjust their decision style depending on the degree to which the quality of the decision is important and the likelihood that employees will accept the decision.

LEADER'S DECISION STYLES   The Normative Decision Model identifies four decision methods available to leaders (Vroom and Jago, 1988). The first method is autocratic (A), in which the leader makes a decision with little or no involvement from followers. The second decision method is consultation (C), which means that the leader consults with followers yet retains the final decision-making authority. The third decision method is group (G). Here, the leader relies on consensus building to solve a problem. The final method involves total delegation (D) of decision making to one employee. The decision styles and their subcategories are summarized in Table 3.

A leader must decide which style to use depending on the situation that the leader and the group face and on whether the problem involves a group or one individual. Individual problems affect only one person, whereas group problems can affect a group or individual. For example, deciding on raises for individual employees is an individual problem, whereas scheduling vacations is a group problem. Similarly, deciding on which employees should receive training or undertake overseas assignment is an individual problem, whereas moving a business to another state or cutting down a city service is a group problem. The distinction between the two is not always clear; individual problems can affect others, and group problems can have an impact on individuals.

CONTINGENCY FACTORS AND PREDICTIONS OF THE MODEL   The two central contingency factors for the Normative Decision Model are the quality of the decision and the need for acceptance and commitment by followers. Other contingency factors to consider are whether the leader has enough relevant information to make a sound decision, whether the problem is structured and clear, the likelihood that followers will accept the leader's decision, whether the employees agree with the organizational goals, whether employees are cohesive, and whether they have enough information to make a decision alone. Table 4 presents the eight contingency factors.

Decision Style	AI	AII	CI	CII	GI	GII	DI
TABLE 3 Decision Styles in the Normative Decision Model							
Description	Unassisted decision	Ask for specific information but make decisions alone	Ask for specific information and ideas from each group member	Ask for information and ideas from whole group	Ask for one person's help; mutual exchange based on expertise	Group shares information and ideas and reaches consensus	Other person analyzes problem and makes decision
Who makes the decision	Leader	Leader	Leader	Leader with considerable group input	Leader and one other person	Group with leader input	Other person
Type of Problem	Group and individual	Group and individual	Group and individual	Group	Individual	Group	Individual

Key: A = Autocratic, C = Consultative, G = Group

Sources: V. H. Vroom and A. G. Jago, *The New Leadership: Managing Participation in Organizations* (Upper Saddle River, NJ: Prentice Hall, 1988); and V. H. Vroom and P. W. Yetton, *Leadership and Decision Making* (Pittsburgh: University of Pittsburgh Press, 1973).

TABLE 4 Contingency Factors in the Normative Decision Model

Contingency Factor	Question to Ask
Quality requirement (QR)	How important is the quality of the decision?
Commitment requirement (CR)	How important is employee commitment to the implementation of the decision?
Leader information (LI)	Does the leader have enough information to make a high-quality decision?
Structure of the problem (ST)	Is the problem clear and well structured?
Commitment probability (CP)	How likely is employee commitment to the solution if the leader makes the decision alone?
Goal congruence (GC)	Do employees agree with and support organizational goals?
Employee conflict (CO)	Is there conflict among employees over a solution?
Subordinate information (SI)	Do employees have enough information to make a high-quality decision?

Sources: V. H. Vroom and A. G. Jago, *The New Leadership: Managing Participation in Organizations* (Upper Saddle River, NJ: Prentice Hall, 1988); and V. H. Vroom and P. W. Yetton, *Leadership and Decision Making* (Pittsburgh: University of Pittsburgh Press, 1973).

QR	Quality requirement:	How important is the technical quality of this decision?
CR	Commitment requirement:	How important is subordinate commitment to the decision?
LI	Leader's information:	Do you have sufficient information to make a high-quality decision?
ST	Problem structure:	Is the problem well structured?
CP	Commitment probability:	If you were to make the decision by yourself, is it reasonably certain that your subordinate(s) would be committed to the decision?
GC	Goal congruence:	Do subordinates share the organizational goals to be attained in solving this problem?
CO	Subordinate conflict:	Is conflict among subordinates over preferred solutions likely?
SI	Subordinate information:	Do subordinates have sufficient information to make a high-quality decision?

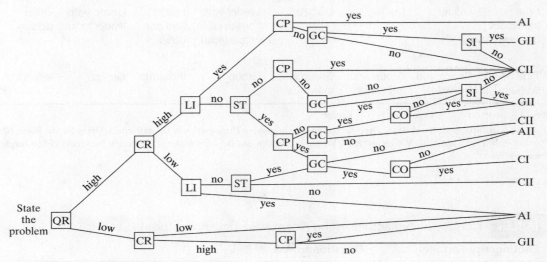

FIGURE 2 Normative Decision Model

Source: "Decision-Process Flow Chart for Both Individual and Group Problems" from *Leadership and Decision-Making* by Victor and Philip W. Yetton © 1973. All rights are controlled by the University of Pittsburgh Press. Pittsburgh, PA 15260. Used by permission of the University of Pittsburgh Press.

The Normative Decision Model is a decision tree, as shown in Figure 2. Leaders ask a series of questions listed in Table 4; the questions relate to the contingency factors and should be asked sequentially. By responding "yes" or "no" to each question, managers can determine which decision style(s) is most appropriate for the problem they face. Figure 2 presents the most widely used Normative Decision Model and is labeled "time efficient," based on the assumption that consultation and participation require time and are not efficient (Vroom and Jago, 1988). Thus, whenever appropriate, the model leans toward more autocratic decision making. A second version of the model, labeled "time investment," focuses on the development of followers at the expense of efficiency. This version recommends more participative decision making whenever possible.

An autocratic decision-making style is appropriate in the following situations:

- When the leader has sufficient information to make a decision
- When the quality of the decision is not essential
- When employees do not agree with each other
- When employees do not agree with the goals of the organization

A consultative style of decision making is appropriate in the following situations:

- The leader has sufficient information, but the employees demand participation to implement the decision.
- The leader has insufficient information, and employee consultation will help the leader gather more information as well as develop commitment.
- Followers generally agree with the goals of the organization.

A group-oriented decision style should be used when the leader does not have all the information, quality is important, and employee commitment is essential. Delegation is used to assign the decision to a single individual who has the needed information, competence, and organizational commitment to make and implement it.

EVALUATION AND APPLICATION   Several research studies support the Normative Decision Model in a variety of settings (Crouch and Yetton, 1987; Tjosvold, Wedley, and Field, 1986), including evaluating historical decisions (Duncan, LaFrance, and Ginter, 2003). The model has also been applied in not-for-profit settings with some success (Lawrence, Deagen, and Debbie, 2001), and recent research on sharing information with followers further support the contingency approach presented by the model (Vidal and Möller, 2007). The decision methods are clearly defined, and the contingency factors included are based on extensive research about group dynamics and participative management.

Some practitioners and theorists argue that the model is too complex to provide practical value. Few managers have the time to work their way through the decision tree. Furthermore, the assumption that leaders have the ability to use any of the decision styles equally well might be flawed. Not all leaders can be autocratic for one decision, consultative for another, and group oriented for still others. In addition, because the model relies on a manager's self-report, it may be subject to some bias (Parker, 1999).

The Normative Decision Model, compared with Fiedler's Contingency Model, takes a narrower focus on leadership decision making. Within that limited focus, the model works well and can be a helpful tool for leaders. The model suggests several practical implications:

- Leaders must understand the situation and understand how and when to use the different decision methods.
- Participation is not always desirable as a leadership style.
- Leaders must pay particular attention to their followers' needs and reactions when making a decision.

In addition to Fiedler's and Vroom and Yetton's theories that focus on how leaders use their resources, three other contingency models hinge on how leaders manage their relationships with followers.

Path-Goal Theory

The Path-Goal Theory of leadership, developed in the early 1970s, proposes that the leader's role is to clear the paths subordinates use to accomplish goals (House, 1971; House and Dessler, 1974). By doing so, leaders allow subordinates to fulfill their needs, and as a result, leaders reach their own goals as well. The concept of exchange between leaders and subordinates, whether it is an implicit or explicit contract, is at the core of this model. The leader and followers establish a relationship that revolves around the exchange of guidance or support for productivity and satisfaction.

THE FRAMEWORK   The major conceptual basis for the Path-Goal Theory is the expectancy model of motivation (Vroom, 1964). Expectancy theory describes how individuals make rational choices about their behavior, based on their perceptions of the degree to which their effort and performance can lead to outcomes they value. The key to motivation, then, is to remove the various obstacles that weaken the linkages between effort and performance and between performance and outcomes. The nature of the task and follower characteristics determine which leadership behavior contributes to subordinate satisfaction. If the task is new and unclear, the followers are likely to waste their efforts due to a lack of knowledge and experience. They might feel frustrated and unmotivated, so the leader must provide instructions and training, thereby removing obstacles to followers' performance and allowing them to do their job. If a task is routine and subordinates performed it successfully a number of times, however, they might face an element of boredom, which would require the leader must show consideration, empathy, and understanding toward subordinates.

Behaviors the leader uses to motivate employees further depend on the employees themselves (Griffin, 1979; Stinson and Johnson, 1975). Some employees need guidance and clear instructions; others expect to be challenged and seek autonomy to do their own problem solving. The followers' need for autonomy and other personal characteristics, such as locus of control, are factors that the leader needs to consider before selecting an appropriate behavior. For example, a follower who likes challenges and needs autonomy will not need or want the leader to be directive even during an unstructured task. For that employee, leader directiveness can be irrelevant or even detrimental because it might reduce satisfaction.

EVALUATION AND APPLICATION   Despite several supportive research studies (e.g., House and Mitchell), the empirical support for the Path-Goal Theory remains mixed (Downey, Sheridan, and Slocum, 1975; Szilagyi and Sims, 1974). The model is generally under-researched, although researchers have proposed several new potential applications (Elkins and Keller, 2003). Notwithstanding contradictory findings, the Path-Goal Theory contributes to our understanding of leadership by once more focusing attention on the behavior of providing guidance and support to followers. It adds to resource utilization models, such as Fiedler's Contingency Model, by including followers' perceptions of the task and the role of the leader in removing blocks to task accomplishment. The Path-Goal Theory's use of employee satisfaction as a criterion for leadership effectiveness broadens our view of leadership. The model's suggestion that not all behaviors will be effective with all subordinates points to the importance of an employee's need for challenge and desire to be autonomous as a determinant of a leader's behavior. Interestingly, the role of the leader in the Path-Goal Theory is that of obstacle remover, which is similar to the role ascribed to team leaders.

The next theory reviews a leadership model that focuses on how leaders interpret their followers' actions and use that information as the basis for their relationship with them.

Substitutes for Leadership

In some situations, a relationship between a leader and the followers is not needed to satisfy the followers' needs. Various aspects of the work environment provide enough resources and support to allow subordinates to achieve their goals without having to refer to their leader. For example, an experienced team of pharmaceutical salespeople, who spend a considerable amount of their time on the road and who have control over their commissions, are not likely to rely much on their manager. Their job provides them with challenges, and their experience allows them to make many decisions on their own. The office is not accessible, and they often rely on other

LEADING CHANGE

Jim Goodnight of SAS

"Creativity is especially important to SAS because software is a product of the mind. As such, 95 percent of my assets drive out the gate every evening. It's my job to maintain a work environment that keeps those people coming back every morning. The creativity they bring to SAS is a competitive advantage for us" (Goodnight, 2010). That statement is one indicator of what Jim Goodnight, CEO of SAS, considers to be important in the success of his company. He further states: "Employees don't leave companies, they leave managers" (Lauchlan, 2007). Goodnight cofounded SAS, the world's largest privately held software company and, with John Sall, continues to fully own the company so that the two can think long term and do what it takes to take care of their employees and their customers. With a 98 percent customer renewal rate, global sales of $1.34 billion (Bisoux, 2004), and a turnover of around 4 percent compared to 20 percent in the industry (Goodnight, 2010), SAS is doing something right. Goodnight is the public face of the company and deserves much credit for that success. SAS has kept its workforce happy by giving its employees challenging work, letting them enjoy a 35-hour workweek, free on-site day care, health care, an extensive fitness center, car detailing, and discounts to country club memberships; and free M&Ms one day a week. Although the candy costs the company $45,000 a year, Goodnight believes it is a small price to show appreciation for his employees and is an indicator of the organization's friendly culture (Bisoux, 2004).

Goodnight believes that when the company removes day-to-day challenges, people can focus on their jobs. He tells his managers, "If you treat people like they make a difference, then they will make a difference" (Lauchlan, 2007). For him, it is about giving people a chance to prove themselves. Valuing employees is as important to him as keeping his customers happy. Goodnight states, "I simply wanted to create a company where I would want to work. Over the years, I've learned how employee loyalty leads to customer loyalty, increased innovation, and higher-quality software" (Faiola, 2006). He considers his employees and his customers the building blocks of the success of his organization (Goodnight, 2005). During his speech after being named as the year's top executive in 2005, Goodnight echoed this theme: "I simply facilitate a creative environment where people can create great software and foster long-term relationships with our customers" (Stevie, 2004). While he stays involved in the daily operations, he has the opportunity to stay close to both employees and customers and hear firsthand about ideas and challenges SAS may face. His formula for success is simple: "Keep your customers happy. Value your employees . . . while you may not grow your profits every quarter, you will grow your business over time" (Bisoux, 2004: 20)

Sources: Bisoux, T., 2004. "Corporate counter culture," *BizEd*, November–December: 16–20; Faiola, A. M., 2006. *Inc.*, June, *xx.*; Goodnight, J., 2005. "Software 2005: Building blocks for success," http://www.sandhill.com/conferences/sw2005_proceedings/goodnight.pdf (accessed July 8, 2007); Goodnight, J. 2010. SAS web site. http://www.sas.com/presscenter/bios/jgoodnight.html (accessed January 20, 2010). Lauchlan, S., 2007. "Interview with Jim Goodnight," *MyCustomer.com*, May 22. http://www.mycustomer.com/cgi-bin/item.cgi?id=133019&d=101&h=817&f=816 (accessed July 8, 2007); Stevie Award. 2004. http://www.crm2day.com/news/crm/EpluuFlFFpWCyCGeTT.php (accessed July 8, 2007).

salespeople for help and information. Similarly, skilled emergency room nurses and technicians do not rely on a leader or manager to take care of their patients. In such circumstances, various situational factors replace the leader's functions of providing structure, guidelines, and support to subordinates.

The Substitute for Leadership Model proposes that various organizational, task, and employee characteristics can provide substitutes for the traditional leadership behaviors of consideration and initiation of structure.

TABLE 5   Leadership Substitutes and Neutralizers

Substitutes or Neutralizers	Consideration	Structuring
Follower Characteristics		
1. Experience and training		Substitute
2. Professionalism	Substitute	Substitute
3. Lack of value for goals	Neutralizer	Neutralizer
Task Characteristics		
1. Unambiguous tasks		Substitute
2. Direct feedback from task		Substitute
3. Challenging task	Substitute	Substitute
Organizational Characteristics		
1. Cohesive team		Substitute
2. Leader's lack of power	Substitute	Neutralizer
3. Standardization and formalization	Neutralizer	Substitute
4. Organizational rigidity		Neutralizer
5. Physical distance between leaders and followers	Neutralizer	Neutralizer

Source: Based on S. Kerr and J. M. Jermier, "Substitutes for leadership: Their meaning and measurement," *Organizational Behavior and Human Performance*, 22 (1978): 375–403.

Such situations led to the development of the Substitutes for Leadership Model (SLM; Kerr and Jermier, 1978). SLM proposes that various organizational, task, and employee characteristics can provide substitutes for the traditional leadership behaviors of consideration and initiation of structure (Table 5). In general, if information about the task and its requirements are clear and available to the subordinates through various means such as their own experience, their team, or through the organization, they are not likely to need the leader's structuring behaviors. Similarly, when support and empathy are not needed or are available through other sources such as coworkers, the subordinates will not seek the leader's consideration behaviors.

In addition to substituting for leadership, some situations can neutralize the effect of the leader. Most notably, the leader's lack of power to deliver outcomes to followers and an organization's rigid culture can prevent a leader's consideration and structuring behaviors from affecting subordinates. For example, a subordinate whose manager is in another state or is powerless to deliver on promises and reward or a subordinate who does not value the rewards provided by the manager is not likely to be affected by the leader's behaviors (see Table 5). The situation neutralizes the leader.

Consider how Ricardo Semler, president of the Brazilian firm Semco, author and proponent of open-book management, set up his company so that it runs with few managers (Leading by Omission, 2005). Workers are trained carefully; provided with considerable information, including detailed financial data and salary information; and left to set their own hours, evaluate and vote for their managers, and make most of the decisions. The workers' training and experience allows the company to function with few senior managers. The structure, training, and teamwork at Semco act as substitutes for leadership.

EVALUATION AND APPLICATION   The SLM has not been tested extensively and needs considerable clarification regarding the nature of the various substitutes and neutralizers and the situations to which they might apply. Because of inconsistent results, some researchers suggest that it suffers from methodological problems (Villa et al., 2003), and the few studies performed in non-U.S. cultural settings failed to yield support for the model (Farh, Podsakoff, and Cheng, 1987). Like the next model we will discuss, the leader–member exchange, however, the SLM is intuitively appealing and addresses processes not taken into account by other leadership models. In particular, it questions the need for leadership in certain situations and points to the difficulty of being an effective leader when many neutralizers are present. Furthermore, the model provides considerable potential for application. Depending on the culture, strategy, and goals of an organization and on a specific leader's personality, the leader might want to set up or remove leadership substitutes. For some control-oriented leaders or in organizations with traditional structures and hierarchies in place, the presence of substitutes could be perceived as a loss of control and authority.

Given the flattening of many organizations and the push toward empowerment and use of teams, judicious use of substitutes can free up the leader for other activities, such as strategic planning, and still allow the organization to achieve its objectives. The use of information technology tools that make information widely available and support work structures, such as telecommuting and outsourcing, further reduces the need for leadership in some situations (Howell, 1997). Consider the case of one of the oldest and fifth-largest breweries in the United States. Despite its 175-year-old history, D.G. Yuengling & Son uses a modern, relatively flat structure that focuses on not becoming bureaucratic. Respect for the individual and a positive work environment are part of its core values (Yuengling, 2007). The company offers relatively high-paying jobs in an area where jobs are scarce and has developed a loyal following (Rubinkan, 2007). Like many other family operations, however, employees and managers found themselves relying too much on the owner, Dick Yuengling. Yuengling recognizes the need to set up substitutes for his hands-on leadership: "You've got to get people in the proper place" (Kurtz, 2004: 71). The company's chief operating officer, David Cainelli, along with Jennifer Yuengling, set up the structures that would allow for decision making to be decentralized and delegated to people closest to the products and markets (Kurtz, 2004).

Autonomous and self-managed teams provide an application of the SLM. The goal of such teams is to function without supervision. The team becomes a substitute for leadership. Extensive technical and team-building training, selection of team members with a professional orientation, intrinsically satisfying tasks for which team members are given considerable autonomy, and direct feedback can be used as substitutes for leadership structuring behaviors. Similarly, a cohesive team replaces the leader's supportive behaviors. The factors identified as substitutes can be used as a guide in setting up such autonomous work teams. One final implication of the SLM is leadership training. Based on this model, leadership training might need to focus on teaching the leader to change the situation as much as it focuses on teaching effective leadership behaviors. Leaders can be taught how to set up substitutes and avoid neutralizers. Such a recommendation is similar to those based on Fiedler's Contingency Model discussed earlier in this chapter.

The next model we consider focuses on the dyadic relationship between leaders and followers. Among the early leadership theories of leadership, it is the only one that continues to draw considerable interest and research.

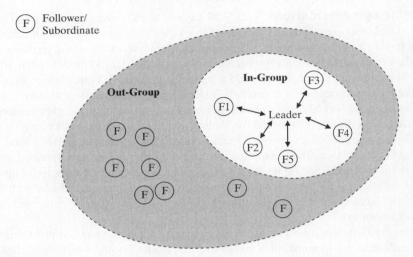

FIGURE 3 Leader—Member Exchange Mode

Leader–Member Exchange

Many of us experience leadership, either as leaders or followers, as a personal relationship between a leader and a subordinate, rather than a group phenomenon. We interact daily with our managers and forge an individual relationship with them. As leaders, we do not experience the same relationship with all of our followers. Each dyadic relationship is different. A leader establishes a one-on-one relationship with each follower (Figure 3), and each relationship varies greatly in terms of the quality of the exchange. Some followers are part of in-group; some are in the out-group. These concepts are at the core of the Leader–Member Exchange (LMX) model, which was called the Vertical Dyad Linkage Model in its earlier versions (Dansereau, Graen, and Haga, 1975; Graen and Shiemann, 1978). The LMX model focuses on the unique, relationship-based exchange between a leader and followers (Graen and Uhl-Bien, 1995).

THE FRAMEWORK   In each exchange, the leader and follower establish a role for the follower. Those followers with a high-quality relationship are in the in-group. High-quality LMX involves mutual respect, anticipation of deepening trust, and expectations of continued and growing professional relationships and obligations. In-group followers enjoy their leader's attention, support, and confidence, and receive challenging and interesting assignments. The leader might overlook their errors (Duarte, Goodson, and Klich, 1994), attribute them to factors outside the followers' control, or recognize their contributions to a greater extent and reward them more (Burris et al., 2009). In exchange for the in-group status, the followers' role is to work hard, be loyal, and support the leader. They are likely to work beyond their formally prescribed job duties (Liden and Graen, 1980) and increase their commitment to their goals (Klein and Kim, 1998).

For the members of the in-group, such a high-quality exchange often becomes a self-fulfilling prophecy and leads to high performance, high satisfaction, and low stress. Studies extend the impact of a positive LMX to safety communication, commitment, and reduction of accidents (Hofmann and Morgeson, 1999). Other studies found that a positive LMX is related to higher frequency of communication, which in turn leads to more favorable job performance ratings (Kacmar, Witt, Zivnuska, and Gully, 2003), It also may lead to higher outputs in research and development teams (Elkins and Keller, 2003) and encourage in-group members to participate more (Burris et al., 2009). Conceptual extensions of the model suggest that the positive work relationship might even extend to social networks, whereby leaders sponsor members of their in-group into various social networks (Sparrowe and Liden, 1997). Research indicates that a positive exchange with a leader plays a role in the extent to which employees feel the organization supports them (Wayne, Shore, and Liden, 1997).

The followers in the out-group face a different situation. The leader might perceive them as less motivated or less competent, interact with them less, provide them with few opportunities to perform, and promote them less often (Wakabayashi et al., 1988). Their role tends to be limited to that defined by formal job descriptions, with little or no expectation of high performance, commitment, or loyalty. They often have to find ways of compensating for the low-quality relationship they have with their leader (Kacmar, Zivnuska, and White, 2007). Regardless of whether the leader's perception and expectations are accurate and fair, members of the out-group are likely to live up, or down, to them. As a result, out-group members who have a low-quality LMX will perform poorly and experience more stress. They also file for grievances more often (Cleyman, Jex, and Love, 1993) and are more likely to take retaliatory actions against the organization (Townsend, Phillips, and Elkins, 2000).

The relationship between the leader and each follower forms early. The LMX model suggests that development of the leader–follower relationship takes place in stages summarized in Table 6. Additionally, leaders create positive relationships with three types of followers: those who are competent and show relevant skills, those whom they can trust, and those who are willing to assume more responsibility. Some research further suggests that followers can create a positive LMX by seeking feedback about their performance as long as the supervisor attributes the behavior to work rather than a desire to make a positive impression (Lam, Juan, and Snape, 2007). Culture can also play a key role in how in-group membership is assigned and which of these three factors is given more weight. In achievement-oriented cultures, such as the United

TABLE 6	Stages of Relationship Development Between Leaders and Their Followers
Stage	**Description**
Testing and assessment	No relationship is yet formed. Leaders consider followers who do not yet belong to a group in terms of objective and subjective criteria for inclusion in either in-group or out-group. Followers' potential, ability, skills, and other psychological factors, such as loyalty, may be tested. Group assignments are made. The relationship with out-group followers does not progress beyond this stage.
Development of trust	This stage only exists for in-group members. Leader provides in-group followers with challenges and opportunities to perform that reinforce development of trust. In return, followers perform and demonstrate their loyalty to the leader.
Creation of emotional bond	In-group followers with a well-established relationship may move to this stage where the relationship and the bond between them become strong and emotional. Followers are highly committed to leader's vision.

Source: Partially based on information in Graen and Uhl-Bien, "The transformation of work group professionals into self-managing and partially self-designing contributors: Toward a theory of leadership-making," *Journal of Management Systems* 3, no. 3 (1991): 33–48.

States and Germany, individuals are evaluated based on their performance and achievement, rather than on their past or their membership in certain castes (Trompenaars, 1994). Therefore, it is expected that leaders select their in-group members based on competence, performance, and commitment to the organization, rather than based on a personal relationship. Anything else would be called favoritism and nepotism. As a result, formal human resource policies and procedures, as well as day-to-day personnel practices, in such cultures focus on fairness, equal opportunity, and hiring those who are most qualified for the jobs based on their personal competence.

In ascriptive cultures, such as many in the Middle East or France, where people are judged and evaluated more based on their group membership, rather than their individual achievement and performance, higher-quality exchange may depend more on the leader's ability to trust followers, which is likely to be based on issues such as social class and birth (Trompenaars, 1994). The concepts of nepotism and inappropriate favoritism to one's in-group do not apply readily in ascriptive and collectivist cultures, where loyalty to one's village, clan, or family is the primary concern. In such cultures, managers hire those they know directly or who are recommended by others they know. Skills and competence are secondary to such personal recommendations. In Hong Kong, for example, leaders are obligated to take care of their own people first (Adler, 1991). Malaysians place a strong emphasis on loyalty and harmony in the work group (Kennedy, 2002). In many Middle Eastern countries, including Arab and non-Arab countries, such as Afghanistan and Iran, leaders surround themselves with family and clan members who can be trusted and who are loyal. Doing otherwise would be disloyal to one's community and even foolish. In such cultures, a wise leader does not allow strangers into the in-group, no matter how competent and qualified they are. Outsiders are hired to help, but access to the in-group is based on community factors. Recent studies further suggest that organizational culture may also affect the quality of the LMX, with better relationships in team-oriented cultures (Erdogan, Linden, and Kramer, 2006).

> In achievement-oriented cultures, such as the United States and Germany, individuals are evaluated based on their performance and achievement, rather than on their past or their membership in certain castes. In ascriptive cultures, such as many in the Middle East or France, where people are judged and evaluated more based on their group membership, rather than their individual achievement and performance, a higher-quality exchange may depend more on the leader's ability to trust followers, which is likely to be based on issues such as social class and birth.

EVALUATION AND APPLICATION   Interest in LMX theory continues to be strong with many recent extensions and testing of its component (e.g., Lam et al., 2007; Sin, Nahrgang, and Morgeson, 2009). Several areas require further clarification. Specifically, researchers question the adequacy of the theory, the multiple measures, and the methods used to test the concepts (for a detailed review, see Schriesheim, Castro, and Cogliser, 1999). In addition, despite continued research, the factors that lead to the development of an in-group versus an out-group relationship need more attention. Some research suggests that similarity in regard to personality plays a key role early in the relationship (Dose, 1999; Murphy and Ensher, 1999; Nahrgang, Morgeson, and Ilies, 2009), whereas performance matters more as time goes on (Bauer and Greene, 1996). More research needs to be conducted in other areas as well, including identifying factors that affect the development of the LMX, assessing the desirability of having the two groups, the conditions under which subordinates move from one group to the other, and exploring the cultural factors that are likely to affect the decision on who belongs to the in-group. The research on the impact of gender similarity on the development of LMX, for example, produced mixed results and requires further clarification (see McAllister, 1995; Tsui and O'Reilly, 1989). The results of at least one study in Mexico, however, show gender similarity to be related to lower absenteeism, particularly with female leaders (Pelled and Xin, 1997) and higher trust (Pelled and Xin, 2000).

From a practitioner and application point of view, the LMX model is appealing. Anyone who has been part of an organization has experienced the feeling of being part of either the in-group or the out-group. Many have seen the departure of a well-liked manager, who is replaced with someone who has his own team. The quick movement from in-group to out-group is felt acutely. The concept of in-group and out-group also can be perceived as violating the norm of equality (Scandura, 1999), which is highly valued in many Western cultures, including the United States. As leaders, most of us can identify our in-group (see Self-Assessment 3). Our in-group members are the people we trust. They are our right-hand assistants. We can give them any assignment with confidence. They will get the job done without us having to check up on them. We also know the members of our out-group. Toward some, we feel neutral; others we dislike and may try to get transferred. In both cases, those individuals do not get many chances to interact with us, and they are not provided with many opportunities to demonstrate their competence on visible and key projects.

The development of an individual exchange with others is a natural part of any interaction. Such a situation can be highly positive for an organization, allowing for the identification of competent individuals and ensuring that they achieve organizational goals. The creation of in-groups and out-groups, however, can also be highly detrimental, leading to feelings and accusations of unfair treatment (Scandura, 1999). Alan Canton, president of Adams-Blake Co., a software company in California, faced considerable obstacles in the development of a new software when three of the five-member team assigned to the task formed a friendship—a clique—and decided to exclude the other two members (Rich, 2005). Canton addressed the problem head-on to get rid of the unproductive in-group/out-group that formed. The key issue is the basis on which such relationships are formed. Researchers suggest that personal compatibility and employee ability are the basis for selection (Graen and Cashman, 1975). Unfortunately, organizational reality does not always match theory. Most of us can identify, or were part of, LMX relationships based on either positive or negative personal feelings, stereotypes, or interpersonal conflicts. Many highly competent and qualified employees are excluded from a leader's in-group based on personal dislike or organizational politics. After all, leaders are subject to human error just like the rest of us.

Abuse of power and membership of some top management teams are examples of the potential negative effects of in-groups. Being able to work with people, you trust and agree with and who share your vision for the organization sounds like an ideal situation for any leader, who would then not face unnecessary arguments and delays. Decisions would be made quickly and efficiently, and goals would be achieved. This ideal situation is exactly what many top-level executives attempt to set up when they select their top management team and the members of their board of directors. They pick people they trust and can work with. Executives rarely consciously and willingly pick members with whom they have major conflicts and differences. The goal is to create a workable team—a team made up of in-group members.

An example of the importance of being part of a team is the now-classic case of Michael Ovitz, who was hired to be Disney's president and was fired 14 months later, receiving a $140-million severance package for his short tenure. During the trial of a lawsuit filed by a Disney shareholder against CEO Michael Eisner for wasting company resources by hiring and then firing Michael Ovitz, Ovitz testified that from the first day, he was left out of decisions and undercut by the Disney management team, who did not report to him (Holson,

2004a). Eisner, for his part, testified that he had to spend too much time managing Ovitz (considered one of the most powerful and successful wheeler-dealers in Hollywood when he headed the Creative Artists Agency before coming to Disney): "Every day I was trying to manage Michael Ovitz. I did little else" (Holson, 2004b: C1). Eisner further accused Ovitz of "un-Disney-like" behavior and of not fitting in with the rest of management team. Eisner cited an example of Ovitz taking a limousine instead of a bus with other executives and states that Ovitz "was a little elitist for the egalitarian cast members" (Holson, 2004b: C12). Although the Ovitz–Eisner case is much more complex than an LMX relationship, the poor relationship and the fact that Ovitz either did not fit in or was not allowed to be part of the in-group clearly played a role in his firing from Disney, a factor that, in turn, was central to the shareholder lawsuit.

Research on friendship patterns and attraction to others indicates that people tend to associate with those who are like them, have similar backgrounds, and share their values and beliefs. To counteract this potential bias, Maggie Widerotter of Wink Communication makes a point of taking time to look for employees she does not see on a regular basis. She takes time to get out of her office and go on a "lion hunt" (McCauley, 2000: 114). She says, "That gives me a chance to connect with employees who I don't usually talk to. . . . I always walk away from the experience having learned something: I have a renewed understanding of what we're doing at my company" (114).

Without a conscious effort to seek out new people, the in-group for most leaders includes people who are like them, with similar backgrounds and views. This homogeneity in top management teams and board membership caught the blame recently for many of the problems in U.S. businesses. Industrial giants such as General Motors, AT&T, and IBM suffered from the lack of initiative and creativity of their top management teams. The members worked well together and disregarded input from outsiders. As a result, they failed to foresee the problems and full consequences of their decisions or inaction. The same pursuit of homogeneity was also seen as a weakness in President George W. Bush's inner circle and administration and its decision making on highly complex issues such as the war in Iraq or the firing of U.S. attorneys. The ease, comfort, and efficiency of working with a cohesive in-group are usually because of the similarity of its members. These advantages, however, are sometimes offset by a lack of creativity and limited decision making. In an ideal case, no in-group or out-group should exist. All of a leader's subordinates should have equal access to the leader and to projects and resources. Those who do not perform well should be helped or moved out of the group altogether. Reality, however, is different, and avoiding the creation of in-groups and out-groups is difficult.

One of the key issues then becomes how members are selected to be in each group. For the individual relationship to be productive, leaders should follow some general principles in creating in-groups and out-groups and in selecting their membership. It is important to note that these guidelines apply mostly to achievement-oriented rather than ascriptive cultures:

- Pick in-group members based on competence and contribution to the organization.
- Periodically evaluate your criteria for in-group and out-group membership.
- Assign tasks to persons with the most applicable skills, regardless of group membership.
- Set clear, performance-related guidelines for in-group membership.
- Avoid highly differentiated in-groups and out-groups.
- Keep membership fluid to allow movement in and out of the groups.
- Maintain different in-groups for different activities.

The concept of exchange in the leadership interaction and the importance of the relationship between leaders and their followers continue to be of interest and are expanded and developed further in a more recent model of leadership, Transactional-Transformational Leadership.

Summary and Conclusions

The scientific approach to understanding leadership that started at about the time of the industrial revolution added rigor and attempts at precise measurement to other already-existing views about leadership. The first modern approaches focused on the identification of traits that would distinguish leaders and followers. Although certain traits were found to be associated with leadership, no simple sets of traits consistently predicted who would be an effective leader. Because of inconclusive results, researchers turned their attention to leadership behaviors. The two major categories of initiation of structure and consideration were established as the central leadership behaviors. The switch from simple traits to simple behaviors still did not account for the complex leadership process and, therefore, did not allow researchers to make strong predictions about leadership effectiveness.

The early theories that are the foundation of modern leadership address either the way leaders use resources or the relationship between the leader and the follower. Fiedler's Contingency Model and the Normative Decision Model consider how the leader uses resources that are available and propose that the leader's style must be matched to the situation to achieve effectiveness. Whereas the Contingency Model assumes that the leader's style (LPC) is determined by internal traits and therefore difficult to change, the Normative Decision Model relies on decision-making styles that are assumed to be learnable. The two also differ on the criteria they use for leadership effectiveness. The Contingency model looks at group performance; the Normative Decision Model focuses on decision quality. Perhaps their most interesting

contribution to leadership application and training is that both models involve a series of well-defined variables that can be used to improve leadership effectiveness.

The relationship-based theories focus on the relationship between the leader and the follower. The Path-Goal Theory proposes that the leader's main function is to remove obstacles in the subordinates' path to allow them to perform their jobs and to be motivated and satisfied. The Substitutes for Leadership Model (SLM) explores situations in which a relationship between the leader and subordinates is not needed and is replaced by individual, group, and organizational factors. Finally, the Leader–Member Exchange (LMX) Model focuses on the dyadic relationship between a leader and each follower and proposes the concept of in-groups and out-groups as the defining element of that relationship.

All the models use a contingency view of leadership, and in all of them, the leader's behavior or style depends on the requirements of the situation. Although the concept of task and relationship orientation continues to be dominant, several of the models consider other factors, thereby expanding our views of leadership. The structure and routine of the task continue to be key situational factors, although other variables such as follower independence and maturity are also introduced.

The contingency models of leadership presented here are the foundation of current theory in leadership and continue to dominate the field of leadership. The models differ in the factors they use to describe the leader's style or behavior and elements of the leadership situation that are considered (Table 7).

TABLE 7 Comparison of the Early Contingency Models of Leadership

	Leader Characteristic	Follower Characteristic	Task	Other Factors	Effectiveness Criteria
Fiedler's model	LPC based on motivation; not changeable	Group cohesion	Task structure	Position power	Group performance
Normative Decision Model	Decision-making style; can be changed	Group cohesion	Available information	Agreement with goals Time	Quality of the decision
Path-Goal theory	Leader behavior; can be changed	Individual follower need to grow	Clarity and routineness of task		Follower satisfaction and motivation
Substitutes	Leader behavior; can be changed	Group cohesion	Clarity of task; availability of information	Organization culture, structure, and processes	Need for leader
LMX					Quality of relationship with follower

For each model, however, whether in resource utilization or in exchange and relationship development models, the focus is on the match between the leader and the situation. The extensive research about the various contingency models, although not always consistent and clear, led to the broad acceptance and establishment of the concept of contingency in leadership. Clearly, no one best way to lead exists. Effective leadership is a combination of and match between the leader and the leadership situation.

Review and Discussion Questions

1. What are the similarities and differences between the trait and behavior approaches to leadership?
2. What are the major assumptions of the contingency approach to leadership?
3. Define the leadership and situational factors included in Fiedler's Contingency Model. What are the primary predictions of the model?
4. After assessing your own style, interview several people with whom you worked to determine whether their perceptions match your score based on the LPC.
5. Provide examples for the situations in which each of the major decision styles of the Normative Decision Model would be appropriate.

6. Provide examples of how the Path-Goal Theory of leadership can be used to improve leadership effectiveness.
7. What are positive and negative impacts of substitutes on leaders and organizations? Provide examples.
8. How does the LMX Model differ from all the other contingency theories of leadership?
9. How can leaders use the LMX Model in improving their effectiveness?
10. Compare and contrast the contingency models of leadership. How do they each contribute to our understanding of leadership?

Leadership Challenge: The in-Group Applicant

You are an expatriate manager sent to work in the Indian operation of your company. As you get settled in, one of your first decisions is to hire an assistant manager. Your efficient office manager, who has been extremely helpful to you already and has been with the company for many years, quickly suggests one of his relatives, who, he tells you, would be perfect for the job. According to him, his cousin just graduated from a top business school and, most important, is trustworthy, loyal, and eager to work and learn. Your office manager tells you that his cousin will be coming shortly to introduce himself. He tells you that you don't have to be inconvenienced any further and won't need to waste your time and risk having an unreliable stranger become your assistant.

1. How do you interpret and explain your office manager's actions?
2. Will you hire the "cousin"?
3. What factors do you need to consider before making your decision?

Exercise 1: The Toy Factory

The goal of this exercise is for each group to produce as many high-quality toy wolves as possible. Your instructor will assign you to a group, designate the leader, and provide you with a list of materials needed for making the toy wolves. Your team leader will give you instructions on how to make the toys. After a 15-minute production run, each group's productivity will be measured.

The Toy Factory Worksheet

1. How would you describe your team leader's style of leadership? Provide several specific behavioral examples.

2. How did you react to your leader's style? How satisfied were you?

3. What improvement suggestions (if any) could you offer your leader?

Exercise 2: Using the Normative Decision Model

This exercise is based on the concepts and principles presented in the Normative Decision Model of leadership. Use the contingency factors presented in Table 4 to analyze each case. Figure 2 along with Table 3 provides a guide to the appropriate decision styles for each case.

Case 1: Centralizing Purchasing

You are the western regional manager in charge of purchasing for a group of hospitals and clinics. Your territory includes eight western states. You recently joined the group but you brought with you nearly 10 years of experience in purchasing with one of the company's major competitors. One of your major achievements in the previous job was the implementation of a highly efficient companywide purchasing system. The health group oversees more than 30 associated health clinics and hospitals in your region alone. Each center operates somewhat independently without much control from the regional purchasing manager. Several of the clinics are cooperating under informal arrangements that allow them to get better prices from suppliers. The purchasing managers from the larger hospitals in your region, on the other hand, have almost no contact with one another or you. As a result, they are often competing for suppliers and fail to achieve economies of scale that would allow them to save considerable costs on their various purchases. In other cases, the managers rely on totally different suppliers and manage to obtain advantageous contracts.

With the pressure to cut health-care costs, the health group's board of directors and the group's president identified purchasing as one area where savings need to be achieved. You are charged with centralizing purchasing, and you are expected to reduce the costs of purchasing by at least 15 percent within a year.

You still need to meet many of the purchasing managers who are supposed to report to you. Your appointment was announced through a memo from the group's president. The memo also mentioned the need to cut costs in all areas and indicated the need to focus on purchasing as first step. The purchasing managers you did meet or contact were civil but not overly friendly. With only six months to show the first results, you need to start planning and implementing changes as soon as possible.

Analysis and Recommendation

Using the problem requirements, decision rules, and leadership styles of the Normative Decision Model, indicate which decision style(s) would be most appropriate.

1. What type of problem is it: group or individual?

2. Contingency Factors:
   Is there a quality requirement?

   Does the leader have enough information to make a high-quality decision?

   Is the problem clear and structured?

Is employee acceptance of the decision needed for its implementation?

Will subordinates accept the decision if the leader makes it by himself or herself?

Do subordinates share the organization's goals for the problem?

Is there conflict among subordinates (are they cohesive) regarding the problem?

3. What are acceptable decision styles? Why?

4. What are unacceptable decision styles? Why?

Case 2: Selecting the Interns

You are the manager of the public relations and advertising department of a large electronics plant. Through your contacts with a local university, you made arrangements for your department to hire several interns in public relations and marketing every summer. Your company supports the idea, because ties with universities are important to you. The interns provide support to your department and work directly with your assistant and report to him. They spend most of their time observing various activities and helping where needed. The interns hired over the past years were all excellent and helpful. Your assistant enjoys working with them and even helped several of them find jobs after they graduated, some within your company.

This year, you received more than twenty applications, but your funding only allows you to hire two. You need to decide which two to hire.

Analysis and Recommendation

Using the problem requirements, decision rules, and leadership styles of the Normative Decision Model, indicate which decision style(s) would be most appropriate.

1. What type of problem is it: group or individual?

2. Contingency factors:
   Is there a quality requirement?

Does the leader have enough information to make a high-quality decision?

Is the problem clear and structured?

Is employee acceptance of the decision needed for its implementation?

Will subordinates accept the decision if the leader makes it by himself or herself?

Do subordinates share the organization's goals for the problem?

Is there conflict among subordinates (are they cohesive) regarding the problem?

3. What are acceptable decision styles? Why?

4. What are unacceptable decision styles? Why?

Case 3: Moving to a New Location

You are the manager of a medium-sized city in the Midwest. Through a number of exchanges between the state, local cities, and several businesses, the city recently acquired a building that could house several departments. The building is within one-half mile of other major municipal offices. Although the building is newer than most of the other city buildings and offers larger offices, it is relatively sterile and does not have the charm of many of the older buildings. You inspected the building and also just received the report from the space allocation committee that is working on the problem of overcrowding of several departments. You identified five departments that could move to the new location. After the initial disruption caused by the move, neither the departments' employees nor their constituents would be affected by the move.

Because of the demand for office space, you must make the decision in the next two days. You are aware of the considerable disagreement among the various departments' employees as to which building is a better location and who would be less negatively affected by the move. Everyone agrees that overcrowding is a problem.

Analysis and Recommendation

Using the problem requirements, decision rules, and leadership styles of the Normative Decision Model, indicate which decision style(s) would be most appropriate.

1. What type of problem is it: group or individual?

2. Contingency factors:
   Is there a quality requirement?

   Does the leader have enough information to make a high-quality decision?

   Is the problem clear and structured?

   Is employee acceptance of the decision needed for its implementation?

   Will subordinates accept the decision if the leader makes it by himself or herself?

   Do subordinates share the organization's goals for the problem?

   Is there conflict among subordinates (are they cohesive) regarding the problem?

3. What are acceptable decision styles? Why?

4. What are unacceptable decision styles? Why?

Self-Assessment 1: Determining Your LPC

To fill out this scale, think of a person with whom you have had difficulty working. That person may be someone you work with now or someone you knew in the past. He or she does not have to be the person you like the least well, but should be the person with whom you experienced the most difficulty. Rate this person on the following scale.

			Score
Pleasant	8 7 6 5 4 3 2 1	Unpleasant	_____
Friendly	8 7 6 5 4 3 2 1	Unfriendly	_____
Rejecting	1 2 3 4 5 6 7 8	Accepting	_____
Tense	1 2 3 4 5 6 7 8	Relaxed	_____
Distant	1 2 3 4 5 6 7 8	Close	_____
Cold	1 2 3 4 5 6 7 8	Warm	_____
Supportive	8 7 6 5 4 3 2 1	Hostile	_____
Boring	1 2 3 4 5 6 7 8	Interesting	_____
Quarrelsome	1 2 3 4 5 6 7 8	Harmonious	_____
Gloomy	1 2 3 4 5 6 7 8	Cheerful	_____
Open	8 7 6 5 4 3 2 1	Guarded	_____
Backbiting	1 2 3 4 5 6 7 8	Loyal	_____
Untrustworthy	1 2 3 4 5 6 7 8	Trustworthy	_____
Considerate	8 7 6 5 4 3 2 1	Inconsiderate	_____
Nasty	1 2 3 4 5 6 7 8	Nice	_____
Agreeable	8 7 6 5 4 3 2 1	Disagreeable	_____
Insincere	1 2 3 4 5 6 7 8	Sincere	_____
Kind	8 7 6 5 4 3 2 1	Unkind	_____
		Total	_____

Scoring Key: A score of 64 or below indicates that you are task-motivated or low-LPC. A score of 73 or higher indicates that you are relationship-motivated or high-LPC. If your score falls between 65 and 72, you will need to determine for yourself in which category you belong.

Source: F. E. Fiedler and M. M. Chemers, *Improving Leadership Effectiveness: The Leaders Match Concept,* 2nd ed. (New York: Wiley, 1984). Adapted with permission.

Self-Assessment 2: Assessing a Leadership Situation

This assessment is based on Fiedler's Contingency Model and is designed to allow you to assess a situation you faced as a leader. To complete the questions in each category, think of a current or past situation at work, in sports, or in social or church events where you were the formal or informal leader of a group of people. You were either successful or not so successful. Rate the situation by circling one of the alternatives for each of the following questions; use the same situation to answer all the questions. You will evaluate your effectiveness, relationship with your followers, the structure of the task, and the power you had.

Self-Rating of Effectiveness

1. Considering the situation and task, how effective were you as a leader?

3	2	1
Very effective	Moderately effective	Not at all effective

2. How effective was your group in completing its task?

3	2	1
Very effective	Moderately effective	Not at all effective

3. How would you rate the overall performance of your group?

4	3	2	1
Very high performance	Moderately high performance	Somewhat low performance	Poor performance

Now add up the score of the three questions. The maximum score is 10; minimum is 3. A high performance score would indicate effectiveness. A score between 7 and 10 indicates high performance; a score between 6 and 4 is moderate performance; score of 3 indicates poor performance.

Total Effectiveness score: _____

Leader–Member Relations Scale (LMR)

Write the number that best represents your response to each item using the following scale:

1 = Strongly agree

2 = Agree

3 = Neither agree nor disagree

4 = Disagree

5 = Strongly disagree.

_____ 1. The people I supervise have trouble getting along with each other.
_____ 2. My subordinates are reliable and trustworthy.
_____ 3. A friendly atmosphere exists among the people I supervise.
_____ 4. My subordinates always cooperate with me in getting the job done.
_____ 5. Friction is present between my subordinates and myself.
_____ 6. My subordinates give me a good deal of help and support in getting the job done.
_____ 7. The people I supervise work well together in getting the job done.
_____ 8. I experience good relations with the people I supervise.

Scoring: Add up your scores for all 8 questions.

Total LMR score: _____ *(Save to enter in Sit Con at the end)*

Early Theories: The Foundations of Modern Leadership

Task Structure Rating Scale—Part I (TS Part I)

Write the number that best describes your group's task using the following scale:

0 = Seldom true

1 = Sometimes true

2 = Usually true

Goal Clarity

_____ 1. A blueprint, picture, model, or detailed description of the finished product or service is available.

_____ 2. A person is available to advise and give a description of the finished product or service, or how the job should be done.

Goal-Path Multiplicity

_____ 3. A step-by-step procedure or a standard operating procedure indicates in detail the process that is to be followed.

_____ 4. A specific way to subdivide the task into separate parts or steps is provided.

_____ 5. Some ways for performing this task are clearly recognized as better than others.

Solution Specificity

_____ 6. It is obvious when the task is finished and the correct solution is found.

_____ 7. A book, manual, or job description indicates the best solution or the best outcome for the task.

Availability of Feedback

_____ 8. A generally agreed understanding is established about the standards the particular product or service must meet to be considered acceptable.

_____ 9. The evaluation of this task is generally made on some quantitative basis.

_____10. The leader and the group can find out how well the task was accomplished in enough time to improve future performance.

Add up your scores for all 10 questions. ***Total for TS (Part I):*** _____

Task Structure Rating Scale—Part II (TS Part II)

Only complete if your score on TS Part I is higher than 6.

Training and experience adjustment (circle a number for each of the following questions)

1. Compared to others in this or similar positions, how much training have you had?

3	2	1	0
No training at all	Very little training	A moderate amount of training	A great deal of training

2. Compared to others in this or similar positions, how much experience do you have?

6	4	2	0
No experience at all	Very little experience	A moderate amount of experience	A great deal of experience

Add the numbers you circled for the two questions. *Total TS (Part II):* _____

Scoring Task Structure

    Total from TS—Part I: _____

    Subtract Total from TS—Part II: _____

    Total TS score: _____ *(Save to enter in Sit Con at the end)*

Position Power Rating Scale (PP)

Circle the number that best describes your answer.

1. As the leader, I can directly or by recommendation administer rewards and punishments to my subordinates.

2	1	0
Can act directly or can recommend with high effectiveness	Can recommend but with mixed results	Cannot recommend

2. As the leader, I can directly or by recommendation affect the promotion, demotion, hiring, or firing of my subordinates.

2	1	0
Can act directly or can recommend with high effectiveness	Can recommend but with mixed results	Cannot recommend

3. As the leader, I have the knowledge necessary to assign tasks to subordinates and instruct them in task completion.

2	1	0
Yes, I have knowledge	Sometimes or in some aspects	No, I do not have knowledge

4. As the leader, it is my job to evaluate the performance of my subordinates.

2	1	0
Yes, I can evaluate	Sometimes or in some aspects	No, I cannot evaluate

5. As the leader, I have some official title of authority given by the organization (e.g., supervisor, department head, team leader).

    Yes = 2   No = 0

Scoring: Add your scores for the five PP questions.

    Total PP score: _____ *(Save to enter in Sit Con at the end)*

Situation Control Score (Sit Con)

Add up the scores of the LMR, TS, and PP scales.

$$\frac{\quad}{\text{LMR}} + \frac{\quad}{\text{TS}} + \frac{\quad}{\text{PP}} = \frac{\quad}{\text{Sit Con}}$$

Using the ranges provided, evaluate the situational control you have as the leader in the situation you described.

Total Score	51–70	31–50	10–30
Amount of Sit Con	High Control	Moderate control	Low control

Source: F. E. Fiedler and M. M. Chemers, *Improving Leadership Effectiveness: The Leaders Match Concept,* 2nd ed. (New York: Wiley, 1984). Adapted and used with permission.

Early Theories: The Foundations of Modern Leadership

Evaluation and Discussion

Self-Assessment 1 provided you with your LPC score; Self-Assessment 2 helped you assess the situational control you have as a leader. Fiedler's Contingency Model suggests that if you are a low-LPC task-motivated leader, you and your group will perform best in high- and low-situational control. If you are a high-LPC relationship-motivated leader, you and your group will perform best in moderate-situational control. If the leader is "in match," the group will perform best.

1. Were you "in match" with the situation you described?

2. To what extent did your level of effectiveness (refer to the self-rating at the beginning of this exercise) match Fiedler's predictions? Why or why not?

Self-Assessment 3: Identifying Your In-Group and Out-Group

This exercise is designed to help you identify the members of your in-group and out-group and your own behavior toward members of each group.

Step 1: Identify the Members

Make a list of the subordinates (or team members) whom you **trust**. Select people who work for you (or with you) whom you like and respect, people who enjoy your confidence.

Make a list of the subordinates (or team members) that you **do not trust**. Select people who work for you (or with you) whom you do not like or respect.

Step 2: Membership Factors

What are the commonalties among the group members for each group? What are the factors that caused them to be in each group? Consider behaviors, personalities, and demographic factors, as well as any other relevant factors.

Step 3: How did You Treat Them?

Describe your own behavior as a leader toward each group and its members:

Leader Behaviors	In-Group	Out-Group
Amount of at-work interaction		
Type of interaction		
Type of assignments given		
How was feedback provided		
Amount of out-of-work		
Performance expectations		
Other factors: List		

Step 4: Self-Evaluation

1. What does it take for a person to move from your in-group to your out-group?

2. How does having two groups affect your group or department and the organization?

3. To what extent is group membership based on organizational versus personal factors?

4. What are the implications for you as a leader?

LEADERSHIP IN ACTION

The Caring Dictator

By any measure, Jack Hartnett, the president of Texas-based D.L. Rogers Corp., is a successful man. D.L. Rogers owns 54 franchises of the Sonic roller-skating nostalgic hamburger chain, which generate $44 million in revenues for the company. Hartnett's restaurants make 18 percent more than the national average, and turnover is incredibly low for the fast-food industry, with a supervisor's average tenure at 12.4 years. He knows what he wants, how to keep his employees, and how to run his business for high profit.

In a management world where everyone will tell you that you need to be soft, be participative, be open to ideas, and empower employees, Jack Hartnett appears to be an anachronism. He runs his business on the Sinatra principle: "My Way!" He tolerates little deviation from what he wants, his instructions, and his training. He is absolutely sure he knows the best way, and more than one employee is scared of disagreeing with him. He likes keeping people a little off balance and a little queasy so that they will work harder to avoid his wrath. Hartnett even has his own Eight Commandments, and he will fire those who break any one of them twice. The last Hartnett commandment is "I will only tell you one time." Interestingly, he believes that his style shows that he really cares about his people: "The success of our business is that we really care about our owner-operators—we don't have managers. Our No. 1 focus is to take care of our people" (Ruggless, 1998).

Hartnett restaurants run like clockwork. He does the top-level hiring himself and is reputed to spend as long as 10 grueling hours with prospective managers and their spouses. He wants to know about their personal lives and their financial health and looks for right responses and any signs of reticence to answer questions. Hartnett says, "I want them to understand this is not a job to me. This is a lifetime of working together. I want partners who are going to die with me" (Ballon, 1998: 67). If you are one of the selected few, you are expected to be loyal and obedient. Once a quarter, you can also expect a Hartnett "lock-in" meeting, where Jack will take you away along with other supervisors to a secret location with no chance of escape. You can expect to be blindfolded, put through survival exercises, and sleep in tents before you go to a luxury resort to discuss business.

For all their trouble and unquestioning obedience and loyalty, D.L. Rogers' employees and supervisors find a home, a family, a community, and a place to grow. If you have problems with your husband, like Sharon, the wife of one of the D.L. Rogers' supervisors, you can call Jack. He will listen to you, chew your spouse out, and send him home for a while. Hartnett says, "I don't want you to come to work unhappy, pissed off, upset, or mad about anything, because I don't think you can be totally focused on making money if you're worried" (Ballon, 1998: 63). He pays his employees considerably above national averages, plays golf with them, and gets involved with their personal lives. Hartnett wants to create a bond that lasts. A few years ago, he spent $200,000 to take 254 managers and their families to Cancun, Mexico, for four days. They got training on better time management and marketing techniques, and on how to be a better spouse.

Hartnett also likes to have fun. Practical jokes, including gluing supervisors' shoes to the floor, are common. But he also works hard. Eighty-hour weeks are common, and he starts his days earlier than most. He is not above taking on the most menial jobs in the restaurants and is willing to show the way, no matter what. His presence, his energy, and his unbending confidence in "his way" make converts. Hartnett has created an organization that is consistent and that simplifies everybody's life.

Questions

1. How would you describe Jack Hartnett's leadership style?
2. Why is he successful? Would you work for him?

Sources: Ballon, M. "Extreme managing," *Inc.*, July 1998, 60–72. Ruggless. R. D.L. Rogers Group. 1998. *Nation's Restaurant News*, January. http://findarticles.com/p/articles/mi_m3190/is_n4_v32/ai_20199540/ (accessed January 20, 2010).

New Models for Leadership

Neocharisma, Inspiration, and the Relationship with Followers

From Chapter 6 of *The Art and Science of Leadership*, 6/e. Afsaneh Nahavandi. Copyright © 2012 by Pearson Education. Published by Prentice Hall. All rights reserved.

New Models for Leadership
Neocharisma, Inspiration, and the Relationship with Followers

The most powerful weapon on earth is the human soul on fire.

—FIELD MARSHAL FERDINAND FOCH

One person with passion is better than forty people merely interested.

—E. M. FORSTER

After studying this chapter, you will be able to:

- Describe the various leader, follower, cultural, and situational characteristics that contribute to charismatic leadership.
- Explain the positive and negative impacts of charismatic leadership on organizations.
- Distinguish between transactional and transformational leadership.
- Understand the key role of contingent rewards and the impact of management by exception.
- Present the elements of transformational leadership and their impact on followers and organizations.
- Describe the elements of value-based and spiritual leadership.
- Identify the components of authentic leadership and the impact of this leadership on followers and organizations.
- Explain the concept of positive leadership and its impact.

For many people, the concept of leadership conjures up images of political or organizational leaders who accomplish seemingly impossible feats. When asked to name leaders, people mention the likes of Martin Luther King, Jr., Mahatma Gandhi, Nelson Mandela, and Barak Obama. These leaders and others like them are passionate and engender strong emotional responses in their followers. They change their followers, organizations, and society and even alter the course of history. They have a relationship with their followers that goes beyond simply setting goals, motivating followers, allocating resources, and monitoring results. The most-current approaches to leadership focus on leaders who create special and long-lasting relationships or deep emotional bonds with their followers and, through such bonds, are able to implement change and, in some cases, achieve extraordinary results. The concepts presented in this chapter address the ways in which leaders establish that bond and the approach they take in engaging their followers.

The models are part of what some researchers have called a "new paradigm for leadership" (Bryman, 1992). Although they have many differences, their common themes are inspiration, vision, and focus on the relationship between leaders and followers. Addressing the relationship with followers relates them to exchange and relationship development models. These models, however, go beyond the study of that relationship by highlighting inspiration and vision. Because they dominate the field of leadership with considerable new research devoted to the concepts and because they do not rely fully on contingency approaches, they are discussed separately.

A BRIEF HISTORY OF NEOCHARISMATIC LEADERSHIP

Although not yet old enough to have a history, the theories and research focused on charismatic, transformational, and inspirational leadership have evolved considerably since their introduction in the 1970s (for a review, see Sashkin, 2004). Such approaches are credited with bringing much-needed new life and enthusiasm to the field, which around the 1970s and 1980s was criticized for being irrelevant, trivial, and inconsequential (see McCall and Lombardo, 1978). Max Weber introduced the concept of charisma in the early 1920s, and social historian James McGregor Burns reintroduced and refined the theory (1978), launching decades of empirical-based investigations. Since then, researchers have developed the concept of charisma for application to organizational contexts (Bass, 1985; Conger, 1989; Conger and Kanungo, 1987; House, 1977) and proposed models of leadership that focus on vision and large-scale change in organizations.

Several well-established researchers such as Bernard Bass and Robert House shifted their attention to these new models, and many of the young researchers entering the field made charismatic, transformational, visionary, and inspirational leadership their area of research. The renewed interest moved the research from purely theoretical and primarily case-oriented research to the much-needed empirical investigations of various constructs. The neocharismatic and inspirational approaches provide several advantages over other views of leadership presented in this text:

- They allow us to look at a different aspect of leaders and their role as inspirational visionaries and builders of organizational cultures (Hunt, 1999).
- They highlight the importance of followers' emotional reactions (Chemers, 1997).
- They focus on leaders at top levels who are the subject of study in strategic leadership, thereby allowing for a potential integration of upper-echelon research with transformational and charismatic leadership.

Research about the models presented in this chapter continues as the concepts evolve; however, their predictions and explanations are a first step in addressing a growing need in today's organizations for understanding how leaders create and implement their vision and how they orchestrate and manage large-scale change.

CHARISMATIC LEADERSHIP: A RELATIONSHIP BETWEEN LEADERS AND FOLLOWERS

The word *charisma* means "an inspired and divine gift." Those who have the gift are divinely endowed with grace and charm. Charismatic leaders capture our imagination and inspire their followers' devotion and allegiance. We describe political and religious leaders as charismatic, but leaders in business organizations can also be gifted. Charismatic leaders are those who have a profound emotional effect on their followers (House, 1977). Followers see them not merely as bosses but as role models and heroes who are larger than life.

> Charismatic leaders are those who have a profound emotional effect on their followers. Followers see them not merely as bosses but as role models and heroes who are larger than life.

Consider the case of President Barack Obama and his election in 2008. Obama presents many of the elements of a charismatic leader. The large number of volunteers who engaged in his campaign and supported him felt a strong emotional connection to him, as witnessed by the many people who attended his events and the high level of emotion they exhibited. Expressions such as "Yes we can" and "This is our time" and powerful messages during his acceptance speech such as "If there is anyone out there who still doubts that America is a place where all things are possible, who still wonder if the dream of our founders is alive in our time, who still questions the power of our democracy, tonight is your answer" (Gibbs, 2008: 34) inspired his followers. Obama's optimism and perceived sincerity connected with the majority of the U.S. electorate and many around the world, for example in Germany, where 200,000 people turned out to see candidate Obama. He became the symbol of change and hope for many who, even without knowing much about him, felt a connection to him.

On the other side of the political divide is Sarah Palin, Republican vice-presidential nominee for the same 2008 U.S. election. Her supporters have the same frenzied devotion for her and her ideals as Obama's do for him. Palin's supporters show up to root for her, recently at rallies in Arizona and Nevada, line up at dawn to purchase her book and get her signature, agree with her vision, laugh at her jokes, and cheer her to her next political campaign. Whether it is because of her political or social beliefs or her ability to hunt and field dress a moose, they feel an intense emotional connection to her.

Obama and Palin are charismatic leaders. They inspire followers who are devoted and loyal to them and their vision. This type of relationship involves an intense bond between leaders and their followers and goes beyond a simple exchange. These two leaders also show that charisma is clearly in the eye of the beholder; followers make the charismatic leader. The charismatic bond is far from typical of leadership situations and neither essential nor sufficient for effective leadership. The following sections consider the three elements that are necessary for the development of charismatic leadership: leader characteristics, follower characteristics, and the leadership situation, including culture (Figure 1).

Characteristics of Charismatic Leaders

Charismatic leaders share several common personality and behavioral characteristics and traits (Table 1). Although many of the traits—such as self-confidence, energy, and the ability to communicate well—are related to all types of leadership, their combination and the presence of followers and a crisis are what set charismatic leaders apart.

One characteristic that defines charismatic leaders is their self-confidence in their own abilities and in the correctness and the moral righteousness of their beliefs and actions (Bass, 1985; Sashkin, 2004). Mahatma Gandhi's unwavering beliefs about the need for change in India and

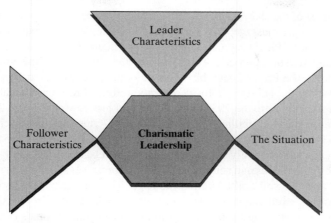

FIGURE 1 Requirements of Charismatic Leadership

Martin Luther King Jr.'s single-minded focus on civil rights are examples of this trait. The self-confidence is accompanied by an apparent lack of internal conflict. Whereas noncharismatic leaders doubt themselves in the face of failure and criticism, charismatic leaders seem to know they are right and project that confidence. Their high level of confidence motivates their followers and creates a self-fulfilling prophecy. The more confident the leader is, the more motivated the followers are, which further emboldens the leader and encourages the followers to carry out the leader's wishes wholeheartedly. The charismatic leader's ability to express positive emotions further encourages followers' positive moods, which increase the attraction to the leader and his or her effectiveness (Bono and Ilies, 2006). Positive expressions, motivation, and hard work increase the chances of success, which provides proof of the correctness of leader's vision.

Steve Case, the highly confident founder of Revolution, a company dedicated to increasing consumer power in health decisions, and former CEO of America Online (AOL), made others believe in his vision of connecting everyone through the Internet. Case believes that three things are most important in success: people, passion and perseverance (Case, 2009). One of Case's former associates explains, "In a little company everybody's got to believe. But there needs to be somebody who believes no matter what. That was Steve. Steve believed from the first day that this was going to be a big deal" (Gunther, 1998: 71). Even though the merger of AOL with Time Warner was unsuccessful and led to a $135-billion loss, Case seemed to put the failure behind him and poured his energy and resources into several new ventures, including Revolution and a free health and medical information Web site, RevolutionHealth. Case's advice to potential entrepreneurs is, "If you feel passionate about a particular business and have the fortitude to break down barriers and redirect when needed, you can do great things" (Edelhauser, 2007).

TABLE 1 Characteristics of Charismatic Leaders

- High degree of self-confidence
- Strong conviction about ideas
- High energy and enthusiasm
- Expressiveness and excellent communication skills
- Active image building and role modeling

Many examples of the charismatic leader's self-confidence can be found in political leaders. President Obama's simple message "Yes we can" is an example of the expression of confidence from a charismatic leader. Fidel Castro has withstood considerable pressure over the past 50 years and remains undaunted in his approach. Aung San Suu Kyi, the leader of the political resistance in Burma and a Nobel Peace Prize winner, has been under house arrest for many years, but remains unwavering in proclaiming her agenda for democratic reform. President Gamal Abdul Nasser of Egypt galvanized Arab pride in the 1950s and 1960s, and his view of a united Arab world dominated the psyche and dreams of millions in the Middle East. Other destructive charismatic leaders use their "gift" to abuse and exploit followers; we discuss them in a later section.

Charismatic leaders generally exhibit high energy levels, along with self-confidence. They are passionate about their ideas and actions, are highly expressive, and use nonverbal cues to lend dramatic support to their well-crafted verbal message. Their exceptional articulation skills that help them express their excitement and communicate the content of their ideas to their followers are a primary tool in persuading followers to join in their vision. Obama's considerable oratory skills provide an example, as do J. F. Kennedy's, Hitler's and Fidel Castro's. With excellent communication skills, charismatic leaders define and frame the mission of the organization or the group in a way that makes it meaningful and relevant to followers. The process of framing puts the leader's goals in a worthwhile context that is used to draw and motivate followers (Conger, 1991; Fairhurst and Sarr, 1996). Charismatic leaders emphasize the group's history and common past, their common identity, and future hopes and common goals (Shamir, Arthur, and House, 1994). In addition, they appeal to their followers' emotion through the use of language, symbols, and imagery. Examples of all of these can be found in President Obama's inaugural speech (Obama's Inaugural speech, 2009).

Charismatic leaders carefully craft their message and present themselves as role models to their followers. They use active impression management to support their image (Conger, 1999; Conger and Kanungo, 1998). They "walk the talk," whether it is through the self-sacrifice that they make and demand of their followers or the self-control they demonstrate. House and Shamir (1993) note that a large number of charismatic political leaders spent time in prison, a sacrifice that demonstrates their willingness to put up with hardship to achieve their vision. For example, Gandhi and Nelson Mandela were imprisoned for defending their beliefs. Other charismatic leaders, such as Martin Luther King, Jr., who role modeled the peaceful resistance he advocated, demonstrate through their actions what they expect of their followers. John McCain, the U.S. senator from Arizona, 2008 presidential candidate, Vietnam war hero, and prisoner of war, considers courage and self-sacrifice to be at the heart of leadership (McCain, 2004).

Carol Bartz, the CEO of Yahoo, talking about making tough decisions states: "It requires role-modeling the behavior you want your leaders to mimic. It means promoting cooperation, communication and making sure everyone is responsible for making things happen. Asking everyone to face their fears and get moving!" (Sellers. 2009c). James E. Rogers, chairman and CEO of Duke Energy adds: "It's one thing to make policy or direction or say, 'Go take this hill.' It's another thing to be there when the hill's being taken" (Bryant, 2009d). Andrea Jung (see Leadership in Action at the end of this chapter) faced the financial problems for her company by reinventing both her company and herself. She states, "Reinvent yourself first before you reinvent your company" (Jones, 2009). Being a role model and "walking the talk" plays a key role in leadership and has become the focus on a new approach to understanding leadership reviewed later in this chapter.

The process of role modeling can also be symbolic, as was the case with the well-publicized $1 salary that Chrysler's Lee Iaccoca accepted while receiving substantial income from stock options and other benefits or John Mackey's $1 salary for 2007 from Whole Foods. Dan Cathy, president and COO of Chick-fil-A and son of the company's founder, is passionate about customer service, and what makes him an effective leader is partly the fact that he is willing to "walk the talk." He is often found in his stores, where he introduces himself to customers with a simple "I'm Dan. I work in customer service" (McGregor, 2004: 83). He believes that "the closer top management is to the customer, the more successful an organization is likely to be" (McGregor, 2004: 84). Whether actual or symbolic, role modeling and powerful verbal messages contribute to the enhanced image of the leader. Cult leaders make use of these behaviors to create a powerful and self-perpetuating mystique that strengthens their relationship and their hold on followers.

Charismatic leaders are masterful impression managers (Conger, 1989; House, 1977). They surround themselves with dramatic and mystical symbols that further enhance the image of the leader as a larger-than-life figure. Bass (1985) cites John F. Kennedy as a case in point. His administration carefully developed the image of Camelot, complete with Guinevere and the knights who were fighting the battle against communism. The competition to conquer space before the Russians further contributed to the mystical and heroic image of a youthful statesman struggling to pull the United States out of the stodgy Eisenhower era. President Obama developed a similar image of youthful enthusiasm by simple gestures such as running up to the podium wherever he was speaking and the presence of his young family beside him. The power of these symbols and their resulting emotional bonds are evidenced by the strong sense of loss after President Kennedy's assassination.

Overall, the characteristics of charismatic leaders are not in dispute; however, they are not the only factor. The next step is describing the development of followers who are devoted to the leader.

Characteristics of Followers

Because charismatic leadership results from a relationship between a leader and followers, the followers of such leaders demonstrate certain characteristics. Without the leader and the followers, no charismatic relationship can form. Take away the frenzied followers, and Hitler would not have been considered charismatic. The same is true for many cult leaders. Even for positive and constructive charismatic leaders such as Gandhi, followers demonstrate particular traits and behaviors (Table 2). First and foremost, followers hold the leader in high esteem. They are strongly devoted to him or her and have a strong sense of loyalty. These followers admire their leader; emulate her behaviors and mannerisms, including talking, dressing, and acting like the leader. They identify with him, a process that further helps followers internalize the leader's values and aspirations as their own. They feel an intense emotional bond and attraction to the leader.

TABLE 2   Characteristics of Followers of Charismatic Leaders

- High degree of respect, affection, and esteem for the leader
- Loyalty and devotion to the leader
- Identification with the leader
- High confidence in leader
- High performance expectations
- Unquestioning obedience

Consider the reaction of employees of Russ Berrie and Co. when the toymaker's founder and namesake died suddenly. Berrie had established a close family bond with his employees. He was the best man at some of their weddings, and one company executive continued to visit his grave regularly because he felt a spiritual bond with the deceased leader (Marchetti, 2005). In addition, followers of charismatic leaders have a high degree of confidence in the vision and direction the leader provides and expectations for high performance. All these characteristics are likely to lead followers to obey calls to actions without question.

Charismatic leaders are able to connect their followers to a common vision. Researchers suggest that charismatic leaders change the followers' perception of the nature of what needs to be done. The expression of positive emotions, which indicates the leader's self-confidence, creates a positive mood contagion (Bono and Ilies, 2006). Leaders offer an appealing vision of the future, develop a common identity, and heighten the followers' self-esteem and sense of self-efficacy (for a review, see Conger, 1999). In addition, one of the key components of the emergence of charismatic leaders is for the followers to perceive a need for change because the current state is unacceptable and because they believe that a crisis either is imminent or already exists (Shamir, 1991; and Beyer, 1993). The case of the 2008 election of Barak Obama presents all these elements. His supporters enthusiastically believed in his vision and their ability to create change to correct a situation they considered unacceptable. The leader, President Obama, provided them with the vision they needed to implement the change. The final element of charismatic leadership is the situation.

The Charismatic Situation

President Obama's case provides yet one more element of charismatic leadership: a sense of crisis and need for change. Perception of crisis leads followers to look for new direction and solutions and prepares them to accept change. If an individual is able to capture and represent the needs and aspirations of the group, that individual is likely to become the leader. In addition, individuals who demonstrate competence and loyalty to a group and its goals are provided with "credit" that they can spend to assume leadership roles. This idiosyncrasy credit allows certain individuals to emerge as leaders and change the direction of the group (Hollander, 1979). Because of the strong emotional impact of charismatic leaders, followers provide them with tremendous leeway (credit) to lead the group into new territory.

EXTERNAL CRISIS AND TURBULENCE At the heart of the issue of charismatic leadership is how certain individuals either emerge as leaders in leaderless groups or replace an appointed leader. Many charismatic revolutionary leaders achieve their status without any formal designation. In organizations, although charismatic leaders are elected or appointed, their followers recognize them as leaders before a formal appointment, the last step in their rise to power, typically during a time of crisis. Popular political and religious leaders, such as Martin Luther King, Jr., Ronald Reagan, or Barak Obama won the hearts and minds of their followers, who then carried them into formal positions.

Charismatic leaders emerge in situations where a change and a new ideological vision need to be articulated and when followers are ready to be saved or more simply moved in a different direction. With an emotionally charged situation, leaders enter the field promising a new beginning, radical solutions, and a break from the unwanted values of the past.

Table 3 summarizes the external situational elements that contribute to the development of charismatic leadership. Although not all researchers believe that a situation of crisis is necessary for the emergence of charismatic leadership, many suggest that a *sense* of distress or crisis is (Bass, 1985; Beyer, 1999a; Shamir and Howell, 1999). Research

TABLE 3 Elements of Charismatic Situations

- Sense of real or imminent crisis
- Perceived need for change
- Opportunity to articulate ideological goal
- Availability of dramatic symbols
- Opportunity to clearly articulate followers' role in managing the crisis

by Roberts and Bradley (1988) suggests that situations of crisis provide more latitude for leader initiative such that the person can demonstrate leadership abilities. Others link resilience and tolerance for ambiguity to charisma and its importance in crisis situations (Hunter, 2006), where followers believe that charismatic leaders are the only ones who can resolve the crisis. Therefore, charismatic leaders emerge in situations where a change and a new ideological vision need to be articulated and when followers are ready to be saved or more simply moved in a different direction. With an emotionally charged situation, leaders enter the field promising a new beginning, radical solutions, and a break from the unwanted values of the past (Boal and Bryson, 1987). They use dramatic symbols to illustrate their goals and point to clear and specific roles that their followers can play in resolving the crisis. As a result, followers are convinced that the charismatic leader is the only one who can help, and the leader helps followers becoming aware of how they can contribute individually.

Historical charismatic leaders emerge in a time of real or perceived crisis. Cyrus the Great of Persia united warring tribes in 1500 B.C.; Napoléon galvanized a fractured postrevolutionary France; the fascist dictators of modern Europe took power during economic and social crises; in the U.S., charismatic civil rights leaders of the 1960s rode on the wave of a cultural and civil unrest; and recently, a sense of crisis and need for change led to the election of Obama to the presidency. These leaders brought a new vision of the future to their eager followers. As a matter of fact, many charismatic leaders fuel the sense of crisis, either sincerely or as a means of manipulation, as one of the reasons why followers need to select them. For example, Sarah Palin and many Republicans in the United States have portrayed the Obama presidency and the Democratic majority as the beginning of Armageddon, enticing voters to the polls. In all cases, the crises and the perceived need for change set the stage for the charismatic leaders' skills and provide the leader with an opportunity to present a vision or solution.

INTERNAL ORGANIZATIONAL CONDITIONS   Researchers suggest that in addition to a sense of external crisis, several internal organizational conditions also facilitate charismatic leadership (Shamir and Howell, 1999).

- *Organizational life cycle.* Charismatic leaders are more likely to emerge and be effective in the early and late stages of an organization's life cycle, when either no set direction is established or change and revival are needed.
- *Type of task and reward structure.* Complex, challenging, and ambiguous tasks that require initiative and creativity and where external rewards cannot be clearly tied to performance can be ideal situations for charismatic leaders.
- *Organizational structure and culture.* Flexible and organic structures and nonbureaucratic organizational cultures are likely to encourage charismatic leadership.

Although some evidence is available to support these propositions, empirical testing is needed before they are established fully as conditions for the emergence of charismatic leadership.

ROLE OF CULTURE   As you have read throughout this text, culture strongly affects what behaviors and styles are considered appropriate and effective for leaders and limits what behaviors people learn and consider acceptable. Based on the nature and processes involved in charismatic leadership, it would stand to reason that cultures with a strong tradition for prophetic salvation, in particular, would be more amenable to charismatic leadership. For example, the Judeo-Christian beliefs of the coming of the savior create fertile ground for charismatic leaders to emerge and be accepted. Prophets by definition are charismatic saviors. Israel, for example, has this type of strong tradition. Another case in point is the recent rise of Islamic fundamentalism, which typically is tied to a prophetic spiritual leader, as is the case in the Sudan and Iran (Dekmejian and Wyszomirski, 1972). The case of Khomeini in Iran illustrates all the elements of a typical charismatic relationship, including leader and follower characteristics, the intense and calculated image management on the part of the leader, and the sense of crisis because of the political climate of the country in the 1970s (F. Nahavandi, 1988; H. Nahavandi, 1994).

In cultures without such prophetic traditions, few charismatic figures are likely to emerge. For example, in China, although periods of crisis and change have certainly occurred, it appears that the relationship between leader and followers is based more on the social hierarchy and need for order, as is prescribed in the Confucian tradition, rather than on the intense emotional charismatic bonds that exist in Judeo-Christian religions. This appears to be the case even for one of the few charismatic Chinese leaders, Mao Zedong. Furthermore, the factors that create the charismatic relationship may differ from one culture to another. The development of a charismatic relationship in a culture such as Japan relies on the leader's development of an image of competence and moral courage, and the securing of respect from followers (Tsurumi, 1982). By contrast, in India, charismatic leadership is associated with a religious, almost supernatural, state (Singer, 1969). In the United States, charisma is assertive and direct, whereas in others it may be more quiet and nonassertive (Scandura and Dorfman, 2004). In any case, even if the concept of charisma is present within a culture, its manifestations may be widely different.

The GLOBE research has studied charismatic leadership in 60 countries (Den Hartog et al., 1999). The basic assumption of the research project is that "charismatic leadership will be universally reported as facilitating 'outstanding' leadership" (Den Hartog et al., 1999, 230). The researchers found that although some attributes are universally endorsed and some are universally negative, several attributes are culturally contingent (see Table 4 for a summary). It is important to note that although several of the behaviors associated with charismatic leadership are universally associated with effectiveness, the term *charisma* evokes mixed reactions in different cultures. In other words, being charismatic is seen as both positive and negative.

In addition to characteristics typically associated with charismatic leadership (e.g., positive and dynamic), there are other characteristics (e.g., being a team builder and being intelligent) that are not part of charisma (see Table 4). Interestingly, although having a vision is universally associated with leadership, how it is expressed and communicated differs greatly across cultures. For example, Chinese leaders are seen as effective if they communicate their vision in a nonaggressive and soft-spoken manner, whereas Indians prefer bold and assertive leaders (Den Hartog et al., 1999). Similarly, followers universally value communication, but the communication style (e.g., level of directness, tone of voice, etc.) that is considered desirable is highly culture specific. For example, Cambodians expressed considerable enthusiasm at the ascendance of their new king Norodom Sihamoni in October 2004, even though he lacked any political experience, partly because they valued his extremely modest and soft-spoken demeanor (Sullivan, 2004). Furthermore, self-sacrifice and risk taking, important components of charismatic leadership in the United States, do not contribute to outstanding leadership in all other cultures (Martinez and Dorfman, 1998).

TABLE 4 Cross-Cultural Attributes of Leadership		
Universally Positive	**Universally Negative**	**Culturally Contingent**
• Being encouraging, positive, and motivational	• Being a loner	• Risk taking
• Having a vision and a plan and being able to make decisions	• Being noncooperative	• Enthusiasm
• Being dynamic	• Being ruthless and dictatorial	• How vision is communicated
• Having integrity and being trustworthy	• Nonexplicit	• What constitutes good communication
• Building teams	• Irritable	• How much leader is seen as equal
• Intelligent		
• Communicator		
• Win–win problem solver		

Source: Based on information in Den Hartog et al., 1999. Culture-specific and cross-culturally generalizable implicit leadership theories: Are attributes of charismatic/transformational leadership universally endorsed? *The Leadership Quarterly* 10: 219–256.

The Dark Side of Charisma

Given the charismatic leaders' strong emotional hold on followers, they can abuse that power easily and apply it toward inappropriate ends. Along with Gandhi, Presidents Kennedy and Mandela, and Dr. King, the list of charismatic leaders unfortunately includes Hitler and Jim Jones (the cult leader who convinced thousands of his followers to commit suicide). The destructive charismatic leaders resemble the positive ones in some dimensions, but several characteristics distinguish them from one another (Table 5; Bass and Steidlmeier, 1999; Conger, 1990; Howell, 1988; Howell and Avolio, 1992).

The major difference between ethical and unethical charismatic leaders is the unethical leaders' focus on personal goals rather than organizational goals. Unethical leaders use their gift and special relationship

> The major difference between ethical and unethical charismatic leaders is the unethical leaders' focus on personal goals rather than organizational goals. Unethical leaders use their gift and special relationship with followers to advance their personal vision and to exploit followers.

TABLE 5 Ethical and Unethical Charisma	
Ethical—Socialized Charisma	**Unethical—Personal Charisma**
• Focus on organizational goals	• Focus on personal goals
• Message built on common goals	• Message built on leader's goals
• Encourage and seek divergent view	• Censors, discourages, or punishes divergent views
• Open and two-way communication	• One-way, top-down communication
• Accepting of criticism	• Closed to criticism
• Impression management used to energize and motivate followers	• Impression management used to deceive followers
• Describe the actual need for change	• Create or exaggerate the sense of crisis

with followers to advance their personal vision and to exploit followers; they follow an internal and personal orientation, behaviors that are similar to narcissistic personality. Ethical charismatic leaders use their power to serve others, develop followers, and build and achieve a common vision. The unethical charismatic leader censors opposing views and engages in one-way communication, whereas the ethical one accepts criticism and remains open to communication from followers. Given the considerable power of some charismatic leaders and their intense bond with their followers, it is easy to see how the line between ethical and unethical behaviors can be blurred. Leaders who are convinced of their vision do not doubt its righteousness, and leaders who have the ability to persuade often will do so without concern for others. The characteristics of self-confidence and skillful role-modeling and persuasion that make a charismatic leader effective can also be the sources of highly destructive outcomes.

Distinguishing between the two types of charismatic leadership further helps explain how negative leadership can develop. Howell (1988) contrasts socialized and personalized charismatic leaders. Socialized leaders focus on satisfying their followers' goals and on developing a message that is congruent with shared values and needs and may be a factor in reducing deviance in their group (Brown and Treviño, 2006a). Personalized leaders rely on getting followers to identify and agree with their personal values and beliefs. Both examples include all the characteristics of charismatic leaders, their followers, and the situation. Personalized leadership situations, however, are more prone to abuse.

In addition to the potential for power abuse and corruption, charismatic leaders also might present other liabilities ranging from a flawed vision that is self-serving to unrealistic estimates of the environment (Conger and Kanungo, 1998). The charismatic leader's skills at impression management and influence can become a liability when leaders mislead their followers with exaggerated estimates of their own or their followers' abilities and the chances for success. The unethical charismatic leader's journey becomes all about the leader. For the ethical one, it is about achieving a common goal. In many cases, the unethical charismatic leader will exaggerate the crisis and fan followers' sense of impending disaster and doom to demonstrate the need for his or her leadership. Other potential liabilities of charismatic leadership include failure to manage details, failure to develop successors, creation of disruptive in- and out-groups, and engaging in disruptive and unconventional behaviors (Conger and Kanungo, 1998). It is important to note that whereas followers often see their charismatic leader as ethical and their savior, detractors perceive him or her as unethical and even evil, both demonstrating very strong emotions. The emotion created by charismatic leaders leaves little room for moderation.

Evaluation and Application

The considerable changes in many organizations in recent years have created a sense of crisis and resulted in a perceived need for revitalization and change. Therefore, it is no coincidence that the concept of charismatic leadership dominates academic and popular views of leadership. The need to revitalize industrial, educational, health care, and governmental institutions creates one of the essential elements for charismatic leadership; many perceive that we are in a time of turbulent change, if not crisis. We make many demands on our leaders to provide us with revolutionary ideas and are often disappointed when they cannot fulfill those expectations. In fact, our expectations are so high that we are bound to be disappointed.

Researchers have developed a number of different approaches to explain charismatic leadership, ranging from an attributional perspective whereby the leader's behavior and the situation persuade followers to attribute charismatic characteristics to the leader (Conger, 1989a; Conger and Kanungo, 1987), to self-concept views that focus on explaining how charismatic leaders can influence and motivate their followers (Shamir, House, and Arthur, 1993), to psychoanalytic perspectives (Kets de Vries, 1993), and self-presentational views (Sosik, Avolio, and Jung, 2002). Much debate centers around the sociological and organizational views of charismatic leadership regarding its contents, focus, and situational antecedents (Bass, 1999; Beyer, 1999a; House, 1999; Shamir, 1999). Various studies have tested the elements of the different views of charismatic leadership; the results are not always consistent (e.g., see Shamir et al., 1998). Continued research, however, provides strong support for the existence and importance of understanding charismatic relationships and how such leaders affect their followers and their organizations. For example, charismatic leadership may lower burnout (De Hoogh and End Hartog, 2009); engender positive effect in followers (Erez et al., 2008); and positively change cooperation in some groups (De Cremer and van Knippenberg, 2002). Charismatic leaders seem to increase followers' efforts and citizenship behaviors (Sosik, 2005) and have been suggested to have a positive impact on external organizational stakeholders as well as immediate followers (Fanelli and Misangyi, 2006).

The charismatic relationship is a powerful and undeniable part of the most celebrated leadership situations, particularly in Western cultures. Charismatic leaders and their followers can achieve incredible feats. Such leadership, however, is not required for an organization to be successful. Indeed, it can be destructive, as is the case of unethical or personal charismatic leadership or even when a charismatic leader is simply wrong and drives the organization to failure. Charismatic leaders can also be powerful agents of change, but an equally powerful obstacle to change (Levay, 2010). In addition, because it is difficult, if not impossible, to train someone to be a charismatic leader (Trice and Beyer, 1993), the phenomenon depends on one individual rather than on stable organizational processes that can be put in place once the leader is gone. Finally, it is important to remember that charismatic leadership is not a cure-all (Trice and Beyer, 1993). With all its potential benefits, charismatic leadership is a double-edged sword that requires careful monitoring to avert abuse. Although charismatic leadership holds a potentially negative side as demonstrated by many destructive charismatic historical figures, transformational leadership, which is presented next, relies on charisma as one element but concentrates on the positive role of leadership in change.

TRANSACTIONAL AND TRANSFORMATIONAL LEADERSHIP

How do leaders create and sustain revolutionary change in organizations? What style of leadership is needed to motivate followers to undertake organizational transformations? Several researchers proposed transformational leadership concepts to answer these questions and to describe and explain how leaders succeed in achieving large-scale change in organizations. First developed by Burns (1978), transformational leadership theory suggests that some leaders, through their personal traits and their relationships with followers, go beyond a simple exchange of resources and productivity.

The leadership models presented in previous chapters focused on the transaction and exchange between leaders and followers. For example, in Path-Goal Theory, the leader clears obstacles in exchange for follower motivation by providing structure to the task or by being considerate. Such basic exchanges, sometimes labeled transactional leadership, are considered an essential part of leadership and leaders must understand and manage them well. To create change, however, they must supplement exchange with transformational leadership. Transformational leadership theory and observation of many leaders suggest that leaders use behaviors that are more complex than initiation of structure and consideration to establish a connection with their followers and transform organizations.

Transactional Leadership

Transactional leadership is based on the concept of exchange between leaders and followers. The leader provides followers with resources and rewards in exchange for motivation, productivity, and effective task accomplishment. This exchange and the concept of providing contingent rewards are at the heart of motivation, leadership, and management theory and practice. Two styles of transactional leadership are Contingent Reward (CR) and Management by Exception (MBE).

CONTINGENT REWARD   Through the use of contingent reward, leaders provide followers with promised rewards when followers fulfill their agreed-upon goals. When well managed, contingent rewards are highly satisfying and beneficial to the leader, the followers, and the organization. The informal and formal performance contracts that result are highly desirable and effective in managing performance (Bass, 1985). Some research indicates that transactional leadership can provide structure and lead to positive outcomes (Walker, 2006) and that individualistic cultures may react more positively to transactional leadership than collectivistic cultures (Walumbwa, Lawler, and Avolio, 2007), whereas other studies (e.g., Rank et al., 2009) indicate that transactional leadership may impede innovation. CR is part of most leadership training whereby leaders are taught to reinforce appropriate behaviors, discourage inappropriate ones, and provide rewards for achieved goals. It is a necessary component of effective leadership and management. For example, transactional leadership successfully motivated remaining employees to decontaminate and tear down the infamous Rocky Flats nuclear site in Colorado. The Environmental Protection Agency certified the nuclear weapons site "clean" in June 2007 after years of mismanagement, accidents, and extensive cleanup. Denny Ferrara, whose whole family worked at the plant, was in charge of getting employees to work themselves out of a job. He accomplished this task by setting clear goals, communicating extensively, allowing employees to provide input into how to do the work, and encouraging them with recognition and generous rewards, which in some cases topped $80,000 a year (McGregor, 2004b).

MANAGEMENT BY EXCEPTION   Management by Exception (MBE) is a leadership style whereby the leader interacts little with followers, provides limited or no direction, and only intervenes when things go wrong. In one type of MBE, labeled "active MBE," leaders monitor follower activities and correct mistakes as they happen (Bass and Avolio, 1990a). In another type, labeled laissez-faire or omission, leaders are passive and indifferent toward followers and their task (Hinkin and Schriesheim, 2008). In both cases, little positive reinforcement or encouragement is given; instead the leader relies almost exclusively on discipline and punishment. Some managers confuse using MBE with empowering followers. After all, it does appear that followers have freedom to do as they please, as long as they do not make a mistake. Such comparisons, however, are not warranted. Encouragement and creating a supportive and positive environment in which risk-taking is encouraged, which are at the heart of empowerment, are clearly absent when a manager relies on MBE. Even though CR can yield positive effects, using MBE, particularly laissez-faire, as a primary leadership style has a negative impact on follower's performance and satisfaction.

Despite the success of some transactional relationships in achieving performance, an exclusive focus on such exchanges and transactions with followers is blamed for low expectations of followers and minimal performance in organizations (Zaleznik, 1990). Transactional contracts do not inspire followers to aim for excellence; rather, they focus on short-term and immediate outcomes. Long-term inspiration requires transformational leadership.

Transformational Leadership

Leadership scholars and practitioners (Bass, 1985, 1990b; Bennis and Nanus, 1985; Conger and Kanungo, 1998) suggest that today's organizations need leadership that inspires followers and enables them to enact revolutionary change. For example, the health-care industry pays attention to the role of hospital administrators in guiding their organizations in uncertain times. Institutions such as Harbor Health Systems focus on clarifying each person's role in the accomplishment of the organization's mission. Pacific Presbyterian stresses strong leadership commitment to the organization's mission and goals. Leaders such as Mark Wallace of Texas Children's Hospital are celebrated for their vision, creativity, and ability to inspire followers (Lutz, 1992), all factors needed to create a new vision to deal with the dynamic and often-threatening environment that characterizes the health-care industry.

Transformational CEOs from the business and nonprofit sectors, who have dramatically changed their organizations, are also celebrated. Many, such as Jack Welch of GE and Andy Grove of Intel, are management gurus who provide others with extensive advice. Transformational leadership includes three factors—charisma and inspiration, intellectual stimulation, and individual consideration—that, when combined, allow a leader to achieve large-scale change (Figure 2).

> Transformational leadership includes three factors—charisma and inspiration, intellectual stimulation, and individual consideration—that, when combined, allow a leader to achieve large-scale change.

CHARISMA AND INSPIRATION   The concept of charisma is one of the three central elements of transformational leadership (Bass, 1985; Bass and Avolio, 1993). The charismatic leadership relationship creates the intense emotional bond between leaders and followers. The result is loyalty and trust in, as well as emulation of, the leader. Followers are inspired to implement the leader's

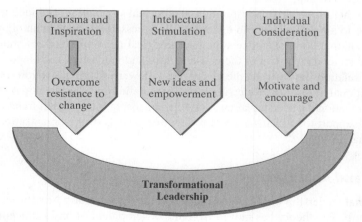

FIGURE 2   Transformational Leadership Factors

vision. The strong loyalty and respect that define a charismatic relationship pave the way for undertaking major change by reducing resistance.

INTELLECTUAL STIMULATION   The second factor in transformational leadership is the leader's ability to motivate followers to solve problems by challenging them intellectually and encouraging them to come up with creative solutions. The leaders and the group question existing values and assumptions and search for new answers (Shin and Zhou, 2003). By encouraging them to look at problems in new ways, requiring new solutions, and by triggering controversial discussions and debates, the leader pushes followers to perform beyond what they previously considered possible (Boerner, Eisenbeiss, and Griesser, 2007). Shantanu Narayen, CEO of Adobe Systems, when focusing on what leadership styles matter, states, "Challenging individual by setting goals and then letting them use their ingenuity to accomplish them is something that I hope I can pass on as part of my leadership style. If you set a common vision and then get really scary-smart people, they do things that amaze you" (Bryant, 2009). The charismatic bond provides support and encouragement in this endeavor and prevents followers from feeling isolated. Intellectual stimulation includes a strong empowerment component, which assures followers of their abilities and capabilities and enables them to search out new solutions. Transformational leadership has been shown to create empowerment that, in turn, increases team effectiveness (Kark, Shamir, and Chen, 2003).

INDIVIDUAL CONSIDERATION   The last factor of transformational leadership, the development of a personal relationship with each follower, is closely related to the Leader–Member Exchange (LMX) Model. The leader treats each follower differently but equitably, providing everyone with individual attention. As a result, followers feel special, encouraged, motivated, and developed, and they perform better (Dvir et al., 2002). The leader's individual consideration further allows for matching each follower's skills and abilities to the needs of the organization. Anne Mulcahy, chairwoman and chief executive of Xerox, brought the company back from the brink of bankruptcy. She believes the most important leadership lesson is followership, ". . . I think it's a lot more about followership—that your employees are volunteers and they can choose to wait things out if they don't believe. And that can be very damaging in a big company. So it is absolutely this essence of creating followership that becomes the most important thing that you can do as a leader" (Bryant, 2009e).

The three factors—charisma/inspiration, intellectual stimulation, and individual consideration—combine to allow the leader to undertake the necessary changes in an organization. The charismatic emotional bond overcomes the psychological and emotional resistance to change. The intellectual stimulation provides the new solutions and innovation and empowers followers. The individual relationship between the leader and follower encourages followers and provides them with additional motivation. Referring back to the definition of leadership effectiveness, we see that transformational leadership allows for external adaptation, whereas transactional leadership behaviors support the maintenance of the routine aspects of the organization necessary to maintain internal health.

Evaluation and Application

Transformational leadership is one of the most popular and currently heavily researched theories of leadership. The theory has moved from the development of basic concepts to the stage where the concepts are critically reviewed and various moderating variables are identified

(Antonakis, Avolio, and Sivasubramaniam, 2003). Therefore, considerable research about the various aspects of transformational leadership is available, several extensions of the model have been proposed (e.g., Rafferty and Griffin, 2004), and applications to broader organizational contexts, such as the public sector, suggested (Denhardt and Campbell, 2006). Several empirical studies have tested the propositions of transformational leadership in a variety of settings (e.g., Hardy et al., 2010; Shin and Zhou, 2003; Yammarino and Bass, 1990). For example, researchers find that transformational leadership can increase employee proactivity by enhancing their commitment to the organization (Strauss, Griffin, and Rafferty, 2009). It is further linked to performance (Colbert et al., 2008), particularly in smaller organizations (Ling et al., 2008). Other studies suggest that there is a positive relationship between transformational leadership, organizational climate, and innovation (Eisenbeiss, Knippenberg, and Boerner, 2008).

Several studies consider transformational leadership theory across gender and cultures. For example, female transformational leaders form a unique relationship with each of their followers, suggesting that women favor an interpersonal-oriented style of leadership (Yammarino et al., 1997). Women leaders often exhibit concern for others, expressiveness, and cooperation (Eagly, Karau, and Makhijani, 1995), traits that are associated with transformational leadership. From a cross-cultural perspective, it appears that ideal leadership characteristics across many countries—such as Canada, South Africa, Israel, Mexico, Sweden, and Singapore—include some transformational leadership elements (Bass, 1997) and that individuals from collectivistic cultures in particular may be most receptive to transformational leadership (Jung and Avolio, 1999; Jung, Bass, and Sosik, 1995; Walumbwa and Lawler, 2003; Walumbwa, Lawler, and Avolio, 2007).

Continued research is needed, especially in regard to the measurement of transactional and transformational behavior (Yukl, 1999) and the factors that lead to the use of transformational behavior by leaders. The primary empirically derived measure, the multifactor leadership questionnaire (MLQ), does not consistently allow for separate identification of the various behaviors (Bycio, Hackett, and Allen, 1995; Keller, 1992; Seltzer and Bass, 1990; Tepper and Percy, 1994), although new research indicates that the measure offers better validity and reliability than previously thought (Antonakis et al., 2003). In addition, despite the focus on behaviors, many of the transformational behaviors include dispositional, traitlike elements and are reported to develop early in life (Bass, 1985). For example, although it might be easy to instruct a leader how to provide contingent rewards, teaching the leader to inspire and intellectually stimulate followers may not be as simple. Furthermore, even though some research links transformational leadership to emotional intelligence (e.g., Gardner and Stough, 2002), the relationship of transformational leadership characteristics with other personality traits such as the Big Five needs further research (De Hoog and Den Hartog, 2009). In addition, as is the case with charismatic leadership, the tendency is to propose transformational leadership as a panacea to organizational problems. A stronger contingency approach, however, would identify various contextual organizational variables that might contribute to the effectiveness of transformational leadership (Pawar and Eastman, 1997). Some researchers further suggest that the transformational leadership theory could benefit from clarification of the difference between charismatic and transformational leadership and the mediating processes and situational variables that lead to transformational leadership (Sashkin, 2004; Yukl, 1999). As is the case with charismatic leadership, transformational leadership involves the potential of leading to followers' excessive dependency (Kark et al., 2003) and negative and unethical behavior (Price, 2003); further research in that area would also enhance the model.

Transformational leadership concepts apply widely to organizational effectiveness and leadership training. Although charismatic leadership sometimes carries negative connotations, transformational leadership generally is perceived as positive. Research findings suggest that organizations can benefit from encouraging their leaders to be less aggressive and more nurturing (Ross and Offerman, 1997: 1084). Other recommendations for leaders based on transformational leadership models include the following:

- Project confidence and optimism about the goals and followers' ability
- Provide a clear vision
- Encourage creativity through empowerment, reward experimentation, and tolerate mistakes
- Set high expectations and create a supportive environment
- Establish personal relationships with followers

The use of transformational leadership can facilitate change in organizations. The next section considers other leadership theories that also focus on how to bring about change.

LEADING CHANGE

Sir Richard Branson and His Vision

The Virgin Group family of 200 companies with over 55,000 employees has been, for many years, a household name in Europe. From record stores to cell phones to airlines, Virgin is a formidable brand now exploring areas such as galactic travel (Foley, 2010) and banking (Dey, 2010). No less formidable is its founder and CEO, Sir Richard Branson, who built an empire by breaking rules and successfully taking on challenges that everyone told him would fail. Running his business from his house on the private Caribbean island of Necker, taking phone calls while resting in his hammock between tennis games, Branson considers profits to be secondary: "The bottom line has never been a reason for doing anything. It's much more the satisfaction of creating things that you're proud of and making a difference" (Deutschman, 2004: 95).

Most often mentioned for his keen marketing skills and his ability to attract attention through his daredevil endeavors such as hot-air balloon trips across the Atlantic, outrageous behaviors such as dressing as a bride or a pirate or being photographed nude for his biography, Branson focuses on ventures he feels passionate about, and he cares deeply about the culture and people in his many companies (Hawn, 2006). With his businesses well established and considerable name recognition, he has turned his attention to social and environmental issues such as climate change, the search for clean fuels, helping social entrepreneurs around the world, and even creating a group called the Elders—with Nelson Mandela as a founding elder—a rapid reaction force that brings together senior world leaders to address global crises such as the situation in Darfur (Rose, 2009).

Branson believes, "You can't be a good leader unless you generally like people. That is how you bring out the best in them" (*Workforce*, 2004). He believes, "It's extremely important to respond to people, and to give them encouragement if you're a leader. And if you're actually turning people down . . . take the time to do it yourself" (Branson, 2007). While recruiting managers and employees for his companies, he looks for the best so he can get the best (*Workforce*, 2004). Encouraging people through lavish praise so they can flourish, allowing them to figure out their mistakes instead of picking on them, and moving employees around to help them to find a job that allows them to excel are all part of Branson's leadership philosophy. He suggests that most employees leave companies when they are frustrated because they are not heard.

Although often considered a control freak for keeping a hand in all his companies (Deutschman, 2004), Sir Richard has learned to delegate and develop the people who work for him. He describes the process: "I come up with the original idea, spend the first three months immersed in the business so I know the ins and outs and then give chief executives a stake in the company and ask them to run it as if it's their own" (*Workforce*, 2004). Branson wants to make sure that whatever he builds or takes part in is something that he can be proud of. He admits, "I made and learned from lots of mistakes. In the end, the key is will power" (Hawn, 2006).

Sources: Branson, R. 2006. "How to succeed in 2007." *CNN Money.com.* http://money.cnn.com/popups/2006/biz2/howtosucceed/4.html (accessed August 14, 2007); Deutschman, A., 2004. "The Gonzo way of branding," *Fast Company*, October: 91–96; Dey, I. 2010. U.S. Tycoon Wilbur Ross is to back Sir Richard Branson bank spree. *New York Times* April 4, http://business.timesonline.co.uk/tol/business/industry_sectors/banking_and_finance/article7086707.ece (accessed on April 4, 2010); Foley, S. 2010. Lift off for space tourism. *Business Week* March 29, http://www.businessweek.com/globalbiz/content/mar2010/gb20100329_092782.htm (accessed on April 4, 2010); Hawn, C. 2006. "Branson's next big bet." CNN Money.com, October 2. http://money.cnn.com/magazines/business2/business2_archive/2006/08/01/8382250/ (accessed August 12, 2007); Rose, C. 2008. An interview with Richard Branson. February 12. http://www.charlierose.com/view/interview/8935 (accessed on April 3, 2010); "The importance of being Richard Branson," *Workforce*, December 2004. www.workforce.com/archive/article/23/91/47.php (accessed January 30, 2005).

VALUE-BASED, AUTHENTIC, AND POSITIVE LEADERSHIP

Leadership is more than a series of behaviors and actions. For many, the leadership process is highly emotional and personal and based on fundamental values such as integrity and caring for others. Such concepts have found their way into leadership theory and research, and some approaches now take into consideration values, emotions, and optimism as primary aspects of leadership.

Value-Based Leadership

The topics of values and spirituality are increasingly finding their way into the workplace, particularly in the United States. Workplace spirituality recognizes that people often have a meaningful inner life that influences their beliefs and actions. Such approaches integrate what some consider the essence of the human existence, the body, mind, heart, and spirit (Moxley, 2000), and the search for the meaning of life and interconnectedness with others (Zinnbauer, Pargament, and Scott, 1999). Spirituality focuses on how leaders and followers tap into their basic values to transform organizations by creating a vision based on deeply held values related to making a difference, and implementing a caring and altruistic culture that supports that vision (Fry, 2003). Value-based and spiritual leaders develop their relationship with followers based on the values they share.

One such value that has particular importance to organizations is integrity. Others would be spiritual values, such as love, hope, humility, and faith. These values are considered key to leadership by some practitioners (e.g., Covey's principle-centered leadership, 1991 and Greenleaf's servant leadership, 1998), researchers (see the special issue of *The Leadership Quarter 2005*, volume 16), and leadership textbooks (e.g., Daft, 2008). Some suggest that spiritual values such as integrity, honesty, and humility are actually an inherent part of effective leadership (Fry, 2005), and research findings imply that value-based leadership practices positively affect leadership effectiveness (Reave, 2005) and are related to improved organizational learning. Although honesty and integrity are part of most conceptions of effective leadership, in the wake of business and political scandals, the call for integrity and ethics in leadership has become louder and the focus of recent research (for a review, see Brown and Treviñno, 2006b). Ethical leaders demonstrate fair, appropriate, and caring personal and social decisions and behaviors and communicate, promote, and reinforce such values and actions with followers and throughout the organization (Brown, Treviño, and Harrison, 2005). Some research shows that attention to moral issues leads to moral behavior (Reynolds, 2008), and ethical leadership creates a trickle down effect in organizations (Mayer et al., 2008). In talking about communicating with employees, Gordon Bethune, the former CEO of Continental Airlines states: "And we never lied. You don't lie to your own doctor. You don't like to your own attorney, and you don't lie to your employers. And if you never lie, then when it hits the fan, and somebody says you're wrong—you can say, 'No, I'm not,' and they'll believe you" (Bryant, 2010a).

Chris Lowney, author of *Heroic Leadership*, applies the teachings of St. Ignatius Loyola—founder of the Jesuits, one of the world's oldest and most successful religious orders—to leadership in today's organizations (2005). Lowney believes that the Jesuits' success is attributed to their focus on self-awareness (based on reflection and accounting for one's actions and goals), ingenuity (innovation, adaptation, willingness to look at new opportunities), love (support and caring), and heroism (willingness to take risks and make the best of situations). Approaches such as Lowney's and other value-based leadership are closely related to both transformational and authentic leadership through the focus on key individual characteristics of leaders regarding integrity, caring for others, and transparency.

Authentic Leadership

"To be a great leader, you need to be yourself" states Padmasree Warrior, chief technology officer at Cisco Systems (Warrior, 2010). Hatim Tyabji, executive at Bytemobile, Inc., a wireless infrastructure provider and a world renowned innovation expert, agrees, "The first principle of leadership is authenticity: Watch what I do, not what I say. Leadership requires moral authority. You can't have moral authority if you behave differently from your people. If you want your people to be frugal, then don't spend money on perks designed to make your life more comfortable" (Tyabji, 1997: 98). Authentic leaders are people who know themselves well and remain true to their values and beliefs. They have strong values and a sense of purpose that guide their decisions and actions (George, 2003). Bill George, the former CEO of Medtronics and one of the strongest proponents of authentic leadership, believes that the most effective leaders, those who have the most long-lasting impact on their followers and their organizations, are those who have a moral compass and have found their "true north" (George, 2007). The key to authentic leadership is understanding personal strengths and developing them. Consultant Marcus Bukingham suggests, "Be authentic. To become a leader, identify where you are strongest and most confident, and then work to expand those areas. If you want to be a better leader, don't try to be all things to all people . . . you will lead best by following who you are" (Bukingham, 2005).

The key to authentic leadership is understanding your strengths and developing them.

To apply the recent research on authentic leadership, practitioners of leadership should

- *Understand their own purpose:* Leaders must understand themselves and their motivation and what they are looking for.
- *Practice solid values:* Leaders must have personal values that guide their decisions and their actions. These values develop based on their personal experiences and challenges.
- *Connect with their followers:* Leaders must disclose appropriate information about themselves with followers to help establish long-lasting relationships.

- *Demonstrate self-discipline:* Leaders must work hard to demonstrate their values and lead by action as well as words.

Howard Schulltz, cofounder and CEO of Starbucks, has created an organization based on what matters most to him. As a child, Schulltz watched his family struggle without health benefits after his father lost his job because of an injury. Those experiences left an indelible mark on Schulltz, who made taking care of employees, providing health benefits, and not leaving anyone behind the core of Starbucks' culture (Meyers, 2005). Schulltz' actions as a leader stem from his beliefs and values, which are the source of his success as a leader. Bill George suggests that Wendy Kopp, founder of Teach For America, is another example of an authentic leader (2007). With a strong desire to change the world and improve K–12 education, she organized conferences that included students and business leaders while she was a senior at Princeton University. Her isolated background from a middle-class family, her consideration of a teaching career, and her passion to make a difference led her to create Teach for America and lead the organization through many turbulent years before it established itself as a model for community engagement (George, 2007). Other leaders who believe that facing a major crisis allows people to find out who they are and what is truly important include Brian Dunn, CEO of Best Buy, whose wife had breast cancer (Bryant 2009f), and John Chambers the CEO of Cisco Systems. Chambers says: "People think of us as a product of our successes. I'd actually argue that we're a product of the challenges we face in life. And how we handled those challenges probably had more to do with what we accomplish in life" (Bryant, 2009g).

In addition to anecdotal and case examples of authentic organizational leaders, researchers have started exploring the concept of authenticity and are working on clarifying its various components and links to other theories. As in the case of spiritual leadership, the prominence of the concept of authentic leadership in research is evidenced by a recent issue of *The Leadership Quarterly* devoted to the topic (2005, issue 16).

DEFINITION AND ELEMENTS Researchers consider authentic leadership to be a continuum where at one end a leader is either unaware of his or her values or does not follow them and at the other end, the person is able to articulate values clearly and use them to guide his or her behavior (Figure 3; Avolio et al., 2004; Erickson, 1995). The roots of authentic leadership can be traced back as far as Rogers' and Maslow's concept of self-actualization and more recently to the positive psychology movement (Seligman, 2002; Seligman and Csikszentmihalyi, 2000), the concept of positive organizational behavior (Luthans, 2002), and optimal self-esteem (Kernis, 2003). Although closely related to practitioner views of authentic leadership, the research-based models offer further clarification. Specifically, the concept is considered highly complex and includes

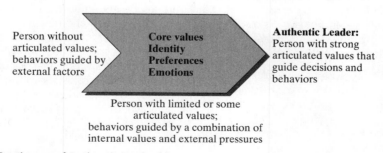

FIGURE 3 Continuum of Authentic Leadership

TABLE 6 Components of Authentic Leadership

Components	Description
Self-awareness	Being aware of and trusting one's emotions, motives, complexities, abilities, and potential inner conflicts.
Unbiased or balanced processing	Ability to consider, within reasonable limits, multiple perspectives and inputs and assess information in a balanced manner both in regard to information about the self and others.
Behaviors are true to self and motivated by personal convictions	Focused by own convictions; unencumbered by others' expectations or desire to please others; decisions and behaviors guided by personal values;
Relational authenticity or transparency	Ability to disclose and share information about self appropriately and openly to relate to others; achieving openness and truthfulness in close relationships.

Source: Based on information in Avolio, B. J., and W. L. Gardner. 2005. Authentic leadership development: Getting to the root of positive forms of leadership. *The Leadership Quarterly* 16:315–338; Kernis, M. H. 2003. Toward a conceptualization of optimal self-esteem. *Psychological Inquiry* 14:1–26.

traits, emotions, behaviors and attributions (Avolio and Gardner, 2005; Cooper et al., 2005; Ladkin and Taylor, 2010). Further, authenticity is differentiated from sincerity, which involves accurate self-presentations rather than being true to oneself (Avolio and Gardner, 2005). Table 6 summarizes the key elements of authentic leadership.

Authentic leadership is still a new theory and remains largely untested (Cooper et al., 2005). Some early research, however, indicates that perception of authentic leadership is related to employee satisfaction (Jensen and Luthans, 2006), and extensions of the model are being proposed and developed in various settings, such as school (e.g., Begley, 2006) and other cultural contexts (Endrissat, Muller, and Kaudela-Baum, 2007).

Applying What You Learn
Developing Authenticity

Being authentic may be related to self-esteem and other traits and therefore may not be something that all of us can simply implement after a few days' practice. It, however, is possible to carefully and mindfully develop more authenticity. Some practical tips include the following:

- Develop a clear sense of your values and beliefs; know what matters to you most and why.
- Understand how your values shape your behavior.
- Seek feedback about your behavior, strengths, and weaknesses.

- Focus on understanding and changing the sources of defensiveness regarding your own values, beliefs, emotions, and behaviors.
- Engage in open and meaningful conversations with your followers and team members regarding your values and your vision.
- Be mindful of any potential real or perceived conflicts and inconsistencies between what you say and what you do.
- Stand your ground on issues that are most important to you. You can disagree without being disagreeable!

Positive Leadership

The newest addition to the neocharismatic approaches to leadership is the concept of Positive Leadership, which has its roots in the positive psychology (Lopez and Snyder, 2009) and positive organizational behavior concepts (POB; Cameron, Dutton, and Quinn, 2003; Luthans, 2002). Instead of focusing on "What is wrong with people?" and on correcting weaknesses, which has been the basis of much of applied psychology, positive psychology focuses on what is right, on things that make life worthwhile, and on human strengths (Seligman, 1998; Snyder and Lopez, 2007). Much like spiritual and authentic leadership, POB and positive leadership have roots in the concepts of self-actualization and the 1960s management approaches of Chris Argyris and Douglas McGregor, who focused on human growth and potential. POB and positive leadership emphasize individual strengths and helping people achieve their highest potential, and what some researchers have called the psychological capital (PsyCap), which includes confidence/self-efficacy, hope, optimism, and resilience (Luthans, Youssef, and Avolio, 2007).

"What I've learned over time is that optimism is a very, very important part of leadership. However, you need a dose of realism with it. People don't like to follow pessimists" says Robert Iger, CEO of Disney (Bryant, 2009h). Author, Carmine Gallo further states, "Inspiring leaders have an abundance of passion for what they do. You cannot inspire unless you're inspired yourself (Gallo, 2007). Tachi Yamada, the president of the Bill and Melinda Gates Foundation echoes their thoughts, "If I spend my time focusing on everything that's bad, I'd get nothing done. . . . If you can bring out the best in everybody, then you can have a great organization" (Bryant, 2010b). Referring to important leadership lessons she learned, Carol Bartz, CEO of Yahoo says, "Just get it done. Pick yourself up. Move on. Laugh" (Bryant, 2009i). These executives practice positive leadership, which includes (Cameron, 2008; Snyder and Lopez 2009):

- *Being optimistic:* looking at the glass as half-full; considering the positive side of events while remaining realistic
- *Encouraging positive deviance:* by promoting outstanding results that change the way things are for the better
- *Focusing on strengths:* having an affirmative bias that promotes what is going well instead of trying to correct what is wrong
- *Creating a positive climate:* where you give people the benefit of the doubt; foster compassion, forgiveness, and gratitude; and celebrate successes
- *Maintaining positive relationships:* with followers and advancing kindness, cooperation, support, and forgiveness in your team
- *Having positive communications:* with affirmative language, open and honest feedback geared towards building on and supporting strengths.
- *Dealing with negativity quickly:* addressing those who behave negatively and sap the energy of the team in a constructive manner.

Positive leadership emphasizes individual strengths and helping people achieve their highest potential and their psychological capital.

Evaluation and Application

The concepts of value-based, authentic, and positive leadership share common elements with other approaches to leadership presented in this chapter. All focus on the relationship between leaders and followers and on the sharing of a vision for the group. Some researchers suggest that authentic leadership is at the root of the other concepts (Avolio and Gardner, 2005). Although charismatic, transformational, spiritual, and positive leaders all have to have some degree of authenticity, authentic leaders do not necessarily need to be charismatic, transformational, spiritual, or positive. In addition, authentic leaders may lead by being task or relationship oriented or by involving and empowering followers to various degrees. Because authentic leaders are true to their own self, it is reasonable to assume that their actions are not guided by the situation. For charismatic and transformational leaders, the connection with followers comes from inspirational appeal, impression management, or focusing on the followers' needs. In the case of authentic leaders, a focus on followers and on attempts to win them over through arguments and rhetoric is usually absent (Avolio and Gardner, 2003). Instead, the authentic leader wins over followers by the strength of his or her own beliefs. The authentic leader does not focus on others' expectations. The essence of authentic leadership is self-awareness, knowing one's values, and remaining true to them. Authentic leaders engage their followers by knowing themselves well and being true to their own beliefs and values.

Positive leadership offers a fresh approach in that the focus is more on how a leader thinks and less on what he or she is—charismatic, value-based, or authentic, for example. Owing to its roots in psychology, positive leadership has a cognitive approach that emphasizes the perspective leaders choose to take, how they analyze and interpret the situation, and how those processes determine their behavior. Specifically, positive leaders take on positive perspective that guides their approach to leading themselves and others.

As research topics, value-based, authentic, and positive leadership present opportunities and challenges. The concepts add considerable richness to the study of leadership by introducing and considering the role of emotions, in the case of value-based and authentic leadership, in the leadership process. In addition, the introduction of hope and optimism, which is the basis of all three concepts, to understanding leadership is a significant contribution (Avolio et al., 2004). At this point in time, however, much of the information about value-based and authentic leadership theories is based either on case studies or on anecdotal accounts. Although the information is rich and provides many avenues for further study, empirical research about the topic is still scarce. Instead, the concepts are in the theoretical development and refinement phases with substantial opportunities for further contributions to the field. Although positive psychology and, to some extent, POB have generated considerable research, positive leadership is yet a relatively unexplored research area. In addition the application of these concepts to nonindividualistic cultures or to cultures that place less emphasis on emotion should yield interesting results. Furthermore, some suggest that concepts such as spirituality may be so broad to make empirical research difficult (Starck et al., 2002), thereby pointing to the need for considerable research to clarify such concepts (Dent, Higgins, and Wharff, 2005). Finally, the lack of a contingency focus and the apparent assumption that these approaches work in all situations also needs further examination.

From a practical point of view, these recent neocharismatic approaches have significant appeal to leaders. With the concept of spirituality playing a greater role, particularly in the United States, value-based leadership allows for approaching leadership from an angle that addresses the needs of many followers. As a root concept for leadership, authentic leadership provides general guidance for what leaders should focus on and avenues for growth. Finally, positive leadership, like its cousins in psychology and organizational behavior, opens up a new perspective on how to lead others by expecting and helping them achieve their highest potential.

Summary and Conclusions

This chapter focuses on recent theories of neocharismatic approaches, which include charismatic, transformational leadership; value-based, authentic, and positive leadership; and their im-

pact on leadership practice. Although the notion of charisma has been a central element of leadership for many years, recent scientific approaches allow for more-thorough descriptions of the process. In particular, current concepts view charismatic leadership as a relationship between leaders and followers, rather than as a combination of leadership traits and behaviors. For the charismatic leadership relationship to occur, leaders need certain traits and behaviors, followers must demonstrate particular traits and frames of mind, and the situation requires an element of crisis. The combination of these three factors allows for the emergence of charismatic leadership.

Charismatic leadership is one of the elements in the transformational leadership model. The model suggests that the transactional views of leadership, which focus on developing an exchange and transaction contract between leaders and followers, must be supplemented with behaviors that lead to organizational transformation. Transformational leaders provide vision and inspiration and engender the intense emotions required to enact such large-scale changes in organizations. Value-based and authentic leadership concepts similarly have a focus on vision and caring for followers and consider the role emotions can play in leadership, whereas positive leadership considers how a leader choosing to take a

positive and optimistic perspective can encourage high performance. Spiritual leadership considers how leaders and followers create organizations based on their common values and search for deep meaning. Authentic leaders build effective organizations based on self-awareness and transparent sharing of their personal values. Positive leaders create a climate where high expectations and optimistic and uplifting perspectives allow followers to achieve their highest potential.

Charismatic, transformational, value-based, authentic, and positive leadership concepts contribute to the demystification and understanding of leadership processes. They have a broad appeal and provide an intuitive understanding of leadership that is applicable to large-scale leadership situations. They are also responsible for a resurgence in the interest in leadership. Because of their relatively recent development, the concepts still require much refinement, and their use in training leaders needs further refinement, particularly with regard to identification of various situations under which change-oriented leadership might be more appropriate and more effective.

Review and Discussion Questions

1. What are the factors that gave rise to the development of neo-charismatic leadership theories?
2. Describe the elements of charismatic leadership.
3. What are the cultural constraints on the development of charismatic leadership?
4. Describe the elements of transactional leadership.
5. How is management by exception different from empowerment?
6. Describe the elements of transformational leadership and its role in enacting organizational change.
7. Compare and contrast value-based, authentic, and positive leadership concepts. Why do these approaches have so much appeal?
8. What are the major contributions and shortcomings of the neocharismatic approaches to our understanding of leadership?

Leadership Challenge: Standing Up to a Charismatic but Unethical Leader

You are one of the lucky people who work with a leader who has considerable personal charisma. She holds a grand vision of the future, communicates with passion, inspires her followers, and makes them feel special. Because of prior knowledge and experience with her, however, you are one of the few people who is aware that she is disingenuous, focused on her personal agenda and career, would not hesitate to sacrifice her followers for her own benefit, and is ruthless with those who disagree with her. You know that it is only a matter

of time before her followers suffer because of her lack of concern and extreme self-interest.

1. What can you do?
2. Should you share your concerns with other department members? With her supervisor?
3. If you decide to act, what are some productive actions you could take?
4. What are the consequences of your action or inaction?

Exercise 1: Do You Know a Charismatic Leader?

Identify a leader you consider to be highly effective. This person may be in your work organization or a leader in your civic, sports, educational, or religious organization.

Step 1: Describe the Leader

Rate the leader you selected on the following items using the following scale.

1 = Never

2 = Occasionally

3 = Often

4 = Always

_____ 1. The leader shows a high degree of self-confidence.

_____ 2. The leader does not show any doubt about his or her ideas.

_____ 3. The leader has a clear, well-articulated vision.

_____ 4. The leader has a high energy level.

_____ 5. The leader shows a lot of enthusiasm about the work to be done.

_____ 6. The leader is emotionally expressive.

_____ 7. The leader expresses his or her ideas well.

_____ 8. The leader is articulate.

_____ 9. The leader does all that he or she requires of followers.

_____ 10. The leader role models the desired behaviors and "walks the talk."

Scoring Key: Add up your scores for all 10 items. The maximum possible score is 40. The higher your leader's score, the more he or she demonstrates charismatic characteristics.

Total: _____

Step 2: Describe Followers' Reactions and Behaviors

Rate the leader's followers (including yourself) on the following items, using the following scale.

1 = Never

2 = Occasionally

3 = Often

4 = Always

_____ 1. The followers respect the leader.

_____ 2. The followers hold the leader in high esteem.

_____ 3. The followers are loyal and devoted to the leader.

_____ 4. The followers like the leader.

_____ 5. The followers believe in their own capability for exceptional performance.

_____ 6. The followers are enthusiastic about the work to be done.

_____ 7. The followers follow the leader's directions eagerly.

Scoring: Add up your rating for all seven items. The maximum possible score is 28. The higher the followers' scores, the more they demonstrate the characteristics of followers of charismatic leaders.

Total: _____

New Models for Leadership: Neocharisma, Inspiration, and the Relationship with Followers

Step 3: Describe the Situation

Consider the situation that the leader and follower face in their day-to-day activities. Rate the situation on the following items using the following scale.

    1 = Never

    2 = Occasionally

    3 = Often

    4 = Always

    _____ 1. Our team/organization needs to change.

    _____ 2. We seem to go from crisis to crisis.

    _____ 3. We could do many things better around here.

    _____ 4. We do not seem to know what we are all about.

    _____ 5. We have not yet explored many opportunities.

    _____ 6. Many of us are not performing to our fullest potential.

Scoring: Add up your rating for all six items. The maximum possible score is 24. The higher your group's score, the more you are ready for change and face a crisis situation.

    *Total:*_____

Step 4: Putting It All Together

Using the scores from the three previous measures, consider whether

1. Your leader has the personal characteristics of a charismatic leader.

2. The group exhibits the behaviors typically associated with charismatic leadership.

3. The group faces a crisis situation that involves a perceived need for change.

Based on these three questions, to what extent is the leader you selected charismatic?

    1 = Not at all

    2 = Has some, but not all elements

    3 = To a great extent

Step 5: Discussion

1. What are the factors that explain your leader's effectiveness?

2. What do you foresee for the future if the situation changes?

Exercise 2: Charismatic Speech

One of the characteristics of charismatic leaders is their ability to articulate their ideas and vision in an inspiring manner. These articulation skills may come easier to some than to others, but they can be learned if practiced.

Two techniques are key to an inspiring message: (1) proper framing of ideas to give them a powerful context, and (2) use of various rhetorical techniques to support the message.

Elements of Framing

Amplify values and beliefs.

Bring out the importance of the mission.

Clarify the need to accomplish the mission.

Focus on the efficacy of the mission.

Rhetorical Techniques

Use of metaphors, analogies, and brief stories

Gearing language to the audience

Repetition

Rhythm

Alliteration

Nonverbal message

Write a short speech that presents your goals (personal or for your team or organization). Revise and practice the message using charismatic speech methods.

Source: This exercise is based on concepts developed by Conger (1989, 1991).

Exercise 3: Analyzing a Charismatic Speech

Charisma has been a much talked about topic in the United States and around the world in the past few years partly due to the election of President Barak Obama. One of the qualities often attributed to him is charisma, which is most evident during his speeches.

[Alternative exercise: Select a leader that you find charismatic and complete the exercise using that person to answer the questions.]

Step 1: Analyzing President Obama's Speeches

Using one of the speeches below or one that you find on your own, analyze the charismatic qualities of President Obama's speeches.

"Yes we can" (Nashua New Hampshire; January 9, 2008): http://www.youtube.com/watch?v=fe751kmbwms

"A more perfect union" (Philadelphia, Pennsylvania; March 18, 2008): http://www.youtube.com/watch?v=pwe7wtvbluu

"Victory speech" (Chicago, Illinois; November 4, 2008): http://elections.nytimes.com/2008/results/president/speeches/obama-victory-speech.html

"Keynote at DNC" (Boston, Massachusetts; August 18, 2004): http://www.youtube.com/watch?v=ewynt87paj0

To what extent did the leader use each of the following?

Elements of Framing	Not at All	To Some Extent	To a Large Extent
1. Amplify values and beliefs	1	2	3
2. Bring out the importance of the mission.	1	2	3
3. Clarify the need to accomplish the mission.	1	2	3
4. Focus on the efficacy of the mission.	1	2	3
Rhetorical Techniques			
5. Use of metaphors, analogies, and brief stories	1	2	3
6. Gearing language to the audience	1	2	3
7. Repetition	1	2	3
8. Rhythm	1	2	3
9. Alliteration	1	2	3
10. Nonverbal messages	1	2	3

Step 2: Other Noncharismatic Leaders

Consider other leaders, who may or may not be effective, but are generally not considered charismatic. For example, neither presidents G.H. nor G.W. Bush was considered a charismatic speaker; nor was Senator Hilary Clinton in most of her speeches.

Using the same scale, evaluate what elements of the charismatic speech are lacking from the way these leaders communicate.

Elements Of Framing	Not at All	To Some Extent	To a Large Extent
1. Amplify values and beliefs	1	2	3
2. Bring out the importance of the mission.	1	2	3
3. Clarify the need to accomplish the mission.	1	2	3
4. Focus on the efficacy of the mission.	1	2	3
Rhetorical Techniques			
5. Use of metaphors, analogies, and brief stories	1	2	3
6. Gearing language to the audience	1	2	3
7. Repetition	1	2	3
8. Rhythm	1	2	3
9. Alliteration	1	2	3
10. Nonverbal messages	1	2	3

What other factors detract from these leaders' charisma?

Self-Assessment 1: Authentic Leadership

Being an authentic leader consists of several different elements. For each of the following items indicate to what extent the statement is descriptive of you, by using the following scale:

1 = Strongly disagree (does not sound at all like me)

2 = Disagree (I rarely behave this way)

3 = Agree (I often behave this way)

4 = Strongly agree (Describes me very well)

_____ 1. I am aware of who I truly am.
_____ 2. I know what matters to me most.
_____ 3. I make my decisions based on my own principles, rather than what others think.
_____ 4. I have trouble handling my weaknesses and faults.
_____ 5. I have trouble opening up to others.
_____ 6. When I am in groups, I like to share as much information as possible with everyone.
_____ 7. Although I respect others' opinions, I tend to stick to things I believe in.
_____ 8. When I get conflicting advice, I have trouble deciding what the best course of action may be for me.
_____ 9. I am skilled at listening to and understanding many different points of view.
_____ 10. I like to hear information from all sides before I make up my mind.
_____ 11. Most people don't really know who I am.
_____ 12. I can tell when I am not being true to myself.

Scoring: Add up your rating for all 12 items. The maximum score is 48. A higher score indicates a higher degree of authenticy.

Add up items 1, 2, and 12 = ***Total:*** _____ *Self awareness*

Reverse score for item 4 (1 = 4, 2 = 3, 3 = 2, 1 = 4) and add up items 4, 9, and 10.
Total: _____ *Balanced perception*

Reverse score for item 8 (1 = 4, 2 = 3, 3 = 2, 1 = 4) and add up items 3, 7, and 8.
Total: _____ *Value-based behavior*

Reverse score for items 5 and 11 (1 = 4, 2 = 3, 3 = 2, 1 = 4) and add up items 5, 6, and 11.
Total: _____ *Relational Transparency*

Add up the total for the four subscales.
Grand Total: _____ *Authentic Leadership*

Interpretation. The range for the total scale is between 12 and 48. The closer you are to 48, the more elements of authentic leadership you have. Consider each of the subscales (scores range from 3 to 12) for areas where your score may be lower.

Source: This self-assessment is based on work by Kernis (2003) and Avolio and Gardner (2005).

Self-Assessment 2: Positive Leadership

Being a positive leader consists of several different elements. For each of the following items indicate to what extent the statement is descriptive of you, by using the following scale:

1 = Strongly disagree (does not sound at all like me)

2 = Disagree (I rarely behave this way)

3 = Agree (I often behave this way)

4 = Strongly agree (Describes me very well)

_____ 1. I am an optimistic person.

_____ 2. Regardless of how bad things are, I generally tend focus at the positive side of things.

_____ 3. I encourage my team members to look for novel solutions to reach the best results.

_____ 4. I expect the best from my team members.

_____ 5. When I give feedback, I focus most on people's strengths and developing strategies to build on them.

_____ 6. I look for ways to provide my team members with what they need to do their best.

_____ 7. I role model treating people well and with kindness.

_____ 8. I emphasize cooperation among my team and throughout the organization.

_____ 9. I behave kindly and with compassion.

_____ 10. When things go wrong, I focus my group on forgiveness and support.

_____ 11. I share information openly and provide honest feedback.

_____ 12. I encourage team members to communicate often and constructively.

_____ 13. I manage team members who do not stay positive.

_____ 14. I quickly address team members who are negative.

Scoring: Add up your rating for all 14 items. Your score can range between 14 and 56. A higher score indicates a more positive approach to leadership. For a finer analysis consider your score in each of the subcategories (refer to information in the section on Positive Leadership)

Optimism: Items 1 and 2

Positive deviance: Items 3 and 4

Focus on strengths: Items 5 and 6

Positive climate: Items 7 and 8

Positive relationships: Items 9 and 10

Positive communications: Items 11 and 12

Managing negativity: Items 13 and 14

Interpretation: Positive leadership is not considered a trait; rather it refers to way of interpreting events and a choice one makes to take on an affirmative perspective. A high score overall (higher than 40) indicates a generally positive approach. However, consider each of the sub categories to identify your strengths.

Source: This self-assessment is based on work by Cameron (2008), Luthans (1992), and Snyder and Lopez (2009).

LEADERSHIP IN ACTION

Andrea Jung Orchestrates Avon's Makeover

Avon's history spans two centuries. The cosmetics company was global before business became global; it served and employed women before diversity became an issue; it was customer focused before the concept became an organizational mantra; and it has been successful longer than most organizations have been around. Interestingly enough, the company that almost exclusively serves women through its cosmetics did not have a female executive until Andrea Jung was appointed CEO and chairman in 2001 (Executive Team at Avon, 2010). Over the past ten years, Jung has successfully undertaken the daunting task of reinventing the company and moving a traditional, door-to-door sales company to the high-tech Internet world without alienating its loyal sales force—the "Avon Ladies" (Sellers, 2000b). She has also successfully reinvented herself by rethinking what her role is and what is most important to her customers and stakeholders. She states: "Leaders on the offense, not the defense, will comes through this recessionary period" (Jones, 2009).

Jung undertook the makeover of Avon by pouring money into research and development, expanding the overseas markets, and focusing on jazzy marketing that included celebrities such as Salma Hayek. "Jung practically reinvented the company. She united its disconnected international operations into what she called a global 'company for women'" (Global Influentials). Her strategies paid off. Soon after she took over leadership, Avon's sales jumped from $5.7 billion to over $10 billion in 2009 (Forbes, 2010). In addition, the company also continues to be a responsible corporate citizen, raising millions of dollars for causes such as the children affected by the September 11, 2001, attacks; "Race for the Cure"; and most recently by joining the campaign to end violence against women with Reese Witherspoon as its global ambassador (Avon Foundation for Women, 2010). One of Jung's personal passions is helping women advance. She

believes that women are the answer to many economic and social challenges. She is also proud of the fact that Avon has more women in management than any other *Fortune* 500 company and that almost half of the company's board are women (Reilly, 2009).

Jung was able to achieve impressive results through dogged determination and unwavering confidence in her strategy, which involved the slow introduction of the Internet and other retail sales and a gradual blending of new retail methods with the traditional direct sales. The company has become one of the world's biggest online retailers (Tedeschi, 2007). Jung strongly believes that the global force of 5.5 million independent Avon Ladies is the backbone of the company (Duffuor, 2008). She demonstrated her commitment to them by increasing the number of and incentives for the direct sales representatives and providing free training online and gas money. In meetings around the world, she involves them in the decision making rather forcing the necessary changes from the top (Menkes, 2006). Kurt Schansinger, a financial analyst, describes Jung as having a "strong vision, high standards, deep knowledge of the business, and enough confidence to delegate key tasks" (Brady, 2001). Birdie Jarworski, an Avon representative who met Jung at a company convention, describes her as "the rock star of Avon"; she was impressed by Jung's friendliness and her dedication to the company (Chandra, 2004). Jung has the attention of her Avon Ladies, who cheered for almost two minutes at the start of her videotaped message at a recent convention. Allan Mottus, editor of a cosmetics newsletter, states that Avon "needed a person with charisma and Jung has that" (Chandra, 2004).

These attributes are mentioned often when people talk about Jung. Born into a highly educated Chinese immigrant family—her father is an architect and her mother was Canada's first female chemical engineer—Jung always was expected to succeed. She received a Princeton education, graduating magna cum laude, and speaks fluent Mandarin and Cantonese as well as some French. When she joined Bloomingdale's, her parents did not originally approve of their daughter lowering herself to become a retailer, although her current position is winning their applause (Executive Sweet, 2005: 1). After Bloomingdale's, Jung followed her mentor Vass to I. Magnin and later to Neiman Marcus. Jung credits Vass with teaching her the art of tactful aggression, a style that matches her cultural roots (Executive Sweet, 2005: 2). She believes that she still has traces of what she calls Asian submissiveness, although she has learned to be tougher in the corporate world (Executive Sweet, 2005: 2). Jung joined Avon partly because of the corporate culture and partly because women being a quarter of the company's board of directors appealed to her. She says, "I'm very selective about the companies I work for. I started at Bloomingdale's because it was committed to developing women" (Executive Sweet, 2005: 3). As a result, she is a strong believer in mentoring and helping others succeed.

Jung states, "I have a love for this business. I have an enormous amount of passion for it. . . . I love managing people. The product is second to managing the people. And marketing to consumers is so challenging because it is evolving constantly" (Executive Sweet, 2005: 3). She also enjoys building consensus among her team and making sure everyone's voice is heard. She makes an extra effort to listen to her team members' suggestions and ideas and believes that communication is one of the most important things she does (Jones, 2009). When her global marketing team was having difficulty finding an appealing name for a new facial cream, she engaged everyone in the discussion. Joking about integrating everyone's ideas, she states, "It was like naming a child after your mother, your husband's mother, your grandmother, and your great aunt" (Morris, 1997: 79). Her constant smile and upbeat approach and attitude set the tone for her company and send a message of confidence and success. Discussing leadership, Jung says, "I think there is a big and significant difference between being a leader and being a manager—leaders lead from the heart. Flexibility is one of the key ingredients to being successful. If you feel like it's difficult to change, you will probably have a harder time succeeding" (Executive Sweet, 2005: 3). Facing new challenges, Jung recommends, "Reinvent yourself before you reinvent your company" (Jones, 2009).

Questions

1. What are the key elements of Andrea Jung's leadership style?
2. How closely does she match elements of charismatic and transformational leadership?
3. What elements of other neocharismatic theories does she present?

Sources: Avon Executive team at http://www.avoncompany.com/investor/seniormanagement/jung.html (accessed April 5, 2010); Avon Foundation for Women at http://www.avoncompany.com/women/news/press20100310.html (accessed April 5, 2010); Byrnes, N., 2007. "Avon: More than cosmetic changes," *Business Week*, April 12: 62–64; Chandra, S. 2004. "Avon's Andrea Jung Pins Hopes on China as Sales in U.S. Fade." *Bloomberg.com*, December 27. http://www.bloomberg.com/apps/news?pid= 10000080&sid=aBrmvGQAml1c&refer=asia# (accessed January 31, 2005); Duffuor, N. 2008. Avon Ladies find financial boost. *Good Morning America* November 7. http://abcnews.go.com/GMA/story?id=6205986&page=1 (accessed April 6, 2010); "Executive Sweet," *Goldsea: Asian American*. http://goldsea.com/WW/Jungandrea/jungandrea.html (accessed January 31, 2005); Forbes. 2010. Avon Products http://finapps.forbes.com/finapps/jsp/finance/compinfo/CIAtAGlance.jsp?tkr=AVP (accessed April 5, 2010); Global Influential. 2001. *Time.com*. www.time.com/time/2001/influentials/ybjung.html (accessed January 31, 2005); Jones. D. 2009. Avon's Andrea Jung: CEOs need to reinvent themselves. *USAToday* Junez 15. http://www. usatoday.com/money/companies/management/advice/2009-06-14-jung-ceo-avon_N.htm (accessed on March 24, 2010); Jung, A. 2006. "How to succeed in 2007." *CNNMoney.com*. http://money.cnn.com/popups/2006/biz2/howtosucceed/40.html (accessed August 12, 2007); Menkes, J. *Executive Intelligence* (New York: Harper Collins, 2006); Morris, B., 2004. "If women ran the world it would look a lot like Avon," *Fortune*, July: 21; Reilly N. 2009. Women: The answer. *Newsweek* September 12. http://www.newsweek.com/id/215305 (accessed on March 24, 2010); Sellers, P., 2000. "The 50 most powerful women in business," *Fortune*, October 16: 131–160; Tedeschi, B. 2007. When beauty is more than a click deep. *The New York Times* October 1. http://www.nytimes.com/2007/10/01/technology/01ecom.html?_r=1 (accessed April 6, 2010).

Individual Differences and Traits

He who knows about others may be learned
But he who knows himself is more intelligent.

—LAO TSU

After studying this chapter, you will be able to:

- Explain the role of individual difference characteristics in leadership.
- Describe the difference between the past and current approaches to leadership traits.
- Discuss the role demographic characteristics play in leadership.
- Identify the impact of values on leadership.
- Present the relationship between emotional intelligence and leadership.
- Highlight the role of the "Big Five" and other personality traits that are relevant in leadership.
- Understand cross-cultural differences in individual difference characteristics.

Even a quick reading of the history and mythology of any civilization indicates that leaders are considered special. Their physical characteristics are described in detail, their personalities dissected, and their actions celebrated. Long lists of traits and personal exploits are provided. The detailed information about leaders focuses our attention on the person. It represents a common belief that leaders possess something out of the ordinary—something within them that makes them special and worthy of our attention. Many believe that good leaders have natural, inborn characteristics that set them apart from others. Most of us can produce a list of personal characteristics of effective leaders. Leaders are courageous; they show initiative and integrity; they communicate well; they are intelligent, perceptive, goal-directed, and so forth. However, research findings do not clearly support many popular theories about personal characteristics of leaders. The results of hundreds of studies do not yield a specific profile for leaders. Traits alone do not identify and define leaders. Barbara Waugh, former director of HP Labs, when discussing leadership states: "It's not bestowed, it's not a gift, and it's something you can choose and if you do, you're in for a ride; it's worth your life" (Marshall, 2009, p. 5). However, certain characteristics are related to leadership, if not directly linked to leadership effectiveness.

In recent years, the interest in understanding the individual characteristics and personalities of leaders has reemerged, with many studies linking personality and other stable individual characteristics to leadership (for reviews, see Judge, Piccolo, and Kosalka, 2009; Zaccaro, 2007). Many new case studies of and interviews with successful business leaders have refocused attention on the role of individual style, demographic background, personality traits, skills, and other individual characteristics in understanding leadership. For example, Warren Bennis (1992), through numerous interviews and observations, highlights leaders' charisma and personal style and their effects on organizations. Other examples of the continued focus on individual traits are theories of charismatic leadership (Conger, 1991), transformational leadership (Bass, 1985), and the work of Kouzes and Posner (1993, 2003b) about the importance of credibility in leadership. The major difference between earlier approaches during the Trait Era and the recent ones is the researchers' more complex approach. The search is not simply for one individual trait or a combination of traits. Instead, modern theorists consider the complex interaction among traits, behaviors, and situational characteristics, such as expectations of followers. Within this framework, it is important to understand the role that several personal characteristics may play in determining leadership style and behavior. Additionally, self-awareness of one's strengths and weaknesses continues to be at the heart of leader development.

This chapter discusses the role of individual characteristics in leadership by considering demographic characteristics, values, abilities, skills, and several personality traits. These individual characteristics do not determine how effective a leader will be. They, however, do affect the way leaders think, behave, and approach problems and their interaction with others. No single individual characteristic is a direct measure of leadership style, but each can allow a better understanding of a person's basic approach and preferences.

ELEMENTS OF INDIVIDUAL DIFFERENCE CHARACTERISTICS

What makes every person unique is a combination of many factors, including demographic, physical, psychological, and behavioral differences. They are at the core of who we are. Figure 1 shows a framework for understanding individual differences and their complex components. Heredity and environment are the two determinants of individual characteristics. The interactionist view suggests that these two determinants interact to influence the development of those characteristics. This view is widely accepted, although experts debate the relative influence of each factor. Heredity consists of an individual's gene pool, gender, race, and ethnic background, and it creates an early, and some suggest indelible, influence on personality. Although genetic studies establish a link between heredity and some personality traits, research also shows that the environment strongly affects us. Influences include physical location, family, culture, religion, education, early experiences, and friends.

To understand individual differences, we must consider the interaction between heredity and the environment. Environmental and social conditions can reinforce genetic patterns to influence a leader's personality, as can cultural factors, the educational system, and parental

Individual Differences and Traits

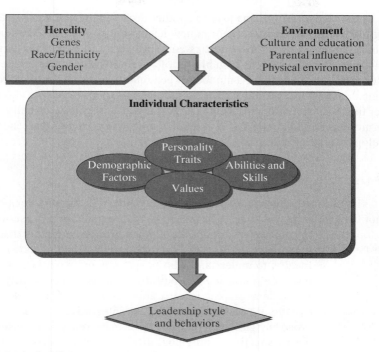

FIGURE 1 Individual Differences Framework

upbringing. For instance, in the United States, the genetic traits typically associated with being male are further reinforced by social norms that encourage boys to be competitive and aggressive. Similarly, although female babies tend to develop language skills earlier than males, parents who speak more to their girls and schools that expect girls to be proficient in language reinforce their verbal skills. These genetic and environmental influences interact and are reflected later in life in leadership styles and behaviors.

As shown in Figure 1, four major individual difference characteristics can affect leadership style: demographic factors, values, abilities and skills, and personality. Demographic factors such as age and ethnic background are individual difference characteristics that may affect individual behavior and to some extent leadership style. Values are stable, long-lasting beliefs and preferences about what is worthwhile and desirable and are closely related to personality. Personality refers to a person's character and temperament, whereas values are principles that a person believes. Like personality traits, values guide a leader's behavior and are influenced by a combination of biological and environmental factors. For example, leaders who hold the value "honesty is the best policy" will attempt to behave fairly and honorably and show integrity in their words and actions. Like personality, values are shaped early in life and are resistant to change. Values also are influenced heavily by one's culture.

Two related individual differences—abilities and skills—play a role in leadership. Ability, or aptitude, is a natural talent for doing something mental or physical. This category includes things such as intelligence. A skill is an acquired talent that a person develops related to a specific task. Whereas ability is somewhat stable over time, skills change with training and experience and from one task to another. You cannot train leaders to develop an ability or aptitude, but you can train them in new leadership skills. Organizations, therefore, recruit and hire leaders with certain abilities and aptitudes and then train them to acquire needed skills. Finally, personality is a stable set of psychological characteristics that makes each person unique. It is made up of a number of personality traits and is the product of inter-acting biological and environmental factors. Although personality is stable and tends to stay the same over time and across situations, it is not rigid and can evolve gradually over the long term. Furthermore, personality consists of a set of characteristics rather than one or two traits. This set develops over time and makes the individual unique.

Multiple Perspectives and the Impact of the Situation

Although individual characteristics are, by definition, stable, this stability does not mean that leaders cannot behave in ways that are different from their personality. A useful approach is to consider a variety of individual difference factors that explain certain aspects of a person's behavior rather than focus on any one trait. Ideally, to understand who people are and what makes them unique, one would consider all possible aspects of personality, values, attitudes, demographic factors, abilities, and skills as well as the various situations a person faces. Such an integrative perspective can provide broad insight into a person. Note that even when considering multiple perspectives, individual difference characteristics do not dictate our behaviors.

> Ideally, to understand who people are and what makes them unique, one would consider all possible aspects of personality, values, attitudes, demographic factors, abilities, and skills as well as the various situations a person faces. Such an integrative perspective can provide broad insight into a person.

When situations provide little guidance and are loosely structured, a person's individual characteristics can have a strong impact (Mischel, 1973; Weiss and Adler, 1984; Zhang, Ilies, and Arvey, 2009). However, when the situation provides strong behavioral cues—cues that signal what behaviors and actions are expected and appropriate—most people behave according to those cues, regardless of their personality traits or other individual characteristics. For example, a highly mechanistic and bureaucratic organization with a strong culture that provides detailed, clear rules of behavior will not encourage its managers to express their individuality. In contrast, a loosely structured, organic organization that provides autonomy will allow leaders the latitude to experiment and show their individual differences.

Individual Characteristics Provide a Range

Although individual characteristics tend to be stable, that stability does not mean that people cannot behave in ways that are inconsistent with their personality, values, and attitudes. Instead, each characteristic provides a behavioral zone of comfort as presented in Figure 2. The zone of comfort includes a range of behaviors that come naturally and feel comfortable to perform because they reflect individual characteristics. Behaving outside that zone is diffi-cult, takes practice, and in some cases might not be possible. Although we are at ease in our behavioral comfort zone, we learn and grow by moving to our zones of discomfort. The be-haviors outside the comfort zone challenge us and push us to our limits. Therefore, although it is difficult to do so, an effective learning tool is to move outside the comfort zone. The re-mainder of the chapter presents individual difference variables that have the potential to affect leadership or that can help in understanding leadership styles, ending with considera-tion of several personality traits.

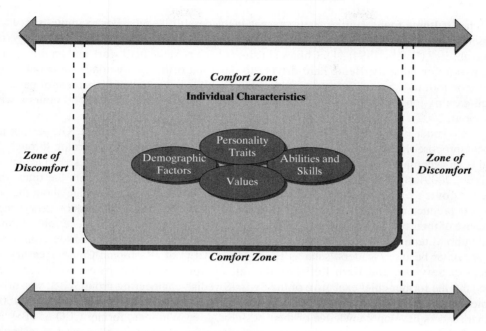

Individual Differences and Traits

Comfort Zone
Individual Characteristics

Zone of
Discomfort

Personality Traits

Demographic Factors

Abilities and Skills

Values

Zone of
Discomfort

Comfort Zone

FIGURE 2 Individual Characteristics and Behavioral Range

Traits Revisited: A Fresh Look at Leaders' Individual Characteristics and Behaviors

Although strong evidence of a consistent relationship between specific traits and leadership effectiveness is lacking, interest in understanding the personal characteristics of leaders continues. In 1974, a thorough review of traits by Stogdill, together with other findings, reestablished the validity of the trait approach, reviving research on the topic. In general, activity level and stamina, socioeconomic class, education, and intelligence, along with a variety of other traits, appear to characterize leaders, and especially effective leaders. The role of situational characteristics, however, is also recognized.

Kirkpatrick and Locke (1991) have proposed a modern approach to understanding the role of traits in leadership: several key traits alone are not enough to make a leader, but they are a precondition for effective leadership. Kirkpatrick and Locke list a number of traits that facilitate a leader's acquisition of needed leadership skills. The key traits are as follows:

- Drive, which includes motivation and energy
- Desire and motivation to lead
- Honesty and integrity
- Self-confidence
- Intelligence
- Knowledge of the business

Some of the traits, namely intelligence and drive, cannot be acquired through training. Others, such as knowledge of the industry and self-confidence, can be acquired with time and appropriate experience. The trait of honesty is a simple choice. Studies of managers and leaders in other cultures found similar traits present in successful leaders. For example, successful Russian business leaders are characterized by "hard-driving ambition, boundless energy, and keen ability" (Puffer, 1994: 41). Chinese business leaders value hard work and an impeccable reputation for integrity. Being hard-driving to the point of being a workaholic is not an uncommon trait in U.S. business executives either. Surveys indicate that 60 percent of people in high-earning jobs work more than 50 hours a week; 35 percent more than 60 hours a week (Armour, 2007).

Consider how many business executives demonstrate the traits that Kirkpatrick and Locke propose. Kathy Wade, who runs a nonprofit organization called Learning through Art and is an accomplished jazz musician, considers passion and initiative to be key to leadership (BizEd, 2009). Similarly, Lisa Harper, CEO of Gymboree Corp., remembers the time when she took over the company with the task of turning it around: "I was passionate about the people, the product, and the customer . . ." (Canabou, 2003a: 58). Small business owners succeed because of their extreme confidence in their own abilities (Wellner, 2004). Steve Jobs of Apple and Fujio Mitarai of Canon are famous for their drive, energy, intelligence, and self-confidence, as are other business leaders, such as Heidi Miller, CEO of JP Morgan Chase Treasury and Security Services, and Herb Kelleher, the famous founder of Southwest Airlines. Goran Lindahl, the former chief executive of the Swiss-Swedish engineering group ABB, was driven almost to the point of obsession to keep his company's stock prices high (Tomlinson, 2000). Other leaders develop knowledge of their business. Meg Whitman, former CEO of eBay and 2010 California gubernatorial candidate, made a point of traveling coach instead of taking the corporate jet. She wore an eBay T-shirt so that she could talk to people about their experience with her company and gather information (Dillon, 2004). Emilio Azcarraga Jean, chair of Grupo Televisa SA, the largest Spanish-language media company in the world, learned all the details of the family business when he took over for his ailing father (Kroll and Fass, 2007). Through his intense drive and motivation, he refocused his organization's culture from loyalty to performance to gain ground in the U.S. market.

Interestingly, integrity, or lack of it, is cited as a key factor in leadership. Many anecdotes about bad leadership contain elements of lack of trust, dishonesty, and unwillingness to be held accountable on the part of the leaders. The corporate scandals have increased and renewed focus on the importance of transparency and honesty. The GLOBE researchers have found that integrity is one of few culturally universal leadership characteristics (House et al., 2004), although other studies found cultural differences in managers' willingness to justify ethically suspect behaviors (e.g, Garibaldi de Hilal, 2006). Followers all over the world complain bitterly when leaders abuse their trust, lie to them, or mislead them. The scandal at the Italian food manufacturer Parmalat provides a striking example of blatant dishonesty. Calisto Tanzi, the company's chief executive, Fausto Tonna, its chief financial officer, and other top executives falsified accounts and embezzled millions of euros, leading to the company's bankruptcy and public outrage. Goran Lindahl, mentioned earlier for his almost obsessive focus, was also severely criticized for taking a large retirement package while the company reported losses.

Just as some traits are necessary for leadership, they can be detrimental when carried to an extreme (Kirkpatrick and Locke, 1991). A leader with too much drive might refuse to delegate tasks, and a desire for too much power can work against a leader's effectiveness (Bennis and Nanus, 1985). For example, Michael Eisner, the president of Disney, was not able to hold on to several talented executives because of his need for control and inability to delegate, which stemmed in part from his drive and motivation to lead. These characteristics were blamed for the high turnover on top. Eisner's tight hold on power also caused bitter disputes with several board members, triggered investor lawsuits, and was one of the factors that led to Eisner's resignation (Holson, 2004a). His replacement, Bob Iger, is known to be understated, calm, diplomatic, and collaborative, all characteristics that Eisner lacked (Steptoe, 2007). Small business owners who are highly driven face similar challenges when it comes to delegation. For example, Andrew Nadel, owner of Pride Products, a promotional and corporate gift company, does everything from calling customers to assembling new office chairs himself, even though he employs a staff to take care of many of these tasks (Wellner, 2004).

The current approach to understanding the role of leadership traits suggests that, as many of us believe, leaders are indeed gifted in at least some areas. Those gifts and talents alone, however, are not enough. Experience, correct choices, and exposure to the right situations are the keys to allowing those gifts to bloom.

DEMOGRAPHIC CHARACTERISTICS OF LEADERS

One approach to understanding the personal characteristics of leaders is to look at their demographic characteristics. Several research projects considering the demographic characteristics of who has and gets power in the United States have yielded consistent results (e.g., Mayo and Nohria, 2006). Kurtz, Boone, and Fleenor conducted one such comprehensive survey of nearly 800 U.S. executives in 1989. All were male. The majority of executives in their sample were first-borns in two-parent, middle-class families living in the rust belt. Close to 90 percent were married, with a median age of 58, and many considered themselves to be religious. Eighty percent were right-handed; they were taller and smoked less than the general population and tended to exercise a fair amount. The CEOs were considerably more educated than the general population, with 47 percent having graduate degrees. The majority studied in public universities, and many paid for their own education, at least to some extent.

The most striking result of this extensive survey is the homogeneity of the executives, despite some differences among industries. Researchers Mayo and Nohria found similar results and conclude that although education opens the door for diverse people to reach leadership positions and although there has been progress in the number of women and people of diverse nationalities in leadership positions, the leadership path is still primarily influenced by birthplace, nationality, religion, education, social class, gender, and race (2006). Other studies further show progress at least in some areas. For example, a U.S. government study indicates that in 2002, women owned 28.2 percent of nonfarm companies (Lowrey, 2006). Reports from the Center for Women's Business Research further indicate that women own part or all of 46 percent of privately held businesses (Franklin, 2003).

Even though women and minorities have made their way up many organizations in the United States and other countries, formal organizational leadership is still heavily dominated by males. Despite some changes, the top executives in the United States, and in many other parts of the world, are still a homogeneous group. The homogeneity in demographic background does not necessarily lead to similar approaches in managing a business and leading followers. It is also unlikely, however, to lead to high diversity of thought and approaches to management. Although homogeneity can be a strength if unity of purpose is needed, it can be a weakness where creativity is required. Many studies (e.g., Hackman, 1990; Nahavandi and Aranda, 1994) propose that lack of support from top management is a key obstacle in the implementation of innovative management approaches. With the current state of flux of public and private organizations, the need for diverse and innovative approaches is strong.

Given the homogeneity of current business leaders in the United States and around the world, it is not surprising that such innovation is sometimes lacking. The homogeneity of executives might be one of the factors that indicate the need to further diversify business leadership.

VALUES

Values are long-lasting beliefs about what is worthwhile and desirable. They are personal judgments about what is right and wrong, good and bad. Understanding values is important for leaders because they affect how leaders lead. This section examines value systems, investigates how culture affects values, and considers the interplay between values and ethics.

Value System and Culture

The ways in which a person organizes and prioritizes values is that person's value system (see Self-Assessment 1). For instance, for one person family may be a central value and a top priority when compared with other issues, such as faith, career, and social relationships. Other people might value their career more than their family or put their faith and spirituality above all else. Each of us has a personal value system around which we prioritize our actions. Some people are aware of their values and their priorities, whereas others are unclear about their own priorities and become cognizant of them only when conflicts arise. Each individual's value system is unique, although members of one family or culture might share certain key values. Many factors influence what an individual's values are. Particularly, researchers have found consistent gender and cultural differences in values (e.g., Golob and Bartlett, 2007; Schwartz, 2005). For example, surveys of political attitudes in the United States consistently reveal what some people call the gender gap, a difference in the value systems of men and women. In the United States, women tend to place a higher value on family and social issues, whereas men focus more on economic problems. In addition to gender-based differences, many generational and culture-based value systems differences also exist. Cultural dimensions include cultural values. For example, individualism is typically highly valued in industrialized Western countries, whereas collectivism is a dominant value in many Eastern cultures. Leaders must understand their own values and those of their followers and how they influence styles and behaviors.

Cultural values indicate what a cultural group considers important, worthwhile, and desirable. We share the values of our culture. The cultural values form the basis for a leader's individual value system. Clearly, not everyone holds the same values (Bigoness and Blakely, 1996). For example, certain values—fairness, honesty, frugality, compassion, and humility—are universal. In contrast, the value of individual dignity—which refers to placing focus on the uniqueness, self-control, and self-governance of individuals—is more prevalent in individualistic than in collectivistic cultures (Anderson, 1997). The GLOBE research indicates that not all cultures value the same traits in their leaders and that many characteristics are culturally contingent (House et al., 2004).

In general, the Euro-American cultures within the United States, as well as many other Western cultures, value individuality. As a result, leaders from these cultures rate personal achievement and recognition highly, and organizations target individuals for rewards and recognition. Displays of individuality are welcomed, as evidenced by the respect many people have for entrepreneurs. By contrast, collectivist cultures place a higher value on the community and a lower value on the individual. For instance, the Japanese value and reward conformity to the group. Parents teach children not to stand out or draw attention to themselves. The Japanese proverb "the nail that stands out will be hammered down" reflects the value system of many Japanese, who believe that they should sacrifice the self for the good of the collective. Leaders are similarly valued for their conformity to the social order as much as their uniqueness. Several Native American cultures, such as the Navajos, have comparable cultural values. Navajos, who are a horizontal collectivistic culture, devalue individualism and standing out in one's community and, indeed, consider such behavior inappropriate. They appreciate leaders primarily for their contribution to their community. Hofstede's other cultural values of avoidance of uncertainty, power distance, and masculinity further influence an individual's value systems. When a culture emphasizes low power distance—such as in Sweden, which is individualistic but horizontal—leaders are likely to be cooperative and avoid status symbols and hierarchy. When the culture is masculine, individuals are likely to emphasize honor and self-reliance. The concept of high and low context can further affect values. In high context cultures, such as Mexico, bending the truth to preserve relationships or protect feelings is much more accepted than in low-context cultures, such as Germany or the United States.

Generational Differences

In addition to national cultural differences, age, ethnic, and other group cultural differences may affect value systems. Research suggests that many people from the older generation in the United States believe that the younger generation has worse moral values, less respect for others, and a lower work ethic than their parents (Taylor and Morin, 2009). However, the younger generations are perceived to have higher social and racial tolerance. Table 1 presents some value differences based on age. Different generations often hold different views of what effectiveness and efficiency mean. Older generations consider loyalty, regular work hours, and consistent attendance to be primary. They are often less optimistic and less confident about their future (Tyson, 2002). Generation Xers and Millennials hop from one job to another, work odd shifts, rely on technology, work late into the night, and may not consider the traditional 8-hour workday appropriate. They have an optimistic view of their future and are bolder, an approach that was reflected, for example, in their initially more positive view of the Iraq war in 2002 (Tyson, 2002). Technology provides another divide where younger workers often are impatient with older workers' perceived lack of expertise in technology. Some, however, believe that although the Millennials may need a lot of attention, they are also high performing. Describing the values and behaviors of that generation, generational researcher Bruce Tulgan suggests, "They walk in with more information in their heads, more information at their fingertips—and, sure, they have high expectations, but they have the highest expectations first and foremost for themselves" (Hira, 2007).

A survey of 66,000 people around the world by the Pew Research Center for the People and the Press indicates that generational value differences are prevalent particularly in Western Europe, but almost nonexistent in Asia, Africa, and the Middle East (Pew Global Attitudes Project, 2004). Older people in the United States and Western Europe express more national pride and are worried about globalization more so than younger generations in those countries. The older generations also demonstrate a stronger sense of cultural superiority, whereas the younger generations feel less tied to their national cultural identity.

Each individual develops a different value system that shapes attitudes and behaviors. Value systems, in turn, affect ethical behavior in organizations, a factor with critical implications for leaders.

TABLE 1 Generation-Based Value Differences in the United States

Generation	Key Social and Historical Influences	Dominant Value System
GI generation, 60+ (born 1940s or before)	Raised by Depression-era parents in post-Depression period or around WW II; Big Band music	Hard work; frugality; patriotism; Protestant work ethic; respect for authority
Baby boomers, 50–65 (born between late 1940s and 1960s)	Raised by WW II parents; grew up during Korean and Vietnam wars; Kennedy assassination; moon landing; rock & roll and Woodstock; cold war energy crisis	Nonconformity; idealism; self-focus; distrust of establishment; happiness and peace; optimism; involvement
Baby Busters, 40–50 (born between the 1960s and 1970s)	Raised by the early hippies; post Vietnam era; Watergate; the Beatles, Grateful Dead, Jimmy Hendrix	The Yuppies; "me" generation; ambitious; material comfort; success driven; stressed out
Generation Xers, 30–40 (born between 1970s and 1980s)	Peaceful era; fall of communism; Iran hostage crisis; recession and economic changes; Bill Clinton; AIDS; MTV; The Eagles, Michael Jackson	Enjoyment of life; jaded; latchkey kids; single-parent family; desire for autonomy and flexibility; self-reliance; spirituality; diversity; balance work and personal life
Millennials or Nexters under 30 (born after the mid-1980s)	A lot of parental focus; Oklahoma bombings; 9/11 World Trade Center attack; school shootings; globalization; George W. Bush; Internet and media; tech savvy; Cold Play, Kanye West	Flexibility; choice; socially conscious; meaningful experiences and work; diversity; achievement; tolerance and openness

Sources: Partially based on N. A. Hira, "You raised them, now manage them," *Fortune*, May 28 2007, 38–43; M. E. Massey, "The past: What you are is where you were when" (videorecording) (Schaumburg, IL: VideoPublishing House, 1986); D. J. Cherrington, S. J. Condies, and J. L. England, "Age and work values," *Academy of Management Journal*, September 1979, 617–623; P. Taylor and R. Morin. 2009. Forty years after Woodstock: A gentler generation gap. *Pew Research Center: Social and Demographic Trends.* http://pewsocialtrends.org/pubs/739/woodstock-gentler-generation-gap-music-by-age (accessed February 21, 2010).

Values and Ethics

One value related to leadership is ethics. Ethics are a person's concept of right and wrong. Two general views of ethics are the relativist and universalist views. Individuals with a relativist view of ethics believe that what is right or wrong depends on the situation or the culture, and research suggest that ethics is strongly influenced by culture (e.g., Hooker, 2009). An index collected by Transparency International, an organization that uses a complex set of data to monitor corruption around the world, shows distinct national differences in ethical behaviors. In their 2009 index, Somalia, Afghanistan, Myanmar, Sudan, and Iraq were ranked as some of the most corrupt nations; New Zealand, Denmark, Singapore, and Sweden were ranked as the least corrupt (Transparency International, 2009). The United States ranked 19 out of 180, behind many Western countries and Canada, which is ranked eighth. To illustrate, business-people in many places consider gifts, bribes, or kickbacks acceptable behavior in contract negotiations, although these activities are unethical and illegal based on U.S. values and laws. A person with a relativist view of ethics would take a "when in Rome, do as the Romans do" approach. That is, a U.S. manager who learns that it is generally accepted to bribe officials in Thailand to secure a contract, would consider bribing a Thai official acceptable and ethical. Note that it is rarely possible for managers of U.S.-based companies to adopt a rela-tivist view of ethics in business situations simply because U.S. laws forbid any form of bribery anywhere in the world. In contrast, a per-son with a universalist view of ethics believes that all activities should be judged by the same standards, regardless of the situation or culture.

> A person with a relativist view of ethics would take a "when in Rome, do as the Romans do" approach, whereas a person with universalist view of ethics believes that all activities should be judged by the same standards, regardless of the situation or culture.

For example, a U.S. oil company manager would appoint a female manager to its Saudi oper-ations, based on U.S. laws of equal opportunity and the principles of cultural diversity, despite the religious and cultural problems it might create.

The value and ethical issues facing leaders are highly complex. Global and cross-cultural issues further add to the complexity. For example, research by Triandis and his asso-ciates (Triandis et al., 2001) indicates that collectivism tends to be related to greater use of deception in negotiation, as well as higher levels of guilt after using deception. Particularly, Koreans and Japanese feel considerable guilt and shame after using deception. Furthermore, based on what a culture values, individuals within that culture might lie for different reasons, such as protecting their privacy in the case of the United States or benefiting family members in the case of Samoans (Aune and Waters, 1994). Other research suggests that organizations from a low power distance, long-term orientation, or highly individualistic cultures may be less likely to engage in giving bribes (Sanyal and Guvenli, 2009). When comparing United States and Hong Kong Chinese, some studies show cross-cultural differences in attitudes to-ward breach of contract (Kickul, Lester, and Belgio, 2004). United States employees re-sponded more negatively to breaches of intrinsic contracts (e.g., autonomy) by displaying lower levels of job satisfaction and commitment. The Hong Kong Chinese are less accepting than U.S. workers of violations of extrinsic contract violations (e.g., salary or job training), but more tolerant of violations of intrinsic contract. The researchers attribute the differences to the Chinese Confucian value to preserve harmony as compared with the U.S. value of indi-vidual success. Still other research shows that different factors motivate managers in different cultures (Mathur, Zhang, and Meelankavil, 2001), and factors that determine commitment to work depend to some extent on cultural values (Andolsek and Stebe, 2004), suggesting a strong link between culture and values.

Because of complex cross-cultural and individual differences in values, handling ethical and value-driven issues will continue to be a major part of every manager's job.

ABILITIES AND SKILLS

Much of the early research in leadership characteristics focused on establishing leadership abili-ties. Although leaders clearly must have some abilities, competencies, and skills, these character-istics do not have high correlations to leadership effectiveness (for a review of the early research, see Bass, 1990a). Intelligence in its various forms and technical, interpersonal, and cognitive skills have received particular attention.

Intelligence

Intelligence is one of the most often used characteristics to describe leaders and is often included in discussions of leadership (Sternberg, 2007). It is clear that the complex task of leading requires a person with a cognitive ability to remember, collect and integrate information, analyze problems, develop solutions, and evaluate alternatives, all of which are related to traditional definitions of intelligence. For most people, intelligence is a factor in leadership; however, the actual link between intelligence and effectiveness is far from clear (Rubin, Bartels, and Bommer, 2002), as they are in other areas of success (Gladwell, 2008). Correlations vary, and many studies suggest that the link is relatively weak (for a review of past research, see Bass, 1990a). To date, only one leadership theory, the Cognitive Resource Model (Fiedler and Garcia, 1987a, b), has used intelligence explicitly as a factor. Reviews of the link between general intelligence and leadership indicate that it is an important aspect of leadership (Cornwell, 1983; Lord, De Vader, and Alliger, 1986). The relationship, however, may be moderated by many factors. For example, when being competent is important, leaders who are more intelligent might do better, but in situations that require interpersonal skills, general intelligence might not be sufficient. The level of leadership also may be a factor. Particularly, intuition may be especially important for leaders at upper organizational levels. Furthermore, some early research shows that a curvilinear relationship may exist between intelligence and leadership (Ghiselli, 1963). Those individuals with either low or high scores are less likely to be effective and successful leaders. Both, for different reasons, might experience difficulty communicating with their followers and motivating them to achieve the task.

Consider Scott Rudin, producer of hit movies such as *It's Complicated, Julie & Julia, No Country for Old Men, Failure to Launch*, and *Clueless*. Some of the people who work with him consider Rudin to be "one of the smartest and most clever and witty guys I have ever met" (Carvell, 1998: 201). He is bright and creative, and many admire his work. However, his intelligence and creativity are not enough and not his only well-known qualities. Rudin is famous for his fiery outbursts, throwing phones and office supplies, outrageous demands, and on-the-spot firing and rehiring of assistants—by some accounts 250 in a 5-year period (Kelly and Marr, 2005). He has been ranked as one of the worst bosses in New York City (Gawker, 2007). As one of Rudin's ex-assistants states, "I think the people that work there—most of them hate him. Nobody likes him. Everybody's miserable" (Carvell, 1998: 201). Rudin simply suggests, "The thin-skinned guys don't like it. The thick skinned people . . . understand that I am working as hard as them" (Kelly and Marr, 2005). Even his mentor, Edgar Scherick, referred to his protégé as "Scott Rude." As this example illustrates, being intelligent is not sufficient for being an effective leader. Many other characteristics play important roles. In Rudin's case, his high level of intelligence and creativity are not matched by his ability to relate to others.

Practical and Emotional Intelligence

In the past few years, other perspectives have been added to the concept of intelligence. Instead of primarily focusing on memory and analytical skills, several researchers have suggested that being able to work well with others or having the skills needed to succeed in life are important components of intelligence. Researcher Robert Sternberg and his colleagues introduced the concept of practical intelligence to address the types of abilities and attributes that people use to solve everyday challenges they may face (Headlund et al., 2003; Sternberg, 2002a; Sternberg et al., 2000). People with this type of intelligence either change their behavior to adapt to the environment, manipulate the environment, or find a new environment in which to succeed (Sternberg, 2007). Sternberg further proposes a model of leadership, WICS, that integrates wisdom, intelligence, and creativity in a systems approach putting intelligence at the center of leadership traits (Sternberg, 2003). Although the concept has received some attention, research about its link to leadership is still scarce (for an example, see Hedlund et al., 2003).

Peter Salovey and John Mayer (1990) coined the term emotional intelligence (EI; or EQ for emotional quotient) to describe the social and interpersonal aspect of intelligence. Whereas intelligence generally is defined in terms of mental and cognitive abilities, some argue that the ability to relate interpersonally contributes another type of intelligence (see Goleman, 1995, 2004). The ability to interact well with followers, satisfy their emotional needs, and motivate and inspire them is another key to effective leadership. Table 2 summarizes the five elements of EI/EQ.

Individuals with high EI/EQ are in touch with their emotions and demonstrate self-management in their ability to control their moods and feelings productively and in staying motivated and focused even when facing obstacles. They can calm themselves when angry and stay balanced. They also are able to read others' emotions, feel empathy for them, and put themselves in their place. The last component of EI/EQ is having the ability to develop productive and positive interpersonal relationships through understanding, conflict resolution, and negotiation (Goleman, 1998; see Self-Assessment 2). Goleman suggests that EI/EQ is important in leadership because of the increased use of teams, globalization, and the need to retain talented followers (Goleman, 1998). Many have explored the relationship between EI/EQ and transformational leadership. Some studies show that EI is essential for effective leadership (Riggio and Reichard, 2008) and is related positively to attitude toward change (Vakola, Tsausis, and Nikolaou, 2004). Others have focused on the role empathy plays in leadership, suggesting that it is a good predictor of leadership emergence in teams (Wolff, Pescosolido, and Druskat, 2003) and the development of

TABLE 2	Components of Emotional Intelligence
Component	**Description**
Self-awareness	Being aware of and in touch with your own feelings and emotions
Self-regulation	Being able to manage various emotions and moods without denying or suppressing them
Self-motivation	Being able to remain positive and optimistic
Empathy for others	Being able to read others' emotions accurately and putting yourself in their place
Interpersonal and social skills	Having the skills to build and maintain positive relationships with others

Source: Based on D. Goleman, "What makes a leader?" *Harvard Business Review*, 82, no. 1 (2004): 82–91; and D. Goleman, R. E. Boyatzis, and A. McKee, *Primal Leadership: Realizing the Power of Emotional Intelligence* (Boston: Harvard Business School Press, 2002).

positive group norms (Koman and Wolff, 2008). Although it may be obvious that the leader's ability to understand followers is a component of relationship-orientation and consideration behaviors (Kellett, Humphrey, and Sleeth, 2002), empathy also plays a role in the leader's task-orientated behaviors (Wolff et al., 2003). Specifically, leaders who show empathy are better able to guide their followers around challenging tasks because they can recognize patterns and coordinate group activities.

A leader's ability to self-regulate and manage his or her emotions, another component of EI, also affects followers. Research by Newcomb and Ashkanasy (2002) indicates that how a leader delivers a message can be more important than the content of the message. When subjects in their study used positive facial expressions, they were rated higher than when they used negative expressions, which led to the suggestion that leadership is an emotional process where a key leadership role is the management of emotions. Furthermore, research in psychology about how people experience emotion (e.g., Gohm, 2003) links it to the abilities to regulate mood and to make judgments, once more emphasizing the potentially strong role emotions can play in leadership.

> The ability to interact well with followers, satisfy their emotional needs, and motivate and inspire them is another key to effective leadership.

Psychologist Daniel Goleman states, "The rules for work are changing, and we're all being judged by a new yardstick—not just how smart we are and what technical skills we have, which employers see as givens, but increasingly by how well we handle ourselves and one another" (Fisher, 1998: 293). Although competence and cognitive ability—namely, traditional intelligence—might be keys for success when working alone, leadership requires successful interaction with others and the ability to motivate them to accomplish goals. Therefore, EI/EQ is a central factor in several leadership processes, particularly in the development of charismatic and transformational leadership where the emotional bond between leaders and followers is imperative. Being able to empathize with followers can further allow a leader to develop followers and create a consensus. Recently, the importance of reading others well, with its potential biological origins, and acting based on such readings, has also been emphasized (Goleman, 2006). Some researchers suggest that emotional intelligence contributes to effective leadership because an emotionally intelligent leader focuses on followers, on inspiring them, and on developing enthusiasm (George, 2007). Whereas leaders with a high IQ lead with their head, leaders with a high EI/EQ lead with their heart and address their followers' emotional needs.

Ken Chenault, Chairman and CEO of American Express (AmEx), one of only a few African American leaders of *Fortune* 500 companies in the United States, is able to win his employees' trust and build cohesion partly through empathy and ability to express his emotions. He is described as understated, modest, and unassuming, with quiet warmth and a style that makes people want to be on his team (Schwartz, 2001). His skills at managing through crisis focus on communication. He states: ". . .you've got to communicate constantly. . ." (Colvin, 2009). He believes that although the rational aspects of leadership are essential, values are what make a leader. He states, "What I have seen in companies throughout my career is that if you are not clear on who you are, on what it is you stand for, and if you don't have strong values, you are going to run your career off a cliff" (*Knowledge@Wharton*, 2005). After AmEx was driven out of its Manhattan headquarters by the September 11 terrorist attacks, Chenault moved into a cramped windowless office with standard issue furniture. While addressing the AmEx employees during a company town-hall meeting after September 11, he openly expressed his emotions, embraced grief-stricken employees, and stated, "I represent the best company and the best people in the world. In fact, you are my strength, and I love you" (Byrne and Timmons, 2001). Tom Ryder, who competed with Chenault for the top AmEx job, said, "If you work around him, you feel like you'd do anything for the guy" (Schwartz, 2001: 62). For Chenault, integrity, courage, being a team player, and developing people are foundations for becoming a leader; all are elements of emotional intelligence.

Because of the potential of EI/EQ to address an important aspect of leadership, many organizations are finding that developing their managers' EI can lead to higher performance. Danny Myers, who owns several highly successful restaurants in New York City, including the Union Square Café and Gramercy Tavern, and who has written a book about delivering first-class service (Meyer, 2006), believes that the secret of his success is that he has surrounded himself with people who have higher EQs than IQs. He looks for people who have natural warmth, optimism, intelligence, and curiosity. Similarly, business education that, for many years, emphasized analytical and numbers-oriented skills is shifting attention to developing interpersonal skills. Well-respected MBA programs at University of Pennsylvania's Wharton Business School, the University of Chicago, and Berkeley's Hass Business School are stressing teamwork and teaching listening skills, mostly in response to employers' need to hire people who have such skills.

Creativity

A leader's ability to be creative is ever more important, given the uncertainty that many businesses face. Creativity—also known as divergent thinking or lateral thinking—is the process of bringing into reality something novel and useful (Maddux and Galinsky, 2009). Lateral thinking focuses on moving away from the linear approach advocated by rational decision making (De Bono, 1992). Caterina Fake, cofounder of the photo-sharing site *Flickr* likes to let her curiosity guide her. She states: "I work on whatever instinctively feels the right thing at the moment" (Buchanan, 2010, p. 69). David Rockwell, the architect who designed the 2009 Academy Award set and the Walt Disney Family Museum say, "The key is to stay curious. As you have success in certain areas, you have to find ways to keep alive that sense of discovery, of not knowing all the answers (Sacks, 2009: 133). Patrick Le Quément, French carmaker Renault's chief designer, is credited with many of the company's cutting-edge and highly unusual designs. He believes that being original is the key to his creativity, stating, "It's worth alienating most of your customers if you can make the rest love you" (Wylie, 2004a: 90). Because creativity is a complex process, leading creative efforts also is a highly complex activity.

Creativity is a necessary component of leadership because leaders are often expected to develop new ideas and directions that others will follow. Creative leaders listen intently to all sources, especially to bad news, in order to know where the next problem is emerging. They value subjective as well as objective information. They turn facts, perceptions, gut feelings, and intuitions into reality by making bold and informed decisions. Other factors found to be important are modeling creative and unconventional behaviors, delegation, monitoring the process, and showing followers how their work affects the organization (Basadur, 2004). Creative leaders must not only be creative, but also have considerable technical expertise to lead their followers through the challenges of creative decision making (Mumford and Licuanan, 2004). Creative leaders typically share four characteristics (Sternberg and Lubart, 1995):

1. *Perseverance in the face of obstacles and self-confidence.* Creative individuals persevere more in the face of problems and have strong beliefs in the correctness of their ideas.
2. *Willingness to take risks.* Creative individuals take moderate to high risks rather than extreme risks that have a strong chance of failing.

3. *Willingness to grow and openness to experience.* Creative individuals are open to experiences and are willing to try new methods.

4. *Tolerance of ambiguity.* Creative individuals tolerate lack of structure and not having clear answers.

As this list suggests, creative leaders tend to be confident in the paths they select and are willing to take risks when others give up. Creative people focus on learning and are willing to live with uncertainty to reach their goals. As with any other characteristic, the organizational setting can have a great impact on allowing creativity to flourish. Some suggest that creative people make a decision to be creative when facing challenging problems (Sternberg, 2002b). Interestingly, some research suggests a link between a leader's EI and the ability to encourage followers to be creative (Zhou and George, 2003). Because creativity is an emotional process, managing emotions well can play a positive role in the creativity process. Teresa Amabile, head of the Entrepreneurial Management Unit at Harvard Business School, believes that creativity is not just the domain of creative people, but requires experience, talent, and motivation to push through problems. She also suggests that people are least creative when they feel time pressure, fear, or intense competitive pressures (Breen, 2004). Other research suggests that exposure to new situations such as living abroad can enhance creativity (Maddux and Galinsky, 2009).

Skills

The research on leadership skills is considerably clearer and more conclusive than that on leadership abilities. Leadership skills are divided into three categories: technical, interpersonal, and conceptual (Table 3).

As leaders and managers move up in their organization, they rely less on technical skills and increasingly more on interpersonal and conceptual skills. Company CEOs, school principals, or hospital administrators do not need to be able to perform various jobs in detail. They, however, should be able to negotiate successfully and effectively and manage various interpersonal relationships inside and outside the organization. Furthermore, top executives more than lower-level leaders and managers need to read and analyze their internal and external environments and make strategic decisions that require considerable problem-solving skills.

The impact of ability and skills on leadership depends to a great extent on the situation. Situational factors, such as the type of organization, level of leadership, ability and needs of followers, and type of task at hand, all influence what abilities and skills leaders will need to be effective. In addition, although skills can be learned and can affect a leader's behavior, research suggests that a lag time occurs between learning skills and translating them into actual behavior (Hirst et al., 2004).

TABLE 3 Leadership Skills

Skills Category	Description
Technical skills	Knowledge of the job processes, methods, tools, and techniques
Interpersonal skills	Knowledge of interpersonal relationships including communication, conflict management, negotiation, and team building
Conceptual skills	Knowledge of problem solving, logical thinking, decision making, creativity, and reasoning in general

RELEVANT PERSONALITY TRAITS

Although a review of early trait research indicates that no specific traits can predict who will become a leader or which leader will be effective, traits do play a role in leadership in several ways (for a review, see Judge et al., 2009; Zaccaro, 2007).

- First, researchers have identified some traits that are consistently associated with leadership.
- Second, a leader's personality influences his or her preferences, style, and behavior.
- Third, personality may affect the ease with which a leader learns skills and is able to implement them.
- Fourth, being aware of key personality traits shown to affect work-related behaviors can help leaders develop their self-awareness and aid them in their learning and development.
- Finally, traits can be strong predictors of leadership when considered in an integrated system that includes several individual difference characteristics and situational and contextual variables.

The next section presents six personality traits with implications for leadership.

The Big Five Personality Dimensions

Over time, psychologists and organizational behavior researchers have condensed countless personality traits into a list of five major personality dimensions, known as the *Big Five* (Barrick and Mount, 1991; Digman, 1990; Norman, 1963). Research shows that these five dimensions are consistent components of personality not only in the United States, but in several other cultures as well (Paunonen, 2003; Schmitt et al., 2007). Table 4 summarizes the key elements of the Big Five personality dimensions.

The Big Five dimensions allow the grouping of many different traits into a meaningful taxonomy for studying individual differences. These five dimensions are relatively independent,

TABLE 4 Big Five Personality Dimensions

Personality Dimensions	Description
Conscientiousness	Degree to which a person is dependable, responsible, organized, and plans ahead
Extraversion/Introversion	Degree to which a person is sociable, talkative, assertive, active, and ambitious
Openness to experience	Degree to which a person is imaginative, broad-minded, curious, and seeks new experiences
Emotional stability	Degree to which a person is anxious, depressed, angry, and insecure
Agreeableness	Degree to which a person is courteous, likable, good-natured, and flexible

Sources: Based on descriptions provided by W. T. Norman, "Toward an adequate taxonomy of personality attributes: Replicated factor structure in peer nomination personality ratings," *Journal of Abnormal and Social Psychology* 66 (1963): 547–583; J. M. Digman, "Personality structure: Emergence of the five-factor model," *Annual Review of Psychology* 41 (1990): 417–440; and M. R. Barrick and M. Mount, "The five big personality dimensions and job performance: A meta-analysis," *Personnel Psychology* 44, no. 1 (1991): 1–76.

with several implications for management. A number of the Big Five personality dimensions have links to work-relevant behaviors such as academic (Poropat, 2009) and career success (Seibert and Kraimer, 2001), the performance of managers who work abroad (Caligiuri, 2000), and use of different types of power (Karkoulian et al., 2009). Additionally, the Big Five have been shown to be good indicators of related behaviors (Fleeson and Gallagher, 2009). None, however, alone strongly predicts performance or leadership effectiveness, even though some links to work involvement have been established (Bozionelos, 2004). Of the five dimensions, *conscientiousness* is the most strongly correlated to job performance. This connection makes sense: individuals who are dependable, organized, and hard working tend to perform better in their job (Barrick and Mount, 1991; Frink and Ferris, 1999; Hayes, Roehm, and Catellano, 1994). Most managers would agree that a good employee is dependable, shows up on time, finishes work by deadlines, and is willing to work hard. For instance, Andy Grove, former CEO of Intel and management guru, used to make a list of which of his employees showed up on time. He believes that dependable employees perform better. *Extraversion* is the Big Five dimension with the second-highest correlation to job-related behaviors and is particularly important in jobs that rely on social interaction, such as management or sales (Anderson, Spataro, and Flynn, 2008). It is much less essential for employees working on an assembly line or as computer programmers (Hayes, Roehm, and Catellano, 1994). Unlike conscientiousness, which can apply to all job levels or occupations, extroversion is not an essential trait for every job, and individuals can succeed without being extroverted. In fact, one of the United States' most-admired business leaders, Lew Platt, former CEO of Hewlett-Packard, is not an extrovert. "Lew Platt isn't a loud, extroverted guy, but he is . . . in his own quiet, blushing way getting his colleagues not only to understand but to agree " (Stewart, 1998a: 82). Another example is Paul Otellini, Intel's CEO, who is known for his quiet and reserved manner and for shying away from the media spotlight, much in contrast with one of his predecessors, Andy Grove (McGirt, 2009).

Openness to experience can help performance in some instances, but not in others. For example, being open to new experiences can help employees and managers perform well in training because they will be motivated to explore fresh ideas and to learn (Goldstein, 1986), and it might help them be more successful in overseas assignments (Ones and Viswesvaran, 1999). E. Neville Isdell, CEO of Coca-Cola believes that openness to experience is key to leadership. Advising business students, he states, "I would want to teach students to understand different backgrounds, cultures, religions, and perspectives even if those perspectives are antithetical to their own" (Bisoux, 2008b, p. 18). In describing the qualities he looks for in new Coca-Cola hires, he adds, ". . . they also must have a sense of curiosity. They must want to travel and discover new societies and see the world. Curious people are engaged" (p. 20). Ken Chenault, CEO of AmEx, suggests that being open to change and able to adapt to it are the most important characteristic today's leaders need to have: "It's not the strongest or the most intelligent who survive, but those most adaptive to change" (Chester, 2005). Bill Gates of Microsoft, is legendary for his intelligence and his thirst for new ideas. After his travel to India in 1997, he observed, "Even though 80 percent of what you hear from customers is the same all over the world, you always learn something you can apply to our business elsewhere" (Schlender, 1997: 81). But the same eagerness to explore new ideas and ways of doing things can be an impediment to performance on jobs that require careful attention to existing processes and procedures.

As one would expect, *emotional stability* also is related to job behaviors and performance. At the extreme, individuals who are neurotic are not likely to be able to function in organizations. Some degree of anxiety and worrying, however, can help people perform well because it spurs them to excel. Andy Grove's (former executive at Intel) book *Only the Paranoid Survive: How to*

Exploit the Crisis That Challenges Every Company and Career is an indication of the sense of anxiety he instilled at Intel to make sure employees perform and the organization excels. Finally, although *agreeableness* is a highly desirable personality trait in social situations, it generally is not associated with an individual's work-related behaviors or performance. Furthermore, some recent research suggests that leaders who are higher on emotional stability, extroversion, and agreeableness, while low on conscientiousness, have followers with higher job satisfaction and job commitment (Smith and Canger, 2004).

The most important managerial implication of the Big Five dimensions is that despite the reliability and robustness of the Big Five as measures of personality, no single trait is linked strongly to how well a leader or manager will perform in all types and levels of jobs. The links to leadership that do exist are relatively weak, and even a broad personality measure such as the Big Five alone cannot account for success or failure in the complex leadership process.

Other Personality Traits

Another approach to understanding the role of traits in leadership is to take into consideration personality traits that may affect the way a person leads. As is the case with the Big Five dimensions, many of the traits fit into the framework and categories proposed by Kirkpatrick and Locke (1991), discussed earlier in this chapter. We consider five such traits that affect leadership style.

LOCUS OF CONTROL The concept of locus of control, introduced by Rotter in 1966, is an indicator of an individual's sense of control over the environment and external events. People with a high internal locus of control (i.e., a high score on the scale; see Self-Assessment 3) believe that many of the events around them are a result of their actions. They feel a sense of control over their lives. They attribute their successes and failures to their own efforts. Because of this attribution, individuals with an internal locus of control are more proactive and take more risks (Anderson, Hellreigel, and Slocum, 1977). As such, they demonstrate the motivation, energy, and self-confidence proposed by Kirkpatrick and Locke (1991) to be central leadership traits. Research indicates that internals are less anxious, set harder goals, and are less conforming to authority than externals (for a review of the literature, see Spector, 1982). In addition, internals make greater efforts to achieve their goals and tend to be more task oriented than externals and are more proactive when managing stress (Nonis and Hoyt, 2004). They also tend to be more ethical in their decision making, harsher on bribery (Cherry and Fraedrich, 2000), and more open to globalization (Spears, Parker, and McDonald, 2004). Some research also indicates that internal leaders of not-for-profit organizations are more successful than externals at generating funding commitments from their members (Adeyemi-Bello, 2003).

Individuals with an external locus of control attribute the events in their lives to forces external to them—to factors such as luck, other powerful people, or a deep religious faith. They attribute their success to luck and interpersonal skills rather than to their intelligence and ability (Sightler and Wilson, 2001). In other words, they do not generally perceive a high degree of control over their lives. Therefore, they are more reactive to events and less able to rebound from stressful situations. They rely on others' judgments and conform to authority more readily than internals (Spector, 1982). As leaders, externally controlled individuals are likely to use more coercive power, a factor that stems from projecting their own sense of lack of control onto others. Because they do not feel they control events and because they tend to be reactive, they believe others will do the same and overcontrol their followers to compensate for how they perceive others.

Several studies have explored the link between leadership and locus of control. Some findings indicate that internals are more likely to emerge as group leaders and that groups led by internals perform better than those headed by externals (Anderson and Schneier, 1978). Other research has looked at the effect of locus of control on CEOs' behaviors and choices of strategy for their organizations. The results indicate that internally controlled CEOs select risky and innovative strategies for their firms to a higher degree than do externals (Miller and Droge, 1986; Miller, Kets de Vries, and Toulouse, 1982). They also tend to be more proactive and future oriented, as indicated by the findings that internals are more entrepreneurial (Hansemark, 2003).

Although research is limited, the pattern of results is highly consistent. A clear difference is evident between the behavior and decision-making patterns of internally and externally controlled individuals. Such patterns are not the only determinant of a leader's behavior, but they potentially affect a leader's actions.

TYPE A   Beginning in the late 1960s, researchers have focused on the concept of the Type A behavior pattern as a risk factor for coronary disease (Glass, 1983; Rosenman and Friedman, 1974). Psychologists and management researchers are also interested in the Type A personality (Baron, 1989). Generally, Type As are described as trying to do more in less and less time. As compared with Type Bs, they are involved in a whirlwind of activity. At the heart of the Type A construct is the need for control (Smith and Rhodewalt, 1986; Strube and Werner, 1985). As opposed to Type Bs, who tend to have less need for control, Type A individuals show a high need for control, which manifests itself in four general characteristics (Figure 3). It is important to note that although Type A and locus of control both rely on the concept of control, the two measures

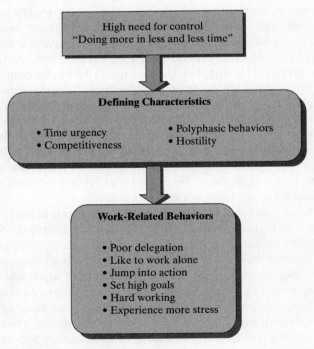

FIGURE 3   Type A Characteristics and Behaviors

are not related. Locus of control indicates the extent to which an individual feels in control of events; Type A indicates the need for control.

The first Type A characteristic, time urgency, leads Type A individuals to be concerned with time. Being in a hurry, impatience with delays, and worries about time are aspects of time urgency. Jordan Zimmerman, CEO of Zimmerman Advertising starts his day at 3:30 a.m. with a three-hour exercise regimen that he believes gives him energy (Buchanan, 2010). Krissi Bar, founder of the consulting firm Barr Corporate Success, forces herself to work faster: "If I think something is going to take me an hour, I give myself 40 minutes. By shrinking your mental dead-lines, you work faster and with greater focus" (Buchanan, 2010, p. 66). Carol Bartz of Yahoo, talking about not too much time to think through issues says, "This fits my impatient nature of 'doing' very well, and my belief that it's always worth spending energy on 'doing' something better" (Sellers, 2009). The second Type A characteristic is competitiveness. Type A individuals are generally highly competitive in work, social, and sport situations. They measure their out-comes against others and keep track of their performance; getting ahead and winning are major concerns. Legendary Boston Celtics basketball star Larry Bird demonstrated many of the Type A characteristics. When talking about playing against Magic Johnson and his relationship with the LA Lakers star, he states: "I had to have him there as someone I can compare myself to" (Heistand, 2010). The third characteristic, polyphasic behaviors, involves doing several things at once. Although everyone is likely to undertake several activities when pressured, Type As often do so even when not required to by work or other deadlines. For example, they might make a list of specific activities to undertake during a vacation. The last Type A characteristic is hostility. It is the only characteristic still found by researchers to be tied to coronary problems and other health problems (Alspach, 2004). It is manifested in explosive speech, diffused anger, intoler-ance for delays or mistakes, and a generally fiery, aggressive (Baron, Neuman, and Geddes, 1999), and sometimes malicious style of interaction (Strube et al., 1984).These four sets of char-acteristics are triggered by the Type A's need for control and are aimed at providing the Type A with a sense of control over the environment (see Self-Assessment 4).

Type A characteristics are neither bad nor good. Type As and Type Bs possess certain traits and behaviors that can either be helpful or provide obstacles to being effective leaders; situational requirements are the key. The relationship of Type A to leadership has not been extensively stud-ied, but a number of findings that link Type A behavior to work-related behaviors provide interest-ing insights. The results of one study suggest that being Type A affects the way CEOs approach organizational strategy (Nahavandi, Mizzi, and Malekzadeh, 1992). Type A executives see more threats in the environment of their organizations and set challenging strategies that still provide them with a sense of control. Furthermore, as compared with Type Bs, Type As tend to be poor delegators and generally prefer to work alone (Miller, Lack, and Asroff, 1985). They like to main-tain control over all aspects of their work. The lack of delegation can be damaging to a leader and often is considered a major pitfall of management. Furthermore, with the increasing focus on co-operation, use of teams, and empowerment as a leadership style, the inability to delegate can pres-ent an obstacle to successful leadership.

As can be seen in the example of Jeffrey Katzenberg, Type As tend to set high perform-ance goals and have high expectations for themselves and those around them. Such high expec-tations may lead to faster promotions at lower organizational levels (Stewart-Belle and Lust, 1999). When taken in a leadership context, such high expectations can lead to high performance and high quality, as well as to overload and burnout when carried to an extreme. Type As, be-sides having high expectations, do not recognize and admit that they are tired. They are hard workers who might not understand other people's less-intense approach to work. Scott Rudin,

LEADING CHANGE

Jeffrey Katzenberg's Transformation

Jeffrey Katzenberg could be a poster child for the ambitious, impatient, competitive, angry, and highly successful Type A executive. He held top jobs at Paramount pictures and Disney, where he was responsible for hits such as *Aladdin* and *The Lion King*, before being publicly and unceremoniously fired from Disney in 1994. Katzenberg then teamed up with Steven Spielberg and David Geffen to start Dream Works Animation SKG, which has produced even bigger hits, including the Shrek movies and *Monsters vs. Aliens*. Aside from his amazing talent and continued success, Katzenberg had a reputation for being demanding, sometimes unreasonable, and having very public outbursts of anger, lashing out at colleagues and Hollywood stars. A Disney official states: "He was a screamer, and he was a shredder and a very tough force to be reckoned with" (Borden, 2009, p. 106).

Katzenberg seems to have changed, to a great extent, according to Katzenberg himself, as a result of his firing in 1994, "Getting fired when you're doing your best work can wake you up pretty well. It's called a swift kick in the butt. But I learned from that experience that change is good. You know the saying, 'What doesn't kill you makes you stronger?' Well, I'm an optimist. My attitude is when one door closes, another opens" (Ten minutes, 2010). Katzenberg fully admits to his drive, which started early in his life. When describing some early leadership experiences he says: "The thing we all actually wished we had more of was time. I've never forgotten that. I'm always very punctual, and when I'm not, I have high, high anxiety (Bryant, 2009). But he has learned to temper his impatience, having become aware of its effects on followers. He uses what he calls a "five-second tape delay" to "self-edit" before he expresses his opinion and is careful to consider that others may not want to work at the same pace he does: "Something that I was kind of oblivious to for a long period of time is that I ended up setting a pace for everyone else, and they assumed if the boss is working 24/7, then we all must work 24/7. That's not such a good thing because not everyone loves it as much as I do, and it's not actually how you get the best out of people" (Bryant, 2009). Although still not mellow by most people's standards, Katzenberg has altered his behavior to focus on valuing those who work for him and keeping some balance in his life and with his wife of 34 years. His biggest leadership lesson is to cultivate his followers: "I started to realize that if I wanted to stay surrounded by great people, I had to get out of their way and create the room and make sure they started to get the recognition and the credit and everything that goes with it. Honestly, it allowed me to stay around longer" (Bryant, 2009).

Sources: Borden, M. 2010. The redemption of an ogre. *Fast Company* December/January: 104–108; Bryant, A. 2009. The benefit of a boot out the door. *New York Times—Corner Office*, November 7. http://www.nytimes.com/2009/11/08/business/08corner.html?_r=1 (accessed March 2, 2010); Ten minutes that mattered. 2010. *Forbes.com* February 5. http://www.forbes.com/2010/02/04/disney-dreamworks-shrek-intelligent-technology-katzenberg.html (accessed on March 2, 2010).

the Hollywood producer we discussed earlier, is at work at 6:30 a.m. and works at high speed until late hours of the night, expecting his assistants to be there with him all along. Avery Baker, senior vice president of marketing at Tommy Hilfiger, and her boyfriend, Tony Kruz, managing director at Capital Alliance Partners, are both in high-pressure jobs they love that require long hours and extensive travel (each log 400,000 and 300,000 miles a year, respectively; Tischler, 2005). Both sleep only a few hours a night as they hop around the globe, not seeing each other for weeks at a time. Gérard Mestrallet, the CEO of the French energy giant GDF Suez, is obsessed with his company's performance so much so that he interrupts interviews to check on stock prices (Tomlinson, 2000). Although he often appears relaxed and can be very patient about achieving his company's goals, one of his primary values is working hard (Davidson, 2009). Carlos Ghosn, CEO of Nissan Motors and Renault, the French car maker, cut back from a 16-hour day to a 14-hour day, stating, "I'm saving energy that I need for the future . . . I'm conscious that what's important is to be able to last" (Alderman, 2005: C8).

One manifestation of the hard-driving Type A behavior in U.S. business is how little vacation time Type A people take. Gian Lombardo, who together with his wife manufactures luxury luggage, hardly ever takes a vacation or enjoys those he takes. During his last one, he spent all his time in his hotel room on his BlackBerry (his wife calls it Pearl, his mistress). He admits that he is a "total nutcase" (Conlin, 2007). Tom DeMarco, a high-tech consultant, suggests that many companies believe that they are "effective only to the extent that all their workers are totally and eternally busy" (Anders, 2001: 28). Such an approach pushes employees and managers to take on many Type A characteristics.

> Type As tend to set high performance goals and have high expectations for themselves and those around them. Such high expectations lead to faster promotions at lower organizational levels (Stewart-Belle and Lust, 1999). When taken in a leadership context, such high expectations can lead to high performance and high quality, as well as to overload and burnout when carried to an extreme.

As is the case with locus of control, the Type A construct is linked directly to leadership in only a few studies. The consistency of the findings that Type As like to maintain control, are active and hard working, and tend to be impatient with delays and with their coworkers, however, allows us to consider the potential implications for leadership. These behaviors are similar to the high energy and motivation that Kirkpatrick and Locke (1991) propose as central leadership traits. Type A leaders are likely to be intense and demanding, set high performance standards, and be intolerant of delays and excuses. They also might find it difficult to delegate tasks or work in a team environment. Some recent research suggests that Type As and Bs both prefer working in teams made up of others similar to them (Keinan and Koren, 2002). Other research indicates that Type As and Bs may be effective in different types of jobs (Rastogi and Dave, 2004). Yet, although some Type A characteristics appear to define effective leaders (i.e., drive, ambition, and energy) others aspects, such as impatience with delays and a tendency to jump into action, are characteristics that do not serve leaders well. One recent study found that Type A personality is related to depression and lower individual performance over time (Watson, 2006).

SELF-MONITORING When observing some leaders, we can identify their style and even personality traits easily. They seem to be an open book, and their behavior is consistent in many different situations. For example, Herb Kelleher, founder of Southwest Airlines, has a forceful but open style in all settings, whether he is dealing with the Southwest employees or stockholders or presenting at a business conference. Similarly, it was never hard for anyone to read Michael Eisner, the former CEO of Disney; he was highly aggressive and demanding in all settings with a take-no-prisoners approach (he was the one who fired Jeffrey Katzenberg described in the Leading Change case). Other leaders are harder to read, or their behaviors appear to change from one situation to another.

One reason it might be easy to read some people and establish their style but difficult to do so for others is self-monitoring. Developed by Snyder (1974), the self-monitoring scale identifies the degree to which people are capable of reading and using the cues from their environment to determine their behavior. High self-monitors (SM)—individuals who score high on the scale (see Self-Assessment 5)—are able to read environmental and social cues regarding what is appropriate behavior and use those cues to adjust their behaviors. They can present themselves, manage impressions (Turnley and Bolino, 2001), and are able to mirror and mimic others' behaviors better than low SMs (Estow, Jamieson, and Yates, 2007). Studies also find that high SMs are particularly good at getting along with others, may be more likely to emerge as leaders because of their ability to get ahead (Day and Schleicher, 2006), and that they may be more adaptive and innovative (Hutchinson and Skinner, 2007). Low SMs either do not read the cues or do not use them to change their behavior. For high SMs, behavior is likely to be the result of a perception of the environment and is therefore likely to change depending on the situation. Low SMs' behaviors are more internally determined and are likely to appear constant across different situations. This internal focus also seems to make them more accurate decision makers regarding performance ratings and personnel decisions (Jawahar, 2001).

Many leadership theories rely on the assumptions that leaders (1) have the ability to evaluate various situations and (2) can change their behaviors to match the requirements of the situation. In that context, being a high SM might become a key leadership trait. Being a high SM should help a leader better perceive and analyze a situation. Furthermore, given SMs' higher ability to adjust their behaviors, it is reasonable to suggest that, at least in situations that are ambiguous and difficult to read, they might be more effective leaders. Some studies support these ideas (e.g., Dobbins et al., 1990). Researchers have found that high SMs emerge as leaders more frequently than do low SMs, leading to the hypothesis that self-monitoring is a key variable in leadership and job performance (Day, Schleicher, Unckless, and Hiller, 2002). The concept has also been linked to transformational leadership behaviors. Interesting findings have further emerged regarding the link between Type A and self-monitoring, as well as the role that gender might play in self-monitoring.

Several studies looked at the impact of gender, self-monitoring, and Type A on conflict management and leadership in organizations (Baron, 1989; Becker, Ayman, and Korabik, 1994; Dobbins et al., 1990). The studies indicated the following results:

- High SMs emerge as leaders more often than do low self-monitors.
- Men emerge as leaders more often than do women.
- Type As are in conflict more often than are Type Bs, particularly when dealing with their subordinates.
- High SMs resolve conflicts cooperatively when dealing with their subordinates and their supervisors.
- Women generally report lower levels of conflict with both their subordinates and their supervisors.
- High self-monitoring women are especially sensitive to various organizational cues and seem to perceive more conflict.

Overall, self-monitoring presents interesting potential applications to leadership, many of which continue to remain unexplored (for a discussion of the potential impact of self-monitoring on leadership, see Bedeian and Day, 2004). Little doubt remains, however, that being a high SM can be a useful characteristic in helping leaders adjust their behaviors and perhaps even in learning new skills. High SMs may be better able to cope with cross-cultural experiences because such situations are ambiguous and require the ability to interpret environmental cues. Similarly, the changing leadership roles are making leadership situations considerably less routine and more uncertain than they were 20 years ago. Modern leaders must deal with diverse cultures and followers' demands for participation and autonomy, and they also need to understand an increasingly complex global environment. Self-monitoring might be a key characteristic in these new tasks.

MACHIAVELLIAN PERSONALITY Do you believe that the end justifies the means? Are you skilled at manipulating others to get what you want? Are you a ruthless, skilled negotiator? Is gaining and retaining power your major concern? If you answer positively to these questions, chances are you have some elements of a Machiavellian personality (see Self-Assessment 6). The concept of the Machiavellian personality, developed by Christie and Geis (1970), is based loosely on Niccolo Machiavelli's work, *The Prince*. The Machiavellian (Mach) scale measures an individual's willingness to put self-interests and his or her preferences above the interests of the group and a person's ability to influence and manipulate others for personal gain (Jaffe, Nebenzahl, and Gotesdyner, 1989; Panitz, 1989).

Individuals with a high score on the scale are comfortable using various means to achieve their personal goals. A high Mach views human nature cynically, shows few scruples, and is willing to step outside the bounds of formal authority. These individuals might lack the honesty and integrity that are requirements of effective leadership. They are also more flexible in the type of behavior they use to influence others, relying on emotional appeals rather than logic and rational argument (Allen, 1990; Reimers and Barbuto, 2002). On the other end of the scale, low Machs tend to be overly naive and trusting. Although research has not established clear linkages to leadership, it can be assumed that high Machs' political and manipulation skills allow them to be successful if not effective leaders (Luthans, 1989). For example, Micheal Eisner of Disney is often considered to be a high Mach. According to a 2005 book about him and the company, he kept people in uncertainty and self-doubt and purposefully created stress to take control away from them and increase his own power (Stewart, 2005). The other many recent examples of self-centered executives who showed little scruples in pursuing wealth may be an indication that high Mach may often succeed in reaching leadership positions. Their aim is to promote themselves rather than support their followers. Low Machs, on the other hand, might not demonstrate enough political savvy and therefore might be unable to provide their group with the necessary resources and visibility.

Neither the high Machs nor low Machs are likely to be effective leaders. High Machs are too focused on their personal goals and lack integrity; low Machs are not skilled at the legitimate influence tactics essential for effective leadership. In general, individuals who are medium Machs tend to be the most effective leaders. Such people are good negotiators and savvy about manipulation of others to reach goals, but they do not abuse their power, and they focus on achieving organizational rather than personal goals. Medium Machs are the ones who are capable of being successful and effective.

It can be expected from a concept that relates to perception and use of power, cross-cultural differences exist with regard to Mach scores. For example, Hong Kong and People's Republic of China (PRC) managers score higher on the Mach scale than do their U.S. counterparts. It appears that the Chinese are more willing to use social power to accomplish their goals (Ralston et al., 1993a, b). This finding fits with the concept of high power distance, where authority is broad and respected.

Our popular press is full of examples of ruthless leaders from both the private and public sectors who wheel and deal their way to achieving their goals with considerable disregard for their subordinates. They bully their employees and can even be abusive, cruel, and threatening to achieve their goals. One study reports that 45 percent of the 1,000 employees surveyed reported having worked with an abusive boss (Daniel, 2009). Some of these bosses are admired for what they can achieve; others are simply feared. Several publications regularly prepare lists of these tough bosses, and numerous Web sites are dedicated to describing power-hungry, controlling, and sometimes abusive bosses and helping employees deal with them (e.g., *Fortune* magazine and CNN.com; and bnet.com). In many cases, as long as the bottom line is healthy and key constituents, such as the board of directors or stockholders, are satisfied, the means used by these leaders are tolerated.

NARCISSISM   We have all worked with people who have an exaggerated need to be the center of attention, an oversized sense of self-importance, and a limited ability to think about others. It is difficult enough to deal with such people as colleagues, but working with them as supervisors and leaders is another challenge altogether. We call them selfish or self-absorbed; however, such behaviors are part of the concept of narcissism, which when occurring to an extreme and in a pervasive manner, has been identified as the Narcissistic Personality Disorder (NPD; American Psychiatric Association, 2000). Recent research suggests that two general themes of grandiosity and entitlement characterize narcissism (Brown, Budzek, and Tamborski, 2009). Some of the characteristics of narcissism are (see Self-Assessment 7):

- A grandiose sense of self-importance and exaggeration of one's achievements and talents
- Preoccupation with power and success
- Arrogance
- Indifference to others and self-absorption
- Inability to tolerate criticism and a fragile self-esteem
- Desire to be the center of attention at all times
- Sense of entitlement
- Exploiting others without guilt to achieve goals
- Lack of empathy for others and inability to understand others' feelings
- Trouble building meaningful relationships

Although these characteristics when all present in excess can be the basis of a psychological disorder, narcissism has also been used to describe a range of "normal" behaviors (Emons, 1987; Morf and Rhodewalt, 2001; Raskin and Hall, 1979) with possible links to and implications for leadership (Popper, 2002; Rosenthal and Pittinsky, 2006). Many narcissistic traits are related to characteristics of leaders, including desire to have power and influence over others and be in a leadership position (Brunell et al., 2008). Several aspects of the construct are part of a healthy and confident self-esteem, whereas others may be related to less-productive aspects of personality. The concept has further been linked to Machiavellianism and a subclinical form of psychopathy (Paulhus and Williams, 2002).

Well-known tyrants of history, such as Hitler and Stalin, exhibit strong narcissistic tendencies. So do other historical, social, and business leaders, including Michael Eisner and Scott Rudin, discussed earlier in this chapter, and leaders such as Alexander Hamilton, Steve Jobs of Apple, and many U.S. and world leaders, including presidents Carter, Clinton, and G.W. Bush (Rosenthal and Pittinsky, 2006). Destructive narcissistic leaders self-promote, deceive and manipulate others, respond poorly to criticism and feedback, and blame others for their failures (Delbecq, 2001; Rosenthal and Pittinsky, 2006). Their apparent high degree of self-confidence and certainty about their decisions are likely to lead to poor decisions and lapses in ethics and personal conduct related to their exaggerated sense of self and entitlement. Several researchers have linked the narcissistic arrogance to a deep sense of inferiority (e.g., Zeiger-Hill, 2006) that such leaders are able to mask with self-promotion and constant attention grabbing. One of the most negative aspects of narcissism, when it comes to leadership, is the lack of empathy for others, which when combined with paranoia and a sense of entitlement can lead to dire consequences (Judge, LePine, and Rich, 2006).

Applying What You Learn

Dealing with Narcissistic and Abusive Bosses

Many of us have been faced with supervisors and bosses who appear to have strong narcissistic characteristics. Here are some suggestions in how to deal with them. These do not all work, and different ones work depending on the situation and the person you are dealing with:

- Keep your cool; do not react with an emotional response. Self-control is essential.
- Remain professional, even if the boss is not. You can't control his or her behavior; but you can control your reaction.
- Make sure you clearly understand and are able to describe the type of behavior you are facing (e.g., too much criticism, inaccurate feedback, yelling).
- Document everything! Keep careful notes of incidents.
- Make sure that your work and behavior are impeccable and beyond reproach.

- Keep track of any feedback from coworkers and customers that can be used to document your good performance.
- Do not get defensive; respond with level-headed comments without taking the abuse.
- Seek help from HR if that is available, especially if there are legal ramifications (e.g., discrimination, sexual harassment, or other ethical or legal violations).
- Maintain good working relationships and a strong network at work.
- Go up the chain of command as a last resort; provide facts and evidence—not just emotional reactions.
- Unless the situation is dangerous, don't make a quick decision about leaving; carefully plan for contingencies and an eventual exit.
- Plan an exit strategy; look for another position.
- Only you can determine when it's too much; with planning, you can leave on your own terms.

Positive narcissistic leaders may have an exaggerated sense of self and entitlement, but they use their self-confidence, power, and influence to achieve goals, much the same way a moderate Machiavellian would. They are often charming and initially well liked (Back et al., 2010). They can therefore be a positive force for their group and their organization. Research about narcissism and its links to other personality traits and leadership is relatively new, but already some findings suggest that the level of narcissism is increasing among college students in the United States (Bergamn, et al., 2010). A link to leadership has been established in the area of charismatic and transformational leadership.

> Positive narcissistic leaders may have an exaggerated sense of self and entitlement, but they use their self-confidence, power, and influence to achieve goals, much the same way a moderate Machiavellian would. They are often charming and initially well liked. They can therefore be a positive force for their group and their organization.

Each of the preceding individual characteristics and traits plays a role in how leaders interact with others or make decisions. Any one trait alone, or even a combination, cannot explain or predict leadership effectiveness. These characteristics can be useful tools for self-awareness and understanding and can be used as guides for leadership development.

CHARACTERISTICS OF LEADERS WHO FAIL

Another way to learn about leaders' individual characteristics is to evaluate leaders who are not successful and who derail. Do they share some common characteristics? Are they any different from those who succeed? The Center for Creative Leadership conducted research tracking leaders who derail (McCall and Lombardo, 1983), and many anecdotal accounts report characteristics of leaders who do not succeed (Hymowitz, 1988; Nelton, 1997). A book by Barbara Kellerman, the director of the Center for Public Leadership at Harvard University, suggests that we can learn as much from bad leaders as we can from good ones (Kellerman, 2004). Excessive greed and corruption, incompetence, rigidity, isolation from others, and lack of caring for others are just some of the characteristics of bad leaders. The following list provides common characteristics of leaders who have failed:

- An abrasive, intimidating style
- Coldness and arrogance
- Untrustworthiness
- Self-centeredness and overly political behaviors
- Poor communication
- Poor performance
- Inability to delegate

As the list indicates, lack of people skills and the inability to manage relationships are central causes of failure. Leaders who are good with followers and other constituents face a better chance of success. Pam Alexander, the CEO of Ogilvy Public Relations Worldwide, a public relations firm that concentrates on building relationships, states, "To build trust, invest in your relationships constantly. Don't sweat the ROI; help people, whether or not they can return the favor. Connect them to appropriate opportunities whenever you can" (Canabou and Overholt, 2001: 98–102). More and more, leaders who rule with an iron fist, exercise power without accountability, and are unwilling or unable to allow followers to contribute and develop are rated poorly. Other key contributors to leadership failure are organizational factors, unrelated to the leader's style and personality. Organizational climates that tolerate or even encourage unethical behavior (e.g., Enron), boards of directors who fail to take action in time (e.g., Disney), and employees who are scared or prevented from taking action all allow the negative characteristics of leaders to affect the whole organization. Alan Greenspan, the former chairman of the U.S. Federal Reserve, observed, "It is not that humans have become any more greedy than in generations past. It is that avenues to express greed have grown so enormously" (Pink, 2002: 44).

The various individual characteristics presented in this chapter do not allow us to develop a clear leadership profile. We still do not know what traits make an effective leader. But we do know that individual difference characteristics do affect leader behavior. The different traits discussed in this chapter are generally independent from one another. In other words, an individual might have an internal locus of control, be a Type B, a high SM, moderate Mach, and positive narcissist. Although certain combinations are intuitively more likely to occur, the scales are not statistically correlated. Research in the area is limited, and it is reasonable to assume that some combinations of traits make certain traits and behaviors more salient and dominant. For example, a low SM Type A, who also happens to have an internal locus of control, is likely to have a highly proactive and aggressive style in many situations. On the other hand, a high SM Type B with low Mach and moderate or low narcissism is likely to come across as low key and considerate of others, especially if the person believes that the situation requires such behavior.

Despite the validity of the constructs presented, it is important to limit their use to the purpose for which they were developed. The characteristics discussed in this chapter are not selection tools and should not be used for promotional or other job-related decisions.

Summary and Conclusions

This chapter presents the current thinking on the role of individual characteristics in leadership effectiveness and identifies several individual differences and personality characteristics that affect a leader's style and approach. Although these individual differences do not dictate behavior, they establish a zone of comfort for certain behaviors and actions. Values are long-lasting beliefs about what is worthwhile. They are strongly influenced by culture and are one of the determinants of ethical conduct. Intelligence is one of the abilities that most affects leadership. On the one hand, even though being intelligent is related to leadership to some extent, it is not a sufficient factor to predict effectiveness. On the other hand, research suggests that the concepts of emotional and social intelligence, which focuses on interpersonal rather than cognitive abilities, may link to leadership emergence effectiveness. Creativity is another ability that might play a role in leadership effectiveness, especially in situations that require novel approaches.

One of the most reliable measures of personality is the Big Five. Although the conscientiousness and extraversion dimensions in the Big Five show some links to work-related behavior, the traits are not linked directly to leadership. Several other individual traits do link to leadership. Locus of control is an indicator of the degree to which individuals perceive that they have control over the events around them. Individuals with internal control are found to be more proactive, more satisfied with their work, and less coercive. Type A behavior also deals with issues of control but focuses on the need for control as demonstrated through a person's time urgency, competitiveness, polyphasic behaviors, and hostility. The Type A's need for control makes it difficult to delegate tasks and pushes the individual toward short-term focus and selection of strategies that maximize control. Another relevant personality trait, self-monitoring, is the degree to which individuals read and use situational cues to adjust their behavior. High self-monitors possess a degree of flexibility that might be helpful in leadership situations.

Machiavellianism focuses on the use of social power to achieve goals. High Machs are adept at manipulating others to achieve their personal goals. The concept is related to the last personality trait we discussed, narcissism. With a grandiose and exaggerated sense of self and low concern for others, those with high narcissistic characteristics have the potential for being highly destructive leaders, although some of the traits associated with the construct are part of leadership.

All the concepts discussed in this chapter allow for better self-understanding and awareness, but none is a measure of leadership style. The measures are well validated, but they are not designed to be used for selection or promotion decisions.

Review and Discussion Questions

1. What is the impact of individual characteristics on behavior?
2. How do values affect behaviors, and what impact does culture have on our value system?
3. How do emotional intelligence and general intelligence affect leadership?
4. What role does creativity play in leadership?
5. Describe the six personality traits and their implications for leadership.
6. In your opinion (or based on your experience), do certain characteristics and traits have a greater impact than others on a person's leadership style? Explain your answer.
7. What are the limitations of the personality approach presented in this chapter, and how should the information about personal characteristics be used in leadership?
8. After completing the personality self-assessment surveys at the end of this chapter, consider your personal profile. What is the impact of this profile on your leadership style?

Leadership Challenge: Using Psychological Testing

Organizations are relying increasingly on psychological tests to select, evaluate, promote, and develop their employees and managers. Although many of the tests are reliable and valid, many others are not. In addition, tests developed in one culture do not always apply or have predictive validity in other cultures. However, such tests do provide a seemingly quick and efficient way to get to know people better.

As a department manager, you are faced with the selection of a new team of 10 members to run the marketing research and advertising campaign for a new product. The ideal employee profile includes intelligence, creativity, assertiveness, competitiveness, ability to

persuade others and negotiate well, and ability to work with a team. Your human resources department conducted extensive testing of 50 inside and outside applicants for the new team. As you review the candidates' files, you notice that the majority of candidates who fit the profile best are young, Caucasian males; whereas women and minorities tend to have low scores, particularly on assertiveness and competitiveness.

1. How much weight do you give the psychological tests? What factors do you need to consider?
2. Who do you select for the team?

Exercise 1 Your Ideal Organization

This exercise is designed to help understand the way different individuals perceive and define organizations.

Part I: Individual Description

Think of working in the organization of your dreams. What would it look like? How would it be organized? How would people interact? Your assignment in this part of the exercise is to provide a description of your ideal organization. In doing so, consider the following organizational characteristics and elements.

1. What industry would it be?

2. What is the mission of your ideal organization?

3. What is the culture? What are the basic assumptions? What are the behavioral norms? Who are the heroes? How do people interact?

4. How would people be organized? What is the structure? Consider issues of centralization, hierarchy, formalization, specialization, span of control, departmentation, and so on.

5. What is the role of the leader? What is the role of followers?

Individual Differences and Traits

6. Describe the physical location, office spaces, office decor, and so on.

7. Consider issues such as dress code, work schedules, and others that you think are important in describing your ideal organization.

Part II: Group Work
Your instructor will assign you to a group and provide you with further instructions.

Self-Assessment 1: Value Systems

Rank the values in each of the two categories from 1 (most important to you) to 5 (least important to you).

Rank	Instrumental Values	Rank	Terminal Values
_____	Ambition and hard work	_____	Contribution and a sense of accomplishment
_____	Honesty and integrity	_____	Happiness
_____	Love and affection	_____	Leisurely life
_____	Obedience and duty	_____	Wisdom and maturity
_____	Independence and self-sufficiency	_____	Individual dignity
_____	Humility	_____	Justice and fairness
_____	Doing good to others (Golden rule)	_____	Spiritual salvation

Scoring Key: The values that you rank highest in each group are the ones that are most important to you. Consider whether your actions, career choices, and so forth are consistent with your values.

Source: Based on C. Anderson, "Values-based management," *Academy of Management Executive* 11, no. 4 (1997): 25–46; M. Rokeach, *Beliefs, Attitudes, and Values* (San Francisco: Jossey-Bass, 1968).

Self-Assessment 2: Emotional Intelligence

Indicate whether each of the following statements is true or false for you.

Self-Awareness

_____ 1. I am aware of how I feel and why.

_____ 2. I understand how my feelings affect my behavior and my performance.

_____ 3. I have a good idea of my personal strengths and weaknesses.

_____ 4. I analyze things that happen to me and reflect on what happened.

_____ 5. I am open to feedback from others.

_____ 6. I look for opportunities to learn more about myself.

_____ 7. I put my mistakes in perspective.

_____ 8. I maintain a sense of humor and can laugh about my mistakes.

Managing Emotions and Self-Regulation

_____ 9. I can stay calm in times of crisis.

_____ 10. I think clearly and stay focused when under pressure.

_____ 11. I show integrity in all my actions.

_____ 12. People can depend on my word.

_____ 13. I readily admit my mistakes.

_____ 14. I confront the unethical actions of others.

_____ 15. I stand for what I believe in.

_____ 16. I handle change well and stay the course.

_____ 17. I can be flexible when facing obstacles.

Self-Motivation

_____ 18. I set challenging goals.

_____ 19. I take reasonable and measured risks to achieve my goals.

_____ 20. I am results oriented.

_____ 21. I look for information on how to achieve my goals and improve my performance.

_____ 22. I go above and beyond what is simply required of me.

_____ 23. I am always looking for opportunities to do new things.

_____ 24. I maintain a positive attitude even when I face obstacles and setbacks.

_____ 25. I focus on success rather than failure.

_____ 26. I don't take failure personally or blame myself too much.

Empathy for Others

_____ 27. I pay attention to how others feel and react.

_____ 28. I can see someone else's point of view, even when I don't agree with them.

_____ 29. I am sensitive to other people.

_____ 30. I offer feedback and try to help others achieve their goals.

_____ 31. I recognize and reward others for their accomplishments.

_____ 32. I am available to coach and mentor people.

_____ 33. I respect people from varied backgrounds.

_____ 34. I relate well to people who are different from me.

_____ 35. I challenge intolerance, bias, and discrimination in others.

Social Skills

_____ 36. I am skilled at persuading others.

_____ 37. I can communicate clearly and effectively.

_____ 38. I am a good listener.
_____ 39. I can accept bad as well as good news.
_____ 40. I can share my vision with others and inspire them to follow my lead.
_____ 41. I lead by example.
_____ 42. I challenge the status quo when necessary.
_____ 43. I can handle difficult people tactfully.
_____ 44. I encourage open and professional discussions when there are disagreements.
_____ 45. I look for win-win solutions.
_____ 46. I build and maintain relationships with others.
_____ 47. I help maintain a positive climate at work.
_____ 48. I model team qualities such as respect, helpfulness, and cooperation.
_____ 49. I encourage participation from everyone when I work in teams.
_____ 50. I understand political forces that operate in organizations.

Scoring Key: For each of the 50 items, give yourself a 1 if you marked "true" and 0 if you marked "false." Consider your total for each of the subscales and your overall total score:

Self-awareness:	_____	out of 8
Managing emotions and self-regulation:	_____	out of 9
Self-motivation:	_____	out of 9
Empathy for others:	_____	out of 9
Social skills:	_____	out of 15
Overall total:	_____	out of 50

Those with higher scores in each category, and overall, demonstrate more of the characteristics associated with high emotional intelligence. Some things you can keep in mind as you focus on developing your EQ:

- Keep a journal to track your behavior and progress.
- Seek help from friends, coworkers, and mentors.
- Work on controlling your temper and your moods; stay composed, positive, and tactful when facing difficult situations.
- Stay true to your words and commitments.
- Build relationships and a wide network.
- Practice active listening and pay attention to those around you.

Source: Based on information in D. Goleman, *Working with Emotional Intelligence* (New York: Bantam Books, 1998); MOSAIC competencies for professional and administrative occupations (U.S. Office of Personnel Management); Richard H. Rosier (ed.), *The Competency Model Handbook*, Volumes One and Two (Boston: Linkage, 1994 and 1995).

Self-Assessment 3: Locus of Control

Read the following statements and indicate whether you agree with Choice A or Choice B.

	A	B	
1.	Making a lot of money is largely a matter of getting the right breaks.	Promotions are earned through hard work and persistence.	____
2.	I have noticed a direct connection between how hard I study and the grade I get.	Many times the reactions of teachers seem haphazard to me.	____
3.	The number of divorces indicates that more and more people are not trying to make their marriages work.	Marriage is largely a gamble.	____
4.	It is silly to think that one can really change another person's basic attitudes.	When I am right I can convince others.	____
5.	Getting promoted is really a matter of being a little luckier than the next person.	In our society a person's future earning power depends on his or her ability.	____
6.	If one knows how to deal with people, he or she is really quite easily led.	I have little influence over the way other people behave.	____
7.	The grades I make are the results of my own efforts; luck has little or nothing to do with it.	Sometimes I feel I have little to do with the grades I get.	____
8.	People like me can change the course of world affairs if we make ourselves heard.	It is only wishful thinking to believe that one can readily influence what happens in our society at large.	____
9.	A great deal that happens to me is probably a matter of chance.	I am the master of my fate.	____
10.	Getting along with people is a skill that must be practiced.	It is almost impossible to figure out how to please some people.	____

Scoring Key: Give yourself 1 point for each of the following selections: 1B, 2A, 3A, 4B, 6A, 7A, 8A, 9B, and 10A. Scores are interpreted as follows:

8–10 = High internal locus of control   5 = Mixed

6–7 = Moderate internal locus   3–4 = Moderate external locus of control of control

1–2 = High external locus of control

Source: Adapted with permission from Julian B. Rotter, "External Control and Internal Control," *Psychology Today*, June 1971: 42. Copyright 1971 by the American Psychological Association.

Self-Assessment 4: Type A

Indicate whether each of the following items is true or false for you.

_____ 1. I am always in a hurry.
_____ 2. I have list of things I have to achieve on a daily or weekly basis.
_____ 3. I tend to take one problem or task at a time, finish, then move to the next one.
_____ 4. I tend to take a break or quit when I get tired.
_____ 5. I am always doing several things at once both at work and in my personal life.
_____ 6. People who know me would describe my temper as hot and fiery.
_____ 7. I enjoy competitive activities.
_____ 8. I tend to be relaxed and easygoing.
_____ 9. Many things are more important to me than my job.
_____ 10. I really enjoy winning both at work and at play.
_____ 11. I tend to rush people along or finish their sentences for them when they are taking too long.
_____ 12. I enjoy "doing nothing" and just hanging out.

Scoring Key: Type A individuals tend to answer questions 1, 2, 5, 6, 7, 10, and 11 as true and questions 3, 4, 8, 9, and 12 as false. Type B individuals tend to answer in the reverse (1, 2, 5, etc. as false and 3, 4, etc. as true and so forth).

Self-Assessment 5: Self-Monitoring

Indicate the degree to which you think the following statements are true or false by writing the appropriate number. For example, if a statement is always true, you should write 5 next to that statement.

5 = Certainly always true

4 = Generally true

3 = Somewhat true, but with exceptions

2 = Somewhat false, but with exceptions

1 = Generally false

0 = Certainly always false

_____ 1. In social situations, I have the ability to alter my behavior if I feel that something else is called for.

_____ 2. I am often able to read people's true emotions correctly through their eyes.

_____ 3. I have the ability to control the way I come across to people, depending on the impression I wish to give them.

_____ 4. In conversations, I am sensitive to even the slightest change in the facial expression of the person I'm conversing with.

_____ 5. My powers of intuition are quite good when it comes to understanding others' emotions and motives.

_____ 6. I can usually tell when others consider a joke in bad taste, even though they may laugh convincingly.

_____ 7. I feel that the image I am portraying isn't working, I can readily change it to something that does.

_____ 8. I can usually tell when I've said something inappropriate by reading the listener's eyes.

_____ 9. I have trouble changing my behavior to suit different people and different situations.

_____ 10. I have found that I can adjust my behavior to meet the requirements of any situation I find myself in.

_____ 11. If someone is lying to me, I usually know it at once from the person's manner or expression.

_____ 12. Even when it might be to my advantage, I have difficulty putting up a good front.

_____ 13. Once I know what the situation calls for, it's easy for me to regulate my actions accordingly.

Scoring Key: To obtain your score, add up the numbers written, except reverse the scores for questions 9 and 12. On 9 and 12, 5 becomes 0, 4 becomes 1, and so forth. High self-monitors are defined as those with score of approximately 53 or higher.

Source: R. D. Lennox and R. N. Wolfe, "Revision of the self-monitoring scale," *Journal of Personality and Social Psychology*, June 1984: 1361. Copyright by the American Psychological Association. Reprinted with permission.

Self-Assessment 6: Machiavellianism

For each statement, circle the number that most closely resembles your attitude.

Statements	Disagree			Agree	
	A lot	**A little**	**Neutral**	**A little**	**A lot**
1. The best way to handle people is to tell them what they want to hear.	1	2	3	4	5
2. When you ask someone to do something for you, it is best to give the real reason for wanting it rather than giving reasons that might carry more weight.	1	2	3	4	5
3. Anyone who completely trusts anyone else is asking for trouble.	1	2	3	4	5
4. It is hard to get ahead without cutting corners here and there.	1	2	3	4	5
5. It is safest to assume that all people have a vicious streak and that it will come out when they are given a chance.	1	2	3	4	5
6. One should take action only when it is morally right.	1	2	3	4	5
7. Most people are basically good and kind.	1	2	3	4	5
8. There is no excuse for lying to someone else.	1	2	3	4	5
9. Most people more easily forget the death of their father than the loss of their property.	1	2	3	4	5
10. Generally speaking, people won't work hard unless they're forced to do so.	1	2	3	4	5

Scoring Key: To obtain your Mach score, add the number you circled on questions 1, 3, 4, 5, 9, and 10. For the other four questions, reverse the numbers you circled: 5 becomes 1, 4 becomes 2, and so forth. Total your 10 numbers to find your score. The higher your score, the more Machiavellian you are. Among a random sample of American adults, the average Mach score was 25.

Source: R. Christie and F. L. Geis, *Studies in Machiavellianism* (New York: Academic Press, 1970). Copyright Academic Press. Reprinted with permission.

Self-Assessment 7: Narcissism

For each of the following statements, indicate the degree to which you think each describes you by writing the appropriate number. For example, if a statement fits you well and sounds a lot like you, you would write 4.

1 = Does not sound like me at all/does not fit me at all

2 = Does not sound like me

3 = Sounds like me

4 = Sounds a lot like me/fits me very well

_____ 1. I see myself as a good leader.
_____ 2. I know that I am good because everyone tells me so.
_____ 3. I can usually talk my way out of anything.
_____ 4. Everybody likes to hear my stories.
_____ 5. I expect a great from other people.
_____ 6. I am assertive.
_____ 7. I like to display my body.
_____ 8. I find it easy to manipulate other people to get what I want.
_____ 9. I don't need anyone to help me get things done.
_____ 10. I insist on getting the respect I deserve.
_____ 11. I like having authority over other people.
_____ 12. I enjoy showing off.
_____ 13. I can read people like a book.
_____ 14. I always know what I am doing.
_____ 15. I will not be satisfied until I get all that I deserve.
_____ 16. People always seem to recognize my authority.
_____ 17. I enjoy being the center of attention.
_____ 18. I can make anybody believe anything.
_____ 19. I seem to be better at most things than other people.
_____ 20. I get upset when people don't notice me or recognize my accomplishments.
_____ 21. I enjoy being in charge and telling people what to do.
_____ 22. I like to be complimented.
_____ 23. I can get my way in most situations.
_____ 24. I think I am a special person.
_____ 25. I deserve more than the average person because I am better than most people.
_____ 26. I have a natural talent for leadership.
_____ 27. I like to look at myself in the mirror.
_____ 28. I know how to get others to do what I want.
_____ 29. The world would be a better place if I was in charge.
_____ 30. I am going to be a great person.

Scoring Key:

Desire for power and leadership (L): add up scores for items: 1, 6, 11, 16, 21, and 26:

Total: _____

Need for admiration and self-admiration (SA): add up scores for items: 2, 7, 12, 17, 22, and 27.

Total: _____

Exploitiveness (EX): add up scores for items: 3, 8, 13, 18, 23, and 28.

Total: _____

Individual Differences and Traits

Arrogance and a sense of superiority (A): add up scores for items: 4, 9, 14, 19, 24, and 29.

Total: _____

Sense of entitlement (ET): add up scores for items: 5, 10, 15, 20, 25, and 30.

Total: _____

Add up the total for the five subscales: (30 lowest to 120 highest possible score).

Interpreting Your Score

The five subscales are the key factors in narcissism. The highest possible total in each subscale is 24, with highest possible total score of 120. The higher your scores, the more narcissistic characteristics you have. Some degree of narcissism is associated with healthy self-esteem and effective leadership.

Sources: Based on Emmons, 1987; Raskin and Terry, 1988; Rosenthal and Pittinsky, 2006.

LEADERSHIP IN ACTION

Pernille Spiers-Lopez Assembles a Winning Team at IKEA

"Leadership is about me. It's about what I stand for and my values. . . . It is about being in front of everybody and taking steps that others can't always see" (Pernille Spiers-Lopez, 2004). Effective leadership starts with self-examination, states Spiers-Lopez, Head of Global Human Resources for IKEA since 2009 and former president of IKEA North America. She attributes her success to her passion about her work (Gutner, 2008). This philosophy leads to clear priorities in her life: her family comes first. "I am very aware of the necessary give-and-take between the importance of my work and of my life at home. . . . I have no illusions about obtaining a complete balance. Ultimately there isn't one" (Marcus, 2007). She was forced to clarify her values in 1999 after she was taken to the emergency room with what first appeared to be a heart attack, but turned out to be an extreme stress reaction. She recalls, "I was going and going and going. . . . I said to myself, 'so this is success'" (Mendels, 2005). Since then she takes time for yoga and meditation, and she has worked on clarifying her values, which has not only helped her to chart the course for her own career, but has also guided her goals and strategies as a leader.

IKEA, the Danish furniture maker, achieved success with customers wherever it opened stores in 31 countries in Europe, Asia, and North America. In North America, the company's success is partly because of the leadership of Pernille Spiers-Lopez since February 2001, when she was appointed president of IKEA North America. Since joining the company, first in human resource management, Spiers-Lopez has made nurturing coworkers, as employees are called, one of her major goals. In addition to flexible and creative work hours, partner's health benefits, full benefits for part-time workers, a generous maternity leave policy, and a family-friendly environment, IKEA is mindful of providing its employees with opportunities to spend quality time with family and friends. Spiers-Lopez believes that "if an employee's personal life is in disarray, it can affect their productivity at work" (Fleury, 2004). So the company does its best to help employees balance their work and life and create an egalitarian workplace both in terms of philosophy and actual physical space. Describing the new IKEA headquarters in Pennsylvania, Spiers-Lopez states, "We wanted a workplace that embraces our 'we are all equal' organization, to be able to live like a family and share our core beliefs; a home that caters to conversation, open ideas and collaboration" (Van Allen, 2007). She further believes, "We empower our coworkers and respect people's personal lives. . . . This has a tremendous influence on job productivity, growth, and development, which ultimately benefits our customers" (Fleury, 2004).

Her efforts have paid off, not only in providing excellent customer service and high sales but also in attracting and maintaining coworkers, who are essential in delivering those results. In October 2004, IKEA was named one of *Working Mother* magazine's 100 best companies for working mothers, and Spiers-Lopez was singled out for the Family Champion Award (Fleury, 2004). During Spiers-Lopez's tenure, staff turnover dropped from 77 to 36 percent (Meisler, 2004). With more than 8,000 workers in 11 states in the United States alone, sales exceeded $2.5 billion in 2006 (Van Allen, 2007). Spiers-Lopez has also influenced IKEA's overall corporate culture. With close to a majority of employees being female, almost half of the company's 75 top earners are also female; the board of IKEA North America has gone from one female member to five (Mieser, 2004).

Spiers-Lopez's focus on employees stems from her personal values and drive. In her mid-forties, she is married to Jason Lopez, a high school principal, and they have two teenagers.

Every day she faces the struggles of balancing her life and career and addressing her personal and career goals. One of her mentors, Ulf Caap, says that she often carries heavier loads than she should and that "she has the guts and fire to go where few people ever go" (Binzen, 2004). Although she strives to maintain the balance in her own life, she is driven to deliver results beyond her own expectations. Her husband and staff remind her to keep her balance and take breaks. They make fun of her being tireless and pushing herself and others too hard (Meiser,

2004). Interestingly, Spiers-Lopez does not like to make too many plans for the future. "We live in complexity and ambiguity, and I have to be comfortable with that. I think leadership today is really about enjoying change."

Questions

1. What are Spiers-Lopez's key individual characteristics?
2. What are the factors that contribute to her effectiveness?

Sources: Binzen, P., 2004. "IKEA boss assembles happy staffs," *Philadelphia Inquirer*, September 29; Fleury, M., 2004. *Working Mother* magazine award winner. http://www.suite101.com/print_article.cfm/3684/110941 (accessed on December 10, 2004); Gutner, T. 2008. Pernille Spier-Lopez, President of IKEA North American. *The Wall Street* Journal, September 15. http://online.wsj.com/article/SB121917019283353835.html (accessed on March 9, 2010); Marcus, M., 2007. "Finding the balance: Pernille Spiers-Lopez," *Forbes*, March 19. http://www.forbes.com/2007/03/19/spiers-lopez-balance-lead-careers-work-life07-cx_mlm_0319spierslopez.html (accessed on July 20, 2007); Meisler, A., 2004. "Success, Scandinavian style," *Workforce Management*, August: 26–32; Women's Leadership Exchange. Pernille Spiers-Lopez President, IKEA North America. http://www.womensleadershipexchange.com/index.php?pagename=la&sectionkey=17#66; Mendels, P., 2005. "When work hits home," *All Business*, March 1. http://www.allbusiness.com/human-resources/employee-development-leadership/366999-1.html (accessed on July 11, 2007); Van Allen, P., 2007. "IKEA tenets part of the its HQ," *Philadelphia Business Journal*, January 19. http://www.bizjournals.com/philadelphia/stories/2007/01/22/story5.html (accessed on July 11, 2007).

Power

From Chapter 5 of *The Art and Science of Leadership*, 6/e. Afsaneh Nahavandi. Copyright © 2012 by Pearson Education. Published by Prentice Hall. All rights reserved.

Power

Nearly all men can stand adversity, but if you want to test a man's character, give him power.

—ABRAHAM LINCOLN

You can have power over people as long as you don't take everything away from them. But when you've robbed a man of everything, he's no longer in your power.

—ALEXANDR SOLZHENITSYN

After studying this chapter, you will be able to:

- Define power and its key role in leadership.
- Understand the cross-cultural differences in the definition and use of power.
- Identify the individual and organizational sources of power available to leaders.
- Describe the consequences of power for the leader, followers, and organizations.
- Understand the role of power in the leadership and effectiveness of teams.
- Identify the power sources available to top executives.
- Explain the causes of power abuse and corruption and present ways to prevent them.
- Trace the changes in use of power and the development of empowerment, and explain their consequences for leadership.

Power and leadership are inseparable. An integral part of the study of leadership is understanding power, how leaders use it, and what its impact is on leaders, followers, and organizations. Power is necessary and essential to effective leadership. Leaders need power to get things done. Without it, they cannot guide their followers to achieve their goals. Without power, things do not get done. We expect great things from our leaders and provide them with wide latitude and power to accomplish goals. They make decisions that have considerable financial and social impact on a wide range of stakeholders inside and outside their organizations. Using their power, department heads, CEOs, and city mayors implement strategies to achieve organizational goals. They influence those around them to take needed action, and they promote, hire, and fire their employees. None of these actions would be possible without power. Along with the power granted to leaders comes great privilege. In addition to high salaries and other financial incentives (some of the highest in the world in the case of U.S. business executives), leaders receive many benefits, such as company cars and planes, luxurious offices, generous expense accounts, and access to subsidized or free housing, just to name a few. The power and privilege are expected to also engender responsibility for the success of organizations and the well-being of followers.

We willingly grant our leaders power and privilege, even in a culture such as the United States, where power distance is relatively low. We understand that leaders need power to get things done. However, in recent years, instances of power abuse and the development of new management philosophies such as teaming and empowerment are leading organizations to reexamine the need for centralized and concentrated power. As a result, we are changing the way we view power and how leaders use it. In addition, research concerning the potential of power to corrupt indicates the need to consider and use power with caution.

This chapter examines the various approaches to power and their implications for leadership. It presents the impact of power on leaders and followers, lists sources of power for individuals and groups, and discusses the potential detriments of excessive and concentrated power. Finally, the chapter analyzes current views of power in organizations in light of cultural differences and the changes in our management philosophies and organizational structures.

DEFINITION AND CONSEQUENCES

The words *power*, *influence*, and *authority* are often used interchangeably. In its most basic form, power is the ability of one person to influence others or exercise control over them. Influence is the power to affect or sway the course of an action. The two terms are therefore almost synonymous, although influence refers to changing the course of an action or opinion. Clearly, power and influence are not exclusive to leaders and managers. Individuals at all levels inside an organization, as well as outsiders to an organization—namely, customers or suppliers—can influence the behavior and attitudes of others; they have power. Authority, on the other hand, is the power vested in a particular position, such as that of a city mayor or hospital manager. Therefore, even though people at all levels of an organization may have power to influence others, only those holding formal positions have authority.

Consequences of Using Power

Power affects both those who exercise it and those who are subject to it. On the one hand, the person who has power changes in both positive and negative ways. On the other hand, being the target of power and influence also has consequences.

> Power changes people. Having the authority to influence others and being able to successfully do so transforms how one thinks about oneself and others and how one acts.

Power changes people. Having the authority to influence others and being able to successfully do so transforms how one thinks about oneself and others and how one acts. Those who think they have power tend to be more action oriented (Galinsky, Gruenfeld, and Magee, 2003), may show more interpersonal sensitivity toward others (Schmidt

Mast, Jonas, and Hall, 2009), focus on rules rather than outcomes (Lammers and Stapel, 2009), and may become more generous (Seely Howard, Gardner, and Thompson, 2007). On the other hand, there may also be some negative consequences. Those with power may focus on retaining their power and acquiring more (Magee and Galinsky, 2008), may start believing that they are more in touch with the opinion of others than they actually are (Flynn and Wiltermuth, 2009), can become oblivious to the needs of those who have less power (Kirkland, 2009), or may even develop an addiction to power (Weidner and Purohit, 2009). A review by Magee and his colleagues (2005) further provides evidence that those who are given power lose their ability to empathize with others and to see others' perspectives and that they are more likely to take credit for their followers' success. Similarly, members of majority groups with more power are more likely to negatively stereotype those in the minority (Keltner and Robinson, 1996). Another consequence of power, be it legitimate or excessive and abusive, is to increase the distance between leaders and followers. Power also can remove leaders from the inner workings of their organizations. Such separation and distance can cause leaders to become uninformed and unrealistic and can lead to unethical decision making, as we will discuss later in the chapter.

The consequences of power on followers depend to a great extent on the source and manner in which leaders use it. The three most typical reactions to use of power and attempts at influencing others are commitment, compliance, and resistance. *Commitment* happens when followers welcome the influence process and accept it as reasonable and legitimate. Consider the employees at Zingerman's Community of Business (ZCoB), a group of seven food-related businesses built around a delicatessen and a highly successful human resource training company, headquartered in Ann Arbor, Michigan. In 2007, the company was named one of the world's most democratic workplaces (WorldBlu, 2007); its management practices and food products continue to draw much praise. The founders, Ari Weinzweig and Paul Saginaw, pride themselves on being close to their community and customers, offering exceptional quality and building strong employee team spirit (Burlingham, 2003). In growing their business, they look for people who work with passion and take ownership. Weinzweig explains, "We wanted people who had vision of their own. Otherwise whatever we did would be mediocre" (Burlingham, 2003: 70). Todd Wickstrom, one of ZCoB's managing partners, who gave up his own business to join the company, says, "I would have come in as a dishwasher to be in this environment. Working here has never felt like a job to me. I'm constantly learning about managing, about food, and about myself" (66).

Another potential reaction to power is *compliance*. In this case, although followers accept the influence process and go along with the request, they do not feel any personal acceptance or deep commitment to carry out the order. Subordinates go along with their boss simply because they are supposed to. An example would be the imposition of unpopular new rules by a school administrator. Because of the administrator's authority, the faculty and staff are required to implement the rules. They, however, do so without any personal commitment; they simply comply.

The third possible reaction to power is *resistance*. The target in this case does not agree with the attempt at influence and either actively or passively resists it. Examples of resistance to a leader's authority abound in our institutions. The most dramatic ones occur in the labor–management disputes, when employees who typically either accept or comply with management's requests refuse to do so and take overt or covert action against management. The 2004–2005 National Hockey League players' strike in the United States represents such overt action. Another labor dispute occurred between the U.S. men's soccer team, which ranked 11th in the world and was a strong contender for the 2006 World Cup, and the U.S.

Soccer Federation. The players asked for a doubling of their salary to bring it up to the level of other players in the world; the federation threatened to hire replacement players. The dispute put in jeopardy the United States' chances of playing in Germany in 2006 (Seigel, 2005). Recent strikes by grocery workers in several parts of the United States are other illustrations of the resistance to power.

As a general rule, a leader's power increases when employees are personally committed and accept the leader's ideas and decisions, as is the case in ZCoB. Based on Fiedler's Contingency Theory, power based on simple compliance does not increase the leader's power. Similarly, some research shows that managers who lead with a firm hand may actually encourage deviant behaviors in their employees (Litzky, Eddleston, and Kidder, 2006). Despite much evidence supporting this assertion, leaders may come to rely excessively on compliance, which, as you will read in this chapter, sometimes leads to dire consequences. In understanding the sources of power, it is important to evaluate individual factors and organizational elements. Power can be drawn from what a person does or is and from the structure of an organization.

Distribution of Power

Traditional organizations typically concentrate power in a few positions. Authority is vested in formal titles, and nonmanagers are given limited power to make decisions. Their role is primarily implementing the leaders' decisions. Despite the vast amount of publicity about the use of empowerment and teams and their potential benefits, not many organizations around the world rely on such methods. Democracy, power sharing, and trust are even less common in business and other types of organizations than they are in political systems, despite research support for its benefits (Deutsch Salaman and Robinson, 2008; Harrison and Freeman, 2004). Interestingly, even before empowerment and teaming became a business trend in the late 1980s, research about the effect of the distribution of power in organizations suggested that concentrated power can be detrimental to organizational performance (Tannenbaum and Cooke, 1974). The more equal the power distribution is throughout the organization, the higher the performance of the organization. At the other extreme, much research indicates that being powerless has many negative consequences for both the individual and the organization (e.g., Bunker and Ball, 2009; Sweeney, 2007). When individuals feel powerless, they are likely to become resentful, may become passive-aggressive, and may even retaliate. Overall, research points to the need to distribute power as evenly as possible within organizations.

> A leader's power increases when employees feel personal commitment and acceptance of the leader's ideas and decisions. Leaders, however, may come to rely excessively on simple compliance, which sometimes leads to dire consequences.

POWER DISTRIBUTION AND CULTURE   One factor to consider in power distribution is culture (see Figure 1). Perceptions of power and egalitarianism vary widely across cultures and even across genders. For example, employees in the United States respond well to managers they like, but Bulgarian employees follow directions when their managers are vested with legitimate power or authority (Rahim et al., 2000). Nancy McKinstry, CEO of Wolters Kluwer, has learned that people in different countries react differently to their leaders. According to her, in the Netherlands you must ". . . invest a lot of time upfront to explain what you're trying to accomplish, get people's feedback, then when they do say yes, the time to implementation is really fast" (Bryant, 2009c).

Power

HIGH

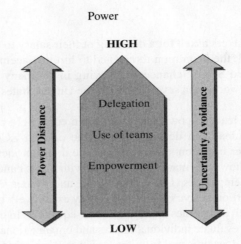

Power Distance

Delegation

Use of teams

Empowerment

Uncertainty Avoidance

LOW

FIGURE 1 Power and Culture

Other research suggests that because of cultural factors, such as paternalism, delegation and power sharing may not be as effective in some Middle Eastern cultures (Pellegrini and Scandura, 2006). Based on research by Hofstede (2001) and others regarding different cultural values in management, the United States tends to be a low to medium power distance culture. The differential of power between the highest and lowest levels of the organization is not great (although the salary differential is one of the highest in the world). The low power distance allows employees in the United States, and in other low power distance cultures such as Australia, to call their bosses by their first name, interact with them freely, and express their disagreement with them. In such cultures, employees do not expect their managers and leaders to know all the answers and accept the fact that leaders, too, can make mistakes (Adler, 1991; Laurent, 1983). Low power distance further facilitates the implementation of participative management and other power-sharing management techniques.

In cultures with high power distance, employees have limited expectations for participation in decision making and assume leaders to be somewhat infallible (e.g., Pelligrini and Scandura, 2006). For example, many Chinese business leaders who operate from a variety of locations around the Pacific Rim work within highly authoritarian-oriented, family-controlled organizations (Kraar, 1994). These leaders make decisions without question or challenge from followers. Even though their approach is contrary to current U.S. thinking about management and leadership, their organizations are successful. Their structure and power distribution fit their culture. The Chinese value order, hierarchy, and a clear delineation of power. Their organizations function in accordance with those cultural values. Likewise, the French, Italians, and Germans expect their managers to provide answers to subordinates' questions and problems (Laurent, 1983). The Eiffel Tower model of organizational culture, used by the French as presented by Trompenaars, for example, concentrates power at the top of the organization. French managers report discomfort at not knowing who their boss is. They also place less emphasis on delegation of responsibility (Harris, Moran, and Moran, 2004). The need for a clear hierarchy is likely to make it more difficult for the French than for Swedes or North Americans to function in a leaderless, self-managed, team environment.

In other countries such as Japan and Indonesia, people value clear hierarchy and authority. For example, Mexican workers may be less comfortable with taking responsibility for problem

186

solving (Randolph and Sashkin, 2002). The Mexican culture, with a family type of organization culture, its strong paternalistic tradition, and the presence of the machismo principle, expects leaders to be strong, decisive, and powerful. Leaders, like powerful fathers, must provide answers, support the family, and discipline members who stray (Teagarden, Butler, and Von Glinow, 1992). Workers feel they owe their loyalty to their boss or "patron" (Harris et al., 2004). In higher power distance cultures, power bases are stable, upward mobility is limited, and few people have access to resources (House et al., 2004). The combination of the culture's power distance and its tolerance for uncertainty determines part of the power structure of an organization. The higher the power distance and the lower the tolerance for uncertainty, the more likely leaders are to hold a high degree of power that subordinates expect them to use. In such cultures, the implementation of power sharing is likely to face more obstacles than in cultures where subordinates do not rely heavily on their supervisor.

The following section considers the sources of power for leaders.

SOURCES OF POWER

Alan Greenspan, who was the chairman of the U.S. Federal Reserve (Fed) from 1987 to 2006 for an unprecedented 19 years, was considered one of the most powerful executives in the United States (Bligh and Hess, 2007). As chairman, Greenspan was able to set policies to sustain low to moderate economic growth, ensuring that the U.S. economy expanded but did not overheat, thereby avoiding high inflation. In a 1996 survey of 1,000 CEOs of the largest U.S. companies, 96 percent wanted him to be reappointed as the leader of the Fed (Walsh, 1996). Greenspan held considerable power with which to chart the course of the U.S. and world economies. He is a well-known economist, is a consummate relationship builder, and is described as low key and down to earth. He stated once that he learned to "mumble with great incoherence" (Church, 1997). Greenspan held no executive power, could not implement a single decision, and employed only a small staff. Nevertheless, he was powerful and had considerable authority. He was able to convince presidents, the Congress, other members of the Fed board, and the financial markets that his policies were devoid of politics and in the best interests of the United States. Where did Greenspan get his power? He relied on individual and organizational sources of power.

Sources of Power Related to Individuals

One of the most widely used approaches to understanding the sources of power comes from the research by French and Raven (1968). These researchers propose five sources of power vested in the individual: legitimate power, reward power, coercive power, expert power, and referent power (see Table 1 for a summary).

SOURCES AND CONSEQUENCES The first three sources of individual power—legitimate, reward, and coercive—are position powers. Although they are vested in individuals, the individuals' access to them depends on the position they hold. In the case of legitimate power, most managerial or even supervisory titles in any organization provide the ability to influence others. When a legitimate authority source asks them to, subordinates comply with requests and implement decisions (Yukl and Falbe, 1991). Alan Greenspan held considerable legitimate power, although his power to reward and punish were limited. In most cases, offering rewards or threatening punishment is another way managers can further convince reluctant subordinates. Managers and executives generally hold all three of these sources of power.

TABLE 1	French and Raven's Sources of Individual Power
Legitimate power	Based on a person holding a formal position. Others comply because they accept the legitimacy of the position of the power holder.
Reward power	Based on a person's access to rewards. Others comply because they want the rewards the power holder can offer.
Coercive power	Based on a person's ability to punish. Others comply because they fear punishment.
Expert power	Based on a person's expertise, competence, and information in a certain area. Others comply because they believe in the power holder's knowledge and competence.
Referent power	Based on a person's attractiveness to and friendship with others. Others comply because they respect and like the power holder.

All three of these sources of individual power depend on the organization that grants them, not the person who holds them. Once the access to title, rewards, or punishment is taken away by the organization, a leader or individual relying on such sources loses power. Because the source of power is related to the individual's position, followers are most likely to react by complying or resisting, as illustrated in Figure 2. Generally, the harsher the source of power that is used, the less willing subordinates will be to comply.

The last two sources of individual power—expert and referent—are based on the person rather than the organization. Access to these two sources of power does not depend solely on the organization. In the case of expert power, people may influence others because of special expertise, knowledge, information, or skills that others need. We listen to the experts, follow their advice, and accept their recommendations. Alan Greenspan provides an excellent example of expert power. His knowledge, expertise, and an established record of success were the bases of his power. Although Greenspan also held legitimate power, in many other cases those with expert power might not hold official titles or have any legitimate power. People, however, will bypass their manager and their organization's formal hierarchy and structure to seek help from those with the expertise they need. For example, a department's computer expert has power even if she is young and relatively inexperienced.

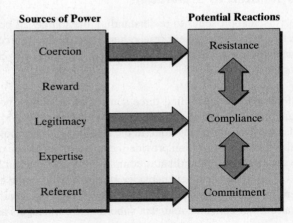

FIGURE 2   Potential Reactions to Individual Sources of Power

Referent power operates in much the same way. Individuals with referent power can influence others because they are liked and respected. As with expert power, this power does not depend on the position or the organization. The person's power stems from being a role model for others. Greenspan was well liked for his ability to work with others. Employees at ZCoB respect Weinzweig and Saginaw for their vision and leadership style. The respect and friendship come on top of other considerable sources of power. In the cases of expert and referent power, followers welcome the influence process and in many cases seek it. As a result, they generally respond with commitment and acceptance. The use of expert and referent power also is related to higher follower satisfaction and performance (Yukl and Falbe, 1991).

USING INDIVIDUAL SOURCES OF POWER Although power and influence are closely related, some research indicates that the two can be treated as separate concepts. A leader with power might not be able to influence subordinates' behaviors, or influence can occur without a specific source of power. Several researchers, most notably Kipnis and his colleagues (Kipnis, Schmidt, and Wilkinson, 1980) and Yukl along with several others (e.g., Yukl and Falbe, 1990, 1991), identified various influence tactics. The result of their work is the classification of influence tactics into nine categories (Table 2). Each tactic relies on one or more of the sources of power related to the individual. Each is appropriate in different situations and carries the potential for leading to commitment on the part of the person being influenced. For example, personal appeal relies on referent power and tends to be appropriate when used with colleagues; it is not likely to lead to a high degree of commitment. Inspirational appeal, which also relies on referent power, leads to high commitment. Rational persuasion relies on expert power and is appropriate to use when trying to influence superiors. The commitment tends to be moderate.

Although leaders must rely on all sources of power to guide and influence their followers and others in their organization, they often have to adjust how they use power, depending on the

TABLE 2 Using Power: Influence Tactics and Their Consequences

Influence Tactic	Power Source	Appropriate to Use With . . .	Effectiveness and Commitment
Rational persuasion	Expert and access to information	Supervisors	Moderate
Inspirational appeal	Referent	Subordinates and colleagues	High
Consultation	All	Subordinates and colleagues	High
Ingratiation	Referent	All levels	Moderate
Personal appeal	Referent	Colleagues	Moderate
Exchange	Reward and information	Subordinates and colleagues	Moderate
Coalition building	All	Subordinates and colleagues	Low
Legitimate tactics	Legitimate	Subordinates and colleagues	Low
Pressure	Coercive	Subordinates	Low

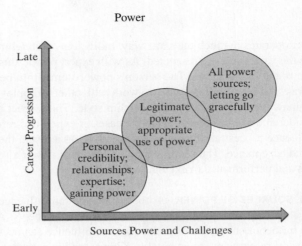

Power

Late

Career Progression

Early

Sources Power and Challenges

- All power sources; letting go gracefully
- Legitimate power; appropriate use of power
- Personal credibility; relationships; expertise; gaining power

FIGURE 3 Potential Reactions to Individual Sources of Power

context and throughout their career. For example, if the leader fits well with the organization, her influence is likely to increase (Anderson, Spataro, and Flynn, 2008). J. P. Kotter, a well-respected researcher on issues of leadership and managerial power, suggests that in the early stages of managers' careers, they must develop an adequate base of power (Kotter, 1985; Figure 3). Managers can be effective by relying on the various bases of personal power. In particular, young leaders must develop a broad network of interpersonal relationships and establish credibility through information and expertise. Other means involve becoming visible by volunteering for challenging and high-visibility projects.

The demonstration of competence and skills is central to the development of power in the early stages of a leader's career. In midcareer, most successful leaders already possess some degree of legitimacy through formal titles, along with other status symbols that demonstrate their power. Their early efforts are likely to establish their credibility and competence within a well-developed network of loyal subordinates, peers, and bosses (Kotter, 1985). Therefore, leaders in midcareer stage already hold considerable power. The challenge at this point is to use the accumulated power wisely and ethically to achieve organizational and personal goals.

Finally, leaders during the late-career stage must learn to let go of power gracefully. By the time they reach retirement age, successful leaders in thriving U.S. public and private organizations enjoy considerable power and influence. To use power well at this career stage, a leader needs to plan for its orderly transmission to others while simultaneously finding new personal sources of power and fulfillment.

Sources of Power for Teams

The differences between organizational and individual sources of power are not always obvious. The structure of an organization provides sources of power to individuals and groups over and above those listed in Table 1. Although individuals can also rely on organizational sources of power, these sources are particularly important for teams. Aside from the expertise of their members, teams have access to power in organizations mainly because of their control of resources and other things that are essential to the organization achieving its goals. These are called strategic contingencies (see Table 3).

TABLE 3	Sources of Power for Teams: Strategic Contingencies
Coping with uncertainty	Based on the ability to reduce uncertainty for others.
Centrality	Based on being central to how the organization achieves its mission and goals.
Dependency	Based on others depending on power holder to get their work done.
Substitutability	Based on providing a unique and irreplaceable service or product to others.

Source: Based on Hickson et al., "A strategic contingencies theory of intra-organizational power," *Administrative Science Quarterly* 16 (1971): 216–229.

The concept of strategic contingencies was originally developed to understand the distribution of power across departments (Hickson et al., 1971; Salancik and Pfeffer, 1977b); however, it also applies well to teams. Strategic contingencies suggest that individuals, teams, or departments gain power based on their ability to address issues that are instrumental or strategic to reaching organizational goals. For example, if a team removes obstacles for others and helps them achieve goals, its leader and members will accumulate power. Table 3 summarizes the sources of power for teams and departments.

> Individuals, teams, or departments gain power based on their ability to address issues that are instrumental to reaching organizational goals.

COPING WITH UNCERTAINTY   The first source of power for teams is their ability to help others cope with uncertainty. With the increased competition and constant changes in the political and economic environments facing many institutions, having information about the changes and alternatives for dealing with them is essential to performance. For example, the leader and members of a cross-functional team designed to provide an organization with market information regarding future products and competitors will gain considerable influence by virtue of the fact that others need that information. The team's product or service reduces uncertainty. A case in point is governmental liaison teams and lobbyists in the United States in a time of change in the healthcare industry. These groups acquire particular power because they help others within the organization reduce or manage the uncertainty they face.

Teams and their leaders can reduce uncertainty through three interrelated methods. First, they can obtain information that others need through market research, polls, contact with key constituents, focus groups, or reliance on external experts. The second method—uncertainty prevention—focuses on the prediction of upcoming changes. For example, a team might research and predict the moves of competitors. Public university administrators rely on their legislative liaison team to predict the mood of the legislature regarding funding of universities. Third, a team reduces uncertainty for others through absorption. In this situation, the team takes certain steps to prevent the change from affecting other teams or departments. The university administrator with information about the legislative mood might try to forestall budget cuts through lobbying. If the cuts happen anyway, various groups within the university might undertake less painful internal budget-reduction mechanisms, such as nonreplacement of retiring employees, thereby preventing more drastic measures from being imposed by outside sources and absorbing uncertainty. Through the use of these three methods, a team and its leader can reduce uncertainty for others and thus acquire power.

CENTRALITY   Another organizational source of power is the centrality to the production or service delivery process. This factor relates to how a team's activities contribute to the mission and goals of the organization. Teams closest to the customer, for example, will gain power. Using the university example again, a recruiting team that is responsible for enrolling new students, which are a primary source of revenue for the university, is central to the survival of the organization. In another example, the librarian team at Highsmith reports directly to the company's executives about connections that can help make important business decisions—a factor that gives its members further power (Buchanan, 1999). Another case in point is the management of diversity in organizations. One of the recommendations for the successful implementation of diversity plans in organizations involves making diversity central to the organization and its leaders. The most successful programs put the individuals and teams in charge of diversity planning and implementation in strategic positions within organizations, reporting directly to the CEO.

DEPENDENCE AND SUBSTITUTABILITY   A final structural source of power available to teams and their leaders closely resembles the reward and expert power of individuals. This source of power depends on the extent to which others need a team's expertise. If employees depend on a team to provide them with information and resources, the team's power will increase. The larger the number of departments and individuals who depend on the team, the greater the team's power will be. In addition, if the tasks performed by the team are unique and not easily provided by others in the organization and if no substitutes are available, the dependence on the team and its power increases. If the team's collective expertise is duplicated in others and its function can be performed easily by another individual or group, however, the team will lack the influence necessary to obtain needed resources and implement its ideas. For example, despite the widespread use of personal computers and information technology tools, many individuals still require considerable assistance to use technology effectively. This factor allows information technology departments, for example, to gain power and obtain resources.

Interestingly, the major complaint from teams in many organizations is their lack of power to obtain resources or implement their ideas (Nahavandi and Aranda, 1994). In the new organizational structures, team leaders often do not have any of the formal powers traditionally assigned to managers. In the best of cases, team members respect their leader because of personal relationships or expertise. These individual sources of power, however, do not translate to power in the organization. As a result, many team leaders express anger and frustration at their lack of ability to get things done. Recommendations on how to make teams more effective often include making them central to the mission of the organization, assigning them to meaningful tasks, and providing them with access to decision makers (Katzenbach and Smith, 1993; Nahavandi and Aranda, 1994).

Special Power Sources of Top Executives

Top executives in any organization, public or private, hold considerable power. One obvious source of power is the legitimacy of their position. A number of symbols establish and reinforce that legitimacy: They have impressive formal titles and separate executive offices, they eat in separate dining facilities, and they are able to maintain privacy and distance from other employees (Hardy, 1985; Pfeffer, 1981). Pictures of past executives that hang in many organizations further signal their importance. Many executives, whether they are city mayors or managers, CEOs of businesses, or presidents of nonprofits, use their powers to benefit their organizations. Dipak

Applying What You Learn
Managing Power When You Are a New Manager

Moving into a managerial position is an important step in any person's career. It comes with many opportunities and challenges. The change in actual and perceived power is one thing that any new manager must handle with care. There is fine balance between no longer being "one of the guys" and overusing one's new power. Here are some guidelines:

- *Know what you know and what you don't know.* Especially in the United States and other low-power-distance cultures, no one expects you to know everything.
- *Get help* from your boss, others at your level, and your reports. Asking questions is not a sign of weakness.
- *Rely on expert and referent power.* You have the legitimate power of a title and can punish and reward others. However, don't forget that other sources are more "powerful." And don't become bossy!
- *Empathize* with your reports about how they might feel. Put yourself in their shoes; the change is hard for them as well. But that does not mean that you will do everything they want or suggest, or continue to listen to

continuous complaints. Empathy shows that you care, but it does not always mean you have to act.
- *Set up new boundaries.* What you set up and how you set them up depends on each individual and may take some time. But you have to realize that things have changed, and you can't continue all the social contact and even work interaction you have had with your reports in the same manner. You won't be able to share as much information as you did in the past or speak as freely, and you are bound to make some unpopular decisions. All these need new sets of rules for interaction.
- *Set up meetings* with your new reports individually and as a team to discuss what they are doing, get their advice for what they can do, share ideas you have, and clarify expectations. This is the first step in establishing trust in the new relationship.
- *Keep your sense of humor* and give yourself time. Like anything else, it will take time for you to learn your new role; practice and be patient.

Jain, the dean of the Kellogg School of Management, has found that "the way to manage your peers—past and future—is through a culture of inclusiveness" (Canabou, 2003b). John Wood, one of the Microsoft alumni and millionaires, is the founder of Room to Read, a not-for-profit group that builds schools and libraries in poor countries. He uses his contacts and power to achieve his goal of helping 10 million children become literate by 2010 (Canabou, 2002). Along with the sources of power we discussed earlier, top executives have four other sources of power:

- *Distribution of resources:* Top managers, either alone or in consultation with a top management team, are responsible for the distribution of resources throughout the organization. This access to resources is a key source of power.
- *Control of decision criteria:* A unique power source available to executives is the control of decision criteria (Nahavandi and Malekzadeh, 1993a; Pettigrew, 1973). By setting the mission, overall strategy, and operational goals of organizations, top executives limit other managers' and employees' actions. For example, if a city mayor runs his or her campaign on the platform of fighting crime and improving education, the city's actions and decisions during that mayor's term will be influenced by that platform. Crime reduction will be one

of the major criteria used to evaluate alternatives and make decisions. For instance, funding requests for increased police training or for building a neighborhood park will be evaluated based on the crime-fighting and education values of the proposals. If the requests address the decision criteria set by the mayor, they stand a better chance of passage, relying on the mayor's weight behind them. If they do not, such proposals might not even be brought up for consideration.

- *Centrality in organization:* Another source of executive power is a top manager's centrality to the organizational structure and information flow (Astley and Sachdeva, 1984). Whether the organization is a traditional hierarchical pyramid or a web, CEOs are strategically placed for access to information and resources. Indeed, new top managers often bring with them a group of trusted colleagues who are placed in strategic locations throughout the organization to ensure their access to information.

- *Access:* Top executives' access to all levels of the organization assists in building alliances that further enhance their power. The most obvious example is the change in personnel in Washington with the election of a new president. Similar personnel changes occur on different scales in all organizations when a new leader is selected. University presidents bring with them several top assistants and create new positions to accommodate them. Other members of the top university administration are slowly replaced with those selected by the new leader. In the private sector, the changes designed to put key people in place are even more drastic and obvious. At General Electric, the selection of Immelt to succeed Jack Welch as CEO led to the turnover of several top management team members who were contenders for the position. Whether new leaders force out several individuals to make room for their own team or whether the individuals leave on their own, the outcome of the personnel shuffle is to allow new leaders' access to trustworthy people and information.

In addition to their considerable power to achieve goals and benefit their various stakeholders, the case of many recent abuses indicates that top executives are not always accountable for their actions. This lack of accountability can lead to abuse and corruption, the topics considered next.

THE DARK SIDE OF POWER: ABUSE AND CORRUPTION

Power allows leaders to influence others and help their team, department, or organizations to achieve their goals; power is essential to effective leadership. The very nature of leading, whether it is a business organization or a social movement, may require some disregard for norms and possible consequences of violating them (Magee et al., 2005). After all, we do not often select leaders so that they can keep the status quo; we expect them to change things. Behaving outside the norms and disregarding some rules may be the only way leaders can implement change, but such disregard can also carry a negative side, as evidenced by the situations at Enron, Tyco, Goldman Sachs, and as some would suggest, even the G.W. Bush administration. These examples illustrate how leaders can defy social convention, established tradition, and even the law. Lord John Brown left British Petroleum in disgrace in 2007, partly because his own behavior did not follow the principles that he loudly proclaimed guide his company's actions (Sonnenfeld, 2007). Conrad Black, CEO of Hollinger International, a newspaper company, billed $2,400 in handbags and the tab for his servants to his company, earning him the title of "kleptocrat" (Chandler, 2004). Richard Fuld, the last CEO of the now bankrupt Lehman Brothers, was nicknamed "the gorilla" for his arrogance and overbearing pride (see the Leadership in Action case at the end of the chapter). The old adage "Power corrupts" appears to be true. Some research indicates that when they become leaders, people may start thinking of themselves, their work, and others differently, and as a result, they change their behavior and become oblivious to the needs of others (Kirkland, 2009). For example, Lloyd Blankfein, the CEO of Goldman Sachs, one of the most successful investment banks in the world, and one of the most criticized for its role the financial crisis of 2008–10, perceives himself as much more than a very rich and thriving CEO. He says he is "doing God's work" (Arlidge, 2009). The hubris and arrogance and a sense of being above the law was further evident when Blankfein and other company executives testified before the U.S. Congress in April of 2010.

Power abuse and corruption are almost synonymous. Abuse involves taking advantage of one's power for personal gain. It includes unethical or illegal actions, taken while in a leadership position and in an official capacity, that affect organizational outcomes, followers, and other stakeholders negatively. It entails using one's title and position improperly to exploit situations and people. It might be in the form of words as well as actions that may injure others. Corruption is abusing one's power to benefit oneself or another person, or getting others to do something unethical or illegal. Whereas power abuse is, unfortunately, not always illegal, corruption is both illegal and unethical. For example, during the 2008–2010 financial crisis and the $85 billion bailout of AIG (American Insure Group) by the U.S. taxpayers, the lavish executive AIG retreat that cost $440,000 was considered unethical and immoral by many, although it was legal. The company's executives bonuses were also considered inappropriate and an abuse of power, but again not illegal or acts of corruption (Elliot, 2009).

Partly because of the potential for abuse and corruption, the privilege associated with power and leadership has come under scrutiny as being at best unnecessary and at worst dysfunctional (Block, 1993). Interestingly, people often have a love–hate relationship with power. Particularly, in the United States, the framers of the Constitution were wary about concentrating power in the hands of one person or one group (Cronin, 1987). Power without accountability is blamed for many excesses, ranging from poor decision making and financial waste to fraud to sexual harassment. Unchecked power is blamed for two of Europe's biggest financial scandals: the Paris-based Credit Lyonnais in the 1990s and the Parmalat case in 2003, as well as the global financial meltdown of 2008–2010. Calisto Tanzi, Parmalat's CEO, was accused of falsifying records and embezzling millions of euros. He fled Italy then returned to arrogantly and shamelessly admit his involvement, whereas his closest associate, Fausto Tonna, wished journalists and their families "a slow and painful death" (Wylie, 2004b: 34). Similarly, in the financial transactions that contributed to the global recession of 2008–2010, as well as other cases such as Enron, WorldCom, and Tyco in the United States, the existing legal requirements and checks and balances did not prevent executives from abusing their power and avoiding accountability for a period of time. Among the executives who are fired in any given year, many are accused of improper and even illegal activities (Brush, 2007). The prevalence of power abuse and corruption warrants understanding factors that contribute to its occurrence. The following sections consider the causes, consequences, and solutions to abuse of power.

> Abuse involves taking advantage of one's power for personal gain. It includes unethical or illegal actions taken while in a leadership position and in an official capacity that affect organizational outcomes, followers, and other stakeholders negatively. It entails using one's title and position improperly to exploit situations and people.

| TABLE 4 | Multiple Causes of Abuse and Corruption |

Leader Characteristics and Behavior	Follower Characteristics and Behavior	Organizational Factors
• Inflated view of self • Arrogant and controlling • Rigid and inflexible • Sense of entitlement • Willing to use and exploit others • Lack of empathy and caring for others • Disinhibited, vicious, ruthless • Overly concerned with power	• Fear • Silence • Agreement • Compliance • Inaction • Flattery	• Organizational culture • Separation of leaders and followers • Hiring practices based on personal relationships rather than objective criteria • Short-term-oriented reward system with limited criteria • Centralized organizational structure • High uncertainty and chaos • Highly unequal power distribution

Sources: N. Brown, *The Destructive Narcissistic Pattern* (Westport: Praeger, 1998); A. Delbecq, "'Evil' manifested in destructive individual behavior: A senior leadership challenge," *Journal of Management Inquiry* 10 (2001): 221–226; and M. F. R. Kets de Vries, *Leaders, Fools, and Imposters: Essays on the Psychology of Leadership* (San Francisco: Jossey-Bass, 1993).

Causes and Processes

Characteristics of leaders and followers and organizational factors contribute to power abuse and corruption (see Table 4 for a summary).

LEADER CHARACTERISTICS   The leadership characteristics that affect corruption closely relate to the Machiavellian and narcissistic personality traits. Several researchers (e.g., Brown, 1998; Delbecq, 2001; Kets de Vries, 1993) have identified individual characteristics of leaders that make them likely to abuse power. These managers are called "evil" (Delbecq, 2001), destructive narcissists (Brown, 1998), tyrants (Ali, 2008), or simply bullies (Hodson, Roscigno, and Lopez, 2006). Often bright and initially likeable, they have an inflated view of themselves and are controlling, rigid, power hungry, and ruthless. They work well with supervisors and impress them, but they are uncaring and vicious with their subordinates. Their sense of entitlement and their belief that they deserve special treatment (Lubin, 2002) make them comfortable with abusing their power and their followers. Their world is divided into those who agree with them and the rest, whom they view with excessive suspicion and even paranoia. Those who are on their side are supported, at least temporarily; those who are not are denigrated, ridiculed, and eventually moved out.

Unfortunately, these types of managers are often able to climb the corporate ladder because others see their self-confidence as evidence of ability (Lubin, 2002). Some research suggests that conditions of uncertainty and chaos, which are highly prevalent in many of today's organizations, further give rise to executive bullies (Hodson et al., 2006). Once in power, they maintain it by surrounding themselves with weak followers, ruthlessly attacking those who disagree with them and managing their superiors so that they can continue their quest for power. Classic cases of evil, or destructive, narcissistic leaders include Al Dunlap (nicknamed "Chainsaw Al"), who ruthlessly cut jobs and abused followers in one job after another until he was fired as CEO of Sunbeam Corp. Philip Agee is another case. As CEO of Morrison Knudson (MK), he not only abused and fired employees based on personal animosity, but is also accused of using company funds for his personal gain. When he was finally fired after much manipulation of board members, the company employees cheered in the parking lot (Lubin, 2002).

FOLLOWER CHARACTERISTICS   Although followers rarely consider their contribution to the power abuse and corruption process, and they are not the starting point for corruption, they do play a significant role. Through their silence, agreement, and compliance they sent a clear message to the narcissistic leader that she is right and that the followers are not capable of independent thought. In the mind of such a leader, follower compliance is further reason to make unilateral decisions and used as a justification for abuse.

ORGANIZATIONAL FACTORS   A person's individual characteristics may make him or her more willing to abuse power, but he can only do so when the organization allows it. In some cases, the organizational culture and practices may even encourage power abuse. The most important determinant of power abuse is the culture of an organization. What is tolerated, accepted, encouraged, and rewarded determines whether a destructive leader can survive and thrive. Creating clear physical and psychological separation between leaders and others, while further isolating leaders from followers, is one indication that leaders are special and deserve exceptional treatment. Hiring practices, the characteristics and style of upper management, and the focus on short-term financial performance, without consideration for much else, all contribute to allowing a destructive leader to last and even flourish. The more centralized and concentrated the power and hierarchy and the more closed the communication within an organization, the less likely that power abuses will be noticed or reported, further perpetuating the abuse. Centralized structures create distance between leaders and followers, allow them to make decisions without consultation and input, and may isolate the leader from others. Closed communication networks further reinforce the isolation and prevent followers from reporting abuses of power easily. Additionally, organizations where power is concentrated in the hands of a few and organizations that face uncertainty and chaos provide fertile grounds for power abuse (Hodson et al., 2006). When power is unequal or when there is high uncertainty, and rules are unclear, abuse can take place or to go unnoticed.

The Abuse and Corruption Cycle

Whether it is the narcissistic leader who creates a corrupt organization or whether it is the organizational culture that creates the abusive leader is difficult to establish. Rather, individual leader characteristics, follower reactions, and organizational factors combine to create an abuse and corruption cycle described in Figure 4. The leader's increasing power, real or perceived, to act without accountability and with impunity leads to followers' compliance. In some cases, subordinates may follow leaders because of personal commitment and acceptance of their decisions, or they might truly respect their leaders' expertise. In other cases, compliance simply comes from fear of retribution or the desire to obtain resources and rewards from the leader. The subordinates' continued compliance can cause leaders to believe that their actions and decisions are always correct, thus reinforcing their inflated view of themselves.

The power, the compliance, and the physical and psychological distance between leaders and followers all contribute to the development of leaders' inflated views of themselves. By virtue

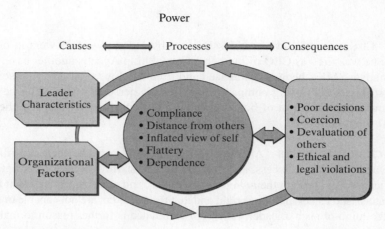

FIGURE 4 Power Abuse and Corruption Cycle

of the hierarchical structure of many organizations, powerholders are separated from those they lead. Based on psychological effects of power, leaders may have the tendency to devalue their subordinates. Both of these can contribute to the corruption cycle. Even though the press and the public appear to value leaders such as Meg Whitman of eBay, who worked in a cubicle and often took commercial flights instead of flying the corporate jet (Dillon, 2004), and despite changes made in many organizations, leaders still occupy offices on separate floors, park their cars in reserved areas, eat in executive dining rooms, and spend a great deal of their time with other power holders. All these symbols of power increase the legitimacy of leaders. The distance and separation can be justified based on the need to protect the leaders' valuable time and to allow them access to other powerholders with whom they need to work to make decisions. These symbols, however, can also corrupt leaders by providing them with an overly inflated view of themselves.

From fear, desire to ingratiate themselves, or simple weakness and incompetence, subordinates submit to the abusive leader's whim and adopt flattery as a means of influencing their leader concerning their ideas or for obtaining the personal or departmental resources that they need. Few dare argue or disagree. Even when they express disagreement, they do so in the softest, most roundabout ways, after praising the leader's ideas and painstakingly recognizing that the leaders are correct. Most of us have witnessed or even been party to such political behaviors, which are considered essential to obtaining needed resources. The insincere flattery, however, can further feed into a potentially destructive leader's sense of self-importance and entitlement and reinforce the devaluation of followers, thereby creating a self-fulfilling prophecy.

Consider the case of Donald Carty, former CEO of American Airlines, who subsequently became the chief financial officer at Dell Computers. While American Airlines was experiencing serious financial trouble in early 2000, seeking $410-million help from the U.S. Congress, he successfully convinced union members and other employees to agree to considerable cuts in pay, benefits, and jobs worth $1.8 billion. Carty conveniently never informed union leaders that airline executives had already assigned themselves lucrative bonuses for the same period (Zellner, 2003). As the union concessions were becoming final, the executive bonuses were revealed, throwing months of painstaking negotiation off course (Meyerson, 2003). Company executives attempted to delay the required announcement of their bonuses until the unions formally approved the concessions, but miscalculated their timing. Under public outrage, Carty recalled a few of the bonuses, but he protected most of the pension funds for executives. His deception eventually cost him his job in April 2003.

Another example of blatant abuse because of power without accountability is Richard Scrushy, former CEO of HealthSouth Corporation, a multibillion-dollar health-care company, who was famous for wielding tremendous power while in office. He intimidated his employees, going as far as sending them out of meetings if he did not like their clothing (Jones, 1998). He was ousted when accused of a $2.7-billion accounting fraud along with perjury, obstruction of justice, money laundering, and wire and securities fraud (Ryerson-Cruz, 2004) and was eventually sentenced to seven years in prison in 2007 (Carrns and Bauerlein, 2007). With more HealthSouth executives indicted for fraud, Scrushy's successor, Jay Grinney, CEO since 2004, states that the company was "managed from the top down" and that "those days are over" (Reyerson-Cruz, 2004).

Consequences of Abuse and Corruption

The excessive power and accompanying corruption of leaders can lead to serious consequences for an organization. Several studies show impact on organizational performance and the increase in deviant behaviors (Tepper et al., 2008, 2009). The most common consequence is poor decision making. Leaders' lack of relevant information because of their distance from others in the organization puts them in the danger of poor decision making. Employees filter information, avoid giving bad news, and hide their mistakes, providing an overly rosy picture of the organization. As a result, leaders lose touch with their organization and its customers. Because of the compliance of followers, leaders might see their followers as dependent and incapable of autonomous behavior and decisions. Leaders then come to see themselves as the source of all events in the organization and consequently might rely less on persuasion and more on coercive methods to get followers to comply. These processes are supported further by a general devaluation and denigration of followers. Leaders come to see their subordinates as less than competent and therefore unable to function without the leader's strong guidance. This devaluation of followers carries a potential for a self-fulfilling prophecy. The leader continues to maintain total control, not allowing followers' input into decisions. The followers comply and encourage such behavior, further proving to the leader the futility of power sharing. The leader sees such compliance as evidence of subordinates' weakness and incompetence, thereby centralizing decision making even further. This self-fulfilling prophecy can become a major obstacle in the successful implementation of various organizational initiatives.

The development of a separate sense of morality based on all the other factors allows the leaders to easily fall into unethical decision making and actions. Such leaders come to believe that regular rules simply do not apply to them. Scrushy's and Carty's actions, as well as in those of many other executives who lie and steal from their company, are examples of such situations. Tyco's executives firmly believed that their outrageous salaries and bonuses were justified. The former CEO, L. Dennis Kozlowski, convicted in 2005 of misappropriation of funds, had no qualms about using and showing his power. "I worked my butt off and it was all based on my performance in Tyco's long-established pay-for-performance culture" (Maull, 2005: D5). There is little doubt that he used money from the company, but it is less clear whether he was authorized to do so. His $30 million apartment in New York City was reputed to have been paid for the company, as was a $2 million bill for his wife's birthday party (Top 10 crooked CEOs, 2009). In another example, James McDermott, Jr., former CEO of Keefe, Bruyette & Woods, was convicted of insider trading for providing secret information to his mistress about pending mergers in which his investment bank was involved. While disagreeing with his portrayal as a corrupt and arrogant executive, he stated: "I'm just an average person who's tried to work hard and to give back," a defense that played a part in the judge reducing his sentence from twenty-four to eight months. Referring to the success of the defense at convincing the judge, McDermott's attorney was overheard saying: "She bought it hook, line and sinker" (Top 10 crooked CEOs, 2009).

Leaders who are caught in the corruption cycle become poor role models and lose their credibility and their ability to be effective in the long run. Amiable negotiation and win–win strategies to resolve conflict and disagreements are replaced with executive fiats and intolerance of diverse opinions. This negative shift, in turn, leads to further bad decisions, to follower resistance and reactance, and to followers' unwillingness to take any risks. The power–corruption cycle, if not stopped, feeds on itself and can lead to dire consequences for any organization.

Solutions

Preventing abuse and corruption requires addressing the leadership, follower, and organizational factors. Identifying individuals with a propensity for power abuse early is one obvious solution; however, it is not always possible or feasible. After all, many narcissists are charming and much liked initially (Back et al., 2010). There are no magic formulas that will prevent the rise of destructive managers and power abuses. Some solutions are presented in Table 5.

As organizations try to reduce if not stop power abuse and corruption, a clear message of the value placed on ethical behavior and integrity is essential. The message that power abuse will not be tolerated accompanied by consistent practices demonstrating such stances are essential (Misangyi et al., 2008). Leaders who know that they will be held accountable for their actions are much more likely to consider the consequences of their actions and act thoughtfully. Although many mechanisms are in place to monitor the behavior of leaders in for-profit, not-for-profit, and governmental organizations, these mechanisms need be implemented to hold leaders accountable. Maintaining checks and balances in the public sector and reinforcing the power of board of governors and directors in other organizations so that they can be independent from the leader are necessary steps toward holding leaders accountable (Colvin, 2007). Organizations can further prevent abuse by reducing uncertainty whenever possible. When there are no clear rules of behavior, the Machiavellian leader is more likely to exploit the situation and his followers (Hodson et al., 2006). Chaotic situations allow bullies to operate freely, so providing order and clear rules can address abuse and corruption.

Much research supports the effectiveness of providing ethics training to employees as a way of decreasing the occurrence of ethical violations. The same has been recommended in trying to address power abuse (Uhl-Bien and Carsten, 2007). Employees who are able to recognize

TABLE 5 Solutions to Corruption

- Clear message and consistency
- Accountability
- Reducing uncertainty
- Training for leaders and followers
- Protecting employees
- Open communication
- Leader involvement in day-to-day activities
- Reducing follower dependence on leader
- Empowerment
- Objective performance measures
- Involvement of outsiders
- Changing the organizational culture

abuse and know what actions may be effective are more likely to resist their leader's abuse. In addition to training in ethics, organizations must be ready to act decisively to protect those who are abused and the employees who stand up to their abusive leaders (Hodson et al., 2006). The more followers and others are able to provide feedback both to the leader and to other powerful members of the organization, the more likely it is that destructive leaders will be detected and power abuses stopped. A recent study suggests that the presence of intranets and other technology-based communication tools encourages flexible control and empowerment equalizing power in an organization (Denton, 2007). Additionally, open communication and transparency regarding financial information further increases the leader's accountability (Welch and Welch, 2007).

The closer the leader is to the day-to-day activities of followers and to the organization's customers, the less likely is leader corruption (Block, 1993; Prendergast, 1993). In addition, the more independent the followers are, the less likely they are to contribute—intentionally or unintentionally—to the corruption cycle. If a person's pay, promotion, and career depend entirely on the manager's subjective opinion and rating, a person is more likely to comply with that manager (Prendergast, 1993). Training followers on how to develop and use personal sources of power can help reduce power abuse by leaders (Uhl-Bein and Carsten, 2007). Followers who have their own sources of power can better resist their leader's bullying. Instituting objective measures of performance, either through precise measurement or based on direct feedback from relevant constituents, is one way to curtail the excessive power of the leader and ensure proper and accurate flow of information. The subordinate can act for the benefit of the customers with feedback from them, rather than for the benefit of the boss.

By opening up the decision-making process to outsiders, an organization can get an objective view and prevent inbreeding. Outsiders can bring a fresh perspective that can break the corruption cycle. For example, the presence of outsiders on a company board of directors contributes to keeping executive salaries more in line with company performance (Conyon and Peck, 1998). Finally, the most difficult and most effective solution to preventing power corruption is a change in the culture and structure of organizations (Delbecq, 2001). The change should focus on performance, productivity, and customer service, rather than on satisfying the leaders.

The new CEO of American Airlines, Gerard Arpey, who was also voted as chairman in 2004, provides an example of the challenge of correcting power abuses by attempting to change the culture while trying to maintain the organization intact (Flint, 2006). After Carty's departure, among its other challenges, the new management desperately needed to rebuild badly eroded trust. Arpey's approach, called "working together," is simple and focuses on rebuilding the culture based on openness and participation (Cameron, 2007). He explains, "I think you will make better decisions and execute better on those decisions if you involve the people who actually do the work . . . the process of listening to each other can't help but lead to better outcomes, no matter which way you go" (Tahmincioglu, 2004). Arpey has made particular efforts to build bridges with labor groups. He states, "If you even allow yourself or your management to identify labor as the problem, you are not only wrong, you also cause everyone else to wait for the solution" (Flint, 2006: 41). He has implemented the new culture by getting to know employees and managers, instituting an open-door policy with union leaders and seeking their advice, promptly returning phone calls, turning down a raise, and agreeing to an initial $110,000 annual salary. Other culture-building mechanisms include use of innovative human resource management techniques and joint decision making through "Joint Leadership Teams" (Tahmincioglu, 2004). Despite all these actions and the fact that the airline showed a profit in 2006, problems are not yet over. Anger over high executive pay and bonuses resurfaced in 2007, evidence of the difficulty of changing the culture of an organization (Cameron, 2007). Grinney, the new CEO of HealthSouth, is taking similar actions to open up the culture and rebuild trust. He says, "Paying up the sins of the past is a process" (BW: "The cleanup crew," 2005: 72).

Partly because of many abuses of power and partly because of philosophical and structural organization changes, the face of power is changing in many of today's organizations.

EMPOWERMENT: THE CHANGING FACE OF POWER

One of the major forces for cultural and structural changes in organizations comes from the empowerment movement. Empowerment involves sharing power with subordinates and pushing decision making and implementation power to the lowest possible level. Its goal is to increase the power and autonomy of all employees in organizations. Its roots lie in perceptions of Japanese management, the quality circle efforts of the 1970s and the quality of work life (QWL) approach (Lawler and Mohrman, 1987), and the psychological concept of self-efficacy (Bandura, 1977). The underlying theme of empowerment is the giving away to and sharing of power with those who need it to perform their job functions. Such power sharing provides people with a belief in their abilities and enhances their sense of effectiveness. Research on the distribution of power (Tannenbaum and Cooke, 1974) and anecdotal and case evidence (Bennis and Nanus, 1985; Block, 1987) strongly suggest that equal power sharing contributes to an organization's effectiveness.

Empowerment of employees can be a powerful motivational tool because it provides them with control and a sense of accomplishment. Business organizations of all sizes, organizations in the nonprofit sector, as well as schools and governmental agencies have all implemented various aspects of empowerment (for examples, see Klidas, van den Berg, and Wilderom, 2007; Marshall, Talbott, and Bukovinsky, 2006; Silver, Randolph, and Seibert, 2006). Keys to empowerment are giving employees control over how they perform their work and over their work environment and building a sense of self-efficacy or competence by providing them with opportunities to succeed. In addition, encouraging participation in goal setting helps followers internalize the goals and builds commitment to them, an important factor in producing a feeling of empowerment (Menon, 2001). The continued emphasis on teams, flexibility, and quick response to environmental change further make empowerment an effective tool for organizations (Callanan, 2004). When Linda Ellerbee, television reporter and CEO of Lucky Duck Productions, an award-winning television production company, learned of her cancer diagnosis, she gave up the reins of her company to her employees. Although she previously involved herself in every aspect of her company, she found out that "I had hired really good people who were good at their job, and what they needed was for me to get out of their way. The company continued to thrive in my absence. I never tried to micromanage again" (Ellerbee, 1999: 81).

Steps to Empowerment

Once managers and leaders decide to adopt and implement empowerment as a management technique, they must adjust the culture and structure of their organization. Many managers talk about empowerment, but few fully accept the concept and implement it completely. Several leadership and organizational steps must be taken to implement empowerment (Table 6).

THE LEADERSHIP FACTORS   The style of leadership potentially creates considerable impact on followers' perception of being empowered and on how effective teams can be (Ozaralli, 2003; Srivastava, Bartol, and Lock, 2006). When empowering employees, the role of the leader is to provide a supportive and trusting atmosphere that encourages followers to share ideas, participate in

TABLE 6	Leadership and Organizational Factors in Empowerment	
Leadership Factors	**Organizational Factors**
• Creating a positive emotional atmosphere	• Decentralized structure
• Setting high performance standards	• Appropriate selection and training of leaders and employees
• Encouraging initiative and responsibility	• Removing bureaucratic constraints
• Rewarding openly and personally	• Rewarding empowering behaviors
• Practicing equity and collaboration	• Expressing confidence in subordinates
• Careful monitoring and measurement	• Fair and open organizational policies

decision making, collaborate with one another, and take risks. Allowing employees closest to the customer to make decisions is crucial. The leader can achieve empowerment through various means, such as role modeling, openness to others, and enthusiasm. Leaders who want to implement empowerment successfully must "walk the talk," be aware of their verbal and nonverbal signals, and believe in the empowerment process. They must encourage experimentation and tolerate mistakes. Leaders can further encourage an atmosphere of openness by increasing their informal interaction with subordinates in and out of the workplace. High work and productivity standards, clarification of organizational missions and goals, and clear and equitable rewards for proper behaviors and proper productivity outcomes must accompany the positive atmosphere the leader creates. Empowerment does not mean a lack of performance or standards. Rather, it involves providing employees with many opportunities to set high goals, seeking out resources they need, supporting them in their decisions and actions, and rewarding them when the goals are achieved. The leader needs to convey high expectations and express confidence in the followers' ability to deliver high performance.

Roy Vagelos, former CEO of Merck and currently chair of Regeneron Pharmaceuticals, insisted on the impossible when he set out to eradicate river blindness, a disease that had long gone without a cure. The price of the project was an apparently unmanageable $200 million for a drug whose customers were unlikely to be able to afford it. Vagelos forged ahead and continued to expect that the project would succeed. His high expectations paid off when the drug was developed and distributed to reach 19 million people (Labarre, 1998).

THE ORGANIZATIONAL FACTORS   In addition to the leader's role in empowerment, the organization also needs to take steps to empower employees (see Table 5). First and foremost, the structure of the organization must encourage power sharing by breaking down formal and rigid hierarchies and by decentralizing decision making (Menon and Hartmann, 2002). It is difficult for a leader to empower employees to make decisions when the organizational structure does not recognize the empowerment. The traditional lines of authority and responsibility do not lend themselves well to the empowerment process, so before new techniques can be implemented, organizations must evaluate their structure with an eye for removing bureaucratic barriers. In many cases, the physical office space must be changed to accommodate the new way people will be working. Formal offices and cubicles indicate hierarchy and individual work, so encouraging interaction will require a different work space that promotes flexibility and cooperation. Several organizations found that changing their office layout was the key to better performance (Goldstein, 2000).

To empower people, the structure of the organization must encourage power sharing by breaking down formal and rigid hierarchies and by decentralizing decision making.

LEADING CHANGE

Sharing Power and Reaping Profits

"As long as we know what each member of staff agrees to deliver in a period of time, their working hours or where they work are no longer important" (Glamoran, 2006). Such a statement is typical of Ricardo Semler, CEO of Semco, a Brazilian company that produces marine and food processing equipment. He is used to being called a maverick. He actually wrote a book on the topic (Semler, 1993). One of the early proponents of open-book management, a method based on sharing financial information with employees and training them to interpret and use it to set and achieve performance goals, Semler believes in sharing information and power. He proposes that people who make far-reaching and complex decisions in their own lives every day are fully capable of managing themselves at work. He believes, "Freedom is the prime driver of performance" (Shinn, 2004: 18). He also believes that even though most people want democracy as a political system, most organizations do not run democratically. At Semco, employees not only pick the color of their uniforms and their work hours, but also vote on adopting new products and undertaking new ventures. Semler states, "At Semco, employees decide where they work and what needs to be done" (Fisher, 2005). The company has set up hammocks in offices to allow employees to relax, so that they can be more creative. Employees can also take sabbaticals and "Retire-A-Little" time, where they can take time off to do what they would do when they retire.

All the freedom and participation are coupled with high performance expectations. Employees who cannot work in the culture or who do not perform do not survive. The company has grown 900 percent under Semler's leadership, is either number one or number two in all the markets in which it competes, and has grown 27.5 percent a year for 14 years (Fisher, 2005). Semler succeeded in creating a culture where performance matters and people have freedom to do what they think is right and have the power to do it without asking their boss. He suggests that his management philosophy is not easy to implement everywhere because of two lacking elements: "One, the people in charge wanting to give up control. This tends to eliminate some 80 percent of businesspeople. Two, a profound belief that humankind will work toward its best version, given freedom; that would eliminate the other 20 percent" (Fisher, 2005). Both these elements make empowerment possible at Semco.

Sources: Colvin, G., 2001a. "The anti-control freak," *Fortune*, November 26: 60; Fisher, L. M., 2005. "Ricardo Semler won't take control," *Strategy and Business*, Winter. http://www.strategy-business.com/media/file/sb41_05408.pdf (accessed July 13, 2007); Glamorgan University international business speaker, September 2, 2006. http://news.glam.ac.uk/news/2006/sep/07/international-business-speaker-glamorgan/ (accessed June 23, 2007); Shinn, S., 2004. "The Maverick CEO," *BizEd*, January/February: 16–21.

Another organizational step is the selection of leaders and employees who are willing to share power. The change in structure and empowerment can be difficult for leaders and followers who are not comfortable with such a process (Frey, 1993). Along with proper selection, appropriate training can introduce the new behaviors of collaboration, encouragement, participation, and openness.

Setting high standards is a requirement for success of empowerment. Equally necessary, however, is the ability to monitor and measure performance and improvement. McDonald's, like many other retailers, has implemented elements of empowerment to engage and motivate employees with the belief that such programs improve morale of the frontline and the quality of service they deliver to customers. To keep track of its efforts and monitor performance, in addition to regular profit and quality measures, the company uses employee surveys and welcomes outsiders who are interested in studying its operations, thereby allowing itself to get feedback about climate and performance (Blundell, 2007).

Finally, just as leaders have to "walk the empowerment talk," so do organizations, by implementing appropriate reward structures and fair policies that allow for experimentation, initiative, making mistakes, and collaboration. Intense focus on the short-term financial outcomes can be deadly to an empowerment process that needs time to take hold. One of the ways organizations can start the process of empowerment is by recognizing and identifying the potential blocks to empowerment. Some consultants and academics even recommend that organizations and employees be encouraged to reject authority outright. Overall, empowering employees requires sharing information, creating autonomy, and holding employees accountable (Seibert, Silver, and Randolph, 2004).

Impact of Empowerment

Empowering employees is a difficult process, but it continues to be recognized as a key factor in today's new structures and a requirement for leaders (Harrison and Freeman, 2004). Leaders in large and small organizations are encouraged to give up power to their followers and rely on democratic practices. Many case examples and anecdotes illustrate that empowerment can be a motivational tool and lead to increased performance. It might even be that empowerment (or its opposite, too much control) can create a self-fulfilling prophecy (Davis, Schoorman, and Donaldson, 1997). On the one hand, the less a leader controls employees, the more likely they are to accept control and responsibility. On the other hand, increased control can cause followers to become passive and, in the extreme, can lead to corruption. The idea of self-leadership is partially based on the concept of empowerment.

There appears to be a resurgence in interest in empowerment, with many recent studies evaluating its impact, application, and effectiveness in a number of settings both in the United States and in others countries (e.g., Bording, Bartram, and Casimir, 2007; Singh, 2006). Despite the reported positive benefits of empowerment, however, research on the subject remains relatively scarce and mixed. Research conducted on the benefits for high-involvement organizations that use empowerment and employee participation to various degrees is increasing, but still includes few director empirical tests (Konrad, 2006; Lawler, Mohrman, and Ledford, 1995). Nevertheless, despite the many obstacles and difficulties and the limited empirical evidence, empowerment is a permanent feature of many organizations in the United States and many other Western countries (Randolph and Sashkin, 2002). When applied well and in culturally compatible institutions, empowerment can powerfully affect a leader's and an organization's effectiveness.

Summary and Conclusions

This chapter focuses on the link between power and leadership. A leader's power to influence others is the key to achieving goals and to being effective. In this influence process, a leader accesses a number of personal and organizational sources of power. Power changes people. The effect on those who hold power ranges from becoming more generous to abusing their power to exploit others. Those who are subject to it can commit to what is being asked of them or resist passively or actively. In either case, equal distribution of power tends to have positive effects in organizations. The more leaders rely on power sources vested in themselves, such as expertise or a relationship, the more likely it is that subordinates will be committed to the leader's decisions and actions. Reliance on organizational sources of power, such as legitimacy, reward, or punishment, at best leads to temporary employee commitment and at worst to resentment and resistance. Given the increasing use of teams in many organizations, it is also important for teams and their leaders to develop sources of power by coping with uncertainty, becoming central to their organization's mission and goals, and providing unique products or services that make them indispensable to others in their organization.

Although power is necessary to accomplish organizational goals, power also leads to abuse and corruption. Excessive power can cause leaders to develop inflated views of themselves due to compliance of the followers, flattery and compliments, the separation of leaders from their subordinates, and their access to too many resources without much accountability. In addition to the ethical consequences, such excessive power can impair the leader's ability to make good decision making, increase their reliance on

authoritarian leadership, engender adversarial interactions, and ultimately, cause subordinates to resist their leader's requests.

The face of power is changing in many organizations. The key aspect of this change is the sharing of power to allow subordinates to participate in decision making, thereby leading to higher-quality decisions and subordinates' sense of accomplishment. This empowerment movement can have many positive consequences. Its success depends on the leader and the organization creating a positive atmosphere in which structures are decentralized and employees are encouraged to experiment and innovate; employees also must be well trained and supported. In addition, high performance standards need to be set, with rewards tied clearly and fairly to performance. Despite the bad press the abuse of power received recently, the proper application of power in organizations is essential to a leader's effectiveness. Power is at the core of leadership.

Review and Discussion Questions

1. How does power impact the power holders and those who are subject to it?
2. Provide examples for each personal source of power. Why are some forms of power more influential than others?
3. Provide scenarios for the appropriate use of each source of power.
4. Provide examples of how teams can use the sources of power available to them.
5. How are the team sources of power different from those available to individuals?
6. Provide examples of the use of different influence tactics.
7. What are the factors that contribute to abuse and corruption?
8. What can be done to prevent or eliminate abuse of power and corruption?
9. What are the key roles of a leader in implementing empowerment?
10. Could empowerment lead to powerless leaders? Why, or why not?

Leadership Challenge: How Much Is Enough?

Business executives, particularly in the United States, commandeer incredibly high salaries and compensation packages. The numbers are approaching and surpassing the $100-million mark without including many other perks and bonuses, in some cases in companies that are performing poorly. A number of arguments explain the rise in compensation packages, including market forces and competition for the few talented executives. Where do you draw the line?

If you were offered an outrageous compensation package to join a company that is laying off employees, declaring bankruptcy, and performing poorly overall, would you take it?

1. What factors contribute to high compensation packages?
2. What are the personal and organizational implications of your decision?

Exercise 1: Words of Wisdom

Following are quotes by historical figures, scholars, and world leaders about power and its impact.

1. Be the chief, but never the lord. (Lao Tzu)
2. There is danger from all men. The only maxim of a free government ought to be to trust no man living with power to endanger the public liberty. (John Adams)
3. I know of no safe repository of the ultimate power of society but people. And if we think them not enlightened enough, the remedy is not to take the power from them, but to inform them by education. (Thomas Jefferson)
4. Justice without force is powerless; force without justice is tyrannical. (Blaise Pascal)
5. Knowledge is power. (Francis Bacon)
6. Power tends to corrupt, and absolute power corrupts absolutely. Great men are almost always bad men. (Lord Acton)
7. Power consists in one's capacity to link his will with the purpose of others, to lead by reason and a gift of cooperation. (Woodrow Wilson)
8. I suppose leadership at one time meant muscles; but today it means getting along with people. (Gandhi)
9. The problem of power is how to achieve its responsible use rather than its irresponsible and indulgent use—of how to get men of power to live for the public rather than off the public. (John F. Kennedy)
10. Those who seek absolute power, even though they seek it to do what they regard as good, are simply demanding the right to enforce their own version of heaven on earth. And let me remind you, they are the very ones who always create the most hellish tyrannies. Absolute power does corrupt, and those who seek it must be suspect and must be opposed. (Barry Goldwater)
11. The first principal of nonviolent action is that of non-cooperation with everything humiliating. (Cesar Chavez)
12. Authority doesn't work without prestige, or prestige without distance. (Charles De Gaulle)
13. Power is the ultimate aphrodisiac. (Henry Kissinger)
14. If you can, help others; if you cannot do that, at least do not harm them. (Dalai Lama)
15. One of the saddest lessons of history is this: If we've been bamboozled long enough, we tend to reject any evidence of the bamboozle. The bamboozle has captured us. Once you give a charlatan power over you, you almost never get it back. (Carl Sagan)

Step 1: Individually

Select two of your favorite quotes. Briefly jot down the reasons why they appeal to you. Consider what their implications would be for organizational leadership.

For example, Napoleon Bonaparte said: "A soldier will fight long and hard for a bit of colored ribbon." Based on this approach, it is important to have goals and rewards, even if not very significant, and leaders must clarify the rewards associated with achieving the goals. As a leader, being encouraging is essential and using reward power is important. This may appeal to you because you like having concrete and clear goals and work best when you have external rewards.

1. _____

2. _____

Power

Step 2: In Groups

Review all the members' favorite quotes and select two that the group agrees on. For each, discuss the potential consequences for organizations and the reasons why your group has selected the quotes. Be ready to make a 2- to 3-minute presentation to the class.

1. _____

2. _____

Exercise 2: Who Holds Power in Your Team/Organization?

You have learned about various sources of power available to individual and groups. The goal of this exercise is for you to consider individuals in your team or organization who are powerful—able to influence others—and analyze their sources of power.

Step 1: Select People

Select three to five individuals from your team, department, or organization and identify which sources of power and influence they use and the impact it has on others. Provide an example for each.

	Individual (First Name)	Source of Power	Most used Influence Tactic	Impact on Others	Example
1.					
2.					
3.					
4.					
5.					

Step 2: Evaluate Impact and Lessons Learned

Next consider whether these individuals are effective in their use of power and influence. What do they do well? What could they do differently? What lessons can you take away from studying them?

Self-Assessment 1: Understanding Your Sources of Power and Influence

For each of the following items, please select the rating that best describes **what you actually do**, rather than what you would like to do. *"Organization" refers to your coworkers, team, department, or whole organization depending on which level you are.*

    1 = Strongly disagree

    2 = Somewhat disagree

    3 = Neither agree nor disagree

    4 = Somewhat agree

    5 = Strongly agree

_____ 1. I strive to be friendly and supportive.

_____ 2. I include as many people as I can in decisions I make.

_____ 3. I strive to be positive.

_____ 4. I am an expert in my area.

_____ 5. I actively build my networks inside the organization.

_____ 6. I have access to resources that other people need or want.

_____ 7. I work hard on staying in my superiors' good graces.

_____ 8. I have a formal title.

_____ 9. I can, directly or indirectly, punish my coworkers (e.g., bad evaluation, not promoting, firing).

_____10. I work on building relationships with people at all levels.

_____11. I prefer to make decisions in a group.

_____12. I am a cheerleader for my coworkers and employees.

_____13. I try to convince people with facts and figures.

_____14. I do favors whenever I can so people owe me.

_____15. I can directly or indirectly help people get what they want (e.g., money, resources, perks, promotions).

_____16. I take care of what my superiors' need.

_____17. I am comfortable pulling rank to get people to do things.

_____18. I put pressure on people until they do what I want.

_____19. I manage to do something nice to thank people who help me or my team members.

_____20. I like to involve people in the decisions that affect them.

_____21. I am good at focusing people's attention on the mission of the organization.

_____22. I am known for my creativity and ability to solve problems.

_____23 I am good at compromising with others to get what I need.

_____24. I do many favors so that others owe me if I need something.

_____25. I do my best to agree with people who have power over me, to keep them on my side.

_____26. I make the final decision because that is my responsibility as a leader.

_____27. I am comfortable threatening people to get them to do what I want.

_____28. I am friendly and approachable.

_____29 I almost always get information from my coworkers before I make a decision.

_____30. People often come to me when they need to regain their motivation.

_____31. My skills and knowledge are at the cutting edge of my field.

_____32. When I need something done, I go around and seek support ahead of time.

_____33. I have information that others need.

_____34. I make sure that my superiors are aware of my accomplishments.

_____35. I rely on the chain of command and the organizational hierarchy to get things done.

_____36. People know that being on my bad side can have bad consequences.

Scoring: To calculate your score, add the items as follows:

Items 1, 10, 19, and 28	=	Total:	_____	*Personal Appeal*
Items 2, 11, 20, and 29	=	Total:	_____	*Consultation*
Items 3, 12, 21, and 30	=	Total:	_____	*Inspiration*
Items 4, 13, 22, and 31	=	Total:	_____	*Rational persuasion*
Items 5, 14, 23, 32	=	Total:	_____	*Coalition building*
Items 6, 15, 24, 33	=	Total:	_____	*Exchange*
Items 7, 16, 25, 34	=	Total:	_____	*Ingratiation*
Items 8, 17, 26, 35	=	Total:	_____	*Legitimate tactics:*
Items 9, 18, 27, 36	=	Total:	_____	*Pressure*

Interpretation: Your total in each of the preceding nine categories indicates the extent to which you use each source of influence. Your score will range from 4 to 16 in each. A higher score in each indicates that you use that tactic more. A balanced score (approximately the same score in all categories) indicates that you tend to use all influence tactics to the same extent. If you have much higher scores in one or more category, consider why you prefer those methods, whether they are effective, and how you could expand your sources of power and influence.

Self-Assessment 2: Views of Power

This self-assessment is designed to provide you with insight into your attitude regarding power. Indicate your opinion on each question, using the following scale:

1 = Strongly disagree
2 = Somewhat disagree
3 = Neither agree nor disagree
4 = Somewhat agree
5 = Strongly agree

_____ 1. It is important for a leader to use all power and status symbols that the organization provides to be able to get his or her job done.

_____ 2. Unfortunately, for many employees, the only thing that really works is threats and punitive actions.

_____ 3. To be effective, a leader needs to have access to many resources to reward subordinates when they do their job well.

_____ 4. Having excellent interpersonal relations with subordinates is essential to effective leadership.

_____ 5. One of the keys to a leader's influence is access to information.

_____ 6. Being friends with subordinates often increases a leader's ability to influence them and control their actions.

_____ 7. Leaders who are reluctant to punish their employees often lose their credibility.

_____ 8. It is difficult for a leader to be effective without a formal title and position within an organization.

_____ 9. Rewarding subordinates with raises, bonuses, and resources is the best way to obtain their cooperation.

_____10. To be effective, a leader needs to become an expert in the area in which he or she is leading.

_____11. Organizations need to ensure that a leader's formal evaluation of subordinates is actively used in making decisions about them.

_____12. Even in most enlightened organizations, a leader's ability to punish subordinates needs to be well preserved.

_____13. The dismantling of formal hierarchies and the removal of many of the symbols of leadership and status caused many leaders to lose their ability to influence their subordinates.

_____14. A leader needs to take particular care to be perceived as an expert in his or her area.

_____15. It is essential for a leader to develop subordinates' loyalty.

Scoring: Add your scores on each items as follows:

Legitimate power: add items 1, 8, and 13. Total: _____

Reward power: add items 3, 9, and 11. Total: _____

Coercive power: add items 2, 7, and 12. Total: _____

Referent power: add items 4, 6, and 15. Total: _____

Expert power: add items 5, 10, and 14. Total: _____

Interpretation: Your total in each of the preceding five categories indicates your belief and attitude toward each of the personal power sources available to leaders.

Self-Assessment 3: Recognizing Blocks to Empowerment

This exercise is designed to help you recognize organizational readiness for empowerment and the potential blocks to its implementation. For each question, think about the current state of your organization or department and check the appropriate box.

Questions	Yes	No
1. Is your organization undergoing major change and transition?	❏	❏
2. Is your organization a start-up or new venture?	❏	❏
3. Is your organization facing increasing competitive pressures?	❏	❏
4. Is your organization a hierarchical bureaucracy?	❏	❏
5. Is the predominant leadership in your organization authoritarian and top down?	❏	❏
6. Is there a great deal of negativism, rehashing, and focus on failures?	❏	❏
7. Are employees provided with reasons for the organization's decisions and actions?	❏	❏
8. Are performance expectations and goals clearly stated?	❏	❏
9. Are goals realistic and achievable?	❏	❏
10. Are rewards clearly tied to performance or the accomplishment of organizational goals and mission?	❏	❏
11. Are rewards based on competence and accomplishments?	❏	❏
12. Is innovation encouraged and rewarded?	❏	❏
13. Are there many opportunities for participation?	❏	❏
14. Are resources generally appropriate for performing the tasks?	❏	❏
15. Are most tasks routine and repetitive?	❏	❏
16. Are opportunities for interaction with senior management limited?	❏	❏

Scoring: For items 1 through 6 and 14 and 16, give a score of 1 if you have marked Yes, 0 if you have checked No. For items 7 through 14, reverse scoring, giving a 0 to Yes and 1 to No.

Interpretation: The maximum possible score is 16. The closer you have rated your organization to that maximum score, the less ready it is for implementation of empowerment. An analysis of individual items can point to specific blocks to the implementation of empowerment.

LEADERSHIP IN ACTION

The Last CEO of Lehman Brothers: Richard Fuld

Among the most dramatic stories of the 2008–2010 global financial crisis was the sudden and unexpected demise of the Lehman Brothers, a financial services firm founded in 1850, in September 2008. After many years of success, the company was brought down by an accounting scheme, dubbed Repo 105, that allowed it to shuffle and hide its risks and bad assets (Johnson, 2010). Its downfall in September 2008 was one of the primary triggers of the global crisis. Leading the company since 1994 and through is bankruptcy was the flamboyant Richard Fuld, who by most accounts was and still is a force to be reckoned with. Although he accepted responsibility for the demise of his company, he steadfastly has refused to admit any wrongdoing or any mistakes (NYT, March 12, 2010) and even denied having knowledge of the shady transactions (Gallu and Scheer, 2010). A serious and intense man who was considered one of the best traders at Lehman's, he seemed to have had the ability to make others want to follow him (NYT, March 12, 2010). He also brought considerable profitability to the company.

Those working with Fuld gave him the nickname of "Gorilla" for his habit of grunting instead of talking and his intimidating presence (Plumb and Wilchins, 2008). He quickly warmed up to the label and kept a life-size toy gorilla in his office (Fishman, 2008). One financial analyst states: "He had the typical hubris that any long-term CEO has: 'I built this thing, and it's got more value than the marketplace understands'" (Plumb and Wilchins, 2008). Several years before the collapse, Fuld refused several offers that could have saved his company, against the advice of many advisors, because he did not agree with them. He then was outraged that the U.S. government did not bail his company out and believes he is being used as a scapegoat because people need someone to blame, although some of his associated believe that Fuld was fully aware of what was going on in his company (Clark, 2010a). During the last days before the company went bankrupt, Fuld used all his political connections, calling U.S. Treasury Secretary Paulson, Jeb Bush (the president's brother), and others to pressure both the U.S. and British governments to intervene on behalf of his company (Clark, 2010); his charm and pressure did not work.

While CEO, Fuld was not shy about using his power. He once berated one of his employees for wearing the wrong colored suit and is reputed to have fired another for using an "appalling" shade of lipstick (Pressler, 2010). Describing an interaction with Fuld, one of Lehman's former executives states: ". . . he made it seem like [a situation] will lead to physical violence if you didn't relent" (Fishman, 2008). He approached his job as CEO with a strong "us vs. them" philosophy, adopting some of his mentor's (and previous Lehman's CEO, Glucksman) working-class suspicion of Wall Street and paranoia about his company being under attack (Fishman, 2008). His intimidating take-no-prisoners approach and sometimes explosive behavior—he once knocked down the papers from an executive's desk—was balanced with generosity to those he liked and those who performed well (Fishman, 2008). Fuld surrounded himself with highly skilled, often non–Ivy league performers—an unusual occurrence in Wall Street—who received some of the highest incentives in the industry for high performance.

With a new report out about the process and causes of the company's downfall and Lehman's in bankruptcy, Fuld spends his time in an office in the Time Life building in New York City, a space that once served as overflow for the company, wrapping up what is left of the company, continuing to replay how things went so wrong, and worrying about the possibility of charges brought against him (Fishman, 2008; Ray, 2010).

Questions

1. What are the sources of Dick Fuld's power?

2. What elements of power corruption are present in this case?

Sources: Clark, A. 2010a. Could Lehman's Dick Fuld end up behind bars. *Guardian.com*. March 12 (accessed on March 24, 2010); Clark, A. 2010b. Lehman Brothers bosses could face court over accounting gimmicks. *The Guardian,* March 12, http://www. guardian.co.uk/business/2010/mar/12/lehman-brothers-gimmicks-legal-claims (accessed on March 18, 2010); Fishman, S. 2008. Burning down his house. *New York Magazine,* November 30, http://nymag.com/news/business/52603/ (accessed on March 18, 2010); Gallu, J. and D. Scheer. 2010. Lehman's hidden leverage "Shenanigans" may haunt Fuld. *Bloomberg.com,* March 13, http://www.bloomberg.com/apps/news?pid=20601108&sid=aQSvfN5gUfoE (accessed on March 18, 2010); Johnson, F. 2010. SEC concedes Lehman shortcomings. *The Wall Street Journal*, March 18, http://online.wsj.com/article/ SB20001424052748704743404575127521800628924.html (accessed on March 20, 2010); New York Times (NYT). 2010. Richard Fuld, Jr., *New York Times* March 12, http://topics.nytimes.com/top/reference/timestopics/people/f/richard_s_fuld_jr/index. html (accessed March 18, 2010); Plumb, C. and D. Wilchins. 2008. Lehman CEO Fuld's hubris contributed to meltdown. *Reuters*, September 14, http://www.reuters.com/article/idUSN1341059120080914 (accessed on March 18, 2010); Pressler, J. 2010. Former Lehman Brothers CEO Richard Fuld has a passion for fashion. *New York Magazine*, March 1 (accessed online on March 18, 2010); Ray T. 2010. Lehman: "Colorable claims" against Dick Fuld. *Barron's* March 11, http://blogs.barrons.com/ stockstowatchtoday/2010/03/11/lehman-colorable-claims-against-dick-fuld/ (accessed on March 24, 2010).

Other Leadership Perspectives
Upper Echelon and Leadership of Nonprofits

Setting an example is not the main means of influencing another; it is the only means.

—ALBERT EINSTEIN

*There are those who look at things the way they are and ask why. . . .
I dream of things that never were and ask why not?*

—ROBERT KENNEDY

After studying this chapter, you will be able to:

- Differentiate between micro and upper-echelon leadership.
- Describe the domain and roles of strategic leaders in the management of an organization.
- Identify the external and internal factors that impact strategic leaders' discretion.
- List the individual characteristics of strategic leaders and their impact on leadership style.
- Contrast the four strategic leadership types and discuss the role of culture and gender in strategic leadership.
- Explain the processes through which strategic leaders manage their organization.
- Review issues of executive compensation and accountability.
- Describe the characteristics and challenges of leadership in nonprofit organizations.

We have many daily conversations about leaders. Our press is full of examples of good and bad leaders from all sectors. We read about business leaders, city mayors and managers, hospital administrators, politicians, and leaders in the nonprofit sector. Many publications and professional associations present yearly awards for the best leaders in their industry. The health-care industry

From Chapter 7 of *The Art and Science of Leadership*, 6/e. Afsaneh Nahavandi. Copyright © 2012 by Pearson Education. Published by Prentice Hall. All rights reserved.

awards a "best health care administrator award"; best and worst city mayors are ranked regularly, as are best and worst business leaders. Based on the amount of attention given to top executives, one can deduce that we clearly believe the top leader of an organization is important. However, the academic research about top leaders' impact on organizational elements such as performance, culture, strategy, and structure is relatively new. With the exception of some of the leadership models, none of the leadership theories presented so far directly addresses the role and impact of upper-echelon leaders; most apply to supervisors, team leaders, and midlevel managers. This chapter will clarify the differences between mid-level (micro) and upper-echelon (macro) strategic leadership and consider individual characteristics of strategic leaders and the processes through which they affect their organization. We will also address the special characteristics and some of the challenges leaders of nonprofit organizations face.

DIFFERENCES BETWEEN MICRO AND UPPER-ECHELON STRATEGIC LEADERSHIP

The reviews of the role of upper-echelon leadership in organizations suggest that efforts at understanding executives are justified (see Finkelstein and Hambrick, 1996; Hambrick, 2007; Hambrick and Mason, 1984; Nahavandi and Malekzadeh, 1993a). Although somewhat fragmented, the research results show that the CEO has impact on the direction an organization takes, on its strategy, and on its performance; CEOs and other top leaders matter (Holcomb, Homes, and Connelly, 2009; Mackey, 2008; Marcel, 2009). Many of the leadership concepts and processes presented in previous chapters operate regardless of the level of the leader. For example, the basic definition of leadership and leadership effectiveness can be transferred from small groups to upper echelons with only minor adjustments. Upper-echelon leaders are still the people who guide others in goal achievement, and their effectiveness depends on maintaining internal health and external adaptability. Therefore, the major differences between micro and macro leadership are not in the nature of the process, but rather in the level and scope of leadership. We call upper-echelon leaders "strategic leaders" because they shape the whole organization. Strategic leadership is a leader's ability to anticipate events and maintain flexibility and a long-term perspective in order to guide the organization. Table 1 summarizes the differences between micro and strategic leadership.

TABLE 1 Differences Between Micro and Strategic Leadership

	Micro (Group)	Strategic (Upper Echelon)
Who is the leader?	One person heading a group, team, or department	A person heading a whole organization with a variety of titles (president, CEO, COO); Top Management Team (TMT); governance body such as board of directors
What is the scope?	Small group, team, or department	Entire organization
Where is the primary focus?	Internal	Internal and external
What are the effectiveness criteria?	Productivity; quality; employee satisfaction and motivation; turnover; absenteeism	Stock prices and other financial measures; overall performance; stakeholder satisfaction

One of the first differences between micro and strategic leadership involves identifying who the leader is. In the case of micro leadership, the person leading the group, team, or department is clearly the leader. In the case of strategic leadership, the issue is often not that simple (O'Reilly et al., 2010). The leader of a business organization might be the president, CEO, or chief operating officer (COO), or it could be a top management team (TMT) made up of division heads and vice presidents. In some cases, such as nonprofits, the relevant strategic leadership may be a governance body such as the board of directors, board of regents, or supervisors. Any of these individuals or groups might be the senior executives who make strategic choices for the organization. Research indicates that the makeup and characteristics of the TMT relate to factors such as degree of globalization (e.g., Levy, 2005; Nadkarni and Perez, 2007), the success of turnaround strategies in organizations that face performance challenges (e.g., Lohrke, Bedeian, and Palmer, 2004), corporate social responsibility (Simerly, 2003), and other financial performance measures (Marcel, 2009).

A second difference in leadership at the two levels is the scope of the leader's impact. Whereas most micro leaders are concerned with small groups, departments, or teams, upper-echelon leaders have jurisdiction over entire organizations that include many smaller groups and departments. Because of this broader scope, upper-echelon leaders have discretion and power over many decisions. Alan Mulally, president and CEO of Ford Motor, describing how job as a top-level leader differs from others, states, "I realized very early that what I was really being asked to do was to help connect a set of talented people to a bigger goal, a bigger program and help them move forward to even bigger contributions (Bryant, 2009i). James E. Rogers, CEO of Duke Energy, says, "I think it's important, if you are going to lead an organization, to have some sense of what everyone does every day. If gives you an empathy that really helps you in terms of telling a story about the company and leading them in terms of where you're trying to go" (Bryant, 2009k).

A third difference between the two groups is their focus. The micro leaders' focus is typically internal to the organization and includes factors that affect their teams or departments. Part of their job may involve dealing with external constituents, as may be the case with a customer representative or a sales manager, or they might be under pressure to take on a more strategic view, even in their small department. They, however, generally do not need an external view to perform their job. In comparison, the job of the upper-echelon leader requires almost equal attention to internal and external factors. Dealing with outside constituents, whether they are stockholders, governmental agencies and officials, or customers and clients, is central to the function of executives. Alan Mulally of Ford says, "The more senior your management position is, the more important it is to connect the organization or the project to the outside world" (Bryant, 2009i).

The effectiveness criteria are also different for the two groups. Although, in a general sense, they are both effective when they achieve their goals, micro leaders focus on department productivity, quality of products and services, and employee morale. Effectiveness for the upper-echelon leader is measured by overall organizational performance, stock prices, and satisfaction of outside constituents. The hospital administrator has to integrate internal productivity issues with overall performance. The CEO of a major corporation does not focus on turnover of employees as a measure of effectiveness. Instead, the criteria are likely to be return on investment and the corporation's growth.

THE DOMAIN AND IMPACT OF STRATEGIC LEADERSHIP

What is the role of senior executives? Do they simply provide direction, or do they stay involved in the day-to-day operations of their organization? The answer depends in part on the leader's style and personality. The six strategic forces depicted in Figure 1 are the primary

FIGURE 1 The Domain of Strategic Leaders: The Six Strategic Forces

domain of strategic leadership (Malekzadeh, 1995). *Culture* is defined as a common set of beliefs and assumptions shared by members of an organization (Schein, 2004). *Structure* is comprised of the basic design dimensions (centralization, formalization, integration, and span of control) that organize the human resources of an organization (Pugh et al., 1968). *Strategy* addresses how the organization will get where it wants to go—how it will achieve its goals. The *environment* includes all the outside forces that may potentially shape the organization. *Technology* is the process by which inputs are transformed into outputs, and *leadership* includes managers and supervisors at all levels.

Any strategic effort requires a balance and fit among the strategic forces. When the fit is good, the organization possesses a greater potential to be effective (Nahavandi and Malekzadeh, 1999). Consider the example of Jagged Edge Mountain Gear (JEMG), a Colorado-based company that specialized in fashionable mountaineering clothing. Twin sisters Margaret and Paula Quenemoen founded the company in 1993 based on the Asian philosophy that focused on the journey and process (Nahavandi and Malekzadeh, 1999: 108–109). JEMG's goal was to become a nationally recognized competitor in their industry. As the Quenemoens state, however, "We are our own competition. We do what we think is right" (Nahavandi and Malekzadeh, 1999: 108). To achieve their goal, the sisters attracted a group of passionate mountain enthusiasts who perform the many business functions while remaining dedicated to cold-weather, extreme sports. The JEMG owners, managers, and employees worked together and played together. The culture of the organization was informal and exuded the members' passion for their sports. The structure, although formally stated, remained informal, with a heavy reliance on participation and empowerment. In addition, because of the company's relative isolation in Telluride, everybody depended on information technology to stay in touch with the marketing division located in Salt Lake City and their suppliers in Massachusetts, Tennessee, and China. The Quenemoens ran JEMG successfully by creating a fit among the six strategic forces.

Any strategic effort requires a balance and fit among the strategic forces. When the fit is good, the organization possesses a greater potential to be effective.

The simultaneous management of the six forces is the essence of strategic management (Malekzadeh, 1995). The upper-echelon leader's role is to balance these various factors and

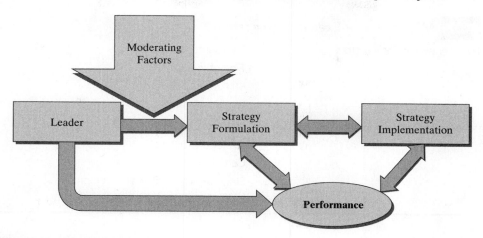

FIGURE 2 Dual Role of Strategic Leaders

set the direction for the organization. Once a direction is selected, internal forces (e.g., culture, structure, and leadership) come into play once more to move the organization toward its selected path.

Role of Strategic Leaders

Strategic leaders (CEO or the TMT) are the ones in charge of setting and changing the environment, culture, strategy, structure, leadership, and technology of an organization and motivating employees to implement the decisions. Their role is to devise or formulate the vision and strategy for their organization and to implement those strategies; they play the dual role of strategy formulator and implementer (Nahavandi and Malekzadeh, 1993a). If an organization has not drafted a strategy or is looking for major changes and strategic redirection, the leaders have a vital role in formulating the direction of the organization based on their reading of the environment. If, on the other hand, the organization has a well-established, successful strategy already in place, the leaders become a key factor in implementing that strategy. The dual role of strategic leaders is depicted in Figure 2.

Although they play a central role in creating and maintaining major organizational elements, the top managers' influence often is moderated by a number of organizational and environmental factors. Therefore, although leaders are highly influential in many aspects of organizational decision making, many circumstances and variables limit a leader's discretion. The next section considers these factors.

Executive Discretion: Factors That Moderate the Power of Leaders

Upper-echelon leaders do not have unlimited power to impact their organization. The research about the limits of their power comes under the label of managerial or executive discretion (Finkelstein and Hambrick, 1996; Hambrick and Finkelstein, 1987) and is the subject of considerable research in strategic management for its impact on firm performance in a variety of areas (e.g., Aragon-Correa, Matias-Reche, Senise-Barrio, 2004; Bates, 2005) and CEO compensation

TABLE 2 Moderators of Executive Discretion	
External environmental factors	Environment uncertainty
	Type of industry
	Market growth
	Legal constraints
Internal organizational factors	Stability
	Size and structure
	Culture
	Stage of organizational development
	Presence, power, and makeup of TMT

(e.g., Cho and Shen, 2007). Table 2 presents the factors that moderate a leader's discretion. They are divided into external environmental and internal organizational factors. Both sets operate to limit the direct or indirect impact of senior executives on their organization.

EXTERNAL ENVIRONMENTAL FACTORS   Several researchers suggest that the leader's role becomes more prominent when organizations face an uncertain environment (Gupta, 1988; Hall, 1977; Hambrick and Finkelstein, 1987). For example, in highly dynamic industries such as high technology, computers, or airlines, top managers must scan and interpret their environment actively and make strategic decisions based on their interpretations. Such activities provide many opportunities for a leader to shape the organization. Bill George, former CEO of Medtronics and professor of management at Harvard, addressed the key role of leaders in the 2008–2010 economic crisis, "The root cause is failed leadership. New laws, regulations, and economic bailouts won't heal wounds created by leadership failures. They can only be solved by new leaders with the wisdom and skill to put their organizations on the right long-term course" (George, 2009a). External forces include market growth and legal constraints. In fast-growing markets, strategic leaders have considerable discretion to set and change the course of their organization (Haleblian and Finkelstein, 1993). Legal constraints, such as environmental laws, health and safety regulations, and international trade barriers, however, limit the discretion of leaders. In such environments, many of their decisions already are made for them, leaving less room for action.

Consider the case of utility companies that, up until some years ago, faced a stable and calm environment. As competition increases and governments deregulate the industry, leaders of these utility companies are becoming more prominent. Similarly, the leaders of the computer industry, such as Steve Jobs (Apple), Bill Gates (Microsoft), and Michael Dell (Dell Computers), have become household names, as have current and former leaders in many of the Internet companies, such as eBay's Margaret Whitman and Amazon's Jeff Bezos.

INTERNAL ORGANIZATIONAL FACTORS   When organizations face internal uncertainty, organizational members question existing practices and decisions and rely more heavily on the leader to provide direction and guidance. In routine situations, organizational rules and regulations and a well-established culture in effect become substitutes for leadership (Kerr and

Jermier, 1978). One example of a situation in which leaders are heavily relied on would be during a threatened or actual merger. The employees are likely to seek direction from their CEO, whose every word and action will be interpreted as a signal and whose attitude toward the merger will be a role model for the employees. Professor Mike Useem, director of the Center for Leadership and Change at the University of Pennsylvania's Wharton School of Business, suggests that a leader's calm and confidence is a key factor in managing during times of crisis (Maruca, 2001). The sense of crisis provides the stage for leaders to increase their impact or to demonstrate charismatic leadership behaviors, which influence followers to a high degree.

Size and structure are the second set of internal moderators of discretion. The larger an organization is, the more likely it is that decision making is decentralized. As an organization grows, the impact of the top managers on day-to-day operations declines. In small organizations, the desires of a top manager for a certain type of culture and strategy are likely to be reflected in the actual operations of an organization. In large organizations, however, the distance between the leader and other organizational levels and departments leads to a decline in the immediate effect of the leaders. For example, the U.S. Postal Service is one of the largest employers in the United States, with more than 650,000 employees. The postmaster's influence is diffused through numerous layers of bureaucracy and probably is not felt by local post office employees. This filtering also could be one reason it is difficult to change large organizations. Even the most charismatic, visionary leader might have trouble reaching all employees to establish a personal bond and energize them to seek and accept change.

One of the causes of internal and external uncertainty is the organization's life cycle or stage of development (Miller, 1987; Nahavandi and Malekzadeh, 1993a). When an organization is young and in its early stages of development, the impact of a leader's personality and decisions is pervasive. The personality and style of the leader/entrepreneur are reflected in all aspects of the organization. The younger an organization is, the more likely it is that its culture, strategies, and structure are a reflection of its leader's preferences. As the organization matures and grows, the leader's influence decreases and is replaced by the presence of a strong culture and a variety of well-established, successful routines. It is often at this stage that the founders of an organization leave and move on to new ventures. The leader's influence, however, becomes strong once again when the organization faces decline. The lack of success and the perceived need to revitalize the organization increase the reliance on the top managers. They once again have the opportunity to shape the organization. The case of A. G. Lafley, former CEO at P&G, illustrates this point. When Lafley become CEO in 2000, P&G faced a crisis in performance and employee morale. Lafley was the center of attention inside and outside the company as he slowly changed the culture and led the company to profitability. Lafley saw himself as a change agent who focused on the longer-term good of the company (Jones, 2007).

Mickey Drexler, current CEO at J. Crew and former chief executive of Gap, Inc., was credited with Gap's success in the late 1990s. Some even claim that he invented casual chic by providing fashionable clothes at a reasonable cost (Gordon, 2004). He is also known for having considerable power. One former Gap employee states, "Mickey is omnipotent. There is nobody who is his equal. There is nobody who is near his equal" (Munk, 1998). Both at Gap and J. Crew, Drexler exercises considerable control over his organization; he is known as a micro manager (Rose, 2008). He makes decisions regarding even minute details of the products and likes to communicate instantly using the public-address system (Kiviat, 2007). Because the Gap was relatively new at the time and was experiencing a revival, Drexler's influence was pervasive.

Another example of the leader's impact in the early stages of an organization's life is Oprah Winfrey—the first African American and the third woman to own a television and film production studio with more than $300 million in annual revenue, she runs an organization that reflects her high-energy, supportive style. She states: "It's all about attracting good people. I've always tried to surround myself not only with people who are smart but with people who are smarter in ways I am not" (Howard, 2006).

The last moderator of power and influence of top managers of an organization is the presence, power, and homogeneity of a TMT (Hambrick, 1987). As noted at the beginning of the chapter, upper-echelon leadership often involves working within a team; the presence of the team and how it interacts with the CEO has a strong impact on an organization. If an organization does not have a TMT or if it is weak, the impact of its CEO is likely to be more direct. If, on the other hand, the organization is managed by a powerful TMT, such a team will moderate the power and discretion of the individual leader. For example, in 2005, Carl Vogel, the CEO of Charter Communication, a cable company, quit his job partly over frustration over the lack of support from several of the company board members (Grant, 2005). Douglas Pertz was ousted by the company's board only four months after becoming CEO because the company's shares plummeted as soon as he took over (Dash, 2007). On the other hand, an example of a functioning partnership that increases a leader's power is the case of Oracle. Part of the success of the company is due to a strong relationship and match between its CEO, Larry Ellison, and president, Safra Catz. He is an extraverted, easily distracted, media celebrity; she is a quiet and highly focused manager (Lashinsky, 2009). One company executive describes their relationship, "Safra allows Larry to work 30 hours a week but have the effectiveness of a CEO who works 100 hours a week. Ninety-eight percent of the time she'll just do things and inform him after the fact. Two percent of the time she'll ask him what he wants" (Lashinsky, 2009).

An interesting twist on the role and power of the TMT is the degree to which the members are similar to the leader and the diversity of the board. Much research indicates that leaders often pick board of director members and other top advisors who are similar to themselves (McCool, 2008). The more similar the TMT is to the leader, the greater the power of the leader (Miller, 1987). Diversity in the board can have both good and bad consequences and has an impact on how the company makes decisions (e.g., Jansen and Kristof-Brown, 2006). Many organizations take into account the importance of heterogeneity in the makeup of the TMT or board of directors. When Mercedes, the German automobile manufacturer, built a plant in Vance, Alabama, the heart of the Deep South, the executive leaders deliberately pieced together a diverse team of executives. It included managers with Detroit automobile experience, several who had worked for Japanese plants in North America, and four Germans (Martin, 1997). The team was designed to provide the best possible mix of experience for running a successful foreign automaker in the United States. Because of the importance and potential power of the TMT, it has been the subject of considerable research in the past few years (for a review, see Carpenter, Geletkanycz, and Sanders, 2004). In addition, many shareholders and stakeholders are increasingly calling for more powerful and involved board members who can closely oversee the actions of the CEO, making board memberships both riskier and more time consuming (Raghavan, 2005).

These external and internal moderating factors limit the power and discretion of strategic leaders and can prevent the leader from making a direct impact on the organization. The next section considers the key relevant, individual characteristics of upper-echelon leaders.

Applying What You Learn
Managing in Times of Crisis

Leaders at all organizational levels have to manage difficult or crisis situations. No book knowledge replaces experience, but knowing what to do and having some guidelines makes handling crises a bit easier. The first step is to take a hard look and gain as good an understanding of the situation as possible. Here are some additional guidelines for handling crisis situations:

- *Be realistic* about how serious the situation is. Some people tend to sugarcoat too much and avoid problems; others tend to see everything as a crisis. Do a reality check.
- *Face the situation;* do not postpone or avoid dealing with the crisis.
- *Do your research and gather facts and information;* it is easier to make a hard decision when you have solid facts to back you up.
- *Seek help and support* from your supervisor if you can, or mentors and colleagues around the organization.

- *Be a role model;* make sure that you do what you are asking others to do; walk the talk.
- *Tell the truth;* communicate honestly and behave with integrity. If you have information you cannot share, simply say so; do not lie or make up what you don't know.
- *Remain calm and professional;* followers will react to your emotions and behaviors; be very deliberate about the tone of your verbal and nonverbal messages.
- *Practice kindness* and give people the benefit of the doubt and support when you can.
- *Listen to concerns and have empathy;* put yourself in other people's shoes. You do not have to agree with or address everything they need, but you do have to listen.
- *Act!* As a leader you must decide and do something. It does not have to be spectacular and solve everything, but you cannot sit idle and avoid dealing with the crisis.

CHARACTERISTICS OF UPPER-ECHELON LEADERS

What impact do executives' personality and other individual characteristics have on their style and the way they run the organization? Are some characteristics or combinations of characteristics more relevant for upper-echelon leadership? Information about upper-echelon leadership characteristics is somewhat disjointed. Research about micro leadership presented throughout this book identified several important dimensions in predicting and understanding small-group leadership; the task and relationship dimensions, in particular, have dominated much of leadership theory for the past 40 to 50 years. Despite the success of those dimensions, however, they do not necessarily provide predictive value when dealing with upper-echelon leadership (Day and Lord, 1988). A number of different studies identify the individual characteristics of upper-echelon leaders (e.g., Simsek, Heavy, and Veiga, 2010).

Demographic and Personality Traits

Older CEOs are generally more risk averse (Alluto and Hrebeniak, 1975), and insider CEOs (as opposed to those who are brought in from outside) attempt to maintain the status quo and are, therefore, less likely to change the organization (Kotin and Sharaf, 1976; Pfeffer, 1983). Researchers also considered the impact of an upper manager's functional background on an organization's strategic choices (Song, 1982), and a body of research explored the various personality characteristics with a recent focus on the impact of charismatic and transformational leadership (e.g., Ling et al., 2008), emotions (e.g., Kisfalvi and Pitcher, 2003), and emotional intelligence (e.g., Scott-Ladd and Chan, 2004). The concept of locus of control is one variable that has shown links to upper-echelon decision making. Managers with internal locus of control emphasize research and development (R&D) and frequent product changes. They also tend to be more innovative than those with an external locus of control (Anderson, Hellriegel, and Slocum, 1977).

Two common themes run through the research about individual characteristics of strategic leaders. They are the degree to which they seek challenge and their need for control.

Most of the leader's personal characteristics studied have some impact on organizational decision making, although the effect is not always strong. Two common themes run through the research about individual characteristics of strategic leaders. They are the degree to which they seek challenge and their need for control (Nahavandi and Malekzadeh, 1993a).

CHALLENGE SEEKING   A number of researchers considered the upper-echelon leader's openness to change to be an important factor of strategic leadership. Upper-echelon management's entrepreneurship (Simsek, Heavy, and Veiga, 2010), openness to change and innovation, futuricity (Miller and Freisen, 1982), risk taking (Khandwalla, 1976), and transformational and charismatic leadership (Ling et al., 2008) are all part of this theme. The common thread among these constructs is the degree to which leaders seek challenge. How much is the leader willing to take risks? How much will the leader be willing to swim in uncharted waters? How much does the leader lean toward tried-and-true strategies and procedures? A more challenge-seeking person is likely to engage in risky strategies and undertake new and original endeavors (Nahavandi and Malekzadeh, 1993a). A leader who does not seek challenges will be risk averse and stick with well-established and previously proven methods. The challenge-seeking dimension is most relevant in the way a leader formulates strategy. For example, one leader might pursue a highly risky product and a design strategy that will help produce and market such a product by accepting a high level of failure risk.

Challenge-seeking executives are celebrated in the current climate of crisis in many institutions. Richard Branson's willingness to take risks has been key to his success and his fame. David Rockwell, the visionary behind many of New York's trendiest restaurants, is in high demand because of his creativity and his ability to harness the energy of 90 designers who work for him (Breen, 2002). Monica Luechtefeld, who has worked at Office Depot since the late 1990s and became the e-commerce vice president in 2009, is one of the "fearless mavericks" of e-commerce (Tischler, 2002: 124). She attributes her willingness to take on tasks that others shun to her parents' constant messages of "You can do anything" and "Figure it out," an approach she passed on to her son, who was raised hearing "Why not?" from her (Tischler, 2002).

NEED FOR CONTROL   The second theme in research about CEO characteristics is the leader's need for control, which refers to how willing the leader is to give up control. The degree of need for control is reflected in the extent of delegation and follower participation in decision making and implementation of strategy. Other indicators are the degree of centralization and formalization or encouragement and the degree of tolerance for diversity of opinion and procedures. Issues such as the degree of focus on process and interpersonal orientation (Gupta, 1984), tolerance for and encouragement of participation and openness, and what one researcher has called "organicity," which generally refers to openness and flexibility (Khandwalla, 1976), are all part of this theme.

The leader with a high need for control is likely to create an organization that is centralized, with low delegation and low focus on process (Nahavandi and Malekzadeh, 1993a, b). The culture will be tight, and focus will be on uniformity and conformity. The leader with a low need for control decentralizes the organization and delegates decision-making responsibilities. Such a leader encourages an open and adaptable culture, with a focus on the integration of diverse ideas rather than conformity to a common idea. The culture will encourage employee involvement and tolerance for diversity of thought and styles (Nahavandi and Malekzadeh, 1993a).

No apparent pattern emerges regarding how controlling the upper echelons of successful organizations are, despite the empowerment trends. In some cases, such as the CEO and TMT of Johnson & Johnson, decentralization and autonomy of various units are built into the credo of the organization and are central to the success of the company (Barrett, 2003). In other cases, such as Mickey Drexler, the CEO controls most of the decisions (Rose, 2008).

Strategic Leadership Types

The two themes of challenge seeking and need for control affect leaders' decision making and managerial styles and the way they manage the various strategic forces (Nahavandi and Malekzadeh, 1993a, b). First, the upper-echelon leader must understand and interpret the environment of the organization. Second, as the primary decision maker, the leader selects the strategy for the organization. Third, the leader plays a crucial role in the implementation of the chosen strategy through the creation and encouragement of a certain culture and structure and the selection of leaders and managers throughout the organization.

Challenge seeking and need for control combine to yield four strategic leadership types. Each type represents an extreme case of strategic management style, and each handles the strategic forces in a manner consistent with his or her basic tendencies and preferences.

Challenge seeking and need for control combine to yield four strategic leadership types (Figure 3). Each type represents an extreme case of strategic management style, and each handles the strategic forces in a manner consistent with his or her basic tendencies and

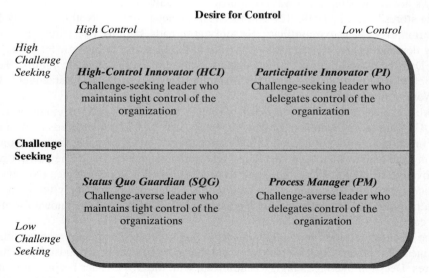

FIGURE 3 Four Strategic Leadership Types

preferences. Given the pressure toward empowerment, employee participation, and the perceived need by many to be unconventional and innovative in all aspects of an organization, it might appear that some types of leaders are more desirable than others. The participative innovator (PI), in particular, could be perceived as ideal. Such an assumption, however, is inaccurate; different leadership styles fit different organizations based on their long-term strategic needs.

STRATEGIC LEADERSHIP TYPES AND THEIR IMPACT ON ORGANIZATIONS   The first strategic type is the high-control innovator (HCI). The HCI leader is a challenge seeker who likes to maintain tight control over organizational functioning. This type of leader sees opportunities in the environment and is willing to use technological advancements to achieve goals. HCIs look for risky and innovative strategies at the corporate and business levels that involve navigating uncharted territories and entering new markets or new industries. (See Table 3 for a summary of leaders' impact on an organization and how they perceive and manage the six strategic forces.)

As opposed to the need for innovation when concerned with external factors, HCIs tend to be conservative in the management of their organization. The HCI leader has a high need for control that leads to the creation of a highly controlled culture in which adherence to common goals and procedures is encouraged and rewarded. Decision making is likely to be centralized, with the leader delegating few if any of the major decisions. The ideal organization for an HCI leader is one that is innovative and focused. The employees share a strong common bond and believe in "their way" of managing. Mickey Drexler, discussed previously, provides an example of an HCI. He has been described as a "visionary *and* a control freak" (Gordon, 2004). Although innovative and a risk taker in his strategies and marketing, he keeps a tight control over his organization. Drexler is described as a relentless "store walker," who picks on every detail (Kiviat, 2007). He is also known for his creativity and his ability to pick successful new trends. He states, "I like to race, run and compete. . . . I'd rather make quick mistakes than have long slow successes" (Dicocco, 2006). His COO at the Gap described him this way: "Mickey's always looking for a way to improve. He is always on the road, always talking to people in stores" (Munk, 1998: 82). Another Gap manager noted, "Nothing gets by Mickey. His attention to detail is extraordinary. He looks at threads, buttons, everything. He's difficult and very demanding. He can attack" (71). Both at the Gap and in his new leadership role at J. Crew, Drexler is known for his knowledge and control of every detail. He admits, "I spot details quickly" (Gordon, 2004). Another example of a HCI is Jeffrey Katzenberg, CEO of DreamWorks Animation SKG.

Unlike the HCI, the status quo guardian (SQG) does not seek challenge; however, like the HCI, SQGs want to maintain control (see Figure 3). This type of leader needs control over the internal functioning of the organization and is risk averse. SQGs perceive their environment as threatening and tend to want to protect their organization from its impact. They do not seek new and innovative strategies, but rather stick to tried and well-tested strategies (Nahavandi and Malekzadeh, 1993b). The organization run by an SQG leader is not likely to be an industry leader in new-product development and innovation. It, however, might be known for efficiency and low cost.

The ideal organization for an SQG leader is highly focused and conservative with a tight, well-defined culture that expects employees and managers to conform to existing practices and procedures. Decision making is highly centralized, with the SQG leader keeping informed and involved in the majority of decisions. Janie and Victor Tsao, *Inc.*, magazine's 2004 entrepreneurs

TABLE 3 The Impact of Strategic Leadership Types on the Six Strategic Forces

Leader	Perception of Environment	Technology	Strategy	Culture	Structure	Leadership
HCI	Presence of many opportunities for growth and threats from others	Innovation and use of high-technology	High-risk; product innovation; stick to core	Strong dominant culture with few subcultures	Centralized decision making by a few people	Leaders and managers with similar styles and views
SQG	Many threats; desire to protect organization from outsiders	Little focus on innovation unless it helps control	Low risk; few innovations; focus on efficiency	Strong dominant culture; low tolerance for diversity	Centralized decision making by a few people	Leaders and managers with similar styles and views
PI	Many opportunities; tendency to open organization to outside	Encouragement of experimentation; wide use of technology	High risk; product innovation; open to new areas	Fluid main culture; many subcultures; high tolerance for diversity	Decentralized decision making to lowest levels: empowerment and participation	Leaders and managers with many diverse styles and views
PM	Threats and tendency to protect organization from outside	Moderate use of technological innovation	Low risk; few innovations; focus on efficiency	Fluid culture with focus on "no change"; tolerance for diversity	Decentralized decision making; participation	Leaders and managers with many diverse styles and views

Source: Partially based on information in Nahavandi, A., and A. R. Malekzadeh. 1993. Leader style in strategy and organizational performance: An integrative framework. *Journal of Management Studies* 30 (3): 405–425; Nahavandi, A., and A. R. Malekzadeh. 1993. *Organizational Culture in the Management of Mergers.* New York: Quorum Books.

of the year, built their $500-million, 300-person company, Linksys, on frugality, hard work, and tight control of every operation and decision (Mount, 2004). Although they develop networking products and allow employees to run their own projects, the husband-and-wife team believes that their product is neither spectacular nor involves any particular genius—just a good business plan and tight execution. One of their employees described their style: "Victor and Janie really like to see people execute" (Mount, 2004: 68). Tootsie Roll Industries, Inc., is another company run by SQG leaders: Ellen Gordon, president, and her husband Melvin, chair of the board, along with four other executives, fully control all operations. Tootsie Roll is named repeatedly as one of the best-run small companies in the United States. Much of the credit for its success goes to the Gordons for their single-minded focus on their business and their benevolent, authority-oriented styles. Ellen states, "We encourage a lot of new ideas, we create teams and we invite challenges, but we always have to make sure we stay on our overall goals" (Murrill, 2007). The company has managed to focus on the candy-making business for 100 years and through a number of defensive moves, warded off acquisition attempts. With a narrow strategy and tight controls, the Gordons encourage openness and feedback from employees and continue to build a strong, conservative culture.

The participative innovator is diametrically opposed to the SQG. Whereas the SQG values control and low-risk strategies, the PI seeks challenge and innovation on the outside and creates a loose, open, and participative culture and structure inside the organization. PIs view the environment as offering many opportunities and are open to outside influences that could bring change in all areas, including technology. Similar to the HCI, the PI is a challenge seeker and is likely to select strategies that are high risk. An organization run by a PI is often known for being at the cutting edge of technology, management innovation, and creativity.

The ideal organization for a PI leader is open and decentralized, with many of the decisions made at the lowest possible level, because the leader's low need for control allows for delegation of many of the decisions. The culture is loose, with much tolerance for diversity of thought and practice. The only common defining element might be tolerance of diversity—a *vive la différence* mentality. Employees are encouraged to create their own procedures and are given much autonomy to implement their decisions. The key to PI leadership is allowing employees and managers to develop their own structure and come up with ideas that lead to innovative products, services, and processes.

Ricardo Semler is celebrated for his willingness to give up control and empower his employees while implementing innovative management strategies. Not only is Roy Wetterstrom, an entrepreneur who created several businesses, a high risk taker, but he also believes that "to make a big strategic shift, you'll need to take a breather from day-to-day stuff" (Hofman, 2000: 58) and push responsibility down the chain of command. John Chambers, CEO of Cisco Systems since 1995, often introduces himself as the "corporate overhead," serves ice cream to his employees, is open to ideas, is willing to adapt, and relies heavily on others to make decisions (Kupfer, 1998). One Cisco employee described the culture: "John has instilled a culture in which it's not a sign of weakness but a sign of strength to say, 'I can't do everything myself'" (86).

The last type of strategic leader, the process manager (PM), has the internal elements of PI leadership and the external elements of SQG leadership. The PM leader prefers conservative strategies that stick to the tried and tested. PMs are likely to shy away from risky innovation. The PM's low need for control, however, is likely to engender diversity and openness within the organization. Employees are not required to adhere to common goals and culture. As such, they have autonomy, and day-to-day operations are not highly standardized; the basic condition for decision making is not to create undue risk for the organization.

Jon Brock, who was the CEO of the world's No. 1 beer maker until 2005, is a process manager. His company, InBev, is part Brazilian and part Belgian with headquarters in Louvain, Belgium. It produces the famous Belgian beer Stella Artois and the Brazilian beers Skol and Brahma. Brock is informal, easygoing, and relaxed and makes it clear that he does not want to be the world's biggest brewer, just the best. His strategy focuses on efficiency and increasing profits by cutting costs. He wants to avoid hornets: "We're not going head-to-head with Budweiser, Miller, and Coors. That would be suicidal" (Tomlinson, 2004: 240).

As the former president of American Express and RJR Nabisco and CEO of IBM from 1993 to 2002, Lou Gerstner has a well-established and enviable track record as a strategic leader. He joined IBM at a time when the company was facing one of the most serious crises of its history. Gerstner is a cautious leader. While at RJR Nabisco, he opened the way for reconsideration of many internal processes. He is intelligent and has exceptional analytical skills, but he is careful about change. He strongly believes that change cannot happen unless it is balanced with stabilization (Rogers, 1994), and he is particularly skilled at letting his expectations be known. His approach is to improve existing processes slowly. He changed some elements of IBM and is proud of the company's slow and steady progress. Some call him an incrementalist rather than a revolutionary who avoids big mistakes but is moving too slowly.

All types of successful and effective leaders can be found in organizations. The need to revitalize our organizations is likely to be the reason we are celebrating innovators. The health-care industry's award to best administrators regularly goes to innovators. The most-admired business executives are those who push their businesses through change. Many uncelebrated SQG and PM leaders, however, are managing highly effective and efficient organizations. For example, the leaders of the much-publicized Lincoln Electric Company are consistently SQGs or PMs. Their organization is a model for using financial incentives in successfully managing performance. Our current tendency to appreciate only change could make us overlook some highly effective managers and leaders.

Strategic Leadership: Culture and Gender

Given the cross-cultural differences in micro-leadership style and the importance and impact of culture on leadership behaviors, one would expect that strategic leadership also differs across cultures to some extent. Cultural values, in particular, can be expected to influence a top manager's decisions and style (Finkelstein and Hambrick, 1996).

EFFECT OF CULTURE With little empirical research conducted about the direct effect of culture on executive style, considerable anecdotal evidence suggests similarities and differences across cultures. As organizations become more global, their strategic leaders are also increasingly global, a factor that can attenuate cross-cultural differences. Consider that Lindsay Owen-Jones, who is Welsh, is the current chairman of the French cosmetics company L'Oreal. Nissan, which is owned by French car maker Renault, is run by Carlos Ghosn, who was born in Brazil from Lebanese parents and was educated in France. Swiss Nestlé is headed by Austrian Peter Brabeck-Lethmathe. Other companies actively seek to build diverse and multicultural TMTs. For example, half of the senior managers at Citibank and P&G are not from the United States.

Models of cultures, such as those proposed by the GLOBE research (House et al., 2004) and Trompenaars (1994), suggest that patterns of leadership differ from one country or region to another. Particularly, the GLOBE research identified cultural clusters within the countries they researched, each with different implicit leadership theories or CLTs (culturally endorsed

Although most cultures value leaders who have a vision and are inspirational, Anglos, Latin Americans, Southern Asians, and Germanic and Nordic Europeans do so to a greater extent than Middle Easterners.

leadership theories; Dorfman, Hanges, and Brodbeck, 2004). For example, although most cultures value leaders who have a vision and are inspirational, Anglos, Latin Americans, Southern Asians, and Germanic and Nordic Europeans do so to a greater extent than Middle Easterners. Similarly, participation is seen as part of leadership by Anglos and Nordic Europeans, but not as much by Eastern Europeans, Southern Asians, and Middle Easterners. Columbians want leaders who are proactive and recognize accomplishment without being too proactive in terms of change (Matviuk, 2007). Middle Easterners, more than other cultural clusters, consider self-protection (including self-centeredness, status consciousness, and face-saving) to be part of leadership (Dorfman et al., 2004). Based on cross-cultural research and case studies, it is reasonable to suggest that upper-echelon leaders from different cultures will demonstrate different styles and approaches.

For example, being part of the "cadre" (French word for management) in France means having fairly distinct characteristics (Barsoux and Lawrence, 1991). In the United States, upper-echelon managers are from different social classes with many different skills and backgrounds, but the French upper-echelon leaders are much more homogeneous. In a high-power-distance culture, in which leaders are ascribed much authority and many powers, the cadre comes almost exclusively from the upper social classes. Nearly all have graduated from a few top technical universities (*Grandes Écoles*), where entry depends as much on social standing as it does on intellectual superiority. These schools have a strong military influence and continue to be male dominated. Their goal is to train highly intellectual, highly disciplined students who develop close ties and support with one antoher well beyond their years in school. The French cadre is, therefore, characterized by intellectual brilliance, ability to analyze and synthesize problems, and excellent communication skills. Contrary to U.S. leaders, the cadre's focus is not on practical issues or the development of interpersonal skills. Cultures with high power distance show little need to convince subordinates of the leadership's ideas (Laurent, 1983). The cadre is expected to be highly intelligent, and its decisions are not questioned.

Many of the members of French upper management have considerable experience in public and governmental sectors. This experience allows them to forge government–business relationships that do not exist in countries such as the United States. Interestingly, graduates of the *Grandes Écoles* would not consider working for those who received regular university education. This factor perpetuates the homogeneity of the cadre, which in turn creates a group of likeminded executives who agree on many industrial and political issues. By the same token, this like-mindedness can lead to lack of innovation and the focus on intellect at the expense of action can cause poor implementation.

EFFECT OF GENDER Another area of interest is potential gender differences. Unfortunately, research is lacking on the topic of gender differences in strategic leadership. It is evident that many of the top-level female executives in traditional organizations succeed because their style mirrors that of their male counterparts. As Linda Hoffman, a managing partner at PriceWaterhouseCoopers LLP, states, "Many of the things you must do to succeed are more comfortable for men than women" (Himelstein and Forest, 1997: 68). Eileen Collins, commander of the space shuttle *Discovery*, believes that women often try to do too much and that men are more willing to delegate (Juarez, Childress, and Hoffman, 2005), a sentiment echoed by Judith Rodin, former president of the University of Pennsylvania and president of the Rockefeller Foundation. She states, "Women moving up in their careers often feel they have to be more aggressive, be more like men. They ought to find their own voice" (Juarez, Childress, and Hoffman, 2005). Nonetheless, the more recent accounts of female executives and business owners and their focus on openness, participation, and interactive leadership provide some basis to make deductions about gender differences. It appears that the feminine style of leadership is generally low control. Meg Whitman, former CEO of eBay, who was consistently ranked among the most powerful women in business and is running for governor of California in 2010, states, "I don't actually think of myself as powerful"; instead she relies on relationship building, developing expertise and credibility, and enabling—one of her favorite words—her employees (Sellers, 2004: 161). Similarly, Parmount's Sherry Lansing, cofounder of Stand Up to Cancer foundation, is famous for her nurturing style, charm, and ability to show empathy (Sellers, 1998). Gail McGovern, former president of Fidelity Investments and president and CEO of the Red Cross since 2008, observes that "real power is influence. My observation is that women tend to be better in positions where they can be influential" (Sellers, 2000a: 148).

Many female leaders, however, play down the gender differences. Judith Shapiro, former president of Barnard College, suggests, "You need to be supportive of your people because leading is about serving. That's not a girly thing; it's what I believe a strong leader does" (Juarez et al., 2005). She attributes any gender differences to women's social experiences. Chairman of the advertising company Ogilvy & Mather since 1997, Shelly Lazarus asserts, "I don't really believe that men and women manage differently. There are as many different styles and approaches among women as there are among men" (Juarez, Childress, and Hoffman, 2005). Whether they are challenge seekers or risk averse, many upper-echelon women leaders, such as those described in the research by Sally Helgesen (1995), encourage diversity of thought and employee empowerment. Their open and supportive style allows employees to contribute to decision making. In addition, the web structure that some women leaders are reputed to use is flat, with well-informed leaders at the center and without centralized decision making.

As is the case with micro leadership, the type of strategic leadership that is needed depends on the type of environment the organization faces, the industry to which it belongs, and the internal culture and structure that it currently has. Therefore, leaders define and influence strategic forces, and their style also needs to match existing ones. If an organization is in a highly stable industry with few competitors, the need for innovation and openness might not be as great. The appropriate focus in such circumstances would be on efficiency. For such an organization, a highly participative and innovative strategic leadership style might not be appropriate.

HOW DO EXECUTIVES AFFECT THEIR ORGANIZATION?

Regardless of the type of leadership at the top of an organization, the processes through which strategic leaders affect and influence the organization are similar. As the chief decision makers and the people in charge of providing general guidelines for implementation of the strategies, top executives influence their organizations in a variety of ways (Figure 4).

Direct Decisions

Leaders' decisions regarding various aspects of the organization shape the course of their organization. The choices regarding the vision and mission for an organization influence all aspects of an organization's functioning. The vision and mission influence the culture of an organization by determining the basic assumptions, what is important, what needs to be attended to first, and what is considered less valuable. Similarly, the choice of strategy is considered to be the almost-exclusive domain of top management.

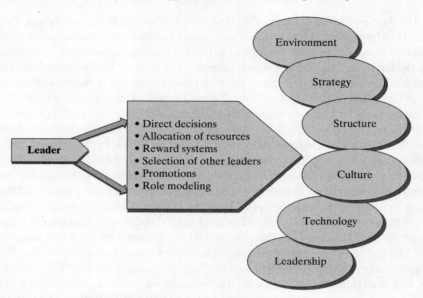

Leader →
- Direct decisions
- Allocation of resources
- Reward systems
- Selection of other leaders
- Promotions
- Role modeling

Environment
Strategy
Structure
Culture
Technology
Leadership

FIGURE 4 Processes Leaders Use to Impact their Organizations

In addition to the vision, mission, culture, and strategy, the decisions to adopt a new structure, adjust an existing one, or make any changes in the formal interrelationship among employees of an organization rest primarily with top management (Miller and Droge, 1986; Nahavandi, 1993; Yasai-Ardekani, 1986, 1989). The leader can determine the structure of the organization through direct decisions on the type of structure or indirectly through the way employees share and use information. Mickey Drexler of the Gap and J. Crew does not e-mail and does not write memos. He likes to use a public-address system to communicate with people in the office and leave voice messages and communicate face-to-face. His employees have learned to check their voice mail on a regular basis and be ready for his questions at any time (Munk, 1998). A leader who consistently communicates only through formal reporting channels sets up a different structure than one who crosses hierarchical lines and encourages others to do so, as well.

Allocation of Resources and Control over the Reward System

In addition to direct decisions, one of the most powerful effects of top managers on their organization is through the allocation of resources and the control they have over the reward system (Kerr and Slocum, 1987; Schein, 2004). A top executive is the final decision maker on allocation of resources to departments or individuals. If leaders want to encourage continued innovation and creativity, they might decide that the R&D and training departments of the organization will get the lion's share of the resources. Such allocations reinforce certain goals and actions, support a particular organizational culture and strategy, and create structures that facilitate desired outcomes and discourage undesirable ones (Kets de Vries and Miller, 1986; Miller, 1987). Consider that Jeff Bezos, CEO of Amazon.com, believes in spending resources on things that matter, which include simple and functional offices rather than luxurious furniture, creating small creative teams, and borrowing competitors' successful ideas (Deutschman, 2004).

The formal and informal reward systems also can have a powerful impact on the culture of an organization and on the behavior of its members (Schein, 2004). For example, top managers can shape the culture of their organization by rewarding conformity to unique norms and standards of behavior at the expense of diversity of behaviors and opinions (Nahavandi and Malekzadeh, 1988). This process could take place not only through encouragement of certain behaviors but also through the selection of other top managers and the promotion of those who adhere to the leader's culture. Such a process is likely to take place regardless of the leader's style of strategic leadership. For instance, an HCI will most comfortable with other HCIs, whereas a PI will prefer other managers with a similar style in key positions. A comparable process is likely to take place on an individual employee level. Employees whose actions fit the vision, mission, and culture of the organization are more likely to be rewarded. These processes create domino effects that further lead an organization to reflect the style and preferences of its leader.

Setting the Norms and Modeling

Rewarding certain types of behaviors and decisions is an overt action on the part of the leader; modeling behaviors and setting certain decision standards and norms, however, provide more indirect ways of affecting organizations. Alan Mulally of Ford Motor says, "I really focus on the values and standards of the organization. What are expected behaviors? How do we want to treat each other?" (Bryant, 2009j). In addition to making decisions, the top managers can set the parameters by which others make decisions. CEOs might tell their vice presidents that they will go along with their choice of a new product while also providing them with clear guidelines on which types of products are appropriate and which types of markets the organization should enter. By setting such standards, even without making a direct decision, the CEO still can be assured that the vice presidents will make the right decision.

Another subtle way in which leaders shape their organization is by the types of behavior they model (Nahavandi and Malekzadeh, 1993a; Schein, 2004). A top manager who believes that physical fitness is important might engage in vigorous exercise and invite members of the TMT to join in. Irishman Feargal Quinn, founder and president of Superquinn, a chain of supermarkets, gained a reputation as the "pope of customer service." He focuses obsessively on making sure his customers come back—an obsession that he transfers to his employees (Customer service, 2007). James E. Rogers of Duke Energy, who was recently appointed to be on the presidential panel on energy policy, emphasizes walking the talk, ". . . as I've been CEO for over 20 years, it's really important to be on the front lines and to remember kind of the sound of the bullets whizzing by, to be on the ground" (Bryant, 2009k). Another area in which role modeling can have a powerful impact is in ethics. A. G. Lafley, former CEO of P&G considers self-sacrifice and integrity to be essential traits of leadership (Jones, 2007). Similarly Gordon Bethune of Continental Airlines emphasizes the importance of integrity (Bryant, 2010a). Bob Moffat, IBM's senior vice president for Integrated Operations, demonstrates the need for hard work by spending 15 to 16 hours a day at the office (Fishman, 2001).

Direct decisions, allocation of resources and rewards, setting of decision norms, and modeling are some of the ways through which a leader affects the organization. Through these various processes, leaders can make an organization the reflection of their style and preferences. They also provide strategic leaders with considerable power and influence. Such power requires some accountability, which is considered in the next section.

STRATEGIC LEADERS' ACCOUNTABILITY

Chief executive officers and TMTs around the world have considerable power and influence over people's lives. Their actions affect the economic health of countries and citizens. For this burden, CEOs are well rewarded financially and achieve considerable status. The topic of executive compensation, another governance mechanism, attracts considerable attention and criticism (e.g., Pfeffer, 2010). The average salary of CEOs in Standard and Poor's top 500 companies in 2008 was $10.9 million, with perks averaging $364,04, which is nearly 10 times the median salary of a full-time worker (Executive pay watch, 2009). According to the Economic Policy Institute, in 1978 CEOs were paid an average of 78 times as much as the minimum wage earner; in 2005, that difference increased to 821 times, leading the average CEO to earn more before lunchtime on the very first day of work than a minimum wage worker earns all year (Mischel, 2006).

Even ousted CEOs fare well. By some estimate, the cost of various severance packages in 2006 for CEOs was over $1 billion in the United States (Dash, 2007). The list includes fired AOL CEO Randy Falco, who will be payed $1 million in salary and $7.5 million in bonuses through 2010 (Carlson, 2009). Seagate Technology is paying its fired Chief Executive $2.5 million and continuing to employ him as a $500-an-hour consultant while also covering the close to $30,000 cost of his health insurance (Davis, 2009). Others include David Edmonston, who resigned from Radio Shack in 2006 after admitting lying on his resume ($1 million severance pay); Home Depot's Robert Nardelli, who is reputed to have refused to have his pay tied to the company performance and received an exit package of more than $200 million in 2007, despite poor stock performance and considerable controversy and criticism (Grow, 2007); Jay Sidhum, who resigned from Sovereign Bancorp amid cricitism ($73.56 million that includes cash and stock options, 5-year free health care, and consulting contract); and Douglas Pertz, who resigned from Harman International Industries after the stocks dropped during his 4-month tenure and still earned $3.8 million in severance pay (Dash, 2007). Those who have kept their job continue to receive highly generous compensation packages. United States executives have some of the highest compensation packages in the world, although political pressure seems to have had an effect and caused a slight drop in average salaries in 2008 and 2009 (MSNBC-Executive Pay, 2010). Japanese and European executives earn between one-half to one-tenth of comparable U.S. CEOs. These differences could have been explained by a higher performance of U.S. executives prior to 2008; however, the pay is generally not closely tied to company performance (Pfeffer, 2010; The Pay at the Top, 2010).

The issue of executive compensation is highly complex. Theoretically, boards of directors determine CEO compensation relative to company performance; the better the financial performance of the company, the higher the CEO's compensation. Therefore, CEO's compensation can be an effective tool for motivating and controlling managers. In many cases, company leaders get fair compensation packages and perform well. The instances of lack of performance and high compensation, however, are hard to ignore. Many executives get pay raises that are considerably higher than their company's performance. For example, in 2008, profit at Archer Daniels Midland fell by 17 percent; CEO Patricia Woertz' salary was increased by close to 400 percent (The pay at the top, 2010). Similarly, while Boeing's profit dropped by 35 percent in 2008, CEO James McNemey got a 14 percent increase in his compensation (The pay at the top, 2010). After pulling Vioxx off the market, shares of Merck slumped 30 percent, but the company board gave the CEO, Ray Gilmartin, a $1.4-million bonus and stock options valued at $19.2 million (Strauss and Hansen, 2005).

TABLE 4	Factors That Determine Executive Compensation
Firm size	The larger the firm, the higher the compensation
Industry competition	Companies often outbid one another to hire top executives
CEO power and discretion	The higher the power of the CEO, the higher the compensation package
Internationalization	Increased internationalization is related to higher executive pay
High stress and instability	CEO jobs are considered high stress, requiring high compensation

Based on these examples and the extensive research about CEO compensation (for a recent example, see O'Reilley and Main, 2007), company performance is not the only determinant of CEO compensation. So what determines an executive's worth? Table 4 gives a summary of factors that determine executive compensation. One factor that seems to explain the size of executive pay in the United States is the size of the organization (for a recent study, see Geiger and Cashen, 2007): the larger the organization, the larger the CEO's compensation package, regardless of performance. Another factor seems to be the competition for hiring CEOs; as organizations outbid one another, salaries continue to increase.

Organizations in which top managers have more discretion also tend to have higher pay (Cho and Shen, 2007). In addition, research shows that top management pay and company performance are more aligned when the company's board of directors is dominated by members from outside the organization (Conyon and Peck, 1998). Other research that considers the impact of internationalization found that increased internationalization is related to higher CEO pay (Sanders and Carpenter, 1998). The thought is that the high demands put on CEOs and the instability of their positions must be balanced with high salaries. These high salaries, now standard in U.S. industry, show no end in their upward trend, even during a time of economic crisis. The result is the creation of a new, powerful U.S. managerial class and a widening of the gap between high and low levels of organizations.

The highly paid top executives have become popular heroes whose names are part of our everyday life. Based on economic and organizational theory, environmental forces will push a nonperforming leader to be replaced. Ideally, elected federal, state, and city officials who do not perform are not reelected. Similarly, the board of directors replaces a CEO who does not manage well. The principal of a school with poor student academic performance and a high dropout rate would be fired by the school board. These ideal situations do not seem to be common, however. Many powerful leaders are not being held accountable for their actions. They continue to hold positions of power and influence regardless of their organization's poor performance, ethical abuses, and social irresponsibility. It is not common in the United States for a company CEO or public officials to resign when they fail to live up to the promises they made. When their organizations cause major disasters or commit illegal acts, the CEOs escape unscathed. The CEO of Exxon accepted none of the responsibility for the *Valdez* fiasco. After the Bhopal disaster, with several thousand dead and hundreds of thousands injured, the CEO of Union Carbide was not replaced. The public firing of the CEO of General Motors by the U.S. government in 2009 and the replacement of BP's CEO Tony Hayward in 2010 are the exception rather than the rule.

For the benefit of organizational and social functioning and well-being, it is essential that the tremendous power, influence, and status of CEOs be accompanied by accountability and responsibility to their various constituents. Such accountability exists on paper but is hardly ever executed. The power and impact of upper-echelon leaders are undeniable. Their credibility and ability to further affect their organizations, however, can increase only with more accountability.

UNIQUE CHALLENGES OF NONPROFIT ORGANIZATIONS

Nonprofit organizations are private organizations that cannot make a profit for its owners or members but can charge fees for services or membership. Other terms used to describe such agencies that are private, nonprofit, and with a public purpose include voluntary, not-for-profit, philanthropic, and nongovernmental organizations (NGOs; Weiss and Gantt, 2004). Although many of the leadership and organizational principles that apply to business and other organizations are also relevant in nonprofit organizations, some of their distinguishing characteristics present them with unique leadership challenges. The case of Kavita Ramdas in Leading Change in this chapter provides an example of a leader of a nonprofit organization. The primary purpose of her organization is public good, and its source of funding is donations through grants, foundations, and individuals.

Characteristics of Nonprofit Organizations

Many of the characteristics that identify nonprofit organizations are related to tax status. Other characteristics include

- *Operate without profit.* Although nonprofit organizations charge for services or membership and many generate and use considerable sums of money, all the funds are reinvested to support the operations of the organization. Many nonprofits are highly "profitable"; however, all excess funds are reinvested to achieve their mission.
- *Public service mission.* The primary mission of a nonprofit organization is to serve the public good, whether it is health care (hospitals), education (schools and universities), churches, community improvement, or foundations with a broad purpose.
- *Governed by voluntary board of directors.* As opposed to business organizations that have paid board of directors, the governing boards of nonprofits are staffed by volunteers with a stake or interest in the mission of the organization.
- *Funded through contributions.* Whereas charging fees is a source of revenue for many nonprofit organizations, their primary sources of funding are contributions, grants, and donations from individuals, government agencies, and other foundations.

There are many organizations around the world that fit into the nonprofit category. Examples in the United States include the American Cancer Society, National Geographic Society, the Metropolitan Museum of Art, Stanford University, Planned Parenthood, the Ford and Rockefeller Foundations, the National Association for the Advancement of Colored People (NAACP), and the YMCA and YWCA. Around the world, NGOs make considerable contributions to improving social, human, political, economic, and ecological conditions. Organizations such as Doctors without Border (*Médecins sans Frontières*); OXFAM, an international relief agency; the International Red Cross; and the World Wildlife Fund are just a few that encourage development and support communities in crisis around the world. These organizations survive and achieve their goals by using funds they obtain through various means. For example, physicians volunteer their time through Doctors without Borders and provide health

LEADING CHANGE

Kavita Ramdas at the Global Fund for Women

The Global Fund for Women is a San Francisco-based nonprofit organization committed to equality and social justice focused on helping women achieve full equality and participation worldwide by making grants to support women's groups around the world (Global Fund for Women, 2010). The organization was founded in 1987 to raise funds to support women-led enterprises and activities that promote better health, economics, education, and social welfare for women (Social Capitalist, 2007). Since its creation it has awarded $71 million to 3,800 women's organizations in 167 countries (Global Fund for Women, 2010). The organization embraces such principles as freedom and liberty for individuals, dignity for people, tolerance, education, economic independence, nonviolence, and peace. It has granted funds to causes including a Buddhist orphanage in Sri Lanka, an organization for coordination of peasant women in Bolivia, empowering women in Nepal, legal aid for women in China, and a women's rights organization in Guatemala (Global Fund for Women, 2010; Patel, 2007)

The fund's current president and CEO, Kavita Ramdas, named one of the world's top 20 entrepreneurs in 2002 and holder of many other international awards, is a tireless advocate for changing women's situation in all aspects of life around the world. She suggests that there has been an undeclared "war" against women around the world through increases in abuse, health crises, silence in case of abuse and neglect, and lack of resources going to support women worldwide (Now with Bill Moyers, 2004). Ramdas leads the effort to change the situation of women one person and one organization at a time, advocating for the cause she passionately represents.

Ramdas was born into a prominent secular Hindu family in Mumbai, India. Her father is a retired former head of the Indian navy turned peace and antinuclear activist, and her mother is highly active in social causes. Ramdas is married to a Pakistani man, Zulfiqar Ahmad, raised in a secular Muslim family and himself a peace advocate (Curiel, 2002), a union that has generated many concerns and comments in both India and Pakistan. At 18, Ramdas volunteered to work in a small farm in India until a village elder told her to use her education and compassion to tell the world about them (Sowing the seeds, 2006). Ramdas was educated in the United States (bachelor's degree from Mount Holyoke and master's from Princeton) and represents her organization with as much ease to U.N. officials and CEOs of major philanthropic organizations, as to villagers in all parts of the world. One of her colleagues states, "Kavita is one of the very few people who, when she enters a room, you know there's a presence. It's important in this work that we do to have that type of presence and grace—to hold people's attention" (Curiel, 2002).

Ramdas says, "For me, what I do at the Global Fund is so deeply connected to my sense of who I am and what I can give back to this world and what my responsibilities are to this world. It's a deep sense of commitment. It's not a 9–5 job" (Curiel, 2002). Ramdas' passion for what she does allows her to lead her organization to make changes to improve women's lives one step at a time.

Sources: Social capitalists: Global Fund for Women, 2010. http://www.globalfundforwomen.org/cms/ (accessed April 8, 2010); Now with Bill Moyers, 2004. http://www.pbs.org/now/politics/ramdas.html# (accessed April 8, 2010); Entrepreneurs who are changing the world, 2007. http://www.fastcompany.com/social/2007/profiles/profile17.html (accessed April 8, 2010); Curiel, J., 2002. "A woman's work," *San Francisco Chronicle,* November 10. http://www.sfgate.com/cgi-bin/article.cgi?f=/chronicle/archive/2002/11/10/CM148265. DTL&type=news (accessed April 8, 2010); Hatnell, C., 2004. "Kavita Ramdas on feminist philanthropy," *Alliance,* September. http://www.allavida.org/alliance/sep04b.html (accessed April 8, 2010); Patel, P., 2007. "Money makers: Five questions for Kavita Ramdas," *Houston Chronicle,* June 12. http://www.chron.com/disp/story.mpl/business/4884490.html (accessed April 8, 2010); Empowering women. 2004. *The Common Wealth.* http://www.globalfundforwomen.org/cms/content/view/63/98/ (April 8, 2010); Sowing the seeds of global change, 2006. www.mtholyoke.edu/cic/about/reasons.shtml?num=2 (accessed April 8, 2010).

care in remote areas of the world; OXFAM provides funds and resources to combat global poverty and social injustice.

Leadership Challenges

The leadership of nonprofit organizations involves the same principles as other organizations. Their leaders must help individuals and groups set goals and guide them in the achievement of those goals. The public-good mission of nonprofits, along with the voluntary participation of many of their employees, contributors, and other stakeholders, creates a particular burden on leaders of such organizations to lead through a collaborative and trust-based style. In most cases, individual donors, except for tax benefits when applicable, do not get tangible benefits from their donation, and the resources they contribute do not always stay in their community. The nonprofit is based to a great extent on the principles of altruism and selfless contribution.

> The public-good mission of nonprofits, along with the voluntary participation of many of their employees, contributors, and other stakeholders, creates a particular burden on leaders of such organizations to lead through a collaborative and trust-based style.

As much as integrity, trustworthiness, and self-sacrifice are elements for all leadership situations, they are even more so in the nonprofit organizations. Without the profit motive, which legitimately guides business organizations and the rewarding of its leaders (e.g., top leaders being compensated with company shares), nonprofit organizations are likely to attract leaders with a stronger focus on civic contribution. The role of leaders in nonprofit organizations is that of an intermediary (Butler and Wilson, 1990). The leader guides the organization to allocate the resources, such as donations or grants, to various receivers turning the resources that are trusted to the organization into social good (Figure 5). Kavita Ramdas and her Global Fund for Women distribute the resources they gather throughout the world to improve women's lives. In his commencement address at the University of Maryland, Brian Gallagher—president and CEO of the United Way, the $5-billion umbrella organization for large number of charities—emphasized the importance of service to the community and stated that his organization "improves lives by mobilizing the caring power of communities" (Gallagher, 2006: 6). Luis A Ubiñas, president of the Ford Foundation—a resource for

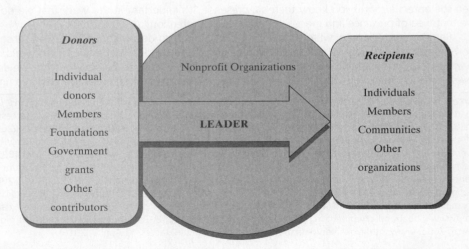

FIGURE 5 Role of Leaders in Nonprofit Organizations

innovative people and institutions worldwide, leads an organization that has as its mission to strengthen democratic values, reduce poverty, promote international cooperation, and advance human achievement (Ford Foundation Mission, 2007). The organization aims to achieve these goals by providing grants to qualified groups and organizations.

One of the major challenges that leaders of nonprofit organizations face is how to recruit, retain, and motivate employees, many of whom are volunteers, without having access to substantial monetary rewards. Even in the case of paid employees, salaries are often lower than comparable positions in business organizations. The leaders of nonprofits, therefore, require considerable skills in motivating and inspiring their followers. In many cases, followers have joined the organization because they are passionate about its mission; however, passion alone does not always lead to effectiveness. An additional factor is that the structure of many nonprofits is relatively flat, with few employees and few layers of management. Effective leadership requires empowerment; use of all available resources, often by harnessing the power of teams; and participation to creatively solve problems without many resources.

According to recent studies, nonprofit organizations are facing a leadership crisis because of a significant shortfall of qualified leaders (Tierney, 2006). As more nonprofit organizations are created and step in to address growing social challenges not addressed by government or business organizations, the need for effective leadership increases. According to the Bridgespan Group's 2006 study, the total number of nonprofit organization has tripled over the past 20 years, but because of demographic shifts, retirement, and lack of active recruitment and development, the supply of potential leaders has not kept up (Tierney, 2006). One of the challenges leaders of nonprofits, therefore, face is the recruitment, retention, and development of future leaders. Such a task is much simpler in a business organization, where considerable resources are dedicated to recruitment and development and access to a pool of leaders from competitors is much greater.

Although many of the processes involved in leading nonprofit organizations are similar to those used in a business organization, leaders of nonprofits need a particular emphasis on building relationships and trust and on the development of future leaders.

Summary and Conclusions

Upper-echelon or strategic leadership has many commonalities with leadership at lower levels of organizations. Upper-echelon leadership, however, adds a new level of complexity to the process by focusing the leader on a whole organization rather than a small group or department and by giving the leader discretion with far-reaching influence over decisions. In addition, upper-echelon leaders focus on external constituencies as well as the internal environment and in so doing are required to lead with a team of other executives.

An integrated approach to upper-echelon leadership considers the leader to be a formulator and implementer of strategy. Therefore, in addition to considering the need to match the leader to existing strategy and other organizational elements, the integrated approach also considers the role of the leader's individual characteristics and style in the selection of various organizational elements and the implementation of decisions. The matching concept, which views the CEO primarily as an implementer of existing strategy, is also useful when selecting a leader to implement a newly charted course.

Two major themes run through the diverse research about top management characteristics. The first theme is the leader's degree of challenge seeking and preference for risk and innovation. The second is the leader's need for control over the organization. The combination of these two themes yields four types of strategic leaders: HCI, SQG, PI, and PM. These four types each exhibit different preferences for the direction and management of their organization. They exert their influence through direct decisions, allocation of resources and rewards, and the setting of norms and the modeling of desired behaviors. Through these processes, strategic leaders gain considerable power and influence. Such power is accompanied by generous compensation packages. Accountability for the actions of top executives, however, is still limited.

Although many of the processes involved in leading nonprofit organizations are similar to those used in business organization, leaders of nonprofits need a particular emphasis on building relationships and trust and on the development of future leaders. Overall, the area of strategic leadership, whether in business or nonprofit organizations, provides a different and important perspective to the study of leadership. Strategic leaders face many challenges that micro leaders do not. The study of strategic leaders is also a fertile area for integrative research linking micro and macro factors.

Review and Discussion Questions

1. What are the differences between micro and macro leadership?
2. What are the strategic forces that affect strategic leadership in organizations?
3. What is the role of the upper echelon in managing the strategic forces in the formulation and implementation of strategy?
4. Provide examples for each of the moderating factors on the impact of leadership in organizations.
5. What are the major themes that are used to describe upper-echelon leaders?

6. Describe each of the four strategic leadership types. Provide examples of each type.
7. How do culture and gender affect strategic leadership?
8. Describe each of the processes used by leaders to influence strategic forces in their organizations. Which of the processes is most important? Why?
9. What is the upper echelon's responsibility in organizational actions and performance?
10. What are the unique characteristics and challenges of nonprofit leadership?

Leadership Challenge: The Board of Directors (BOD) and CEOs

Public corporations are led by CEOs and other upper-echelon leaders who, in turn, report to shareholders and boards of directors (BODs). Interestingly, even though the board oversees the CEOs, decides on terms of employment and salaries, and monitors their performance, the CEOs are, more often than not, the people who nominate board members. The justification is that CEOs are well placed to know what type of expertise they need on the board and should have a BOD they can work with. The relationship between BOD and CEO is a complex and interesting one.

1. What are the potential ethical and conflict-of-interest issues arising from CEO involvement in the selection of board members?
2. How can these issues be addressed?

Exercise 1: Understanding Strategic Forces

This exercise is designed to help you understand the role of leaders in managing the six strategic forces of environment, strategy, culture, structure, technology, and leadership presented in the chapter.

The Scenario

You are a member of a school board for a medium-sized middle (junior high) school in a major western city. The city has experienced tremendous growth in the past 5 years, and as a result, the student body increased by 20 percent without much change in facilities and relatively limited increases in funding. The classrooms are overcrowded, much of the equipment is old, teachers have limited resources to enrich the curriculum, and the sense of direction is unclear. During the same time period, the school slowly developed one of the poorest records for student academic performance and dropout rate.

Earlier to the past few years, however, the school held a well-established reputation as one of the most creative and academically sound schools in the city. Traditionally, parent involvement and interest in the school varied greatly. Similarly, the faculty are diverse in their approach, tenure, and backgrounds, but the majority demonstrate dedication to their students and are committed to the improvement of the school.

Because of a number of recent threats of lawsuits from parents over equal opportunity issues, several violent incidents among the students, and the poor academic performance, the principal was asked to resign. Many parents, teachers, and board members blame her for a laissez-faire attitude and what appears to be a total lack of direction and focus. Problems and complaints were simply not addressed, and no plan was articulated for dealing with the changes that the school was experiencing.

After a 2-month multistate regional search and interviews with a number of finalists, the school board narrowed its search for the new principal to two candidates.

The Candidates

J. B. Davison is 55 years old, with a doctorate in education administration and BA and MA degrees in education. He previously served as principal at two other schools, where he was successful in focusing on basic academic skills, traditional approaches, discipline, and encouragement of success. Before moving to school administration, he was a history and social studies teacher. The board is impressed with his clear-headedness and no-nonsense approach to education. He readily admits that he is conservative and traditional and considers himself to be a father figure to the students. He runs a tight ship and is involved in every aspect of his school.

Jerry Popovich is 40 years old. She holds MA and PhD degrees in education administration with an undergraduate degree in computer science. She worked in the computer industry several years before teaching science and math. She worked as assistant principal in one other school and is currently the principal of an urban middle school on the West Coast. She successfully involved many business and community members in her current school. The board is impressed with her creativity and her ability to find novel approaches. She considers one of her major strengths to be the ability to involve many constituents in decision making. She describes herself as a facilitator in the education process.

Understanding Strategic Forces Worksheet: Comparing the Candidates

In helping you decide on which person to recommend, consider how each would handle and balance the six strategic management forces of environment, strategy, culture, structure, technology, and leadership.

Strategic Forces	J. B. Davison	Jerry Popovich
Environment		
Strategy		
Culture		
Structure		
Technology		
Leadership		

Discussion Items

How are the two candidates different?

What explains the differences between them?

Your Choice

Who would you recommend for the job? Why?

Exercise 2: Your Organization

This exercise is designed to illustrate the potential impact of an upper-echelon leader on the organization. Before starting this exercise, clearly define the department, team, or organization that you are rating. Your instructor may also provide you with several vignettes to use in your evaluation.

Rate your organization or team on the following items, using the following scale:

1 = Strongly disagree

2 = Somewhat disagree

3 = Neither agree nor disagree

4 = Somewhat agree

5 = Strongly agree

_____ 1. Decision making in my organization is centralized.

_____ 2. A strong, thick culture exists in my organization.

_____ 3. We are always coming up with new ways of doing things.

_____ 4. A few people make most of the important decisions.

_____ 5. The organization consists of many subgroups and cliques.

_____ 6. Our primary concern is efficiency.

_____ 7. We are known for our ability to innovate.

_____ 8. We are open to differing points of views.

_____ 9. Employees are empowered to make many decisions without checking with management.

_____ 10. We have not changed our course much in the past few years.

_____ 11. We take many risks.

_____ 12. Many rules and procedures are established for our tasks.

_____ 13. People are encouraged to do their own thing.

Scoring: Reverse score for items 5, 6, 8, 9, and 13 (1 = 5, 2 = 4, 3 = 3, 4 = 2, 5 = 1).

Organizational structure: Add items 1, 4, 9, and 12. Maximum score is 20. A higher score indicates a more centralized, control-oriented structure.

Total: _____

Organizational culture: Add items 2, 5, 8, and 13. Maximum score is 20. A higher score indicates a unicultural organization where diversity is not encouraged.

Total: _____

Strategy: Add items 3, 6, 7, 10, and 11. Maximum score is 25. A higher score indicates risk taking and innovation.

Total: _____

Discussion Issues

Based on your organization's score on the structure, culture, and strategy scales, what would you predict the organization leaders' strategic leadership style to be?

Exercise 3: Influence Processes

This exercise is designed to help you identify the processes that upper-echelon leaders use to influence their organization and most particularly its culture. After reading each of the following scenarios, identify the processes that the leaders and TMT are using to influence the organization.

Brain Toys Executives

Stanley Wang, the CEO of Brain Toys, joined the organization a few years before the founder, J. C. Green, decided to retire. It became clear early on that Stanley was destined to rise fast. With a BS degree in engineering and graphic design, an MBA, and several years of experience in computer software design, he fit right into the Brain Toys culture. He was bright, witty, analytical, and competitive. J. C. took a liking to him and put him in charge of several high-visibility projects with potential for high impact and big budgets. Stanley performed every time. Within the first 2 years, Stanley won all the internal awards that Brain Toys gives its managers. Several of his peers maliciously credited Stanley's love of running rather than his technical and managerial competence as the cause of his success. Stanley ran with the boss every day before work, and they trained for many races together.

The Soft-Touch Leader

Leslie Marks was proud of her accomplishments as one of the few executives in the male-dominated information technology field. As the president of Uniform Data Link, she describes herself as a "soft-touch" leader. "I just don't believe in heavy-handed leadership. People have to be able to express themselves and that is when you get the best out of them. Our best ideas come from all levels." She keeps an open door for all employees and has moved her office from the third floor to the first. She often comes to work in jeans and spends a lot of time with the engineers brainstorming on technical problems. She changed many of the evaluation and promotion procedures and asked several less-educated but highly experienced employees to work with her on important projects.

The Hospital Economist

Joseph Hadad graduated with a doctorate in economics and health-care administration from a major southwestern university, and after many years of work in various health-care organizations, Hadad was named as the top administrator of a major Phoenix hospital. As an economist and a strong believer in fair pay, Hadad focused much time with the human resource managers, revamping the hospital's compensation and benefit plan. The old system based on seniority was all but dismantled and replaced with a pay-for-performance system that ties the pay of all employees, including the physicians, partially to the hospital's financial performance. The plan allows for some flexibility for 2 years, whereby employees are not penalized for poor performance, but only rewarded for good financial health. After 2 years, they shared in the good and the bad. Most of the hospital's employees complain that Hadad seemed to care about nothing else. Many also note a major change in everybody's behaviors.

Influence Process Worksheet

Influence Method	Stanley Wang	Leslie Marks	Joseph Hadad
Direct decisions			
Allocation of resources			
Reward system			
Selection and promotion of other leaders			
Role modeling			

Self-Assessment 1: What Is Your Strategic Leadership Type?

This exercise is a self-rating based on the four strategic leadership types presented in the chapter. You can also use the scale to rate your organizational leaders. For each of the items listed, please rate yourself using the following scale. (You can also use the items to rate a leader in your organization.)

0 = Never

1 = Sometimes

2 = Often

3 = Always

_____ 1. I enjoy working on routine tasks.

_____ 2. I am always looking for new ways of doing things.

_____ 3. I have trouble delegating tasks to my subordinates.

_____ 4. I like my subordinates to share the same values and beliefs.

_____ 5. Change makes me uncomfortable.

_____ 6. I encourage my subordinates to participate in decision making.

_____ 7. It is difficult for me to get things done in situations with many contrasting opinions.

_____ 8. I enjoy working on new tasks.

_____ 9. I feel comfortable giving power away to my subordinates.

_____ 10. I consider myself to be a risk taker.

Scoring: Reverse scores for items 1, 5, 6, 7, and 9 (0 = 3, 1 = 2, 2 = 1, 3 = 0).

Challenge-seeking score: Add items 1, 2, 5, 8, and 10. Your score will be between 0 and 15. Transfer the score to challenge-seeking line (vertical line) on the following grid.

Total: _____.

Need-for-control score: Add items 3, 4, 6, 7, and 9. Your score will be between 0 and 15. Transfer the score to control line (horizontal line) on the following grid.

Total: _____.

What Is Your Strategic Leadership Type?

Where do your two scores intersect? For example, if you have a score of 5 on control and 10 on challenge seeking, your scores indicate that you are a participative innovator.

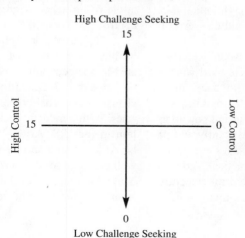

LEADERSHIP IN ACTION

The Leadership at P&G

The venerable consumer goods company Procter & Gamble (P&G) was founded in 1837 and is known globally for its products primarily directed at women, with brand such as Tide, Ivory, Pampers, Crest, Clairol, Cover Girl, and Pantene, just to name a few. Despite its history and well-known brands, P&G faced turbulent times in the 1990s. Particularly, it lost market share in many areas and failed to successfully launch new products for a number of years. With a focus on internal promotions and sets of guidelines called "Current Best Approaches" that informed employees on how to do most everything, the company was comfortably on its way to joining other disappearing business dinosaurs.

Those days are long gone. First under the leadership of A. G. Lafley—a company veteran of over 20 years—until 2009, and now with Bob McDonald at the helm, P&G is once again highly profitable and growing. Company observers and insiders agree that P&G has changed significantly: It has energy, enthusiasm, hope, a new openness, and an outward-looking focus that were sorely lacking just a few years ago (Buckley, 2005). The man credited with much of the success is the soft-spoken and understated A. G. Lafley, who was CEO from 2000 to 2009 and was named one of the best CEOs for 2006 by Harvard's Kennedy School of Government and *U.S. News and World Report* (Jones, 2007). He quietly and effectively changed the culture and the performance of the company.

Lafley's actions that so drastically changed P&G were deceptively simple. He used what he called "Sesame Street language" to "make things simple because the difficulty is making sure everybody knows what the goal is and how to get there" (Markels, 2006). He consistently and patiently repeated those same messages any chance he gets. In a highly symbolic, practical, and well-publicized move, he transformed the executive offices in the top floor of the company's head-quarters into a leadership training center and moved the senior executives to the same floors as their staff. He created open offices, including one for himself and a couple of other executives. Lafley believed that the arrangement is not only symbolic of the new openness in the company and shows the importance of learning at P&G, but also conducive to collaboration, creativity, and flexibility, "I wanted an environment that would be more collaborative, more in touch, more designed to bring human beings together. . . . I wanted a place that was low tech and high touch" (@*Issue*, 2004).

Lafley's ability to transform P&G so quickly is even more surprising, given Lafley's quiet leadership, or maybe precisely because his style seems to so well fit the family culture at the company. He states, "I'm a low-ego guy. I don't have problems putting the greater good of the company or the P&G brands way ahead of my personal aspirations or achievements" (Jones, 2007). Words such as *quiet*, *soft-spoken*, *affable*, *calm*, and *consensual* are often used to describe Lafley along with mentions of his sharp focus and unbending resolve. Describing himself, he says, "I'm not a screamer, not a yeller. But don't get confused by my style. I am very decisive" (Berner, 2003). Regarding power, he believes, "The measure of a powerful person is that their circle of influence is greater than their circle of control" (Sellers, 2004: 162).

His successor, Bob McDonald, inherited a healthy organization but is facing challenges created by the economic crisis. Also a P&G veteran of 30 years, McDonald was most recently vice chairman of global operations in charge of world sales. With a military background—he was a captain in the U.S. Army—and a focus on value-based leadership and strong determination, he is well prepared for the job (Schlosser, 2006). Anne Mulcahy, chairman of Xerox describes him as smart and serious. She says, "You can just read in his face how desirous he is to be an asset to this company" (Schlosser, 2007). Like his predecessor, McDonald is an observer, serious, quiet, and a teacher. He carries with him a list of ten leadership lessons that include, "Everyone wants to succeed," "Success is contagious," "Character is the most important trait of a leader," and "Organizations must renew themselves" (Dana, 2007) and takes every opportunity to teach in P&G training classes and anywhere else he visits (Kimes, 2009).

Just like Lafley, McDonald has very strong values of integrity and taking care of people, things that were reinforced in the Army and throughout his career in P&G. He states, "We teach that the best leaders are those who have ambition for the organization, but not for themselves. If an individual's ambition is for himself or herself, chances are people will not want to follow them." (Goldsmith, 2008). He also believes in the importance of being an effective follower and having a diverse team. He says: "I try to surround myself with people who are different than I am. ... I want to surround myself with people who don't talk like me, who didn't grow up like me and who don't think like I do" (Goldsmith, 2008). McDonald has big goals,"What I want to do is change people's lives, even if it's just in very small ways" (Goldsmith, 2008).

Questions

1. What strategic forces affect P&G?
2. How are Lafley and McDonald's strategic leadership style similar or different?
3. What are the factors that contributed to their success at P&G?

Sources: Berner, R., 2003. "P&G: New and improved," *Business Week Online,* July 7. www.businessweek.com/magazine/content/03_27/b3840001_mz001.htm (accessed December 7, 2007); Buckley, N., 2005. "The calm reinventor," *The Business Standard,* January 31. http://www.businessstandard.com/ft/storypage.php?&autono=179421 (accessed February 9, 2005); Byron, E. 2009. P&G chooses new CEO as it adapts to Era of thrift. *The Wall Street Journal* June 9. http://online.wsj.com/article/SB124449397535495339.html (accessed April 8, 2010); Dana, D. 2007. Bob McDonald CEO of P&G, on value-based leadership. *The Harbus* October 15. http://media.www.harbus.org/media/storage/paper343/news/2007/10/15/News/Bob-Mcdonald.Coo.Of.Procter.Gamble.On.valuesBased.Leadership-3028093.shtml (accessed April 8, 2010); Goldsmith, A. 2008. Executive spotlight: Bob McDonald. *The Monroe Street Journal* October 6. http://media.www.themsj.com/media/storage/paper207/news/2008/10/06/Features/Executive.Spotlight.Bob.Mcdonald.Pgs.Chief.Operating.Officer-3472259.shtml (accessed April 9, 2010); Jones, D., 2007. "P&G CEO wields high expectations but no whip," *USA Today,* February 19. http://www.usatoday.com/money/companies/management/2007-02-19-exec-pandg-usat_x.htm (accessed July 25, 2007); Kimes, M. 2009. A tough job for P&G's new CEO. *Fortune.* June 10. http://money.cnn.com/2009/06/10/news/companies/pandg_mcdonald.fortune/index.htm (accessed April 8, 2010); Markels, A., 2006. "Turning the tide at P&G," *U.S. New and World Reports,* October 22. http://www.usnews.com/usnews/news/articles/061022/30lafley.htm (accessed July 25, 2007); Schlosser, J. 2007. Rising star: Bob McDonald—P&G. *Fortune* January 24. http://money.cnn.com/2006/01/23/magazines/fortune/stars_mcdonald_fortune_060206/index.htm (accessed April 8, 2010); "Corporate design foundation: Procter & Gamble's A.G. Lafley on design," *@Issue: The Journal of Business and Design,* 9, no. 1 (2004). www.cdf.org/9_1_index/lafley/lafley.html (accessed February 8, 2005); Sellers, P., 2004. "eBay's secret," *Fortune,* October 18: 160–178.

250

Participative Management
and Leading Teams

From Chapter 8 of *The Art and Science of Leadership*, 6/e. Afsaneh Nahavandi. Copyright © 2012 by
Pearson Education. Published by Prentice Hall. All rights reserved.

Participative Management and Leading Teams

Coming together is a beginning. Keeping together is progress.
Working together is success.

—HENRY FORD

When we are debating an issue, loyalty means giving me your
honest opinion, whether you think I'll like it or not. Disagreement,
at this stage, stimulates me. But once a decision has been made,
the debate ends. From that point on, loyalty means executing
the decision as if it were your own."

—COLIN POWELL

After studying this chapter, you will be able to:

- Understand when and why participation should be used to improve leadership effectiveness.
- Explain the role of culture in the use of participative leadership.
- Specify the elements of effective delegation.
- Consider the issue of participative management.
- Explain the principles of self-leadership.
- Discuss the types of dysfunctions that may occur in teams and how leaders can help resolve them.

Teams and employee participation have been a central issue in leadership for many years. Almost all our past and current models address this issue in some form. For example, Theory Y of management recommends a higher level of employee participation than Theory X does. The Theory Y manager allows employees to set the direction for their development and provides them with support, whereas the Theory X manager controls employees rather than involving them in decision making. Likewise, the initiation-of-structure construct from the behavioral approach assumes that the leader is the one who provides the structure; no mention is made of subordinate participation in the development of the structure. The consideration behaviors in the same model contain a stronger participation component. Fiedler's task-motivated leader makes decisions alone; the relationship-motivated leader involves the group. Finally, the degree of follower participation in decision making is the pivotal concept for the Normative Decision Model.

This chapter focuses on the concept of participative management and leading teams in their past and current uses in leadership. It discusses the use of participation and delegation and the challenges they present for leaders, and it considers the special characteristics of teams and the importance of self-leadership.

WHEN SHOULD PARTICIPATION AND TEAMS BE USED?

The idea of using teams rather than relying only on the individual leader to make decisions in organizations has been at the forefront of management practice for many years (for a review, see Ilgen et al., 2005). Use of team and participative management occurs along a continuum. On one end, the leader retains all control and makes all decisions without any consultation or even information from the subordinates; on the other end, the leader delegates all decision making to followers and allows them the final say. Few leaders use extreme autocratic or delegation styles; rather, most rely on a style that falls somewhere in between. Similarly, few organizations are either entirely team based or make no use of teams at all. Most fall near the middle of the continuum, with a combination of teams and traditional hierarchical structures (Figure 1). For example, although still maintaining many elements of traditional structures, Ford Motor Company relies on teams for many tasks while maintaining a traditional centralized structure. Nancy Gioia, director of director of Global Electrification (all vehicles with electric drive; Voelcker, 2010) at Ford Motor Company, states, "As a director I'm very participative and hands-on when my team needs me to be. Ford's hybrid team has some of best and brightest minds around. I have complete confidence in their technical breadth and depth" (Peterson, 2005). Space X is a company at one extreme of the participation continuum. The company is trying to build faster, cheaper, and better rockets that will allow for commercial space travel (Space X, 2010). Founder and CEO Elon

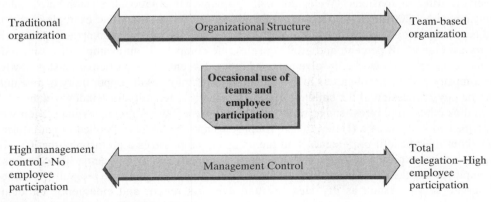

FIGURE 1 Continuum of Participation

Musk, who was *Inc.* magazine's 2007 entrepreneur of the year, relies on small groups of smart, motivated people to provide the creativity and innovation essential to the company. With a horizontal structure, no organizational charts, no red tape, and a culture that values teamwork and intelligence, employees are required to work together. Musk states, "I think it's really unacceptable here for anyone to bear a grudge" (Reingold, 2005: 78). Novartis, the drug manufacturer similarly relies on teams. Chairman Daniel Vasella says, "We abolished walls and cubicles and we created the lab of the future. . . . If you're in the lab here in Basel, without taking off your glove, you push a button and talk to a colleague in the United States and exchange structures and talk about them" (Salter and Westly, 2010).

Longitudinal research about employee involvement conducted by researchers at the University of Southern California indicates that organizations can reap many benefits from employee participation and involvement initiatives, which include such methods as information sharing, group decision making, and the use of teams, empowerment, profit sharing, and stock-option plans (Lawler, Mohrman, and Ledford, 1995). Their goal is to increase employee involvement and participation in the organization. Studies show that the adoption of such programs results in clear, positive impact on performance, profitability, competitiveness, and employee satisfaction (Carson, Tesluk, and Marrone, 2007; Lawler, Mohrman, and Ledford, 1995). Other research further suggests that using teams, participation, and engagement provide a positive impact (e.g., Forde, Slater, and Spencer, 2006) and can be used effectively in a number of business and not-for-profit organizations, such as schools (San Antonio and Gamage, 2007), health care (e.g., Mosadegh-Rad and Yarmohammadian, 2006), and urban planning (Repetti and Prélaz-Droux, 2003). Yet, others argue for using participative management and democratic systems within organizations as the only way to harness the talents of employees (Manville and Ober, 2003).

Organizations of all sizes and from many different sectors rely on teams and participation. Clarence Otis, Jr., CEO of Darden Restaurants, describes how much his business relies on teams, "It's less and less about getting the work done and more and more about building the team—getting the right people in place who have the talent and capability to get the work done and then do it" (Bryant, 2009l). Royal Phillips Electronics, Europe's largest electronics outfit, is counting on cross-boundary cooperation and conversations and employee participation to revive the company. In his attempts to reenergize Phillips, CEO Gerard Kleisterlee gathered people who wanted to make a contribution, regardless of rank and position in the company. Kleisterlee states that "these meetings result in very clear goals and much better cooperation between the different divisions" (Wylie, 2003: 45). Genencor International, a health-care products company with 1,200 employees located in Palo Alto, California, is another example of the use and benefits of employee participation. With turnover rates of 4 percent compared with the industry average of 18 percent, and growing sales, the company is an example of a successful business that relies on worker involvement and input. The employee participation started when the company built its headquarters in 1996 and offered employees the opportunity to give input into the physical design of the building. Research scientists' requests for windows in their labs as well as other employees' suggestions for a "main street" that encourages interaction were implemented with success (Haley, 2004). Employees are now regularly polled to get information about their benefit preferences, and the company emphasizes a philosophy that Cynthia Edwards, the vice president for technology, believes supports employees' entire lifestyle. Based on employee suggestions, Genencor provides various commuter assistance programs, a number of on-site services such as dry cleaning and eyeglass repair, and emergency childcare. Employees get to nominate exceptionally productive colleagues for recognition and celebrate their success during Friday afternoon parties, where they have the chance to mingle and get to know one another (Haley, 2004). The CEO until 2005, Jean-Jacques Bienaimé, believes, "If you want employees to be productive, you have to create a nurturing environment and let them be creative" (Haley, 2004: 98). Jim Sjoerdsma, the company vice president of human resources, suggests that the $700-per-employee cost for such benefits is a wise investment compared with the average $75,000 cost for recruiting and training a new employee. According to Sjoerdsma, "These programs pay for themselves" (Haley, 2004: 99).

Criteria for Participation

Despite its many potential benefits, participation is not a cure-all. Its use is more appropriate in some situations than in others and should follow a contingency approach. After many years of debate and research about participative management in social sciences and management, clear criteria suggest when participative decision making would be most appropriate (Table 1).

Overall, if the organization, its leaders, and its employees are ready for participative management, if the task is complex and involves no strong time pressures, and if employee commitment is important, leaders should rely on participative decision making. If time pressure is genuine or the leader, followers, or organization are not ready, however, then participation is not likely to yield many benefits. If leaders show a high need for control, are highly task oriented, and were previously successful in using an autocratic style of leadership, they are unlikely to be able to implement participation easily. Furthermore, for followers who show little need to participate or who trust their leader, participation might not be required or at least might not lead to better results than the leader making the decision alone. In addition, some organizational cultures are more supportive of participation than others, thereby making the use of participation

TABLE 1 Criteria for Use of Participation

Criteria	Description
When the task is complex and multifaceted and quality is important	Complex tasks require input from people with different expertise; people with different points of view are more likely to deliver a quality decision.
When follower commitment is needed in successful implementation	Follower participation increases commitment and motivation.
When there is time	Using participation takes time; legitimate deadlines and time pressures preclude seeking extensive participation.
When the leader and followers are ready and the organizational culture is supportive	Participation can only succeed if both leader and followers agree to its benefits, are trained in how to use it, and are committed to its success. The organizational culture must encourage or at least tolerate employee participation.
When interaction between leader and followers is not restricted by the task, the structure, or the environment	Participation requires interaction between leaders and followers; such interaction is only possible if restrictions because of factors such as geographic location, structural elements, or task requirements are minimized.

If the organization, its leaders, and its employees are ready for participative management, if the task is complex and involves no strong time pressures, and if employee commitment is important, leaders should rely on participative decision making. If time pressure is genuine or the leader, followers, or organization are not ready, however, then participation is not likely to yield many benefits.

more or less easy. Another factor in using participation is whether the task or the structure limits its use. If followers cannot interact easily with one another and with the leader, either because of task or because of geographic restrictions, participation might not be appropriate. In some instances, legal and confidentiality requirements, such as in personnel decisions, may preclude participation.

The case of Kiwi Airlines presents a classic example of the potential pitfalls of mismanaged participation (Bryant, 1995). When Kiwi Airlines was founded in 1992, it quickly became the symbol of all that is good about participative and egalitarian leadership. Created by a group of former Eastern Airline pilots and other employees, Kiwi promised not to repeat any of Eastern's mistakes and aimed at creating a family atmosphere for all its employees. The employees were all owners with varying degrees of shares and the corresponding pride and desire for involvement, control, and commitment that come from ownership. All decisions were made with full participation. All employees, regardless of levels, pitched in to get the job done and deliver the quality service that soon earned Kiwi honors in surveys of airline quality. The airline quickly grew to more than 1,000 employees with more than 60 daily flights. One of the pilot-founders and then chairman of Kiwi, Robert W. Iverson, attributed the stunning growth and success to the employees' commitment and the organization's egalitarian culture. Kiwi was truly a symbol of the benefits of participation and involvement. In 1994, the bubble burst. Kiwi's board, which included fellow founders and owners, booted Iverson out of office. This event revealed serious management and organizational deficiencies within the airline. The dark side of participation was an amazing lack of concern for management decisions. Many employee-owners failed to follow management directives if they did not agree with them. Employees demanded input in every decision, a factor that led to stagnation in decision making and an inability to act to solve problems. Iverson admitted, "One of the stupidest things I ever did was call everybody owners. An owner is somebody who thinks he can exercise gratuitous control." The case of Kiwi Airlines demonstrates the ineffective use of participation. A few managers could have handled many of the decisions more effectively and efficiently than the employees did through participation.

The Role of Culture

An important issue when considering the use of participation is national cultural values. Factors such as collectivism and power distance (Hofstede, 2001); team-oriented, participative, and autonomous leadership (House et al., 2004); and cross-cultural organizational cultures (Trompenaars, 1994) affect whether leaders can use participation successfully. The GLOBE research findings suggest that collectivistic cultures tend to emphasize cooperative team processes, compensation, and promotion that take into consideration the group (Gelfand et al., 2004). Furthermore, the more the power distance, the less likely it is that teams will be empowered (Carl, Gupta, and Javidan, 2004). Other GLOBE findings suggest that a humane orientation, which includes concern for others and responsibility for their well-being, may also be a factor supporting team-oriented and participative leadership (Kabasakal and Bodur, 2004).

Japanese culture, with its strong emphasis on conformity, consensus, and collectivity at the expense of individual goals, supports the use of participative management, despite its relatively high power distance. Participation in Japan is a mix of group harmony and consensus, with elements of directive leadership (Dorfman et al., 1997). In this vertical collectivistic culture, individuals are expected to sacrifice their personal goals for the good of the group. In China, establishing cooperative goals and taking care of relationships help participative leadership (Chen and Tjosvold, 2006). Mexico, which is also relatively high on collectivism, power distance, and masculinity, has a well-established tradition of autocratic leadership without a history of participative leadership (Dorfman et al., 1997). Similar cultural patterns are found in Dominicans (Montesino, 2003). In such cultural contexts, neither the leader nor the followers find participation desirable. In addition, in the cross-cultural organizational cultures that Trompenaars labels the Eiffel Tower—France, for example—the focus is on performance through obedience and respect for legitimate authority (Trompenaars, 1994). In this environment, a leader is ascribed great authority and is expected to know much; asking for subordinate participation may be perceived as weakness and as an indicator of lack of leadership ability.

Cultures such as the United States and Australia, with relatively egalitarian power distributions and vertical individualism, pose a different challenge. The low power distance allows for participation, but the value placed on individual autonomy and individual contribution can be an obstacle to cooperation in a team environment. In horizontal individualist cultures such as Sweden, participation and team cooperation are much easier because all individuals are equal. Furthermore, appropriate team behaviors vary considerably from one culture to another (Kanter and Corn, 1993). An effective team member in Japan is above all courteous and cooperative; members avoid conflict and confrontation (Zander, 1983). In the United States, effective team members speak their mind, pull their weight by contributing equally, and participate actively, yet they expect to be recognized individually. German employees are taught early in their careers to seek technical excellence. In Afghanistan, team members are obligated to share their resources with others, making generosity an essential team behavior. In Israel, a horizontal collectivistic culture, values of hard work and contribution to the community drive kibbutz team members. The Swedes are comfortable with open arguments and will disagree publicly with one another and with their leader. Each culture expects and rewards different types of team behaviors.

These cross-cultural differences in team behavior create considerable challenges for leaders in culturally diverse teams. Success depends on accurate perceptions and careful reading of cross-cultural cues. Leaders must be flexible and patient and be willing not only to listen to others, but also to question their own assumptions. In addition, they must keep in mind that many behavioral differences stem from individual rather than cultural sources. The only constant in the successful implementation of teams is the leader's sincere belief in the team's ability to contribute to the organization (Marsick, Turner, and Cederholm, 1989). Such belief is necessary regardless of the cultural setting.

THE ISSUE OF DELEGATION

". . . The trick is to get truly world-class people working directly for you so you don't have to spend a lot of time managing them" says Critóbal Conde, president and CEO of SunGard a software and technology services company (Bryant, 2010c). Gauri Nanda, entrepreneur and creator of Clocky, a robot alarm that rolls around the room, discusses something she would do differently if she could, "I would try to find more good help from the beginning. I tried to do a little too much myself, and while that's a great way to learn the process and every part of your business, I would have stopped and tried to find one good person to help" (Kessler, 2010). These leaders are addressing one of the basic principles of management: delegation. Delegation means appointing someone to as deputy or representative and entrusting them with a task. It differs from participation in a number of ways, although many managers consider it an aspect of participation. For example, many leaders define themselves as participative managers if they delegate tasks to their subordinates. Although this practice might lead to more subordinate participation in decision making, the goal of delegation is not necessarily to develop employees or create more commitment. Neither does delegation always involve power sharing with employees. The goal of delegation can be as simple as helping a leader ease an excessive workload. In its most basic form, delegation is simply handing off a task to someone else; in a more complex form, delegation can resemble participative management.

Benefits of Delegation

Delegating tasks well to subordinates is gaining importance as managerial ranks are thinned and managers see their workloads increase. Production managers find themselves with twice as many subordinates to supervise; sales managers see their territories double in current attempts to develop leaner structures. Organizations undergoing restructuring are testing team-based approaches. Until such techniques are well accepted and implemented, however, judicial delegation is still a basic tool for a leader's success. The potential benefits of delegation include the following:

- Delegation frees up the leader's time for new tasks and strategic activities.
- Delegation provides employees with opportunities to learn and develop.
- Delegation allows employees to be involved in tasks.
- Delegation allows observation and evaluation of employees in new tasks.
- Delegation increases employee motivation and satisfaction.

Aside from being a time- and stress-management tool for leaders, delegation allows subordinates to try new tasks and learn new skills, thereby potentially enriching their jobs and increasing their satisfaction and motivation. When employees perform new tasks, the leader has the opportunity to observe them and gather performance-related information that can be used for further development, evaluation, and preparation of employees for promotions. As such, delegation can be one of the tools available to leaders for succession planning in their organizations. Employees who consistently perform well on new tasks and are willing to accept more responsibility could be the future leaders of the organization. Without the opportunity to grow outside their current job, no data are available for accurate forecasting of their performance in higher-level positions. Debra Dunsire, M.D., CEO of the Millennium: The Takeda Oncology company, talking about learning to delegate, says, "So I learned to step away sometimes and, in the right situation, allow a person to stub their toe . . . in a safe situation, it's O.K. to allow them to present their work with a flaw that you can see clearly, because you've done this more times than they have, and letting them learn from that" (Bryant, 2009m).

The final benefit of delegation is, as is the case with participation, increased employee involvement and commitment. Job enrichment and participative management research (Hackman and Oldham, 1980) indicates that employees who are interested in growth quickly feel stifled and unmotivated if they do not have the opportunity to participate in new and challenging tasks. Delegation of such tasks to them helps increase their motivation and commitment to the organization.

Guidelines for Good Delegation

As with any tool, misuse and misapplication of delegation can be disastrous. Leaders must take into account some relatively simple principles (see Table 2 for a summary). One of the major

TABLE 2	Guidelines for Good Delegation	
Guideline	**Description**
Delegate, do not dump	Delegate both pleasant and unpleasant tasks; provide followers with a variety of experiences.
Clarify goals and expectations	Provide clear goals and guidelines regarding expectations and limitations.
Provide support and authority	As a task is delegated, provide necessary authority and resources such as time, training, and advice needed to complete the task.
Monitor and provide feedback	Keep track of progress and provide feedback during and after task completion at regular intervals.
Delegate to different followers	Delegate tasks to those who are most motivated to complete them as well as those who have potential but no clear track record of performance.
Create a safe environment	Encourage experimentation; tolerate honest mistakes and worthy efforts that may fail.
Develop your own coaching skills	Take workshops and training classes to ensure that you have the skills to delegate.

issues for leaders is to separate delegation from dumping. Leaders need to delegate a mix of easy, hard, pleasant, and unpleasant tasks to their subordinates. If only unpleasant, difficult, and unmanageable tasks are assigned consistently to subordinates, while leaders complete the high-profile, challenging, and interesting projects, delegation becomes dumping. One of the major complaints of subordinates regarding delegation is this exact issue. To reap the benefits of delegation, a variety of tasks should be delegated, and the leaders should pay particular attention that their delegation is viewed as balanced.

Effective delegation requires more than handing off a task. Leaders must be clear about their expectations and support their followers while they perform the task. The support might include informing department members and others outside the department that the task has been delegated. Another aspect of support involves providing training and other appropriate resources that allow the subordinate to learn the needed skills. It also might require regular monitoring and clarification of reporting expectations (Foster, 2004). It is easy for an eager subordinate to make decisions that are inconsistent with the leader's goals if the leader does not properly monitor the situation.

One area that cannot and should not be delegated is personnel issues. Unless an organization or department is moving toward self-managed teams (SMTs) that have feedback and performance-evaluation responsibility, the task of performance management remains the leader's responsibility. For example, it would be inappropriate for a manager to delegate the task of disciplining a tardy employee to a subordinate or to expect the latter to monitor and manage the performance of coworkers. The situation of SMTs often changes this guideline; such changes will be discussed later in the chapter.

Leaders must choose carefully the followers to whom they delegate. The easiest choice for most managers is to delegate to the few people they know will do the job well (the in-group). Although such a position is logical and effective, at least in the short run, a leader must be aware of the in-group/out-group issues. Therefore, leaders must select individuals who, in addition to having shown potential, are also eager and motivated to take on new tasks and have the appropriate skills for the new challenge. A follower who is competent and eager but who failed recently on one assignment might also be a good choice but could be overlooked if leaders keep relying on their few trusted in-group members. Kevin Ryan, CEO of AlleyCorp a group of Internet start-ups, keeps a list of 35 to 40 of his employees. According to him, he always connects with the top ten people on his list, but he makes an effort to see the rest, ". . . there are always 30 or 40 people who are up-and-comers or one or two levels down, and I want them to know I'm paying attention" (Buchanan, 2010: 65). Delegation of tasks to a varied group of followers further provides leaders with a broad view of the performance capabilities and potential of their team or department. Finally, creating a climate that tolerates mistakes and encourages continued training for the leader is essential.

Why Do Leaders Fail to Delegate?

Certain circumstances justify a leader's unwillingness to delegate. In some cases, followers are not ready for delegation, are already overworked, or have such specialized jobs that they cannot be assigned new tasks. Such situations are rare, however, and the considerable benefits of delegation far outweigh many of the arguments typically presented against it (Kouzes and Posner, 1987; Miller and Toulouse, 1986). The most commonly used argument against delegation is "I will get it done better and faster myself." Table 3 presents the typical excuses and counterarguments for not delegating.

> Not only does effective delegation require effort and resources such as training, but it also allows leaders to focus on higher-level strategic issues instead of day-to-day routines.

The excuses for not delegating tasks may be valid in the short run. By taking a long-term view that considers the leader's personal effectiveness as well as the development of followers, however, many of the excuses are no longer valid. Not only does effective delegation require effort and resources such as training, but it also allows leaders to focus on higher-level strategic issues instead of day-to-day routines. One underlying factor that might stop many leaders

TABLE 3 Excuses for Not Delegating

Excuses	Counterarguments
My followers are not ready.	The leader's job is to get followers prepared to take on new tasks.
My subordinates do not have the necessary skills and knowledge.	The leader's responsibility is to train followers and prepare them for new challenges.
I feel uncomfortable asking my followers to do many of my tasks.	Only a few tasks cannot be delegated. Balancing delegation of pleasant and unpleasant tasks is appropriate.
I can do the job quicker myself.	Taking time to train followers frees up time in the long run.
Followers are too busy.	Leaders and followers must learn to manage their workload by setting priorities.
If my followers make a mistake, I am responsible.	Encouraging experimentation and tolerating mistakes are essential to learning and development.
My own manager may think I am not working hard.	Doing busy work is not an appropriate use of a leader's time. Delegation allows time to focus on strategic and higher-level activities.

from delegating is their personality style, their need for control, and their fear of losing it. For example, a Type A's need for control often leads to lack of delegation. Competitiveness also might lead Type A leaders to compete with their followers. Other personal needs, such as a need for power, also might cause leaders to want to maintain power over all activities, preventing them from delegating.

Although for many years management and leadership included participation and delegation, they recently took on a new form in team-based organizations with the introduction of empowerment and concepts such as self-leadership, which are considered next.

LEADING CHANGE

Anne Sweeney of Disney-ABC Television

Anne Sweeny is quick to give her team at Disney-ABC Television credit for her success and for being considered one of the world's most powerful fifty women for several years, most recently in 2009 by *Fortune* magazine. She states, "It's wonderful to be recognized, not just my accomplishments, but for my teams' accomplishments" (Bisoux, 2006: 18). Sweeney started in the entertainment business as a page with ABC and has been credited with success in creating new and unique organizations, including Nickelodeon, where she became a senior vice president, and being a key player in launching the highly successful FX network. She has served as co-chair and president of Disney-ABC Television Group since 2004 and co-chair of the Disney Media Networks. She is considered a turn-around artist and a team player and someone who hires talented people and lets them be creative (The new wave, 2005). She is credited with the revival of the network with shows such as *Desperate Housewives* and *Extreme Makeover: Home Edition* (Streisand, 2005). She has further been part of the creative and risky deal to make the network's most popular shows available to iPod users.

Passion for innovation and ability to embrace change are characteristic of Sweeney. She has heeded her mother's advice to do what she was passionate about, considering the obstacles only those that she created for herself. Sweeney believes, "there's a lot more gratification in trying something that you haven't done and didn't know how to do" (Kantrowitz, Peterson, and Wingert, 2005). "I love the jobs that I don't know how to do. I love getting in there and figuring it out and making some good, big, noisy mistakes along the way, which is really part of the learning process (Bisoux, 2006: 22).

To run her company, she looks to people who, like herself, are able to think differently and outside the box and have passion and excitement for what they do. She is known to be a hands-off manager, who though she is an overachiever, does not grab the limelight and tends to let her people do their job with little interference (Streisand, 2005). As a mother of two, she juggles her personal life and career and talks about herself as one of the most tired person in show business rather one of the most powerful ones. Describing Sweeney, Peter Tortorici, president of MindShare Entertainment and the former head of CBS Entertainment, states, "It's hard when the world is bowing at your feet to remember who you really are besides the person who sits in that chair. Anne seems to never have lost touch with that" (Streisand, 2005). Anne Sweeney believes that her first priority is to create the environment that allows creative people to do their job (Myers, 2006).

Sources: Bisoux, T., 2006. "The change artist," *BizEd*, November–December: 18–24; Kantrowitz, B., H. Peterson, and P. Wingert. 2005. "How I got there: Anne Sweeney." *MSNBC.com: Newsweek*, October 24. http://www.msnbc.msn.com/id/9756479/site/newsweek (accessed July 8, 2007); Streisand, B., 2005. "Learning her ABCs," *U.S. News and World Report*, September 4. http://www.usnews.com/usnews/biztech/articles/050912/12sweeney.htm (accessed July 8, 2007); Myers, J., 2006. "Disney's ABC's Anne Sweeney: Inspiring creativity and embracing technology," *Media Village.com*, February 13. http://www.mediavillage.com/jmlunch/2006/02/13/lam-02-13-06/#continue (accessed July 8, 2007); "The new wave," 2005. *Fast Company*, December: 50.

EVOLUTION OF PARTICIPATIVE MANAGEMENT: TEAMS AND SELF-LEADERSHIP

In many organizations that have made teams a permanent part, if not a cornerstone, of their structures, teams create a formal structure through which participation in decision making can be achieved. The use of teams in U.S. and other Western organizations was triggered to a great extent by Japan's economic success and its reliance on teams and participative management (Nahavandi and Aranda, 1994). Although teams are not uniformly successful and they often pose considerable challenges for organizations (for research about teams and their potential problems, see Allen and Hecht, 2004; Salas, Stagl, and Burke, 2004), a large number of organizations continue to use them as a technique to increase creativity, innovation, and quality.

Characteristics of Teams

Although groups and teams both involve people working together toward a goal, they differ along several dimensions. Table 4 outlines those differences.

Some of the considerable success of Goldman Sachs is attributed to the team approach their employees take to their work. As opposed to many banks, bonuses are not based on individual performance alone, but on overall company performance (Arlidge, 2009). When explaining the importance of teamwork at Goldman, Dane Holmes, the head of investor relations, explains, "You can have a great career in banking as an individual, but it won't be here. The system weeds out those who can't play nicely with others" (Arlidge, 2009). Similarly, Rackspace, a San Antonio-based Web-hosting company, that prides itself on being "fanatical," uses teams to serve its customers (Overholt, 2004: 86). David Bryce, the customer-care vice president who joined the company in 1999, reorganized employees, known as Rackers, into teams of eight. Each team, guided by a team leader, includes account managers and billing and technology specialists, who are able to quickly and fully address their customers' needs without having to refer them to anyone else. Each team is its own profit center and responsible for its own performance, which is measured based on customer retention and satisfaction. Each team and its members can earn considerable bonuses if they perform well. The team approach to outstanding customer service paid off for Rackspace. The company continued to turn a profit

TABLE 4	Groups and Teams
Groups	**Teams**
Members work on a common goal.	Members are fully committed to common goals and a mission they developed.
Members are accountable to manager.	Members are mutually accountable to one another.
Members do not have clear stable culture, and conflict is frequent.	Members trust one another, and team enjoys a collaborative culture.
Leadership is assigned to single person.	Members all share in leadership.
Groups may accomplish their goals.	Teams achieve synergy: $2 + 2 = 5$.

Sources: Hackman, J. R. 1900. *Groups That Work (and Those That Don't)*. San Francisco, CA: Jossey-Bass; Katzenbach, J. R., and D. K. Smith. 1993. *The Wisdom of Teams: Creating the High Performance Organization*. New York: Harper Business.

while its competitors went bankrupt during the dot-com bust; the gift baskets that customers send their service teams to express their gratitude are just an added bonus (Overholt, 2004).

> The first distinguishing characteristic of a team is full commitment of its members to a common goal and approach that they often develop themselves.

As illustrated by the Rackspace example, the first distinguishing characteristic of a team is full commitment of its members to a common goal and approach that they often develop themselves. Members must agree that the team goal is worthwhile and agree on a general approach for meeting that goal. Such agreement provides the vision and motivation for team members to perform. The second characteristic is mutual accountability. To succeed as a team, members must feel and be accountable to one another and to the organization for the process and outcome of their work. Whereas group members report to the leader or their manager and are accountable to this person, team members take on responsibility and perform because of their commitment to the team.

The third characteristic of a team is a team culture based on trust and collaboration. Whereas group members share norms, team members have a shared culture. Team members are willing to compromise, cooperate, and collaborate to reach their common purpose. A collaborative climate does not mean the absence of conflict. Conflict can enhance team creativity and performance if handled constructively (Behfar et al., 2008). Related to the team culture is shared leadership. Whereas groups have one assigned leader, teams differ by sharing leadership among all members. Although this shared leadership is essential, leaders continue to play an important role in the success of teams. Particularly, leaders can help encourage a culture of collaboration (Taggar and Ellis, 2007) and help team learning by empowering members (Burke et al., 2006).

Finally, teams develop synergy. Synergy means that team members together achieve more than each individual is capable of doing. Whereas group members combine their efforts to achieve their goal, teams reach higher performance levels. As groups become teams and reach their peak level of performance potential, they may provide their organizations with benefits such as cost reduction because of less need for supervision, higher employee commitment, enhanced learning, and greater flexibility (Cordery, 2004).

Self-Managed Teams

Whereas traditional managers and leaders are expected to provide command and control, the role of leaders in teams is to facilitate processes and support team members. The leader sets the general direction and goals; the team members make all other decisions and implement them. This new role for leaders is most obvious in self-managed teams (SMTs), which are teams of employees with full managerial control over their own work (for some examples, see Barry, 1991; Spencer, 1995). Numerous organizations, such as Toyota, General Foods, and P&G, have used SMTs successfully for decades. In fact, P&G once claimed its SMTs were one of the company's trade secrets (Fisher, 1993). SMTs exhibit the following characteristics:

- *Power to manage their work.* SMTs can set goals, plan, staff, schedule, monitor quality, and implement decisions.
- *Members with different expertise and functional experience.* Team members can be from marketing, finance, production, design, and so on. Without a broad range of experience, the team cannot manage all aspects of its work.
- *Absence of an outside manager.* The team does not report to an outside manager. Team members manage themselves, their budget, and their task through shared leadership. Stanley Gault, once chairman of Goodyear, the largest tire manufacturer in the United

States, said that "the teams at Goodyear are now telling the boss how to run things. And I must say, I'm not doing half-bad because of it" (Greenwald, 1992).

- *The power to implement decisions.* Team members have the power and the resources necessary to implement their decisions.
- *Coordination and cooperation with other teams and individuals affected by the teams' decisions.* Because each team is independent and does not formally report to a manager, the teams themselves rather than managers must coordinate their tasks and activities to assure integration.
- *Team leadership based on facilitation.* Leadership often rotates among members depending on each member's expertise in handling a specific situation. Instead of a leader who tells others what to do, sets goals, or monitors achievement, team leaders remove obstacles for the team and make sure that the team has the resources it needs. The primary role of the team leader is to facilitate rather than control. Facilitation means that the leader focuses on freeing the team from obstacles to allow it to reach the goals it has set.

The success of the team depends on a number of key factors. First, the members of a team have to be selected carefully for their complementary skills and expertise (for some examples of research findings, see Kang, Yang, and Rowley, 2006; Van der Vegt, Bunderson, and Oosterhof, 2006). The interdependence among the members makes creation of the "right" combination critical. The right combination depends as much on interpersonal skills as on technical skills. Second, the team members need to focus on and be committed to the team goal. For example, individuals from different functional departments such as marketing or production, although selected because of their expertise in particular areas, need to leave the department mind-set behind and focus on the task of the team. Susan Lyne, CEO of the Gilt Groupe, a company that provides its customers with access to luxury goods at a discounted price, looks for team members when she is hiring new employees, "I need people who are going to be able build a team, manage a team, recruit well and work well with their peers. . . . Can they work across the company and get people to want to work with them and to help team succeed?" (Bryant, 2009n). Third, the team task must be appropriately complex, as well as provided with the critical resources it needs to perform the task. Finally, the team needs enough power and authority to accomplish its task and implement its ideas. The sources of team power are available to the team to allow it to perform its job.

Building an effective team is a time-consuming process that requires interpersonal team-building skills and extensive technical support. The development of trust, a common vision, and the ability to work well together all depend on appropriate interpersonal skills. Once the trust and goals are established, tackling complex tasks requires timely technical training. Many of these interpersonal and technical functions traditionally fall on the leader's shoulders. Leadership in teams, however, is often diffused, a factor that puts further pressure on individual team members to take on new tasks and challenges.

Self-Leadership

One of the applications of participative management and teams is the concept of self-leadership. With the increasing use of teams in organizations, many of the traditional roles of leaders are undergoing change. As we empower individual employees and provide them with training in various areas of business, we expect them to make increasingly independent decisions. Teams are designed to complement individual employees' skills. SMTs are responsible for continuous assessment and improvement of their own product, the design of their work, and all other work

---

Applying What You Learn

Using a Sports Team Model in Management

Organizational behavior expert and Harvard professor Nancy Katz suggests that managers can learn from sports teams how to make teams more effective (Katz, 2001). Here are some guidelines based on her work:

- Encourage cooperation and competition. The first leads to cohesion; the second energizes team members to do their best.
- Provide some early wins by assigning smaller, short-term, clearer tasks. Early successes build the team's confidence and create a success spiral.

- Break out of losing streaks through positive thinking, challenging the team to succeed, and focusing team members on external rather than internal causes for failure.
- Take time to practice; during practice the focus should be on learning and experimentation rather than success.
- Keep the membership stable to develop cohesion and give members time to learn to work together.
- Review performance, particularly mistakes and failures; analyze problems, and learn from them.

---

processes that influence them. Leaders are elected or rotated, and individuals are pressured to accept responsibility for their decisions and actions.

These changes shift the focus of attention away from the leader to the subordinates. Charles Manz and Henry Sims first proposed a model for leadership that involves self-leadership and self-management by each team member (Manz and Sims, 2001; for a recent review, see Neck and Houghton, 2006). Self-leadership is the process of leading people to lead themselves (Manz and Neck, 2004). The concept suggests that instead of leaders who rely on fear (the "strong man"), focus on narrow exchange relationships (the "transactor"), or inspire commitment while discouraging thinking (the "visionary hero"), leaders and followers must focus on leading themselves. As a result, team members must be taught and encouraged to make their own decisions and accept responsibility to the point where they no longer need leaders. Self-leadership within teams means that all team members set goals and observe, evaluate, critique, reinforce, and reward one another and themselves. In such an environment, the need for one leader is reduced; team members set goals and decide how to achieve them. Increased use of technology, the information revolution, and the preponderance of knowledge workers all support the need for self-leadership, which involves a focus on behaviors, providing natural rewards, and engaging in constructive thought patterns (for a detailed discussion, see Manz and Neck, 2004). Specifically, self-leaders:

- *Develop positive and motivating thought patterns.* Individuals and teams seek and develop environments that provide positive cues and a supportive and motivating environment.
- *Set personal goals.* Individuals and teams set their own performance goals and performance expectations.
- *Observe their behavior and self-evaluate.* Team members observe their own and other team members' behaviors and provide feedback and critique and evaluate one another's performance.
- *Self-reinforce.* Team members provide rewards and support to one another.

Contrary to views of heroic leadership, whereby the leader is expected to provide answers to all questions and to guide, protect, and save subordinates, the concept of self-leadership suggests that leaders must get their subordinates to the point where they do not need their leader much.

The role of formal leaders is, therefore, primarily to lead others to lead themselves or "to facilitate the self-leadership energy" within each subordinate (Manz and Sims, 1991: 18). Contrary to views of heroic leadership, whereby the leader is expected to provide answers to all questions and to guide, protect, and save subordinates, the concept of self-leadership suggests that leaders must get their subordinates to the point where they do not need their leader much. In effect, through the use of job-design techniques, the development of a team culture, proper performance management, and the modeling of self-leadership, the leader sets up internal and external substitutes for leadership. The right job design and the team are the external substitutes. The employees' developing skills and internal motivation serve as internal substitutes for the presence and guidance of a leader (see Exercise 2). Some of the strategies for the development for self-leaders include the following:

- Listen more; talk less.
- Ask questions rather than provide answers.
- Share information rather than hoard it.
- Encourage independent thinking rather than compliant followership.
- Encourage creativity rather than conformity.

Research on self-leadership continues to show support for the model (for a recent example of the link between self-leadership and entrepreneurship, see, D'Intino et al., 2007). The dimensions of self-leadership are valid and distinct from other personality variables (Houghton and Neck, 2002; Houghton et al., 2004), and some research suggests that the practice of self-leadership can be beneficial to an organization (VanSandt and Neck, 2003). Recent research also considers the applicability of the concept in other cultures (e.g., Alves et al., 2006; Ho and Nesbit, 2009). The concepts provide considerable appeal for the development of leaders and help establish workable leadership roles in organizations that rely on teams and empowerment.

In 2002 when Sam Palmisano, IBM's CEO, presented the initiative that was to jump-start the venerable company, Donna Riley, the company's vice president of global talent, had to work on reinventing its leadership (Tischler, 2004). With help from outside consultants, she set out to identify the set of skills, behaviors, and competencies that IBM leaders needed to help the company survive. The leadership traits they developed included trust and personal responsibility, developing people, enabling growth, collaboration, informed judgment, and building client partnerships. "In a highly complex world, where multiple groups might need to unite to solve a client's problems, old-style command-and-control leadership doesn't work" (Tischler, 2004: 113). The leadership characteristics used by IBM to shape its future are similar to those proposed by Manz and his colleagues.

To be successful, participative management and self-leadership require the empowerment of employees and the changing of an organization's culture. One of the key components of the cultural change is redefining the concepts of leadership and followership. Employees who become self-leaders do not require organizing, controlling, and monitoring from their leaders. Such redefinition requires a reconsideration of many current definitions of leadership.

LEADING TEAMS

Are leaders becoming obsolete? What happens to leadership when all employees become self-leaders and teams fulfill the traditional functions of leaders? How do leaders handle some of the challenges that teams present? Many managers and organizational leaders worry that once teams are successful and they train self-leaders, they may write themselves out of a job. Meanwhile, they often struggle to help their teams become effective.

Role of Leaders in a Team Environment

Some leaders never feel fully comfortable in a team environment, whereas others adapt to it well or even embrace it. Leaders of the first type are likely to feel that they are losing their job and might focus efforts on regaining control. Leaders of the second type might be able to redefine their role and continue contributing to the organization.

> The only certainty is that the role of the leader changes in a team environment but it does not altogether disappear. The leaders are not in charge and are not meant to command and control.

The only certainty is that the role of the leader changes in a team environment, but it does not altogether disappear. The leaders are not in charge and are not meant to command and control. Although an often-used metaphor for team leadership is an orchestra conductor, who is often highly directive, team leadership must be much less hands-on (Hackman, 2005). For this reason, many practitioners (e.g., Katzenbach and Smith, 1993) refer to team leaders as facilitators and coaches. Leaders are caretakers of their teams, the ones who help them achieve their goals by providing them with instructions, conflict management, encouragement when needed, and resources. Leaders/facilitators still fulfill many of the functions of traditional leaders, but they do so to a lesser extent and only when asked. They assist the teams by obtaining the resources needed to solve problems and to implement solutions, and only interfere when needed. The leader's central activities, therefore, become assessing the team's abilities and skills and helping them develop necessary skills, which often includes getting the right type of training (Figure 2). The team leaders also play the role of conflict and relationship manager while they continue doing real work themselves.

Another role for team leaders is to make the team aware of its boundaries. Many teams fail because they take on too much or ignore organizational realities and constraints. For example, a team of schoolteachers assigned the role of revising the social studies curriculum for fourth and fifth graders might propose changes that influence other parts of the curriculum and

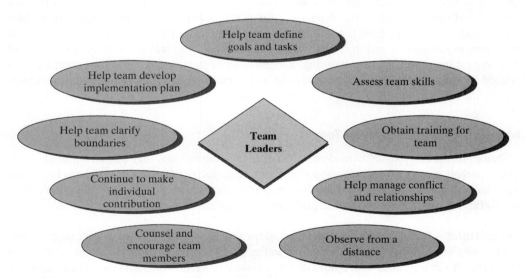

FIGURE 2 New Roles for Leaders in a Team Environment

then be disappointed when its recommendations are not fully implemented. The role of the team leader would be to keep the team focused on its specific task or to integrate the team with others who can help it with its wider recommendations.

A recent review of leadership in teams proposes that in addition to the traditional view of leaders being considered to be an input into the team (e.g., the leader does what is needed to help the team), team leaders should also be viewed as an output or product of team processes (Day, Gronn, and Salas, 2004). Leadership is created by the team and then used as a resource or capital in accomplishing its tasks. As such, all team members share leadership as a distributed function to help the group perform. Another interesting development in the use of teams stems from the view that such structures might not be fully compatible with the Western cultural value of individualism. Some sources describe teams, although needed as a structural element, as already passé and state that the focus needs to shift to individual contributions within teams. The use of teams in the United States and many other Western industrialized nations was spurred by the West's interpretation of Japanese management style. The Japanese continue to dominate many sectors of the global economy and give much of the credit for that success to their participative, team-based decision making and management style. It stands to reason, then, that adoption of some of the same management techniques and tools should help the Western industrialized nations regain their global economic positions. Whereas production and technological tools such as just-in-time (JIT) systems have been implemented successfully in the West, the people- and team-management issues have found considerably less success.

The relative failure of Japanese-style teams in the West and most notably in the United States can be blamed partially on lack of cultural fit. The collectivist Japanese culture fits well within and supports its management styles. The Western cultures by and large are considerably more individualistic, and their values often conflict with team-based approaches. Australians might have come up with a new concept: *Collaborative individualism* could be the buzzword of the future in the West (Limerick, 1990). Collaborative individuals are not limited by the boundaries of the group. They are cooperative and helpful to their team and organization while maintaining their internal motivation and conflict-tolerant skills. Based on a cultural analysis, such an approach could be much more suitable to many Western cultures, particularly those that are vertical individualists, than the Japanese search for consensus and conformity in a team (Nahavandi and Aranda, 1994). Australian researchers propose that empathy with an ability to transform organizations and to be proactive with excellent political and conflict management and networking skills, creative thinking, and maturity is at the core of the new competencies needed by future managers. Teams still exist and continue to play a key role, but individuals will be the focus for performance.

Managing Dysfunction in Teams

Although teams can provide considerable benefits to organizations, they can also provide challenges to their leaders. Not all teams function well; some fall prey to various problems that cause them to spend more time in conflict than in performing activities necessary to achieve their goals. Table 5 summarizes the typical problems that may occur in teams.

GROUPTHINK   Being cohesive is a valued goal for any team. Team members strive to get along, reduce conflict, and keep their membership in the group. Smaller groups with clear norms and members who share similar characteristics and a history of success are more likely to develop cohesion. Such cohesion can provide many benefits such as a supportive environment for learning

TABLE 5	Typical Team Problems
	Groupthink
	Free-riders
	Negativity—Bad apples
	Lack of cooperation and trust

and potential for high performance. However, it can also present one major problem: groupthink. The concept of groupthink was first proposed by Irvin Janis (1982) to describe dysfunctional group processes that can occur when group members focus on being cohesive, do not express disagreement or think critically, and as a result, make bad decisions. The process of groupthink is presented in Figure 3. When cohesive groups face a complex situation, they insulate themselves from outsiders and fail to consider alternatives, instead reaching for quick agreement that protects the group sense of cohesion. A key antecedent of groupthink is directive leadership that further encourages quick agreement. Once these conditions are in place, groups that fall prey to groupthink show a number of symptoms, including the illusion of invulnerability and unanimity, collective rationalization, self-censorship and pressure on dissenters. As a result, alternatives are not evaluated, the group strives toward quick agreement, and the group fails to develop contingency plans, all leading to poor decision making. Janis used several historical examples such as the Bay of Pigs and Cuban Missile crises to illustrate the groupthink process. Other examples where Groupthink can be applied to explain poor decisions include the space shuttle *Challenger* disaster and the decision for the United States to invade Iraq.

Many researchers believe that autocratic and directive leadership play a critical role in the development of groupthink (e.g., Chapman, 2006; Hackman, 2009). In addition to encouraging dissent, building diverse membership, and bringing outsiders to the group, one of the primary

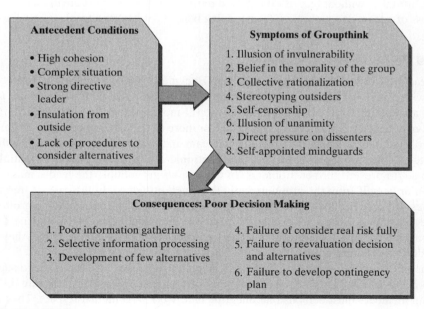

FIGURE 3 Groupthink

solutions to avoiding groupthink is for the leader to avoid pushing the group to reach a consensus, to assign members to be critical evaluators, and in some cases, even to stay away from the group as it considers alternatives and deliberates.

FREE RIDERS   One of the common complaints people have when working in groups is the presence of people who do not contribute to the group but still benefit from its work (Comer, 1995; Mulvey and Klein, 1998; Taggar and Neubert, 2008). Often called free-riders, these individuals appear to be more common in individualistic cultures. In collectivistic cultures, the sense of group and the need to be part of the group often prevents people from free-riding. In individualistic cultures, the focus on individual contribution reinforces the need to have equal and similar contributions from all team members, causing them to feel a sense of unfair advantage when facing potential free-riders. The actual or perceived presence of free-riders can be highly detrimental to team effectiveness, potentially leading other members to reduce their input and contribution for fear of being taken advantage of or even looking to punish the free-rider, which can backfire and further damage the group's effectiveness (Hopfensitz and Reuben, 2009).

NEGATIVITY AND BAD APPLES   As is the case of with positive behavior and attitudes, negativity can quickly spread and damage the cohesion, effectiveness, or even ethical behavior (Kish-Gephart, Harrison, and Treviño, 2010) of a team. One unhappy and unmotivated team member can have a disproportionate negative effect on her team (Felps, Mitchell, and Byington, 2006; Myatt and Wallace, 2008). The "bad apples" are often focused on their own goals, uncooperative or domineering, and unwilling to contribute. Their constant complaining and lack of motivation draw the group down and prevent other team members for achieving the group's goals.

LACK OF COOPERATION AND TRUST   An effective team is one in which members trust one another to work toward a common goal. Trust allows group members to safely experiment, learn, and make mistakes without fear of ridicule and retribution. Lack of trust greatly hampers the effectiveness of a team and prevents it from reaping benefits of having a team.

Helping Teams Become Effective

Several factors can help make teams effective (Hackman, 2005). Specifically, teams must be created with a real and challenging purpose in mind, be empowered to take action, and have the right amount and type of support. Even when teams have the right size and composition, they still may become dysfunctional due to one or more of the factors presented earlier. One of the key roles of a team leader is to monitor the team and continuously assess its health and effectiveness. If the group develops any dysfunctional characteristics, it is essential for the leader to act to prevent further problems. In the case of groupthink, the leader must often remove him or herself from the group to avoid too much influence. In the case of free-riders or bad apples, the leader must take an active role in enforcing team norms, helping other members take leadership to stop the problem, or remove the noncontributing members. Even in a self-managed team environment where leaders are facilitators, it is important that they take action to address problems quickly.

One of the important roles of leaders in helping teams become effective is to support the group to develop trust. Trust requires a number of factors as presented in Figure 4. To build trust, team members must demonstrate integrity, hard work, and mutual respect. They must reward cooperation rather than competition, be fair to one another, and communicate openly. They,

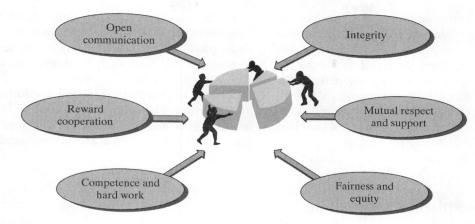

FIGURE 4   Building Trust

further, must believe that their leaders—inside and outside the team—are predictable, have their best interests at heart, and will treat them fairly (Cunningham and MacGregor, 2000).

In addition, even though strategies to make individuals more competent and effective will affect a team's overall ability to be productive, teams often need specialized support and interventions to develop synergy. Possible team-training activities include the following (Day, Gronn, and Salas, 2004):

- *Team building* to clarify team goals and member roles and set patterns for acceptable interaction
- *Cross training* to ensure that team members understand one another's tasks
- *Coordination training* to allow the team to work together by improving communication and coordination
- *Self-guided correction* to teach team members to monitor, assess, and correct their behavior in the team
- *Assertiveness training* to help team members express themselves appropriately when making requests, providing feedback, and other interactions among themselves.

Summary and Conclusions

This chapter presents the concepts of participative management and its extension and application to the use of teams in organizations. Although many benefits can be drawn from the use of participative management, its success depends on appropriate application. Cultural and organizational factors should determine the use of participation as a management tool. A basic application of participation is the use of delegation by a leader. Delegation must be implemented carefully and

judiciously to ensure fair application; leaders must consider which tasks they should and can delegate and the individuals to whom they are delegating. Thorough feedback and monitoring are also important.

Many organizations formalize the use of participation through the creation of teams. The successful implementation of SMTs and self-leadership demonstrates the role of teams in revitalizing organizations. As teams continue to be

271

used, their nature and role change, as does the role of leadership in a team environment. Despite the need for a contingency view in the use of participative management and teams, teams provide a basic management tool in many parts of the world. More-focused attention on cultural factors, along with a continued analysis of the success of participative management and teams, should lead to continued evolution of the concepts.

The role of leaders often changes in a team environment to that of facilitator or coach, but the leader must continue to closely monitor the team to avoid dysfunctions such as groupthink, the presence of free-riders or negative members, and the erosion of trust that is essential to effectiveness of teams. The team leader must also help members gain the right training to allow them to self-manage and self-lead in a team environment.

Review and Discussion Questions

1. What are the factors that determine the use of participation and what are the potential benefits and disadvantages of participation?
2. How does culture affect an organization's ability to implement employee participation?
3. What organizational strategies can be used to help leaders delegate more often and more effectively?
4. Compare and contrast groups and teams. Provide an example of an effective team. What are the elements that contribute to its success?

5. What is the difference between delegation and implementation of self-managed teams?
6. What are the steps to leadership and self-leadership?
7. What are some typical dysfunctions that teams may face? What is the role of the leader in managing them?
8. How has the role of leaders changed in team environments? What functions remain?

Leadership Challenge: Who Gets the Project?

Your department includes 15 members, all of whom have been with you for at least a year. Although the department is generally cohesive and performs well, you are grooming four "stars" for promotion because you believe they are the best performers. You just landed a new account with a lot of potential, a tight deadline, and the need for considerable grooming and development. The success not only will give the person in charge of the project a lot of visibility, but also could affect your career in the company. Everyone in the department is aware of the importance of the project, and several people, including your four stars, volunteered to take it on. In particular, one of the members with the most tenure and experience (but not one of the four

stars) is pushing to get the project. Given the project's importance, you want it to be handled well and without too much direction from you.

As you are about to delegate the project to your top star, you receive a call from the human resources director telling you that one of the department members filed an informal complaint against you, accusing you of favoritism. The director can't tell you the name, but wanted you to be aware of potential problems and that HR would be conducting informal fact-finding interviews.

1. Who will you assign to the project?
2. Consider the implications of your decision.

Exercise 1: To Delegate or Not to Delegate?

This role play is designed to provide you with an opportunity to experience the challenges of delegation either as a leader or as a follower. Read the following situation and description of team members.

Situation

You are a team manager in the public relations and marketing department at a major resort, Sunshine, Inc. Your organization specializes in all-inclusive package vacations and has a reputation for excellent customer service. As a team manager, you are responsible for the supervision and development of four account managers in the corporate area. Your team's role is sales and service to corporate clients.

Your manager, the marketing director, just handed you a new account that she inherited from another of the resort's partners. The client has been problematic in terms of payment and somewhat unreasonable demands, but it has a lot of potential. It is an entrepreneurial firm that your manager referred to as "spoiled brats." However, successful handling of this client, you are told, is important. "We don't want to lose them; in fact, we really want them to be happy! Nobody seems to have figured out how, but I'm sure you will come up with something."

You have four people in your team:

Fran Smith: Fran has been with Sunshine for 4 years. She recently obtained a bachelor's degree in marketing from a major state university. Her prior work experience was with a restaurant supplier, where she was a good performer with a lot of ambition, creativity, and motivation. You previously assigned many different tasks to her, and they were all done well. Fran is one of your in-group people, and you trust her a lot. You have had many discussions about future promotions, and she has followed your advice well. Fran seemed to be in a slump for the past 3 months but has not talked to you about it, and you let it go, assuming it may be a personal issue. Performance is still there, but some of the enthusiasm is gone.

Gerry Narden: Gerry has been with Sunshine for 10 years. He has an AA degree in business and got his first job as a desk clerk at the resort. Gerry has worked in many different parts of the resort and started in corporate sales only 6 months ago. He transferred in with outstanding evaluations from all his previous bosses. Gerry is the newest member of the team and has experienced some ups and downs in sales. One of them almost caused the loss of a major client. You intervened and managed to save the account. He seemed to learn from the experience and has done well in the past 2 months. You have not, however, given him any major accounts since, although he repeatedly asked for more challenge.

Terry Chan: Terry has been with your team for 5 years. Terry has a master's in communication and is a good performer. Her more than 10 years of work experience, most of which were in sales and customer relations within Sunshine, show her knack for working with "big" clients who keep coming back to her. She usually does not ask for assignments and is good at bringing her own. Terry needs little help or management from you and seems to do her own thing successfully.

J. P. Ricci: J. P. has been with the team for over a year. In his first job, he is a major management challenge. A bright, Ivy League graduate with a degree in hotel and restaurant management and marketing, he has considerable sales skills. J. P. wants to do things his own way. J. P.'s clients are delighted with him when he puts his heart into things, but motivation seems to be lacking sometimes. Your discussions with J. P. lead you to believe that he is bored and needs to be challenged. J. P. often talks about trying to find another job that would fit better, but he really likes the sales and resort environment. J. P. seems to be in search of direction. Despite these issues, he is a good performer and delivers when it counts.

Role Play

After reading the scenario, please wait for further information from your instructor.

Participative Management and Leading Teams

To Delegate or Not to Delegate: Worksheet for Managers

  1. Who would you select to manage the account? What are your reasons?

  2. Plan the meeting during which you will delegate the task. What do you need to say? What areas do you need to cover? How are you addressing your employees' needs?

To Delegate or Not to Delegate: Worksheet for Employees

  1. What do you need to do a good job?

  2. Has your manager provided you with clear information about the task and expectations? What is done correctly? What is missing? Do you feel ready and motivated to take on the task?

Exercise 2: Strategies for Becoming a Self-Leader

Changing Behaviors

1. Observe yourself

   Identify specific behaviors that are related to becoming a self-leader. (List at least three.)

   →

   →

   →

   Set specific goals for yourself for each behavior. (List at least three.)

   →

   →

   →

   Include a time line for each goal.

   →

   →

   →

   How will you measure your goals?

2. Set up opportunities for rehearsal.
Identify settings where you can practice the new behaviors. (List at least three.)

→

→

→

Identify and work with individuals who can help you rehearse.

3. Establish reminders.
Establish reminders in your work environment to encourage the new behaviors. (List at least three.)

→

→

→

List individuals who can help you. (List at least three.)

→

→

→

4. Set up reward and "punishments."
List rewards that would encourage you to use self-leadership behaviors. (List at least three.)

→

→

→

Clarify when each should be used.

List things that would stop unwanted behaviors. (List at least three.) Clarify when each should be used.

→

→

→

Changing Cognitive Patterns

1. Focus on natural rewards in tasks.
List aspects of your job that can naturally encourage self-leadership behaviors. (List at least three.)

→

→

→

2. Establish constructive thought patterns.
Look for opportunities rather than obstacles.

3. Use positive mental imagery.
Reevaluate your priorities, beliefs, and assumptions.

Source: Based on self-leadership concepts developed by Manz and Sims (1987, 1991).

Self-Assessment 1: Delegation Scale

Using the following scale, indicate how much you agree with the following items.

1 = Strongly disagree
2 = Somewhat disagree
3 = Neither agree nor disagree
4 = Somewhat agree
5 = Strongly agree

_____ 1. I can do most jobs better and faster than my subordinates.

_____ 2. Most of my tasks cannot be delegated to my subordinates.

_____ 3. Most of my subordinates do not have the appropriate level of skills to do the tasks that I could delegate to them.

_____ 4. I feel uncomfortable delegating many of my tasks to my subordinates.

_____ 5. I am responsible for my subordinates' mistakes, so I might as well do the task myself.

_____ 6. If my subordinates do too many of my tasks, I may not be needed any longer.

_____ 7. Explaining things to subordinates and training them often takes too much time.

_____ 8. My subordinates already have too much work to do; they can't handle any more.

_____ 9. If my subordinates do the tasks, I will lose touch and be out of the loop.

_____ 10. I need to know all the details of a task before I can delegate to my subordinates.

Scoring Key: Your total score will be between 10 and 50. The higher your score, the less inclined you are to delegate, and you agree with many of the common excuses used by managers not to delegate tasks to their subordinates.

    Total: _____

Self-Assessment 2: Are You a Team Leader?

Rate yourself on each of the following items using the scale provided here:

1 = Strongly disagree

2 = Somewhat disagree

3 = Neither agree nor disagree

4 = Somewhat agree

5 = Strongly agree

_____ 1. I enjoy helping other get their job done.

_____ 2. Managing others is a full-time job in and of itself.

_____ 3. I am good at negotiating for resources.

_____ 4. People often come to me to help them with interpersonal conflicts.

_____ 5. I tend to be uncomfortable when I am not fully involved in the task that my group is doing.

_____ 6. It is hard for me to provide people with positive feedback.

_____ 7. I understand organizational politics well.

_____ 8. I get nervous when I do not have expertise at a task that my group is performing.

_____ 9. An effective leader needs to have full involvement with all his or her team's activities.

_____ 10. I am skilled at goal setting.

Scoring Key: Reverse score for items 2, 5, 6, 8, and 9 (e.g., 1 = 5, 5 = 1). Add your score on all items. Maximum possible score is 50. The higher the score, the more team leadership skills you have.

Total: _____

LEADERSHIP IN ACTION

John Mackey of Whole Foods

"I am now 53 years old and I have reached a place in my life where I no longer want to work for money. . . . Beginning January 1, 2007, my salary will be reduced to $1, and I will no longer take any other cash compensation" (Mackey, 2007). The statement is part of a letter John Mackey, the founder and CEO of Whole Foods, wrote to his employees when the sales were below expectations and the stock prices dropped. His company and highly unique management style are a model of innovation and customer service around the world. He considers his company and his over 50,000 employees to be his children, says he does things for fun, and is considered by some to be a "right-wing hippy" (Paumgarten, 2010). His views, which he calls conscious capitalism, see business as having a higher purpose; he states: "We're trying to do good. And we're trying to make money. The more money we make, the more good we can do" (Paumgarten, 2010).

Although he says that his views and those of his company do not always match, he believes that: "We're changing the experience (of shopping) so that people enjoy it" (Sechler, 2004: 1). With bright facilities, wide aisles, rich colorful displays, expert employees, and lots of help and information for customers, Whole Foods has changed the way many people shop for food. John Mackey started the company in 1980 in Austin, Texas, with the first organic food store; it now numbers more than 150 stores with earnings of nearly $3 billion and is making a move to become a global company with the first store opening up in the United Kingdom (Duff, 2005).

"Mackey is hardly a manager at all . . . he's an anarchist" is how a former Whole Foods executive describes the company president (Fishman, 2004: 73). The CEO, who is now in his 50s, visits his stores in shorts and hiking boots and is equally as passionate about egalitarianism and democracy in the workplace and the humane treatment of animals as he is in his opposition to the new U.S. health-care plan (Mackey, 2009). He interacts freely with employees and is eager to learn from them and from his customers. Wendy Steinberg, who has worked at Whole Foods since 1992, describes him as an "observer" (Fishman, 2004: 76). A vegan, who changed his vegetarian diet to exclude all animal by-products after working with a group devoted to improving living conditions for farm animals, he still flies commercial airplanes, rents the cheapest cars, and is a shrewd and disciplined businessman leading his company and employees to considerable success (Fishman, 2004). Much of that success is attributed to Whole Foods' team-based culture that empowers employees and involves them in all aspects of decision making while demanding performance and customer service.

The basic decision-making power at Whole Foods rests with the teams that run each department (e.g., bakery, produce, seafood) in each store. The teams decide whom to hire, whether to retain members, what products to carry, how to allocate raises, and so forth. All teams together also make strategic decisions, such as the type of health insurance the company will offer. The National Leadership Team of the company makes the overall decision based on majority vote. Mackey says, "I don't overrule the National Leadership Team. . . . I've done it maybe once or twice in all these years" (Fishman, 2004: 74). He admits making some top-down decisions, but only when time to consult is not available.

Whole Foods has a "Declaration of Interdependence" that affirms the interdependence of all stakeholders and clearly states the goals of satisfying and delighting customers and of team-member happiness and excellence (Whole Foods philosophy, 2007). Building healthy relationships with team members, getting rid of the "us versus them" management mentality, and a deep-seated belief in employee participation are also highlighted. The core values regarding working at Whole Foods include the following (Whole Foods philosophy, 2007):

- Self-directed teams that meet to solve problems and appreciate members
- Increased communication through open-book management and "no secrets" management that allow employees access to financial data, salary and raise information, and so forth.
- Profit- and gain-sharing to provide team members incentives to perform and build the team through shared fate (nonexecutive employees hold 94 percent of the company's stock options); a salary cap that limits the salary of any team member to fourteen times the average total compensation of all full-time team members.
- Employee happiness through fun and friendship at work with liberal dress codes, ability to do volunteer work on company time, full health benefits, and emphasis on taking responsibility for successes and failures and celebration and encouragement of employees.
- Continuous learning for employees about the products they sell and the job they do.
- Promotion from within to appreciate and encourage employee talent and development and a strong equal opportunity policy.

Although the positive work culture, fun, and friendship are key to the company's ongoing success, competition and focus on performance are not lost. Because individual raises are tied to their team's performance, team members want good workers on their team. Mackey, who wants his company to be based on love rather than fear, is also clearly in charge and in the forefront representing his company in the community. As he battles the animal rights groups that continue to criticize Whole Foods for being hypocritical and counterculture groups that accuse him of having become too corporate, or defending against the anti-union charges leveled at the company. Mackey responds, "We're in the business of selling whole foods, not holy foods" (Overfelt, 2003). The corporate side of the CEO became clearly evident when he had to apologize for having assumed an online alias "Rahobdeb" (an anagram of his wife's name) to bash his competitor Wild Oats Markets for years (Kesmodel, 2007; Stewart, 2007).

Questions

1. What are the elements of John Mackey's leadership?
2. What makes the teams at Whole Foods effective?

Sources: Duff, M., "The perils of the imperial reach," *DSN Retailing Today* 44, no. 1 (2005): 10; Fishman, C., 2004. "The anarchist's cookbook," *Fast Company*, July: 70–78; Kesmodel, D., 2007 "Whole Foods sets probe as CEO apologizes," *The Wall Street Journal*, July 18: A3; Mackey, J., "I no longer work for money," *Fast Company*, February, 112; Mackey, J.," The Whole foods alternative to ObamaCare," *The Wall Street Journal*, August 11. http://online.wsj.com/article/SB1000142405297020 4251404574342170072865070.html (accessed April 16, 2010); Overfelt, M., 2003. "The next big thing: Whole Food Market," *Fortune,* June 2. http://www.fortune.com/fortune/print/0,15935,456063,00.html (accessed January 27, 2005); Paumgarten, N., 2010. The food warrior. *The New Yorker*, January 4. http://www.newyorker.com/reporting/2010/01/04/100104fa_fact_ paumgarten? currentPage=all#ixzz0baVWuHq0 (accessed on April 16, 2010); Sechler, B., 2004. "Whole Foods picks up the pace of its expansion," *Wall Street Journal*, September 29: 1; Whole Foods philosophy at http://www.wholefoodsmarket.com/ company/philosophy.html (accessed August 5, 2007); Stewart, J. B., 2007. "Whole Foods chief disappoints by sowing wild oats online," *The Wall Street Journal*, July 18: D5.

Leading Change

Be the change that you want to see in the world.

—MAHATMA GANDHI

When you're finished changing, you're finished.

—BENJAMIN FRANKLIN

After studying this chapter, you will be able to:

- Define change and explain the forces for change.
- Describe types of change and explain the change process.
- Summarize the reasons for resistance to change and possible solutions.
- Present the leadership practices necessary to implement change, including the importance of vision.
- Explain the importance of creativity and improvisation in managing change.
- Apply the principles of learning organizations and positive leadership to leading change.

"Permanent white water" and "turbulent" are some of the terms used to describe the environment that today's organizations face. Their environment is changing at a rapid pace, leading to the need for flexibility, innovation, and nimbleness. The effectiveness and very survival of most of our organizations depend on their ability to successfully adapt to changes in their environment while still maintaining internal health. Leading change is therefore a leader's most challenging and vital responsibility. Whether to implement new technology, update existing products or services, launch new ones, or put in place new administrative and management systems, leaders must guide their followers through change, which is more often than not perceived as painful, often resisted, and difficult to implement. Whereas managing change well is essential to the survival of the organization, some surveys indicate that many organizational leaders are not satisfied with how well their organizations can innovate and adapt to change, and they fully realize that implementing change is a long-term process with many risks of failure (McGregor, 2007).

This chapter looks at the change process and the role that leaders play in leading and implementing change in their organizations.

FORCES FOR CHANGE

Change is the transformation or adaptation to a new way of doings things. Innovation is the use of resources and skills to create an idea, product, process, or service that is new to the organization or its stakeholders. For example, when in 1992 Procter & Gamble (P&G) introduced its latest innovation, liquid detergent, to be a high-priced limited-production item, it triggered changes in the whole industry that in turn affected how P&G marketed its new product and pushed the company to change its plan and eventually mass produce liquid detergent.

Internal and External Forces

When do organizations change? What makes leaders decide to implement change? Forces for change are both external (in the environment) and internal (Figure 1). Changes in the environment include factors such as social trends, cultural and demographic changes, political shifts, the economy, and technological advances. For example, in the United States and in many other parts of the world, demographic diversity related to both ethnic groups and age forces organizations to consider new ways of addressing their constituents' needs. The case of Avon shows how the company had to change because, in part, demographic and social changes led many women to work outside of the home, disrupting the home-based distribution of the company's products. The CEO, Andrea Jung, has focused on introducing new distribution and marketing methods, changing how her employees think about the products, and getting them to accept the changes. In a similar situation, the public interest in sustainability and demand for safe products have triggered the growth of organizations such as Ecover, the Belgian-based company, which is now the world's largest producer of ecological household cleaners and products. The success of Ecover, in turn, has forced changes in other consumer-good companies. Changes in the local and global political environments compel organizations to look for innovative ways of dealing with new problems. JetBlue was one of

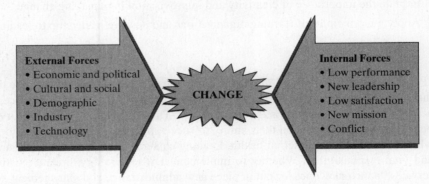

FIGURE 1 Forces for Change

the first airlines to install reinforced doors to their planes' cockpits in response to the terrorist attacks of 2001. To take advantage of the Internet to connect with young voters, all the 2008 U.S. presidential candidates actively used social networking tools to campaign, pushing their political organizations to change.

The internal forces for change closely follow external forces. For example, a new service from one hospital will push others to consider changing their offerings, or wide uses of new technology such as the Web, or poor economic conditions, may lead city and state governments to expand their online services, requiring new hires, training, and new management processes. One of the most common forces for change inside organizations is the performance gap—the difference between expected and actual performance. Another potent internal force for change is new leadership at any level. Therefore, not only do leaders guide organizations through change, but they are also frequently the cause of change.

Consider the forces that pushed the U.S. Federal Bureau of Investigation (FBI) to undergo extensive changes with varying degrees of success since the 9/11 attacks on the United States. The external forces for change were global politics, considerable political pressure in the United States, public demand for security, and changing technology among others. Internally, the FBI faced a performance gap (a glaring failure by some accounts), presence of old technology, antiquated management and administrative systems, and extensive employee dissatisfaction (Brazil, 2007). In addition, the agency has shifted its focus from reactive criminal investigations to proactive intelligence and counterterrorism (Vizzard, 2006). Former U.S. Attorney Dick Thornburgh, who chaired a panel that reviewed the FBI, stated, "It's almost a total transformation of what the bureau does and how it does it. It's staggering" (Brazil, 2007). FBI Director Robert Mueller, a decorated ex-marine who took leadership a week before the 9/11 attacks, was in charge of orchestrating the massive transformation. Talking about the challenges of transforming the organization, he stated: "I've come to find that one of the most difficult things one has to do is to bring an entity through the development of a change of business practices" (Ragawan, 2005). The case of the FBI illustrates the many forces that push organizations to change.

Culture and Change

As pressure for change increases from inside and outside organizations, not all leaders react and respond the same way. Some perceive the pressure as a threat; others see it as an opportunity. One factor that determines the way leaders and their followers perceive pressures for change is culture, both at the national and organizational levels. We consider the importance of organizational culture later in this chapter. From a broader perspective, national cultural values of tolerance of ambiguity and perception and use of time can shape how leaders view change. In cultures such as Greece, Guatemala, Portugal, or Japan, where people do not easily tolerate uncertainty and ambiguity, pressure for change is seen as a threat and is either ignored or carefully planned and managed. A Japanese business leader is likely to manage change through extensive and detailed long-term planning and forecasting supported by governmental organizations such as the Ministry of International Trade and Industry (MITI). MITI targets certain industries for growth and supports them through various economic and political actions, thereby reducing the potential negative impact of change triggered by global competition. Similarly, in countries such as Malaysia and Thailand, with cultures that are risk averse, governmental centralized planning helps support business leaders reduce uncertainty and ambiguity. On the other end of the spectrum, in Sweden, the United States, and Canada, where change is tolerated and perceived as an opportunity, leaders deal with change by making quick changes to their organizations and

National cultural values of tolerance of ambiguity and perception and use of time influence how leaders view change. In cultures such as Greece, Guatemala, Portugal, or Japan, where people do not easily tolerate uncertainty and ambiguity, pressure for change is seen as a threat and is either ignored or carefully planned and managed.

implementing short-term strategies that address the immediate pressures relatively more quickly than in other cultures.

The perception of time further affects how leaders implement change. Leaders from present-oriented cultures, where time is linear, are likely to react fairly quickly to change and focus on short-term planning. The short-term orientation leads to a state of constant change that many U.S. organizations are experiencing. For example, when, in 2000, James McNerney became the first outsider to lead the 100-year-old 3M company, he immediately announced that he would change the DNA of the company. He implemented substantial changes that deeply affected 3M and left 4 years later to lead Boeing (Hindo, 2007). Leaders from past- and future-oriented cultures are less likely to react quickly to change, taking time to plan and to consider the long-term impact of their actions.

TYPES AND PROCESS OF CHANGE

Change is stressful and usually met with some resistance, as you will read later in this chapter. Different types of changes, however, affect people differently and require different types of leadership. Change that is sudden and drastic is more likely to cause stress and resistance, whereas gradual and programmed change is easier to implement.

Types of Change

In some cases, leaders can carefully plan and execute change; in others, leaders and followers are caught by surprise and have to react without specific preparation. Table 1 summarizes the different types of changes organizations face.

Whereas many organizations try to carefully analyze their environment and internal conditions, through methods such as customer- and employee-satisfaction surveys or complex performance measures, to foresee changes and to plan their course of action, many more face changes that they do not expect or are unable to anticipate. In addition, both planned and unplanned change may happen, either gradually or rapidly, leading to dramatic impact on the

TABLE 1 Types of Change

Type of Change	Description
Planned	Change that occurs when leaders or followers make a conscious effort to change in response to specific pressure or problem.
Unplanned	Change that occurs randomly and suddenly without the specific intention of addressing a problem.
Evolutionary	Gradual or incremental change.
Convergent	Planned evolutionary change that is the result of specific and conscious actions by leaders or follower to change the organization.
Revolutionary or frame-breaking	Change that is rapid and dramatic.

Sources: Partially based on work by Tushman, M. L., W. H. Newman, and E. Romanelli. 1986. Convergence and upheaval: Managing the unsteady pace of organizational evolution. *California Management Review*, Fall: 29–44.

organization. In the 3M example presented earlier, James McNerney planned the changes he wanted to implement to move the organization to improved efficiency through careful monitoring, measurement, and implementation of a process called Six Sigma, which relies on precision, consistency, and repetition (Hindo, 2007). The existing 3M culture, known worldwide for its ability to be creative and innovative, was based on experimentation and tolerance for trial and error, all factors that eventually led to innovative products and process. McNerney moved to remove any variability from organizational processes, focusing instead on analysis, control, and efficiency. Although it was planned, the change was revolutionary and felt like a complete cultural transformation (Hindo, 2007).

> The different types of change may require different actions from leaders. For example, in the case of planned and evolutionary change, a leader's ability to structure tasks may be important. When facing unplanned and revolutionary change, charismatic and transformational leaders who make an emotional connection with followers and help them whether the change may become more central.

The different types of change may require different actions from leaders. For example, in the case of planned and evolutionary change, a leader's ability to structure tasks may be important. When facing unplanned and revolutionary change, charismatic and transformational leaders who make an emotional connection with followers and help them whether the change may become more central. In addition, based on the change process considered in the next section, the options that are available, and actions that are required from a leader may be different in each type of change. One factor that remains constant regarding the role of leadership is the need to set a vision and to help followers through the resistance that is likely to take place.

Model for Change

Understanding the course of change can help leaders plan and implement change more successfully. In the 1950s, social psychologist Kurt Lewin proposed a theory of organizational change that continues to influence current thinking (Lewin, 1951). Lewin's Force Field theory proposes that organizations contain forces that drive change and forces that resist change. When the two forces are balanced, the organization maintains its status quo. When the forces for change are stronger than those that resist change, leaders can overcome inertia and implement changes. So to successfully change, leaders must either increase the forces for change or reduce the forces that resist change. Lewin further suggests that change takes place in a three-stage process presented in Figure 2.

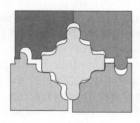

Unfreezing
Preparing people to understand the need for change

Changing
Implementing actual change

Freezing
Providing time and support to ensure change becomes permanent

FIGURE 2 Lewin's Model of Change

In the first, unfreezing state, the existing practices and behaviors are questioned and motivation to change develops. Unfreezing is likely to be easier when the forces for change, whether internal or external are strong and organizational members and leaders are aware of them. One of the major tasks of any leader is to help followers "unfreeze" and realize that there is a need for change. The readiness for change can help reduce resistance that is likely to happen (Self and Schraeder, 2009). In the FBI example presented earlier, Director Robert Mueller was dedicated to communicating consistently and repeatedly about the need for changing the culture and mission and the reasons why the FBI must "chart a new course" and "establish a new mission and priorities" (Brazil, 2007). When the Hanover Insurance Group was close to bankruptcy, CEO Fred Eppinger spent a considerable amount of time selling his new vision for the company to demoralized employees before moving ahead with necessary changes (Byrnes, 2009). In the 3M case, the company's growth had slowed and the stock was performing poorly, prompting McNerney to implement drastic changes such as laying off 8,000 employees (11 percent of the workforce) and putting controls on the creative inventors (Hindo, 2007). Based on all accounts, however, the employees never quite fully grasped the need for change; there had been no "unfreezing."

The second stage according to Lewin is the change itself, where new practices and policies are implemented and new behaviors and skills are learned. The change can involve technology, people, products, services, or management practices and administration. The leader's role continues to be essential, supporting followers, emphasizing the importance of the change, correcting course as needed, and so forth. Most organizations focus on this stage, actually making the change without paying enough attention to either preparing the organization for the change or to the last phase, freezing. In the last phase of change, the newly learned behaviors and freshly implemented practices are encouraged and supported to become part of the employees' routine activities. The leader's role in this stage is coaching, training, and using appropriate reward systems to help solidify the changes that have been implemented.

Organizational researcher Kim Cameron believes that managing change requires fixed points. He states, "Unfortunately, when everything is changing, change becomes impossible to manage. Without a stable, unchanging reference point, direction and processes are indeterminate" (Cameron, 2006: 317). Although change is essential to survival, constant change that is not given time to take hold is likely to be ineffective. It is important for employees to know what is not changing and to be allowed to practice the new behaviors long enough to learn them before something new is introduced. According to Harvard Business School professor John Kotter, a well-known authority on organizational change, leaders must also celebrate early successes and short-term progress to keep followers motivated (Brazil, 2007). In the case of the FBI, the ongoing transformation that took place had an impact on morale, causing heavy turnover (Brazil, 2007). For 3M, although the implementation of the new efficiency-oriented systems lasted for 4 years and stock prices did rebound, the architect of the change, McNerney, left, and most long-time employees did not fully adopt the change. The current CEO, George Buckley, a soft-spoken company insider, has changed course to refocus on the innovation process that 3M is so famous for. He says, "Perhaps one of the mistakes that we made as a company . . . is that when you value sameness more than you value creativity, I think you potentially undermine the heart and soul of a company like 3M" (Hindo, 2007). He has also made leadership training a priority, slowing the pace of moving top executive around and allowing them to savor their successes and learn from their mistakes before they are moved (Jones, 2009).

Lewin's model of change has four key characteristics that leaders must consider:

- The importance of recognizing the need for change and preparing and motivating followers to implement it
- The inevitable presence of the resistance to change
- The focus on people as the source for learning and change
- The need to support new behaviors and allowing them to take hold

The typical model for implementing planned change and ways of managing unplanned change are presented next.

Process of Planned Change

Planned change follows a general process outlined in Figure 3. The process has six steps, each of which requires different types of resources and leadership skills. The first step in the process mirrors the unfreezing phase of Lewin's model. Leaders and followers must become aware of the need for change and recognize its importance to the organization's effectiveness or survival. There may be a performance gap, or employee dissatisfaction, or external pressure from customers or competitors.

The second step involves developing alternatives and ideas for change. This step can be done by organizational leaders at different levels, through small groups or teams, or even with participation of outsiders. Any process that encourages participation and input from those who are affected most by the change is likely to facilitate the implementation process. For example, most municipalities systematically gather input from the public about projects such as parks, freeways, or other developments. Similarly, school boards ask for feedback from parents when planning changes. The use of team and empowerment in organizations can be one mechanism for allowing input into the development of alternatives. In addition, although there may not be a choice on whether or not to change, there are always many alternatives and paths to accomplish the goals; step two of the change process is an ideal opportunity to get involvement and buy-in.

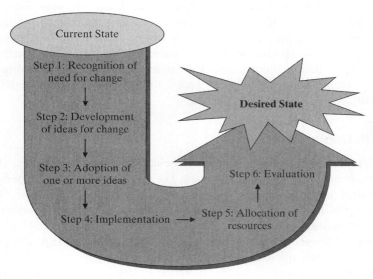

FIGURE 3   The Process of Planned Change

The next two steps are adoption of ideas and implementation of the change plan. These two steps mirror Lewin's change phases. The fifth step is allocation of resources to support the change. Leaders have to either allocate new resources or shift current resources to help implement change and "freeze" the change. For example, FBI Director Mueller shifted resources from fighting crime to counterintelligence to support the new direction, and the FBI started training its executives through additional week-long courses on leading strategic change (Brazil, 2007). The allocation of resources is a potent message from leadership that the change matters and should be taken seriously. Finally, the last step in the process is evaluation of the change process and its outcomes. The process of planned change is a continuous and dynamic loop. After change is implemented, the organization must review and evaluate its effectiveness and assess whether the objectives are met. Did the performance gap narrow or close? Are various constituencies, including employees, more satisfied? Did the new products and services address stakeholders' needs? Are processes more efficient? Does the new technology work? If the goals are not achieved, the change process starts over with the recognition once again that change is needed.

The process of change either can take place in top-down manner with leaders initiating and driving the process or can be bottom-up with individuals and teams throughout the organization starting and implementing the process. A top-down change fits well with traditional, hierarchical, command-and-control organizations and tends to force rapid change. However, it also may engender more resistance. The bottom-up approach creates more involvement and participation, thereby reducing resistance. Yet, the risk of such an approach is not enlisting leadership support, which is essential to the success of any change. The case study of Best Buy at the end of this chapter illustrates a bottom-up approach to change that eventually needed top management support. Another example is Toyota taking over one of the lowest performing and most hostile Chevrolet plants from General Motors in Fremont, California, in the 1980s; no one expected much success. After renaming the plant New United Motor Manufacturing, Inc., or Nummi (sounds like *new me*) and keeping the same workers and the same technology, it took 3 months after the plant started to roll out cars again with almost no defects (the plant had previously averaged 40 defects per car; Deutschman, 2007). Absenteeism and costs were also down dramatically. The key to the successful change was that the workers came up with ideas on how to change things, improve quality, and cut costs (Deutschman, 2007). This bottom-up approach to change, fully supported by top management, was the magical ingredient. Although Nummi produced some of the highest quality cars and had the lowest defects of any Toyota plant, it was closed in 2010, some suspect because of problems between the union and the company (Gonzales, 2010).

Dealing with Unplanned Change

Whereas models of planned change help leaders chart the course for change, change is frequently sudden, unpredictable, and not planned. The economy changes, competitors come up with a new product, an environmental disaster happens, or unions go on strike. Managing unplanned change falls into the domain of crisis management. A crisis occurs when leaders and their organization substantially misread their environment or are caught off guard by events they could not have foreseen. Once crisis occurs, it is difficult to control. The cost to the organization, its employees, and its various stakeholders is likely to be high. Leaders can manage unplanned change to some extent by taking the following steps before a crisis develops (Mintzberg, Quinn, and Voyer, 1995; Starbuck, Greve, and Hedberg, 1978). As you will see, the steps have much in common with learning organizations, a topic we review at the end of this chapter.

- Avoid becoming too formal, hierarchical, rigid, and inflexible.
- Infuse moderate amounts of uncertainty, unpredictability, and spontaneity into decisions to help prevent complacency.
- Stay on the offensive and be proactive with introducing new strategies, products, services, or processes.
- Replace and rotate leaders to bring in fresh ideas, methods, and visions.
- Experiment often with new methods, products, processes, structures, and so forth to help followers practice dealing with change.

Bill George, former CEO of Medtronics, further suggests that crises often present opportunities for organizations to change course for the better and for leaders to focus on their most important values (George, 2009). Whether planned or unplanned, and even with the most careful implementation, people are likely to resist change. The next section considers resistance to change, its solutions, and the role of leaders in the process.

RESISTANCE TO CHANGE AND SOLUTIONS

Change is one of the main causes of stress in our lives. Even positive changes such as receiving a promotion or getting married can create anxiety, lead to stress, and therefore engender resistance, which stops or slows the movement forward (Maurer, 1996). Making major changes in one's life, for example changing your lifestyle after having a heart attack, are extremely difficult (Deutschman, 2007). Although people adjust to minor changes after a brief period of time, large-scale changes in life or work require long adaptation periods and much encouragement and support. Therefore, all changes, especially large-scale ones, meet with some resistance, especially when people do feel ready for the change (Self and Schraeder, 2009).

> Although people adjust to minor changes after a brief period of time, large-scale changes in life or work require long adaptation periods and much encouragement and support. Therefore, all changes, especially large-scale ones, meet with some resistance.

Causes of Resistance

Three general causes explain resistance to change: organizational factors, group factors, and individual factors. (Table 2 presents the causes of resistance to change.) While planning and implementing change, leaders must consider all three causes. The primary organizational cause for resisting change is inertia, which is a tendency for an organization as a whole to resist change and want to maintain the status quo. Closely related to inertia are the culture and structure of the organization, which, if well established, are hard to change. Challenges faced by Ford Motor Company include fighting declining sales for years and most recently being further battered by the recession. With the leadership of CEO Alan Mulally since 2006, the company has refused to accept government help and has instead worked with its stakeholders to find ways to save money and has instilled considerable fiscal discipline (Taylor, 2009). When Mullaly joined Ford, the company provided a perfect example of inertia and the power of organizational culture, with entrenched management, fierce loyalties, and frequent turf battles (Taylor, 2009). The company's previous CEO and now chairman of the board, Bill Ford, Jr., gave up his job believing that an insider could no longer fix the problems and promising that the new CEO "knows how to shake the company to its foundations" (Kiley, 2007). Mulally, who had little experience in the car industry, faced what some considered Ford's dysfunctional and

TABLE 2	Causes of Resistance to Change		
Organizational Causes	**Group Causes**	**Individual Causes**	
Inertia	Group norms	Fear of the unknown	
Culture	Group cohesion	Fear of failure	
Structure	Leadership	Job security	
Lack of rewards		Individual characteristics	
Poor timing		Previous experiences	

defeatist culture. To convince employees and leaders at Ford to change, he repeated the message: "We have been going out of business for 40 years" (Kiley, 2007). Ford's complacent culture, its highly rigid structure with a hierarchical pecking order that discourages sharing ideas, and its well-established leadership-training practices that placed leaders in many jobs for short periods of time, all discouraged openness and cooperation and present a barrier to change.

In addition to inertia and culture and structure, organizations can provide barriers to change by not rewarding people for change or implementing change at inappropriate times, for example when the previous change has not had time to "freeze." Other causes of resistance to change are related to group norms and cohesion. Cohesive groups with strong norms present many benefits. Members stick together, work well together, and can provide a supportive environment for learning. Strong group norms, however, can also be a formidable obstacle to change (Judson, 1991). In addition, the presence of strong charismatic leaders who do not support the change can also be an obstacle (Levay, 2009). When Marc Fields, now president of Ford Americas, joined the company in 1989, he was informed of group norms in the executive suites, which included making sure to get approval from his boss before he brought up any problems at meetings (Kiley, 2007). Ford's Mulally worked on changing such group norms of secrecy and hiding mistakes to encourage people to admit mistakes and share information (Fields, 2006).

The final cause of resistance involves individual factors, such as fear of the unknown, of failure, and of job loss. Individual characteristics can also play a key role. For example, individuals who are open to new experiences, those with internal locus of control, or high self-monitors are more likely to be comfortable with change and able to adapt to it more quickly. Similarly, entrepreneurs, who tend to be characterized by flexibility and willingness to try new ideas, are more comfortable with change. In addition, a person's culture, particularly the degree of tolerance of ambiguity, may play a role. Finally, the person's previous experience with change may present an obstacle to change. If an individual has experienced job loss or has been through other painful organizational changes in the past, he or she is more likely to be wary of implementing change in the future.

Solutions

As we will consider in the next section, the leader of an organization can do much to initiate change, inspire followers to implement it, and reduce resistance to change through inspiration, improvisation, creativity, and motivating followers. Overall, resistance can be reduced if employees learn to change their perception of change as negative and instead reframe it by seeing its potential benefits. Such change in perception can be encouraged by engaging employees in the change process and by rewarding behaviors and norms that support the change. Several specific methods for managing resistance are presented in Table 3.

TABLE 3	Methods of Dealing with Resistance to Change		
Methods	**When to Use**	**Advantages**	**Disadvantages**
Education and communication: Provide information	When there is lack of information and fear of the unknown; in all phases of the change process	Provide facts and once persuaded, people are less likely to resist	Time-consuming when large number of people are involved
Participation and involvement: Engage employees	When people do not have all the information or when they have power to block implementation; in all phases of the change process	Lead to commitment and can provide richer alternatives and ideas	Time-consuming; risk of inappropriate change being implemented
Facilitation and support: Understanding and providing support	When people are resisting because of factors such as fear; during the change and refreezing phases	The only option when adjustment is the cause of resistance	Time consuming and high-risk of failure
Negotiation and agreements: Engage parties who can block change	When there can be winners and losers and groups and individuals have power; during the change and refreezing phases	Relatively easy to implement; only option to balance power	Can be expensive, time consuming and lead to continued and further negotiation
Manipulation and cooptation: Bypass resistance through promises	When nothing else works or other options are too expensive; during the change phase	Relatively quick and inexpensive	Can lead to mistrust and resentment
Explicit or implicit coercion: Impose change through authority and fear	When there is no time and nothing else works; when others have power; use occasionally; during unfreezing and change	Can be fast and effective in short term to end resistance	Can lead to resentment and morale problems; only effective in the short-run

Source: Based on Kotter, J. P., and L. A. Schlesinger. 1979. Choosing strategies for change. *Harvard Business Review* March–April.

Leaders can prevent, manage, or reduce resistance to change by using a variety of these methods. The importance of engagement and communication are very clear. A global survey conducted by McKinsey indicates that one of the keys to successful change is engaging employees to work collaboratively through the transformation (McKinsey, 2010). Alan Mulally has been successful in slowly changing Ford by focusing heavily on communication to make sure everyone understood the extent of the problem, the need for change and by setting a new mission and printing it on cards that he distributed to employees. He also made structural changes, "So I moved up and included every functional discipline on my team because everybody in this place had to be involved and had to know everything" (Taylor, 2009). Considering Mulally's effectiveness, Howard Schultz CEO of Starbucks states, "I've been studying the turnaround at Ford. The reason it has outpaced [GM and Chrysler] is because of the leadership and focus that Alan has brought" (Schultz, 2010). The next section focuses on the specific role of leaders in the successful implementation of change in organizations.

LEADING CHANGE

One of the most important components of leading change is providing inspiration and vision for employees. Other factors include creativity, improvisation, and the processes for changing organizational culture as a requirement to successful change.

Vision and Inspiration

"You have to share the vision you want to accomplish and get everybody on board and enthusiastic about it. When you can get them to march in the same direction, you can really move mountains," states Carl-Henric Svanberg, CEO of the Swedish telecom giant Ericsoon (Bisoux, 2009). Ford's Mulally agrees, "Everyone has to know the plan, its status, and areas that need special attention" (Taylor, 2009). These executives know that providing a vision and inspiring followers are the most important functions of leaders during change. A clear vision provides followers with reasons for change. It further supports the actual change process by helping followers keep the goal in mind and helps them stay focused during refreezing. The inspiration that a leader can provide to his or her followers sustains the followers and helps reduce the resistance to change. Several themes emerge in the visionary leadership essential to change:

A clear vision provides followers with reasons for change. It further supports the actual change process helping followers keep the goal in mind and helps them stay focused during refreezing.

- *Importance of vision.* Successful and effective leaders provide a clear vision or help followers develop a common vision. Whether developed by the leader alone or with engagement with followers, vision is key to effectively leading change.
- *Empowerment and confidence in followers.* Visionary leaders empower followers to allow them to act autonomously and independently from the leader. This empowerment engages followers in the change, reducing resistance.
- *Flexibility and change.* The fast-changing environment requires leaders to develop and encourage flexibility and openness to change in their organization.
- *Teamwork and cooperation.* Successful leaders emphasize teamwork and, maybe more important, the development of shared responsibility, as well as the need for trust and cooperation between leaders and followers and among followers.

Leaders play a key role in the development and communication of the vision. Some leaders, for instance, communicate their vision and values through stories. Patrick Kelly, CEO of Physician Sales and Services (PSS), relies on his storytelling skills to remind employees what is important (Weil, 1998). Whenever he repeats one of his favorites, "PSS employees chuckle. . . . And they learn, or relearn, an important lesson: No matter how badly other people treat you, no matter how confident you get about your future, never burn your bridges" (38). Researcher Noel Tichy recommends that leaders develop three stories. The first one, the "Who I am" story, should tell who the leader is. The second story is about "Who we are." Finally, the leader must have a "Where we are going" story (Weil, 1998). Others agree that storytelling can be one of the most powerful ways for leaders to communicate their vision to their followers. According to Harvard

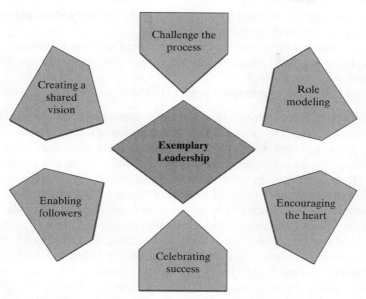

FIGURE 4 Practices of Exemplary and Visionary Leadership

professor Howard Gardner, "Stories of identity convey values, build esprit de corps, create role models, and reveal how things work around here" (Stewart, 1998b: 165). For example, Howard Schulltz of Starbucks is a master storyteller who relies on sharing his personal experiences as a way of explaining his vision for the company.

Similar to the ideas proposed by charismatic, transformational, value-based, and spiritual leadership, the leader's vision is vital to creating change. A motivating vision is clear and understandable, challenging, idealistic yet achievable; it appeals to emotions and is forward looking. Andrea Jung of Avon, Bob McDonald of P&G, or Alan Mulally of Ford do not rely on personal stories, but keep their message simple and repetitive to ensure that their followers hear it and understand it as a priority. Having a forward-looking vision is essential for transforming organizations and enacting large-scale change. Kouzes and Posner (2007) propose one of the most clearly developed models of visionary leadership. In addition to presenting the practices of what the researchers call exemplary leadership (Figure 4), the model considers the followers' points of view and their expectations of leaders. Leaders have to model the way, develop and inspire a shared vision, challenge the status quo, empower and enable their followers to act, and motivate and support them (Kouzes and Posner, 1993).

Kouzes and Posner (2003a, 2007) emphasize the importance of motivation, reward, and recognition—in their words "encouraging the heart"—as key aspects of empowerment, confidence in followers, and development of trust. They specifically suggest that to truly motivate and inspire followers, the leader must do the following:

- Set clear standards for behavior and performance that are accepted by all followers.
- Expect the best from followers through a genuine belief in their abilities. This strong belief creates a self-fulfilling prophecy in followers, who will, in turn, perform better.
- Pay attention by being present, walking around, noticing followers, and caring about their behaviors, actions, and results.

- Personalize recognition not only by considering each follower's needs and preferences, but also by making them feel special in the process.
- Tell a story about followers, events, and performances as a way to motivate and teach.
- Celebrate together. Leaders must look for many opportunities to celebrate the team and the individual's success together.
- Role model the preceding principles to gain credibility and reinforce the message.

To be exemplary and visionary, leaders need to commit themselves to continuously questioning old beliefs and assumptions. This process leads to the creation of a new common vision. Through empowerment, encouragement, and proper role modeling, leaders can motivate followers to implement the vision. The driving force behind a leader's ability to fulfill this commitment is his or her credibility (Kouzes and Posner, 1993). By asking followers about the characteristics they admire most and expect from their leaders, Kouzes and Posner suggest that honesty, the ability to be forward looking, and the capacity to be inspiring and competent are the pillars of a leader's credibility. Leaders' ability to change followers and the organization depends on their credibility.

When Rob Waldron became CEO of JumpStart in 2002, he took over a successful organization that was sending AmeriCorps volunteers and college students to teach Head Start programs in various cities to combat the rising trend of preschoolers in low-income communities entering school without the skills needed to succeed (Overholt, 2005). With the mandate to grow the organization, Waldron admits, "This is the greatest management and leadership challenge I've ever faced. . . . I had to learn how to lead people and persuade them to a common end" (55). Waldron tackled the goals by decentralizing decision making, giving power to each center to encourage its employees to bring out their best ideas, and cutting staff at headquarters to raise everyone else's salary and attract fresh talent. His strategies paid off, and JumpStart grew 33 percent in 2003. Talking about his organization's achievement, Waldron said, "Our legacy is real social change. To have the joy of knowing your day-to-day struggles are turning into something that is life-changing. . . . I just wish everyone got to feel that way about their work" (55).

The visionary approach to leadership and change allows us to explain one of the most interesting and visible sides of leadership. It lets us talk about the leaders who everyone would agree are the real leaders—those who transform their organizations. Despite some survey-based studies, however, this approach generally lacks strong empirical research needed to establish its validity and to clarify and refine its propositions.

It is clear that visionary leadership is needed in times of crisis and that it plays an essential role in implementing change. The effect of such leadership in times when consolidation and status quo are needed, however, is not as clear. Change-oriented leadership, by definition, works in times of change; the role of such a leader when change is not the focus is not clear. Anecdotes of the disastrous effects of change-oriented leaders in times when change is not needed are common and point to the limitations of visionary leadership. The current discussions of visionary leaders do not address these limitations. In addition, no research looks at the fate of organizations and employees who either do not buy into the leader's vision or who buy into an inappropriate vision, as may have been the case at 3M. Many historical and political examples can be found, though. The extent to which similar events would occur in organizations needs to be explored.

Despite these shortcomings, visionary leadership provides guidelines for managing change. Accordingly, leaders must have passion, develop their credibility, develop and clarify their vision, share power with their followers, and—perhaps most important—role model all the attributes that they expect in their followers.

LEADING CHANGE

Jeff Immelt

Replacing someone who was touted as one of the best business leaders in the world and has become an icon in leadership and management is no easy feat. Jeff Immelt, who stepped in after Jack Welch to become CEO of General Electric (GE) in September of 2001, however, has taken on the task with apparent ease and comfort. He is implementing changes that are unpopular and were voted down by the executive committee (MacMillan, 2008). Immelt is focusing on changing the leadership culture at GE by instituting a team culture (Nocera, 2007). He further wants his company to be a role model for sustainability, implementing the concept of Ecomagination, and is reaching out to a wide range of constituencies beyond the shareholders (Murray, 2006). His soft approach and understated style are big assets to him in this process. Whereas Welch was loud, domineering, and impatient, Immelt is quiet, is self-confident, and has a good dose of "people" skills. He believes the key to getting people onboard is that "People want to win. And if people think they've been given the capability to win and are the winner, that's how you get people in the game" (Byrne, 2005).

Although much different than his predecessor, Immelt is said to be equally tireless, dedicated, intelligent, and disciplined, as well as relaxed and charming (Colvin, 2005). John Chambers of Cisco says: "The job that GE and Jeff Immelt have done is the best in the business. You learn a lot about a person and a company during the tough times" (Chambers, 2010). Immelt is keenly aware of the importance of getting people onboard and the challenge in managing the change process. Discussing what university students should learn, he states, "I'd really want to re-engage people around innovation and risk-taking . . . emphasize team building. Good business is about good ideas, and good ideas come when people work together" (Bisoux, 2006: 22). He approached his green ideas the same way, carefully building his base and aligning his stakeholders (MacMillan, 2008). At GE, everything is carefully planned and measured, so creating a team environment is no different. Employees are being taught team skills, managers and leaders are carefully evaluated on those skills, and those who show the best potential and performance are promoted to lead others. Through this careful process, the organization can slowly change its culture. Although innovation is Immelt's primary focus, he also considers that change needs to be focused and that people cannot take on too many initiatives at any one time. For him, the role of the leader is to keep that focus and communicate the new direction often. He states, "This is a company where we want people to make a difference. We want them to be proud of where they work" (Byrne, 2005).

Immelt's leadership is a well-thought-out process. He explains, "I always say that good leaders tend to be good students of leadership. . . . Leadership is ultimately a journey into itself" (Bisoux, 2006: 22). His low-key style and his focus on process and innovation have earned him the rank of the world's best CEOs only a few years after taking on a tough leadership challenge (Murray, 2006).

Sources: Bisoux, T., 2006. "Idea man," *BizEd*, May–June: 18-22; Byrne, J. A., 2005. "Jeff Immelt," *Fast Company*, July. http://www.fastcompany.com/magazine/96/jeff-immelt.html (accessed July 10, 2007); Colvin, G., 2005. "The bionic manager," *Fortune*, September 19. http://jcgi.pathfinder.com/fortune/fortune75/articles/0,15114, 1101055,00.html (accessed July 10, 2007); MacMillan, D. 2008. The issue: Immelt's unpopular idea. *Business Week*, March 4. http://www.businessweek.com/managing/content/mar2008/ca2008034_906295.htm (accessed April 21, 2010); Murray, A., 2006. "A tale of two CEOs: How public perception shapes reputation," *Wall Street Journal*, July 12: A2; Nocera, J., 2007. "Running G.E., comfortable in his skin," *The New York Times*, June 9. http://select.nytimes.com/gst/abstract.html?res=FA0B1FFC3D5B0C7A8CDDAF0894DF404482 (accessed July 10, 2007).

CREATIVITY AND IMPROVISATION

As proposed in visionary leadership, modeling the way is crucial in leading change. Leaders must show followers through their own actions how change can be implemented and how it can successful. To that end, the leader's creativity and ability to improvise become exemplary.

Creativity

Creativity, also called *divergent* or *lateral thinking*, is the ability to link or combine ideas in novel ways. Creativity for leaders and followers is a key factor in organizational ability to innovate and change (see Self-Assessment 2). Creative people tend to be confident in the paths they select and are willing to take risks when others give up. They focus on learning and are willing to live with uncertainty to reach their goals. These traits and behaviors help when facing change. For P&G's cognitive science group, creativity sometimes means borrowing ideas from others. Pete Foley, the group's associate director, found some answers to challenges in the feminine products division in the San Diego Zoo by considering the biomimickry of geckos (Heath and Heath, 2009). Instead of inventing new solutions, this form of creativity involves looking for existing solution in other areas. Harvard Professor Karin Lakhani says: "You can't image that someone else may have a different perspective. But problems that are difficult in one domain may be trivial to solve from the perspective of a different domain" (Heath and Heath, p. 83). Leaders can put in place several processes to help their followers be more creative and accept change more readily:

- *Leadership style.* Autocratic leaders who demand obedience impede the creative process and open exchange that encourage creativity.
- *Flexible structure.* Less centralized and less hierarchical structures allow for free flow of ideas.
- *Open organizational culture.* Being creative and seeking novel solutions is more likely in a culture that values change and constructive deviance rather than tradition and conformity.
- *Questioning attitude.* Leaders can encourage and inspire followers to question assumptions and norms and look for novel alternatives instead of rewarding agreement and obedience.
- *Tolerating mistakes.* By encouraging experimentation, tolerating, and even rewarding some mistakes, the leader can send a strong message about the importance of taking risks.

Many decision-making tools, such as brainstorming, can be used to enhance followers' creativity. In brainstorming (or brainsailing), team members are encouraged to generate a large number of ideas and alternatives without any censorship. Another method called *cooperative exploration* requires individuals to consider a problem by taking different positions and perspectives (De Bono, 1999). Instead of looking at an issue from the typical positive and negative points of view, lateral thinking encourages people to consider a problem from neutral, emotional, optimistic, cautious, creative, and analytical perspectives. By using such techniques, leaders can encourage their followers to take broader perspectives and build a culture experimentation and creativity.

Improvisation

Closely related to creativity is improvisation. According to researchers Robert and Janet Denhardt, authors of *The Dance of Leadership*, "improvisation is a vital leadership skill, one essential to the process of emotionally connecting with and energizing others" (2006: 109). These researchers liken leadership to art, particularly dance, focusing on the intuitive nature of leadership and the need to master its rhythms. Improvisation, a term often used for artists rather than leaders, involves creation of something spontaneously and extemporaneously without specific preparation. Denhardt and Denhardt suggest that it occurs without a script and without perfect information and requires a combination of pre-planned and unplanned activities and materials. Having expertise, knowledge, and perspective on the situation are also required, because without these elements, the leader is not likely to understand the leadership situation and environment enough to be able to lead. Improvisation is not "winging" a solution. It is based on deep preparation, self-knowledge, self-reflection, experience, and confidence, all also elements of authentic leadership. A musician states, "an ability to improvise . . . depends firstly on an understanding, developed from complete familiarity, of the musical context within which one improvises" (115).

> Improvisation involves creation of something spontaneously and extemporaneously without specific preparation. It occurs without a script and without perfect information and requires a combination of preplanned and unplanned activities and materials. Having expertise, knowledge, and perspective on the situation are also required, because without these elements, the leader is not likely to understand the leadership situation and environment enough to be able to lead.

To be able to change their organizations, leaders themselves must be able and willing to take risks. As do artists, leaders must hone their skills, practice often, develop competence, and be willing to work with their team of followers to experiment and transform themselves and their organization.

CHANGING HOW ORGANIZATIONS APPROACH CHANGE

To implement change successfully, most organizations must change their leadership and culture in fundamental ways. Although the various methods described earlier all support change, the most basic and essential steps to successful change is to design organizations that are built to change (Worley and Lawler, 2006) and have cultures that approach change positively (Wall, 2005). The concept of learning organizations has been proposed to address the importance of flexibility and the ability to learn, adapt, and change continuously (Senge, 2006) and more recently, positive organizational behavior and leadership provide a fresh approach to leading organizational change.

Learning Organizations

Learning organizations are organizations in which people continually expand their capacity to create, where innovation and cooperation are nurtured, and where knowledge is transferred throughout the organization. Such an organization learns and creates faster than others, and this ability becomes a major factor in its survival and success. Learning organizations do not simply manage change; their goal is to become a place where creativity, flexibility, adaptation, and learning are integral parts of the culture and everyday processes.

The elements that make up the core of learning organizations are presented in Table 4. For organizations to learn and accept change as part of their routine, the leaders and members must have a shared vision of the current and future states. Charismatic, transformational, authentic, visionary, and positive leadership are all elements of building that vision. It is essential that leaders and followers understand how the organization functions as a system both internally and within its environment and be aware of the stated and unstated assumptions that make up the culture of their organizations. Without understanding how the organization truly functions, it is hard to implement change. The vision and the knowledge of the organization and its culture allow

TABLE 4 Core Elements of Learning Organizations

Element	Description
Shared vision	Using cooperation and openness to build a shared vision through a common identity and a common goal of the future that leads to commitment.
System thinking	Understanding interrelations and the invisible and visible bonds that connect people inside and outside the organization.
Mental models	Being aware of stated and unstated assumptions and mental models that guide behaviors and decisions and developing new ones based on openness and cooperation.
Personal mastery	Continually clarifying and developing personal visions and goals, and expanding skills sets and levels of proficiency.
Team learning	Developing synergy and the ability to think and work together to question assumptions and build new processes.

Sources: P. M. Senge, *"The Fifth Discipline: The Art and Practice of Learning Organizations,"* New York: Doubleday, 2006; P. M. Senge, "Leading learning organizations," *Training and Development*, 1995, 50(12), 36–37; P. M. Senge and J. D. Sterman, "System thinking and organizational learning: Acting locally and thinking globally in the organization of the future," *European Journal of Operations Research*, 1992, 59 (1), 137–140.

organizational members to identify what needs to be changed and the best ways to approach the transformation. Finally, successful change requires expertise and continuous development of new skills and competencies for individuals and for teams.

Figure 5 presents the factors that prevent organizations from learning. These factors are organizational learning disabilities of sorts. They are patterns of thinking and behavior that members have adopted that block change. According to Senge (2006), these blocks or disabilities, stem from lack of system thinking and lead to looking at tasks, jobs, problems, and goals as separate and isolated from one another. In addition, leaders that are focused on large-scale change may fail to ignore the gradual and incremental change that may be occurring and likely to lead to the same outcome. They also may focus on specific events or causes of problems without considering the context in which they may be occurring or all the systemwide factors that may be contributing to them. The focus on events results in trying to find someone or something to blame for

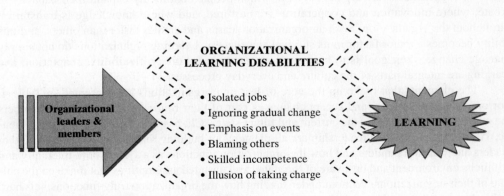

FIGURE 5 Blocks to Learning in Organizations

the problems. Identifying these enemies detracts from fully considering the problems and focusing on solutions. Another organizational learning disability is skilled incompetence, which refers to relying on people with highly developed but narrow expertise who are celebrated and expected to provide answers. Because they are there to solve problems, they often cannot admit to lack of understanding or knowledge or to making mistakes. They, therefore, cannot learn and become incompetent despite their considerable skills. The situation becomes even more precarious if leaders are those who have skilled incompetence. Finally, another factor related to leadership is the illusion of taking charge and of one person being responsible to lead all others through the problem, instead of having shared leadership, empowerment, and cooperation.

To support their organizations in being change-ready and becoming learning organizations, leaders can take several actions to build an open and supportive culture that will support ongoing transformation. Actions include openness to new ideas, encouraging followers to develop local solutions rather than pushing standardization, providing time for learning and experimentation, and developing leaders who are open to participation and follower engagement.

The example of McNerney in 3M provides a case for obstacles and support for learning organizations. Based on its creativity and track record for innovation, 3M had many of the elements that encourage learning in organizations. Before McNerney took leadership, the organization focused on local solutions, open communication among inventors, and plenty of time and tolerance for learning and experimentation. In his search for efficiency, McNerney replaced many of the elements that made 3M a learning organization with factors that blocked learning. Implementation of a one-size-fits-all Six Sigma process, focus on specific events rather than looking for systemwide causes of problems, and an imposed vision from the top rather than a shared vision, all eroded the culture and 3M's ability to learn. Whereas the company continues to face challenges in maintaining its growth and profitability, the current leaders are reinstituting many of the elements that gave the company its innovative culture (Hindo, 2007).

Herman Miller, the office furniture maker, provides another example of a learning organization (Glaser, 2006; Herman Miller Culture, 2010). The company has been recognized as one of the best in its industry for its innovation and unique culture. It is known for its focus on its employees through flex-time, telecommuting, and employee learning and ownership. It works with clients to develop distinctive solutions to their unique problems (Salter, 2000b). But what makes the company truly a learning organization is the focus on curiosity and learning. Author Glaser describes the culture in her book *The DNA of Leadership*: "To encourage a wonderful sense of curiosity, leaders focus on helping Herman Miller employees experiment and take lessons from those experiments. This is such a strong part of the culture that's built into everything they do and say—it's embedded in their genetic code" (Glaser, 2006: 180).

Positive Approach

We have reviewed the positive organizational behavior and positive leadership approaches. Many of their concepts and findings readily apply to leading change in organizations. Best-selling authors and reporters Chip and Dan Heath consider the importance of positive thinking and positive role models in creating and sustaining change (Heath and Heath, 2010). They discuss the case of Jerry Sternin, who worked for Save the Children on improving child nutrition in third-world countries. When discussing how to change behavior, Sternin states: "Knowledge does not change behavior. We have all encountered crazy shrinks and obese doctors and divorced marriage counselors" (Heath and Heath, p. 65). Instead, what works is having a role-model of a positive outcome or event and understanding why things worked out and then trying to replicate them. This positive approach looks for "bright spots" that can be the guide of change in behavior.

Role of Leaders in Changing Organizational Culture

There are many ways in which top-level leaders can influence their organizations. In addition, Edgar Schein has identified several specific mechanisms that leaders use to shape the culture of their organization (2004). They include the following:

- *Communicate priorities.* By stating what is important, in terms of a general vision, specific issues that must be addressed, and ways in which they must be addressed, leaders make a powerful impact on their organization. For example, A. G. Lafley, former CEO of P&G, was relentless about repeating the simple message of paying attention to customers.
- *Role model.* Although what the leader says is important, even more powerful is what the leader does. Leaders must be the change they want to see. Their actions demonstrate their values and what is truly important. For example, many historical charismatic leaders, including Mahatma Gandhi and Nelson Mandela, have gone to prison for their beliefs. A particular opportunity to role model desired behaviors occurs during times of crisis when the focus on and the need for leadership is increased. How a leader acts when facing unplanned change, what she pays attention to, and how her priorities may change all provide authoritative guides for followers.
- *Allocate resources and rewards.* A more practical and equally impacting action is how the leader allocates resources and rewards. By rewarding compliance and conformity, a leader who professes that she values innovation and experimentation shows what she truly values. Similarly, by promoting individuals who demonstrate the values and mission of the organization, the leader can make a clear impact on the culture of the organization.

Applying What You Learn
Change Agents and Peer Pressure

One of the key factors in the success of change is relying on change agents and positive examples as a way of encouraging others to adopt the change. This "peer pressure" can be a positive method of averting resistance to change. Here are some practical pointers on how to use peer pressure in leading change:

- *Don't approach the change alone.* Although leaders have responsibility and authority, successful change is a group effort. Carefully plan how to involve others to help you.
- *Find a few people who are excited about the change* and enlist their help in communicating with other employees.

- *Win over opinion leaders.* In every organization, there are opinion leaders who are respected. Winning them over and enlisting their support for the change will move implementation along much faster.
- *Set up a pilot that can show success.* People may know that the change will be good for them, but that knowledge does not translate into behavior. Seeing a successful example goes a long way to convince employees that things may actually work out.
- *Actions speak louder than words.* Provide concrete examples inside and outside the organization that show how things can work out.

Many other mechanisms that leaders use to shape their organizations are design of the structure and processes, setting design criteria, and even selection of the physical space (Schein, 2004).

Summary and Conclusions

Change has become the only constant in today's organizations. Internal and external forces pressure organizations to be flexible, adapt, and transform themselves. A leader's ability to guide and support followers through change is one of the key leadership roles and may vary depending on cultural factors such as tolerance for ambiguity and perception of time. Even though organizations would like to plan for change and implement change in gradual and incremental ways, many of them face unplanned change that is revolutionary and requires considerable transformation. Regardless of the type of change, leaders need to view change as a three-step process of unfreezing or preparing followers for change, the actual change, and refreezing, which involves providing resources and support to solidify new processes and behaviors.

Planned change often follows six steps from recognizing the need for change; to developing, adopting, and implementing ideas; to allocation of resources; and finally evaluation. In this process, leaders can implement the change from the top down pushing the change faster or allow bottom up input that helps to get commitment and reduces resistance to change. In addition, whereas unplanned change is by definition unpredictable, leaders can prepare their followers by supporting flexibility, introducing gradual change, and experimenting with new methods. Even with careful planning and preparation, resistance to change is likely to occur because of organizational factors such as inertia and culture, group factors such as group norms,

and many individual factors such as fear and individual characteristics. Leaders can use several methods to manage resistance; however, at the core of all successful methods are supporting employees, engaging them in the change, and providing a culture that sustain change.

One of the essential roles of leaders in the change process is to develop a shared vision for the change to help support followers through the implementation phase. Other related roles for visionary leaders are challenging the process, motivating followers, role modeling, and empowerment, all of which can energize followers and establish a culture that can sustain change. Other leadership roles include role modeling and supporting creativity and improvisation. An organization that has flexible and open structures and cultures, where mistakes are tolerated and experimentation and a questioning attitude encouraged, can encourage creativity. Improvisation requires deep preparation, self-reflection, and commitment, all of which are also elements of authentic leadership.

The leader's ability to support followers through organizational change ultimately depends on having an organizational culture that is built and ready for change and continuous learning. The leader plays a critical role in creating a learning organization and in developing followers' ability to think broadly, develop personal mastery, work as a team, and develop as shared vision to ensure that the organization as a whole is ready to learn and change.

Review and Discussion Questions

1. Describe the internal and external forces for change.
2. What role does culture play in how people perceive change?
3. Describe the five different types of changes organizations face.
4. Explain Lewin's model for change and its implications for organizations.

5. Present the six steps in the process of planned change, and describe the role of leaders in each step.
6. What can leaders do to prepare their organization to deal with unplanned change?
7. Present the organizational, group, and individual causes of resistance to change.
8. Describe ways in which resistance to change can be reduced, and explain when each method can be used.

9. What is visionary leadership and how does it relate to change?
10. Compare and contrast creativity and improvisation, and explain their role in leading change.
11. What are the elements of an organizational culture that supports change, and what role do leaders play in developing that culture?

Leadership Challenge: Implementing Unpopular Change

Your supervisor has just informed you of a major restructuring in your area aimed at increasing efficiency. She is assigning you to implement the necessary changes. The plans are coming from headquarters and are not negotiable. In addition to losing a couple of positions, your department will be moved to a new less-desirable location across town and will have to share administrative support with another team. Upper management is further using the restructuring as an opportunity to implement a much-needed new Web-based customer relations system.

Your team of 15 people is cohesive, and you know that letting go of two of your members will be hard on everyone. In addition, the new location is farther for all of you, and your offices will not be as nice.

Although the new technology is welcome, there will be a great need for training and support before it can be fully implemented. On a personal level, you are very upset about the change. This is the second major change in as many years that you have had to implement without having a chance for input. You experience considerable stress and are worried about your team's reaction and ability to pull this through. Yet, your career depends on implementing the change.

1. How should you approach your team?
2. How much of your personal feelings should you share?
3. What are some key actions you should take?

Exercise 1: Analyzing and Planning for Change

This exercise is designed to provide you with the experience of defining a problem and planning for the change. It follows the model presented in Figure 3.

Part I: Form Teams and Select a Problem

In teams of three to five members, select a problem (organizational or personal) that one team member faces that requires change. Potential examples include the following: the sales team you supervise does not work well with the development or manufacturing department; the clerks at your agency do not have a customer-focused approach; the team you belong to in one of your classes is unfocused; the spring program committee that you lead at your child's school has been putting together boring programs for several years; the school board would like to seek more parent input in its decisions, and so on. Note that each of the problems—and any you are likely to identify—involves many different individual and organizational issues.

What problem will your group address?

Part II: Define the Problem

It is important for the team to have a clear idea about what the problem really is. As a team:

Restate the problem in as many different ways as you can.

Consider all the positive and negative aspects of the problem.

Consider all the related issues.

Agree on a final clear description of the problem.

Part III: Plan for Change

Instead of jumping into action and proposing solutions, your team must understand the problem and the process, consider many alternatives, and evaluate them before selecting a solution.

How will you help the organization understand the need for change? What steps will you take? What data do you need?

Identify as many alternative solutions as you can without evaluating each (brainstorm.)

Evaluate each solution carefully; consider the positive and negative aspects of each. Who is likely to be affected if the solutions are implemented? Who will resist? What are the costs? Do they fully address the problem?

Select one solution; it does not have to be perfect, just based on your team's analysis. Explain why it is the best solution.

How will you implement your solution? Consider people and resources, major obstacles, potential solutions, key people to be involved, training needs, timetable, costs, how you will measure success.

Part IV: Presentation

Each team will make a brief presentation of its plan for change.

Source: Based on "Managing Change," in A. Nahavandi and A. R. Malekzadeh *Organizational Behavior: The Person–Organization Fit.* Upper Saddle River, NJ: Prentice Hall.

Self-Assessment 1: Building Credibility

One of the key elements to visionary leadership is the leader's credibility. Having credibility allows a leader to undertake the necessary changes with sincerity and with followers' trust. Following are the elements of credibility. Rate yourself on each of the items using the following scale:

1 = Never

2 = Occasionally

3 = Often

4 = Always

_____ 1. I state my position clearly.

_____ 2. My coworkers and subordinates always know where I stand.

_____ 3. I listen to other people's opinions carefully and respectfully.

_____ 4. I accept disagreement from my coworkers and followers.

_____ 5. I try to integrate my point of view with that of others.

_____ 6. I encourage and practice constructive feedback.

_____ 7. I encourage and practice cooperation.

_____ 8. I build consensus out of differing views.

_____ 9. I develop my coworkers' and subordinates' skills.

_____ 10. I provide frequent positive feedback and encouragement.

_____ 11. I hold myself and others accountable for actions.

_____ 12. I practice what I preach.

Scoring Key: Add up your rating for all 12 items. The maximum score is 48. A higher score indicates behaviors that build credibility.

Total: _____

Self-analysis and Action Plan

Which items have a low score? List those areas that you need to target to build your credibility.

What can you do about them? Focus on clear and specific behaviors. Develop short-term and long-term goals. When will you know that you have improved? How will you measure yourself?

Source: This self-assessment is partially based on concepts developed by Kouzes and Posner (1993, 2003b).

Self-Assessment 2: Creativity

Being open to change is to some extent a function of being creative. Although creativity is partly a personality trait, individuals can enhance their personal creativity in several ways. Rate each statement according to how well it applies to you by using the following scale:

1 = never

2 = some of the time

3 = always

     _____ 1. My life is so hectic; I have no time to pay attention to anything new.

     _____ 2. I set daily goals for myself and focus on getting them done.

     _____ 3. I put considerable effort to do something well when I do it.

     _____ 4. I have clear priorities about what is important to me and what is not. I look for ways to making things I enjoy more complex and challenging.

     _____ 5. I know what I like and don't like in life.

     _____ 6. I face problems head-on and look for solutions immediately.

     _____ 7. I am disorganized and feel that my schedule is out of control.

     _____ 8. I often surprise others with my unexpected actions or words.

     _____ 9. My office/home is organized in a way that calms me and supports my activities.

     _____ 10. I rarely follow through on things that spark my interest.

     _____ 11. I keep routine things simple so that I have energy to focus on what is important.

     _____ 12. I make time for relaxation and reflection.

     _____ 13. I approach problems by trying to develop as many solutions as possible before I try to solve them.

     _____ 14. I stop and look at unusual things, people, and events around me.

Scoring Key: Reverse score items 1, 7, and 10 (1 = 3, 2 = 2, 3 = 1). Total your score for the 14 items. The minimum is 14; the maximum is 42. A score above 30 indicates that you are undertaking many activities and managing your life in ways that enhance personal creativity.

     Total: _____

Self-Analysis and Action Plan

Which items have a low score? List those areas that you need to target to improve your creativity. Which items have a high score? How can you build on them?

Source: Developed based on information in M. Csikszentmihalyi, *Creativity: Flow and the Psychology of Discovery and Invention*, New York: Harper Perennial.

LEADERSHIP IN ACTION

Best Buy Takes on Its Own Culture

The 8-to-5, five-days-a-week workweek is a staple of the U.S. workplace. For most managers and corporate employees, the clock extends well beyond the 40-hour week. Being seen, getting to the office before everyone else, being the last one to leave at night, and working on weekends are all considered a badge of honor and necessary to success in corporate America. At least one U.S. company is changing these traditions with much debate and some undisputable success.

For many Best Buy employees, work is no longer a place where you go, but something that you do. They don't get paid for their time, but rather for their work (ROWE, 2010). The Minnesota-based electronic store has thrown out the time clock for all its corporate employees and is considering doing the same for the store sales staff. There are no set schedules and no mandatory meetings; salaried employees spend enough time to get their work done, wherever they would like. "No one at Best Buy really knows where I am," says Steve Hance, Best Buy's employee relations manager (Kiger, 2006). He and other employees at the corporate office come and go when they want; take afternoons to go to the movies; come in late or leave early during fishing and hunting season; go home to be with their kids in the afternoon; or spend as much time as they can in their cabins in the woods; *and* produce 35 percent more than they used to before they were given the flexibility to set their own work schedule, and process 13 to 18 percent more orders than those not in the program (Conlin, 2006a). The company has further seen an 8 percent decrease in turnover, a factor that helps it manage its hiring costs. CEO Brian Dunn says: "The improvements in turnover were nationwide and at all levels" (Everitt, 2008).

"It used to be that I had to schedule my life around my work. Now I schedule my work around my life," says Hance (Kiger, 2006). This revolutionary approach to work is called Results-Only Work Environment, or ROWE. ROWE focuses on evaluating employees based on meeting their goals

rather than worrying about how much face time they have put in the office. The program has its own set of 13 commandments, including one that states that no one needs to talk about how many hours they work (Conlin, 2006a). Meetings are considered to be "time-sucking crutches for undisciplined managers" (Conlin, 2006b), so everyone instead focuses on understanding what the goals are and actually doing the work. Implementing big changes is nothing new at Best Buy. The company has been instituting many other changes over the past few years. It stopped paying its sales force a commission in 1989, to tackle what some customers perceived as high-pressure sales (Boyle, 2006). It shifted its focus to customers and redesigned stores to address the needs of different types of customers, not just the tech junkies. It made the store more inviting to women, who influence a great majority of electronic purchasing decisions, by widening the aisles to allow baby strollers to go through easily (Fetterman, 2006). It also put much more emphasis on the "blue shirts," the sales force that the former company president, Brad Anderson, believed made up the core of the business (Breen, 2005). The difference between these changes and ROWE is that these changes originated from the top leadership and made their way down. The ROWE program started somewhere in middle and lower management, was intentionally kept secret from upper management, tested in a few teams; and then presented to Anderson. He did not know about the program until two years after it had been implemented in some of the corporate offices with some success.

Results-Only Work Environment is the brainchild of two HR employees, Jodi Thompson, 49, and Cali Ressler, 29, who discovered they shared views about working in cubicles and how technology and wireless access could change how people work (Conlin, 2006a). They also paid attention to the results of a 2001 survey that indicated widespread employee dissatisfaction and a perception of inability to balance work and life (Kiger, 2006). They believed that the typical flex-time solutions did not provide much benefit or flexibility and that the only solution was a radical change to how people work. Meanwhile, they heard of two department managers who were eager to implement any new methods to retain their best employees and improve morale and productivity. Thompson and Ressler suggested that they implement the first version of ROWE by focusing on how much employees produced instead of whether they showed up in the office at 6 A.M. The results were positive, and word got out about the new way to work. Those working under ROWE guarded their secret, fearing a reversal from upper management. Those who didn't convinced their managers to join the program, slowly spreading word about ROWE throughout Best Buy's corporate office.

Although many employees love the program and the results have been very positive with productivity improvements and a reduction in turnover for employees who take part in ROWE, there has been some resistance. Thompson and Ressler are viewed by some as subversives who are "infecting" the company (Conlin, 2006b). More traditional managers feel threatened that they are losing control and power. Others worry about employees never being able to get away from work. Those who are in the program and the company are clearly benefiting.

Implementing ROWE in a department is a lengthy and careful process. Each department interested in implementing the program is carefully evaluated. Employees then receive extensive training that includes role-plays about how to deal with negative comments about the program and those who participate in it and about

how to implement the cultural changes necessary for ROWE to work. Giving up old habits is not easy. The primary drivers, however, are maximum accountability and flexibility (Kiger, 2006). Instead of engaging in tasks to fill up time or make a good impression on their bosses, employees focus on what matters. Ressler states, "You start looking at everything and saying, 'Is this really going to help get me to my desired outcome.' Pretty soon you've cut out 10 of those unnecessary things that use to fill up your week, and you're getting a lot more done" (Kiger, 2006). John Thompson, general manager at BestBuy.com was a late convert who finally bought into the system after seeing the data on the clear performance and morale improvements. He admits, "I was always looking to see if people were here. I should have been looking at what they were getting done" (Conlin, 2006a).

Thompson and Ressler have taken their ROWE concept outside Best Buy and are working on spreading the unique work model to other organizations (ROWE, 2010). Meanwhile, the pressure for more work–life balance, particularly with the millennial generation's desire for flexibility, is leading many other organizations to consider ways to reinvent the traditional work hours (Ludden, 2010).

Questions

1. What are the internal and external forces for change at Best Buy?
2. How was change implemented?
3. What role did various leaders play in the change?

Sources: Boyle, M. 2006. "Best Buy's giant gamble." CNNMoney.com, March 29. http://money.cnn.com/magazines/fortune/fortune_archive/2006/04/03/8373034/index.htm (accessed April 25, 2010); Breen, B., 2005. "The clear leader," *Fast Company*, March: 65; Kiger, P. J., 2006. "Throwing out the rules of work," *Workforce Management*, October 7. http://www.workforce.com/section/09/feature/24/54/28 (accessed April 25, 2010); Conlin, M., 2006a. "Smashing the clock," *Business Week*, December 11. http://www.businessweek.com/magazine/content/06_50/b4013001.htm (accessed April 25, 2010); Conlin, M., 2006b. "How to kill a meeting," *Business Week*, December 11 http://www.businessweek.com/magazine/content/06_50/b4013008.htm (accessed April 25, 2010); Everitt, L. 2008. How Best Buys slays the turnover beast. *BNET* April 16. http://industry.bnet.com/retail/100028/how-best-buy-slays-the-turnover-beast/ (accessed April 25, 2010); Ludden, J., 2010. More employers make room for work-life balance. *NPR* March 15. http://www.npr.org/templates/story/story.php?storyId=124611210 (accessed April 25, 2010); ROWE. 2010. http://gorowe.com/ (accessed April 25, 2010).

Parts of this chapter are based on "Managing Change," in A. Nahavandi and A. R. Malekzadeh, *Organizational Behavior: The Person-Organization Fit*. Upper Saddle River, NJ: Prentice Hall.

Index

Page references followed by "f" indicate illustrated figures or photographs; followed by "t" indicates a table.

A

Abilities, 43-44, 106, 111, 114, 118, 124, 138-142, 147, 149-150, 152, 165, 202, 267, 295
Absenteeism, 85, 218, 290
   trust and, 85
Abstract, 297
Abuse, 7, 85, 108, 113-115, 142, 161, 163, 182-183, 194-201, 206, 239
Accountability, 47, 164, 194-195, 197-198, 200-201, 206, 217, 235-238, 242, 263, 311
Accountants, 31
Accounting, 14, 45, 122, 199, 214-215
Achievement, 3, 5, 7, 22, 34, 83-84, 86, 144, 146, 218, 240-241, 264, 296
Active listening, 171
   Developing, 171
Adaptation, 118, 122, 284, 291, 299
addresses, 14, 32, 74, 81, 126, 218, 220
adjustments, 218
Administrators, 117, 152, 191, 217, 231
Advances, 56, 284
Advantages, 66, 86, 105, 293
Advertising, 92, 157, 166, 233
   corporate, 157
   local, 92
   product, 166
Advertising campaign, 166
Affect, 14-16, 22, 26, 29, 31, 35, 39, 43, 47-48, 55, 59, 67, 74, 84, 98, 101, 115, 121, 138-140, 144-145, 152-153, 155-156, 164-165, 170, 178, 183, 195-196, 205, 210, 218-219, 227, 233, 236, 238, 242, 249, 256, 271-272, 286
Afghanistan, 84, 146, 257
Africa, 119, 145
African Americans, 20, 33
Age, 2, 6, 9, 19-20, 23, 39, 41-42, 51, 139, 143, 145-146, 190, 284
Agencies, 17, 69, 202, 219, 238
agenda, 108, 127
Agent, 223
Agents, 47, 115, 302
aggression, 21, 31, 136
agreement, 38, 88, 196-197, 263, 269, 298
Agreements, 38, 293
AIDS, 146
AIG, 195
Alabama, 224
All-inclusive, 273
Allocations, 234
anecdotes, 142, 205, 296
Anger, 157-158, 192, 201
   teams and, 192
Animals, 281
Animation, 158, 228
Antarctica, 60
antecedents, 115
anticipate, 218, 286
apologies, 32, 60
Application, 8, 32, 72, 77-78, 81, 84-85, 87, 105, 114, 118, 125-126, 205-206, 271
Applications, 78, 92, 119, 160, 264
Arab countries, 84
archive, 121, 239, 311
arguments, 9, 14-15, 22, 85, 126, 206, 257, 260
Art, 1, 29, 31, 63, 103, 136, 137, 142, 181, 217, 238, 251, 283, 298, 300
Asia, 136, 145, 178
Assertiveness, 34, 37-38, 65, 166, 271
Assets, 79, 214, 297
attention, 8, 12-13, 27, 30, 33, 40, 42, 46, 69, 77-78, 82, 84, 87, 105, 117-118, 120, 122, 135, 137-138, 145, 148-149, 151, 154, 162,

170-171, 176, 210, 218-219, 223, 228, 236, 239, 259-260, 265, 272, 288, 294-295, 302, 309-310
   listening and, 171
Attitudes, 47-48, 140, 144-145, 147, 169, 172, 183, 270
Attorneys, 86
Attribute, 14, 82, 115, 147, 155
attributes, 9, 83, 112-113, 135, 149, 153, 178, 226, 233, 296
AU, 29
audience, 130-132
Australia, 34, 37, 60, 186, 257
Austria, 52
Authority, 3, 16, 21, 31-33, 35-36, 41, 44, 51, 74, 81, 98, 122, 146, 155, 161, 176, 183-187, 203, 205, 207, 230, 232, 257, 259, 264, 288, 293, 302
   express, 51, 186, 203
Autocratic, 5, 20, 42, 51, 66, 71-72, 74-77, 253, 255, 257, 269, 298
Autocratic style, 255
availability, 88, 97, 111
   testing, 111
Available, 14, 38, 68, 74, 80-81, 87-88, 97, 111, 119, 163, 170, 182, 192-193, 206, 209, 212, 241, 258, 261, 264, 281, 287
avoidance, 33-34, 37, 48, 145
Awareness, 13, 46, 59-60, 122, 124, 126-127, 133, 138, 149, 153, 163, 165, 170-171

B

Baby boomers, 20, 146
bad news, 151, 199
Bankruptcy, 118, 142, 206, 214, 288
   definition of, 118
Banks, 195, 262
Basic form, 183, 258
Behavior, 8, 12, 21, 30, 32-33, 36, 38-39, 46, 48, 57, 59, 64-67, 73, 78, 80, 83, 86-88, 100, 108, 114, 119, 122-126, 133, 138-140, 145, 147, 149, 152-153, 156-161, 163-165, 170-171, 174, 183, 194-196, 199-200, 214, 235, 257, 265, 270-271, 275, 295, 299-302, 307, 311
   in groups, 133, 270
   morale and, 311
Belgium, 231
Benefits, 7, 21, 27, 45-46, 54, 109, 115, 123, 178, 183, 185, 198, 205, 240, 254-256, 258-260, 263, 268, 270-272, 282, 292
   service, 21, 109, 178, 240, 256, 263
biases, 47
   cultural, 47
Bill and Melinda Gates Foundation, 125
billing, 262
Blending, 135
blogs, 215
   business, 215
   company, 215
board of directors, 13-14, 60, 85, 91, 136, 162, 201, 218-219, 224, 237-238, 242
Boards of directors, 39, 164, 236, 242
Bolivia, 5, 239
Bonds, 60, 105, 109, 112, 300
   performance, 109
Boomers, 20, 146
Borrowing, 234, 298
brainstorming, 246, 298
Brand, 120, 248
Branding, 121
Brands, 248
   family, 248
   importance of, 248
Brazil, 28, 37, 231, 285, 288, 290
Breach of contract, 147
Bribery, 147, 155
Bridges, 51-52, 201, 294

Britain, 33, 35, 66
Budget, 191, 263
Budgeting, 9
Bullying, 201
Burma, 108
Business plan, 230
business plans, 8
Business review, 149, 293
Business Week, 45, 61, 121, 136, 249, 297, 311
Buttons, 18, 228

C

Canada, 19, 30, 33, 119, 135, 147, 285
Capabilities, 5, 118, 260
Capacity, 195, 207, 296, 299
Capital, 125, 158, 268
   growth, 125
   human, 125
   structural, 268
   working, 158
Capitalism, 281
Career, 41-42, 45, 123, 127, 144, 150, 154-155, 169, 178-179, 190, 193, 201, 249, 261-262, 272, 304
Careers, 6, 43, 45, 61, 179, 190, 232, 257
Caribbean, 120
Case Studies, 10, 126, 138, 232
   employees, 10
Case study, 290
Cell phones, 120
Censorship, 269, 298
Central America, 27
Centralization, 167, 220, 226
Centralized organizational structure, 196
Certainty, 162, 267
Chain of command, 163, 211, 230
Change agents, 302
Channel, 3
Channels, 16, 234
Character, 12, 31, 33, 139, 182, 249
   Development, 33, 182
Charismatic leader, 106-108, 111, 114-115, 128-129
Chavez, Hugo, 5
Chief executive officer, 40
Chief financial officer, 60, 142, 198
Chief information officer, 40
Chief operating officer, 17, 81, 219
   COO, 219
Children, 21, 40, 52, 117, 135, 145, 193, 281, 301
China, 32, 37, 112, 136, 161, 220, 239, 257
Chinese, 19, 33, 112, 135, 142, 147, 161, 186
CIC, 239
Civil rights, 4, 107, 111
Claims, 6, 215
   record, 6
Classification, 189
Climate, 11, 15, 51, 112, 119-120, 125, 127, 134, 171, 205, 226, 260, 263
Climate change, 120
clothing, 199, 220
Clusters, 231-232
CMS, 61, 239
Coaching, 259, 288
Coercion, 188, 198, 293
Coercive power, 155, 187-188, 212
collaboration, 178, 203-205, 248, 263, 266
Collapse, 214
Collectivism, 34-35, 37, 144, 147, 256-257
Collectivist cultures, 84, 144
Colleges, 45
Columbia, 60
Commitment, 27, 42-43, 46-48, 51, 55, 74-77, 82-84, 117, 119, 135, 147, 155, 184-185, 188-189, 197, 202, 206, 239, 255-256, 258, 263, 265, 293, 296, 300, 303
committees, 13
Communication, 3, 6, 10, 27, 32-33, 37-38, 42, 46, 48,

61, 82, 86, 107-108, 112-114, 136, 150, 152, 164, 197, 200-201, 224, 232, 271, 273, 282, 293-294, 301
communication skills, 61, 107-108, 232
communication style, 112
Communication styles, 32, 42
  Supportive, 32, 42
Communism, 109, 146
Companies, 6, 8, 17, 21, 32, 40, 45, 47, 60-61, 69, 74, 79, 120-121, 136, 143, 147, 150, 159, 178, 187, 206, 222, 230-231, 236-237, 249, 284
  changing culture, 47
Company stock, 4
compatibility, 25, 85
Compensation, 40, 206, 217, 221, 236-237, 242, 246, 256, 281-282
  of employees, 282
Compete, 228, 261
Competition, 16, 18, 38, 40, 109, 191, 206, 220, 222, 237, 265, 270, 282, 285
Competitive advantage, 79
Competitiveness, 156-157, 165-166, 254, 261
Competitors, 6, 18, 91, 191, 233-234, 241, 263, 289-290
complaints, 44, 48, 193, 243, 259, 270
Compliance, 184-185, 188, 196-199, 206, 302
Compliments, 55, 206
compromise, 72, 263
computer programmers, 154
Computer software, 246
Conceptual skills, 152
Conditions, 14, 84, 111, 138, 196, 238, 269, 281, 285-286
Conference Board, 21
Confidence, 14, 61, 67, 82, 85, 100, 102, 106-110, 120, 125, 128, 135-136, 141-142, 151, 155, 162-163, 196, 203, 223, 253, 265, 294-295, 299
confidentiality, 256
Conflict, 4, 35, 38, 43, 51, 71, 75-76, 92-94, 107, 149, 152, 160, 200, 242, 257, 262-263, 267-268, 284
Conflict management, 152, 160, 267-268
Conflict resolution, 149
Consideration, 12, 46, 67, 78-80, 87, 116-118, 121, 123, 140, 150, 155, 194, 197, 253, 256
Consistency, 9, 159, 200, 287
Consolidation, 296
Constraints, 127, 203, 222, 267
  changing, 203
  creating, 203
Construction, 52, 56
constructive feedback, 308
Consumer goods, 248
Consumers, 60, 136
Contacts, 92, 193
Content, 28, 45, 108, 121, 150, 239, 249, 297, 311
Contingency approach, 64, 67-68, 77, 88, 119, 255
Contingency theories of leadership, 88
  path-goal theory, 88
Contract, 18, 52, 77, 127, 147, 236
Contracts, 33, 51, 91, 116-117, 147
Control, 11, 13, 16-17, 21-22, 40, 42, 56, 69-73, 78, 81-82, 91, 98-99, 108, 121, 142, 144, 149, 155-157, 159, 161, 163-165, 167, 172, 174, 183, 190, 193, 199, 201-202, 204-205, 212, 220, 223, 226-228, 230, 233-234, 241, 245, 247-248, 253, 255-256, 261, 263-264, 266-267, 287, 290, 292, 309, 311
Control continuum, 70
Controlling, 9-10, 12, 17, 19, 70-72, 161, 171, 196, 227, 236, 266
Convergence, 286
Conversation, 178
conversations, 124, 174, 217, 254
Cooperation, 4, 21, 31, 38, 60, 108, 115, 119, 125, 134, 157, 171, 203, 207, 212, 241, 254, 257, 264-265, 269-271, 292, 294, 299-301, 308
Coordination, 239, 264, 271
Copyright, 1, 29, 63, 103, 137, 172, 174-175, 181, 217, 251, 283
Core beliefs, 178
Corporate culture, 17, 136, 178
Corporate social responsibility, 219
corporation, 21, 198, 219
Corporations, 12, 14, 242
Corruption, 114, 146, 164, 182, 194-201, 205-206, 215
Costa Rica, 37
Costs, 6, 79, 91, 231, 290, 306, 310

Countries, 19, 30, 32-33, 36, 38-41, 49, 51, 60, 84, 112, 119, 143-145, 147, 178, 185-186, 193, 205, 231-232, 236, 239, 285, 301
Creativity, 18, 79, 86, 111, 117, 120, 143, 148-149, 151-152, 165-166, 210, 226, 228, 230, 234, 243, 248, 254, 261-263, 266, 273, 283, 288, 292, 294, 298-299, 301, 303-304, 309
  developing, 151, 266, 301, 303-304
  innovation and, 234, 261, 299, 301
credibility, 138, 190, 199, 212, 233, 238, 296, 308
Credit, 14, 69, 79, 110, 158, 184, 195, 230, 261, 268
Crisis management, 290
criticism, 51, 107, 113-114, 162-163, 236
CRM, 79
Cross-functional team, 191
Cultural awareness, 60
cultural context, 29, 48
Cultural differences, 29, 31-32, 35-36, 38, 46, 59, 137, 142, 144-145, 147, 161, 182-183, 231, 257
  business and, 46
  gender and, 29, 144
  in leadership, 29, 137, 142, 147, 182
  in negotiation, 147
Cultural diversity, 12, 19, 31, 147
  in leadership, 12, 19, 147
Cultural factors, 12, 26, 41, 49, 84, 138, 186, 272, 303
Cultural identity, 145
Cultural traits, 30
Cultural values, 30, 34-35, 48, 144-145, 147, 186, 231, 256, 285-286
Culture, 5-9, 11-13, 16-17, 21-22, 25, 28, 29-39, 44-51, 57-59, 79-81, 83-84, 88, 106, 111-113, 120-121, 123, 136, 138-140, 142, 144-147, 165-167, 178, 183, 185-187, 193, 196-197, 199-202, 204, 217-218, 220-223, 227-235, 242-243, 245-246, 248, 252, 254-257, 262-263, 266, 268, 272, 281-282, 285, 287-288, 291-292, 294, 297-299, 301-304, 310
  change and, 5, 17, 106, 111, 287, 291-292, 298, 302-303
  definition of, 5, 7, 22, 218
  high-context cultures, 32-33, 48
  national, 29-30, 32-33, 35-36, 38-39, 48, 145-146, 256, 281, 285
  national cultures, 32
  organizational culture, 5, 11-12, 25, 30-32, 36, 38, 44-45, 47, 84, 186, 196-197, 200, 234, 245, 255, 285, 291, 294, 298, 302-304
  research on, 35, 84, 202, 266
Customer service, 43, 109, 178, 201, 235, 262, 273, 281
Customers, 5-6, 11, 18-20, 27, 69, 79, 109, 135, 143, 151, 154, 163, 178, 183-184, 199, 201, 203-204, 219, 235, 262-264, 281, 289, 302, 310
Customs, 30, 59
  defined, 30

D

Dalai lama, 207
Damage, 270
data, 14, 35, 48, 72, 80, 146, 246, 258, 282, 306, 311
dates, 54
Deadlines, 16, 154, 157, 255
Death, 175, 195
Decentralization, 227
deception, 147, 198
Decision criteria, 193-194
Decision makers, 21, 48, 160, 192, 233
Decision making, 11, 15, 17, 46, 66, 74-77, 81, 86, 135, 151-152, 155, 184, 186, 195, 199, 201-203, 206, 221, 223, 226-228, 230, 233, 243, 245, 247, 253-256, 258, 262, 268-269, 281, 296
Decision-making, 14, 17, 41, 74, 76, 87-88, 156, 201, 227, 281, 298
  group, 14, 17, 74, 76, 87-88, 156, 281, 298
  in organizations, 14, 17, 41
  individual differences and, 156
Decision-making process, 17, 201
Delegation, 74, 77, 143, 151, 156-157, 186, 226-227, 230, 252-253, 257-261, 271-273, 279
  effective, 157, 186, 252, 257, 259-260, 271-272
Demand, 8, 18-19, 21, 42, 77, 93, 108, 226, 284-285, 298
  change in, 284
Democracy, 18, 51, 106, 185, 204, 281
  India, 106

Demographics, 16
Denmark, 37, 147
Depression, 146, 159
design, 52, 73-74, 220, 226, 246, 249, 254, 263-264, 266, 299, 303
  elements of, 299, 303
Determinant, 73, 78, 156, 197, 237
Devaluation, 198-199
Differentiation, 34-35, 37
Directive, 71, 78, 256, 267, 269
disabilities, 47, 61, 300
Disability, 301
Discipline, 116, 123, 187, 243, 291, 294, 300
Discounts, 79
Discrimination, 41, 43-44, 46, 48, 163, 170
Disease, 156, 203
Distance, 31, 33-34, 37-38, 48, 80, 145, 147, 161, 183-184, 186-187, 192-193, 197-199, 207, 223, 232, 256-257, 267
  cultural, 31, 33-34, 37-38, 48, 145, 147, 161, 183, 186, 232, 256-257
Distinctiveness, 33
Distribution, 34, 37, 46, 185-186, 191, 193, 196, 202, 205, 284
Diversity, 12, 19-20, 31, 39, 45-47, 60-61, 135, 143, 146-147, 192, 224, 226-227, 229-230, 233, 235, 245, 284
Divesting, 60
Doctors Without Borders, 238
Dollar, 60, 198
Dollars, 135
Dominance, 21, 66
Door-to-door sales, 135
Draft, 49, 52
Dumping, 259
Duties, 22, 61, 82
Duty, 51, 169
Dynamics, 77

E

Earnings, 281
E-commerce, 226
Economic development, 51
Economic factors, 14, 26
Economic growth, 187
  sources of, 187
Economic policy, 236
Economics, 239, 246
Economies of scale, 91
Economy, 5, 32, 42, 51-52, 187, 268, 284, 290
  team, 5, 52, 268
Education, 1, 20, 22-23, 29, 39, 41, 43, 46-47, 51-52, 63, 103, 123, 135, 137-139, 141, 143, 151, 181, 193-194, 207, 217, 232, 238-239, 243, 251, 283, 293
  change and, 283, 293
Efficiency, 76, 86, 145, 228-229, 231, 233, 245, 287, 301, 304
Egypt, 37-38, 108
Elections, 131
E-mail, 234
emotional appeals, 161
Emotional intelligence, 66, 119, 137, 148-151, 165, 170-171, 226
  in leadership, 66, 137, 148-150, 165
emotions, 12, 107, 110, 114, 121, 123-124, 126-127, 149-150, 152, 170-171, 174, 225-226, 295
Empathy, 12, 78, 80, 149-150, 162, 170-171, 193, 196, 219, 225, 233, 268
emphasis, 31, 35, 84, 126, 186, 202, 241-242, 256, 282, 300, 310
Employee engagement, 21
Employee involvement, 227, 254, 258
Employees, 4, 6, 10-12, 16-22, 27, 29, 31, 33, 39, 45-47, 51, 61, 67-68, 74-79, 81, 83, 85-86, 93, 101-102, 110, 116, 118, 120, 122-123, 147, 150, 154-155, 159, 161, 164, 166, 178, 183-186, 189, 191-193, 197-206, 210, 212-214, 219-221, 223, 228, 230, 233-235, 240-241, 245-246, 248, 252-258, 260, 262-264, 266, 274, 281-282, 284, 288, 290, 292-294, 296-297, 301-303, 310-311
  benefits for, 178, 205
  loyalty, 21, 51, 67-68, 79, 83, 102, 110, 118, 212, 252
  organizational culture and, 45, 197, 234
  selection of, 81, 166, 204, 234-235, 241, 303
Employment, 44, 52, 242
Empowerment, 21, 81, 116-118, 120, 127, 157,

182-183, 185-186, 200-206, 213, 220, 227-229, 233, 241, 254, 261, 266, 289, 294-296, 301, 303
  of leaders, 21, 200, 203-204, 206, 227-228, 241, 266, 294-295, 303
  skills, 21, 118, 120, 241, 266, 289, 294, 296, 301
England, 37, 146
English, 19-20, 33, 52
Enron, 164, 194-195
Entrepreneur, 10-11, 223, 230, 254, 257
Entrepreneurs, 107, 120, 144, 228, 239, 292
Entrepreneurship, 226, 266
Environment, 6-7, 13, 17-18, 30, 32, 38, 48, 61, 69-70, 72, 78-79, 81, 114, 116-117, 120, 138-139, 149, 155, 157, 159-160, 178, 184, 186, 202, 220-222, 227-228, 230, 233-234, 241, 243, 248, 255, 257, 259, 261, 265, 267-268, 270, 272-273, 276, 283-284, 286, 290, 292, 294, 297, 299, 310
  natural, 139, 265
Environmental factors, 15, 139-140, 221-222
Environmental Protection Agency, 116
Equal Employment Opportunity Commission, 44
Equity, 203, 271
ETC, 54, 112, 173
Ethical behavior, 145, 200, 270
Ethical issues, 147
Ethics, 46, 122, 144, 146-147, 162, 200-201, 235
  Bribery, 147
  Contracts, 147
  Gifts, 147
  Internet, 146
  Laws, 147
Ethnicity, 31, 39, 61, 139
Euro, 144
Europe, 111, 120, 145, 178, 195, 254
Evaluation, 35, 48, 66, 72, 77-78, 81, 84, 97, 99, 101, 114, 118, 125, 210, 212, 245-246, 258-259, 289-290, 303
evidence, 15, 39-40, 42-44, 65, 67, 111, 141, 163, 184-185, 196, 199, 201-202, 205, 207, 231
  supporting, 185
exaggeration, 162
Exchange, 7, 75, 77, 81-85, 87-88, 105-106, 115-116, 118, 127, 179, 189, 211, 254, 265, 298
Exchange relationships, 265
Exchanges, 93, 115, 117
Exclusion, 44
Excuses, 159, 260, 279
exit strategy, 163
Expansion, 27-28, 282
expect, 18, 20, 32, 42, 44, 73, 78, 102, 108, 134, 139, 154, 176, 183, 186-187, 194, 203, 231, 257, 259, 264, 286, 295-296
Expectancy theory, 78
Expectations, 16-18, 20, 22, 24-25, 31-32, 44, 58, 82-83, 100, 109-110, 114, 117, 120, 124, 126-127, 138, 145, 157, 159, 179, 186, 193, 203-204, 213, 231, 249, 259, 265, 274, 281, 295
Experience, 7, 23, 38, 40-41, 43-44, 49, 51, 70, 72-73, 78, 80, 82-83, 86, 91, 96-97, 112, 127, 140-143, 148, 150, 152-154, 156, 158, 165, 224-225, 232, 246, 263, 272-273, 281, 291-292, 299, 304-305
expertise, 35-36, 75, 145, 151, 188, 190, 192, 197, 205, 233, 242, 255, 263-264, 280, 299-301
Explanations, 105
Extended family, 34, 51

F
Facebook, 42
face-to-face communication, 10
Facial expressions, 150
Facilitators, 25, 267, 270
Failure, 7, 13, 21, 107, 114-115, 148, 155, 164, 170, 226, 265, 268-269, 284-285, 292-293
fairness, 37, 46, 84, 144, 169, 271
Family, 6, 11, 30-31, 34-37, 42-43, 47, 51, 58, 60-61, 69, 81, 84, 102, 109-110, 116, 120, 123, 135, 138, 142, 144, 146-147, 151, 178, 186-187, 239, 248, 256
  extended family, 34, 51
FAST, 4, 17-18, 20, 27-28, 43, 101, 121, 158, 185, 246, 261, 282, 293-294, 297, 311
Favors, 210
Feature, 47, 205, 311
Federal government, 17
Federal Reserve, 164, 187

structure of, 187
feedback, 12-13, 17, 27, 38, 80-81, 83, 97, 100, 124-125, 134, 162-163, 170, 185, 201, 205, 230, 259, 265, 271, 280, 289, 308
  constructive, 125, 265, 308
  destructive, 162, 201
Fidelity Investments, 233
Fields, 292
Filtering, 223
Finance, 121, 136, 263
Financial crisis, 195, 214
  banks in, 195
Financial issues, 17
Financial markets, 187
Financial services, 214
Financial Times, 6
Fire, 70, 102, 104, 179, 183
Firm performance, 14, 221
Firms, 13, 15, 35, 45, 156
  organizational culture, 45
Flattery, 196, 198, 206
Flexibility, 18, 136, 146, 165, 202-203, 218, 226, 246, 248, 263, 283, 292, 294, 299, 303, 310-311
Flickr, 151
Focus groups, 191
Food, 4, 59-60, 101, 142, 184, 204, 281-282
Forecasting, 258, 285
  sales, 258
Formalization, 13, 80, 167, 220, 226
Foundations, 63-102, 151, 238, 240, 291
France, 37, 84, 111, 231-232, 257
Franchises, 101
fraud, 195, 199
Freedom, 116, 204, 239
Freezing, 287-288
Frequency, 82
Fund, 17, 238-240
Future orientation, 37

G
Gender, 11, 19, 29-31, 34, 37-42, 44, 46, 48-49, 53, 61, 84-85, 119, 138-139, 143-144, 160, 217, 231-233, 242
  in the workforce, 19
Gender roles, 34, 53
Generation Xers, 20, 145-146
generational differences, 145
Germany, 33, 37, 50, 84, 106, 145, 185
gestures, 109
Gifts, 143, 147
Global economy, 268
Global financial crisis, 214
  causes of, 214
Global Leadership and Organizational Behavior Effectiveness, 36, 48
Global marketing, 136
Global recession, 195
Global talent, 266
Global teams, 17
Globalization, 12, 145-146, 149, 155, 219
goal congruence, 75-76
Goals, 3-5, 7, 9, 11, 17, 21-22, 26, 45, 68-70, 74-78, 80-82, 85, 88, 92-94, 105, 108, 110-111, 113-114, 116-118, 120, 122, 130, 150, 152, 155-157, 159, 161-163, 165, 170, 178-179, 182-183, 190-194, 202-207, 213, 219-220, 228, 230, 234, 238, 240-241, 249, 254, 256-257, 259, 262-265, 267-268, 270-271, 275, 281, 289-290, 296, 298, 300, 308-310
  definition of, 3-5, 7, 22, 118
Gold, 51
Golden Rule, 169
Goods, 18, 34, 248, 264
  complement, 264
  complementary, 264
  private, 18
  public, 18
Government, 5, 17-18, 32, 51, 55, 143, 207, 214, 232, 237-238, 240-241, 248, 291
  global financial crisis, 214
Government agencies, 17, 238
Governmental organizations, 40, 200, 285
Grants, 188, 238-241
Great Britain, 33, 35, 66
Greece, 32, 36-37, 56, 285-286
Greenpeace, 18
grooming, 272
Group, 3-12, 14-17, 20, 24, 26, 30-31, 35-37, 39-40,

43-44, 47-48, 53, 60, 65, 67-72, 74-77, 82-93, 96-97, 99-102, 108, 110, 114, 118, 120, 125, 129, 134, 142-145, 150, 156, 161, 163, 168-169, 184, 192-195, 208, 210, 218-220, 225, 232, 241, 253-254, 256-257, 259-261, 263, 268-270, 273, 280-281, 288, 291-292, 298, 302-305
  behavior in, 145
group dynamics, 77
Group membership, 39, 43, 48, 83-84, 86, 101
group norms, 150, 292, 303
Group performance, 3, 87-88
groups, 3, 7, 9, 19, 22, 24-25, 29-32, 39, 43-47, 53, 66-68, 72, 74, 84-87, 101, 110, 114-115, 133, 156, 183-184, 190-191, 201, 208-209, 218-219, 239-241, 254, 262-263, 266, 268-270, 272, 282, 284, 289, 292-293
  development of, 7, 47, 66, 84-85, 110, 183, 190, 241, 266, 269, 289
Groupthink, 268-270, 272
Growth strategy, 13
Guatemala, 239, 285-286
Guidelines, 79, 86, 193, 225, 233, 235, 248, 258-259, 265, 296
  Ethics, 235
  Social contact, 193

H
handshake, 51
Health care, 79, 114, 218, 236, 238, 254
Health insurance, 236, 281
  group, 281
helping others, 136
Hierarchy, 3, 7, 13, 16, 21, 34-35, 39, 112, 145, 167, 186, 188, 197, 203, 211
High-context cultures, 32-33, 48
High-pressure sales, 310
Hiring practices, 196-197
Hong Kong, 37, 84, 147, 161
Hospitals, 91, 238
HTML, 6, 27-28, 79, 121, 131, 136, 158, 179, 215, 239, 249, 282, 297
HTTP, 6, 19, 27-28, 45, 61, 79, 102, 121, 131, 136, 146, 158, 179, 204, 215, 239, 249, 261, 282, 297, 311
Human resource management, 178, 201
  process of, 201
Human resources, 166, 178, 220, 255, 272
human resources department, 166
Human rights, 5, 44, 72
Humane orientation, 37, 256
humor, 13, 65, 170, 193
hypothesis, 14, 160

I
Ice, 230
Idealism, 146
III, 306
IKEA, 178-179
Illegal activities, 195
Image, 25, 34, 47, 60, 107-109, 112, 174, 298
  country, 34, 47, 112
Implementation, 3, 27, 75, 91-94, 143, 185-187, 192, 199, 202, 213, 221, 226-227, 232-233, 241-242, 255, 257, 267, 271-272, 287-291, 293-294, 301-303
implementation plan, 267
Impression, 83, 108-109, 113-114, 126, 174, 311
Inc., 40, 61, 79, 102, 122, 223, 228, 230, 254, 273, 290
Incentives, 135, 183, 214, 231, 282
Income, 39, 51, 108, 296
  differences in, 39
  national, 39
  per capita, 51
India, 37, 60-61, 106, 112, 154, 239
Individualism, 33-35, 48, 144-145, 257, 268
Individualist cultures, 34-35, 257
Indonesia, 30, 37, 186
Industrial Revolution, 9, 64-65, 87
Industry, 27, 79, 101, 117, 121, 141, 167, 191, 214, 217, 220, 222, 228, 231, 233, 237, 243, 254, 284-285, 291, 301, 311
Inequality, 7
Inflation, 187
Information, 5, 10-11, 17, 32, 39-40, 43, 47-48, 51, 65-66, 74-81, 83, 88, 91-92, 94, 107, 113, 122, 124, 126, 133-134, 137, 142, 145, 148,

151, 165, 170-171, 188-194, 199, 201, 204-205, 211-212, 220, 225, 234, 246, 253-254, 258, 265-266, 269, 273-274, 281-282, 292-293, 299, 309
Information gathering, 269
Information processing, 269
Information technology, 81, 192, 220, 246
Infrastructure, 122
Ingratiation, 189, 211
Initiative, 17, 45, 86, 111, 137, 142, 203, 205, 266
Injury, 123
Innovation, 13, 16-17, 21, 79, 116, 118-119, 122, 144, 213, 226, 228-230, 232-234, 241, 245, 254, 261-262, 281, 283-284, 288, 297, 299, 301-302
    creativity and, 226, 228, 254, 261, 283, 301
    importance of, 16-17, 262, 283, 288, 297, 299, 301
Innovations, 229
Innovators, 231
Insurance, 6, 47, 236, 281, 288
Integration, 45, 105, 220, 227, 264
Integrity, 61, 113, 121-122, 137, 139, 141-142, 151, 161, 169-170, 200, 225, 235, 240, 249, 270-271
intelligence, 65-66, 119, 136, 137, 139, 141-142, 148-151, 154-155, 165-166, 170-171, 226, 254, 285
    emotional, 66, 119, 137, 148-151, 154-155, 165, 170-171, 226
Interdependence, 264, 281
Interest, 66, 81, 84, 87, 105, 127, 138, 141, 205, 232, 238, 242-243, 284, 309
Internal control, 165, 172
internal environment, 241
Internal motivation, 266, 268
International business, 204
International trade, 222, 285
International trade barriers, 222
Internationalization, 237
Internet, 27, 107, 135, 146, 222, 260, 285
Interpersonal skills, 46, 148, 151-152, 155, 232, 264
    conflict management, 152
    negotiation, 152
Interviews, 138, 159, 243, 272
Intranets, 201
Investment, 6, 40, 76, 195, 199, 219, 255
Investment banks, 195
Investments, 233
Investor relations, 262
Investors, 6, 8, 51
Iran, 37, 50, 84, 112, 146
Iraq, 32, 86, 145-146, 269
Israel, 35, 37, 112, 119, 257
Italy, 32, 36-37, 195

J

Japan, 32, 34-37, 112, 186, 256-257, 262, 285-286
    culture in, 34, 36
Job description, 97
job descriptions, 83
Job design, 266
Job enrichment, 258
Job loss, 292
Job performance, 67, 82, 153-154, 160
Job satisfaction, 21, 147, 155
Jobs, 18, 20-21, 35, 41, 43, 79, 81, 84, 87, 92, 102, 142, 152, 154-155, 158-159, 162, 197-198, 222, 237, 258, 260-261, 279, 292, 300
    causes of, 41, 292, 300
    cultural differences in, 142
    intelligence and, 154-155
    levels, 20-21, 41, 43, 154-155, 159, 237, 260, 300
    promotion and, 162
    service, 20-21, 43
Jobs, Steve, 142, 162, 222
Joint ventures, 40
Jordan, 157

K

kickbacks, 147
Knowledge, 7, 16, 22, 46-47, 51, 78, 98, 127, 135, 141-142, 150, 152, 188, 207, 211, 214, 225, 228, 260, 265, 299, 301-302
    sharing, 127
    specialized, 260
Knowledge workers, 265
Korea, 32, 35-37
Kuwait, 37

L

Labor, 19-20, 40, 184, 201
    trends in, 19-20
labor force, 19-20, 40
Laissez-faire, 66, 116, 243
Language, 20, 31, 59, 108, 125, 130-132, 139, 142, 248
    authentic, 125
    charismatic, 31, 108, 125, 130-132
    power and, 31
    style, 139, 248
Lawsuits, 143, 243
Layoffs, 21, 27
layout, 203
Leader, 2-5, 7-17, 21-26, 28, 29, 31-32, 35-36, 38-39, 44, 46, 48-49, 51, 53, 65-88, 90-94, 96-101, 104, 106-120, 122-123, 126-129, 131, 133-134, 136, 138-139, 141-142, 144, 148-153, 155-157, 160, 164-165, 167, 176, 178, 182, 184-185, 187-192, 194, 196-203, 205-207, 210, 212, 218-231, 233-235, 237-238, 240-241, 245-247, 249, 253, 255-260, 262-273, 275, 280, 283, 285, 287-288, 292, 294-299, 302-303, 308, 311
    autocratic style of, 255
    behaviors of, 21, 79-80
    empowerment of, 202, 266
    participation of, 240
    traits of, 31, 235
Leadership, 1-28, 29-32, 35-36, 38-50, 53, 60-61, 63-102, 103-136, 137-144, 146-166, 176-179, 181-183, 186, 189-190, 194-196, 200-207, 212-214, 217-228, 230-249, 251-253, 255-257, 261-270, 272, 277-278, 280-282, 283-292, 294-299, 301-304, 308, 310
    motivation and, 21, 35, 122, 141, 268
Leadership ability, 65, 257
Leadership roles, 18, 43, 48, 69, 110, 160, 266, 303
Learning, 7-8, 13, 17, 20, 73, 121, 140, 142, 152-153, 160, 184, 248, 258, 260-261, 263, 265, 268, 282, 283, 289, 291-292, 298-301, 303
Learning organization, 301, 303
Legitimate power, 72, 185, 187-188, 190, 193, 212
Lehman Brothers, 195, 214-215
Leverage, 215
Liabilities, 114
Liability, 114
Lifestyle, 11, 17, 30, 254, 291
listening, 17, 69, 133, 151, 171, 201
    effective, 17, 69, 201
    process of, 151, 201
listening skills, 151
Literacy, 51-52
Lobbying, 191
Locus of control, 78, 155-157, 159, 164-165, 172, 226, 292
Logistics, 6, 74
Loss, 81, 107, 109, 175, 273, 292
    assessment, 175
    control, 81, 292
    direct, 81
    paying, 81
    proof of, 107
Low-context cultures, 32-33, 48
Lying, 174-175, 236

M

Machiavellianism, 162, 165, 175
Magazines, 121, 249, 311
Malaysia, 19, 285
Management, 2, 6, 8-10, 12-14, 17-22, 28, 32, 39-40, 42-43, 47, 61, 64, 71, 77, 80, 83, 85-86, 101-102, 104, 108-109, 112-114, 116-117, 125-127, 135-136, 146, 149-150, 152, 154, 156-157, 160, 169, 171, 178-179, 183-184, 186, 192-194, 196-197, 201-202, 204, 213, 217-222, 226-228, 230, 232-234, 237, 241-243, 245, 249, 251-282, 283, 285-286, 288, 290-291, 296-297, 304, 310-311
    activities of, 201
    functions of, 2, 10, 266-267
    learning organizations and, 283
    organizational behavior and, 80
    organizational culture and, 197, 234
Management issues, 268

Management strategies, 230
Managerial roles, 10, 22
Managers, 2, 4, 7-10, 12-13, 16-18, 21-22, 27, 39-40, 73, 76-77, 79-82, 84, 91, 102, 109, 116, 120, 140-142, 147, 151-152, 154, 159, 161, 166, 183, 185-187, 190, 192-194, 196, 200-202, 217-218, 220-224, 226-228, 230-232, 234-237, 246, 256, 258-259, 262-266, 268, 273-274, 281, 297, 310-311
Manufacturing, 20, 290, 305
Market research, 191
    theory, 191
Market share, 248
Marketing, 92, 102, 120, 135-136, 158, 166, 220, 228, 263-264, 273, 284
    defined, 220, 228
    global, 120, 135-136, 284
    ideas, 136, 264
    people, 102, 120, 135-136, 158, 166, 228, 264, 273
    place, 102
Marketing research, 166
Marketplace, 214
Markets, 81, 135, 187, 204, 222, 228, 235, 282
Massachusetts, 56, 131, 220
Maternity leave, 178
meaning, 7, 72, 80, 121, 127
    understanding of, 127
Measurement, 47-48, 80, 87, 119, 201, 203, 287
Media, 40, 142, 146, 154, 204, 224, 249, 261
median, 143, 236
medium, 93, 161, 186, 243
meetings, 46, 60, 135, 193, 199, 254, 292, 310
    formal, 46, 60
    online, 135
    participation in, 254
    types of, 310
Memory, 21, 148
memos, 234
Mergers, 60, 199, 229
message, 33, 46, 49, 61, 108, 113-114, 130, 135-136, 150, 197, 200, 290, 292, 295-296, 298, 302
    distribution of, 46
    ethical, 113-114, 200
    marketing, 135-136
    negative, 113-114, 150, 200, 292, 298
    positive, 113, 150, 298, 302
    sales, 135-136
metaphors, 130-132
Mexico, 16, 20, 32, 37, 50, 84, 102, 119, 145, 257
Middle East, 84, 108, 145
Millennials, 145-146
Minimum wage, 236
Ministry of International Trade and Industry, 285
Mold, 27
Money, 31, 50, 61, 102, 121-122, 135-136, 172, 199, 210, 238-239, 249, 281-282, 291, 311
Motivation, 16, 21, 35, 68-69, 73, 78, 88, 107, 115-116, 118, 122, 141-142, 149, 152, 155, 159, 170-171, 211, 218, 255, 258, 263, 266, 268, 270, 273, 288, 295
    theories of, 68, 88, 118
Mumbai, 239
Music, 59, 146
Myanmar, 146
Myths, 10

N

National culture, 29-30, 32-33, 35, 38-39, 48
National cultures, 32
Nations, 34, 41, 147, 268
Need for power, 261
Negotiation, 42, 49, 147, 149, 152, 198-199, 293
    Concessions, 198
    Defined, 149
    Process, 152, 293
Nepotism, 84
Netherlands, 37, 185
Networking, 4, 230, 268, 285
New Deal, 49
New products, 204, 248, 290
New York Times, 5-6, 31-32, 121, 136, 158, 215, 297
New Zealand, 43-44, 147
New-product development, 228
Newspapers, 5
Nexters, 146
NGOs, 238
    nongovernmental organizations, 238
Nongovernmental organizations, 238
Nonprofit organizations, 217-218, 238, 240-242

Nonverbal cues, 32-33, 48, 108
Nonverbal messages, 33, 131-132, 225
Norms, 30-31, 34, 37, 139, 150, 167, 194, 235, 242, 263, 268, 270, 292, 298, 303
North America, 178-179, 224
Not-for-profit organizations, 17, 155, 254

O
Objectives, 81, 290
objectivity, 9
Obligation, 12, 35
Occurrence, 195, 200, 214
Offer, 90, 110, 123, 170, 188, 281
Offset, 86
Oil, 147
Open-book management, 80, 204
Operations, 5, 11, 27-28, 69, 79, 81, 135, 147, 205, 219, 223, 230, 235, 238, 248, 300
Opinion leaders, 302
Opportunities, 13, 20, 38, 47, 51-52, 61, 65, 83, 85, 122, 126, 129, 164, 170, 178, 193, 202-203, 213, 222, 228-230, 258, 276, 278, 291, 296
Optimism, 14, 106, 120-121, 125-126, 134, 146, 151
Oracle, 40, 224
Organic organization, 140
Organization, 3-7, 10-15, 17, 21-22, 31-32, 36, 38-40, 44-47, 49, 52, 61, 70, 76-77, 79-81, 83-86, 88, 92-94, 98, 101-102, 108-109, 111, 115-119, 122-123, 125, 128-130, 134, 140, 142, 146, 151-152, 155, 163-164, 167-168, 178, 183, 185-194, 197, 199-203, 205-206, 209-210, 212-213, 217-225, 227-231, 233-235, 237-242, 245-249, 253-259, 262-263, 266-268, 272-273, 284-292, 294, 296-297, 299-304, 306-307, 311
    definition of, 3-5, 7, 22, 118, 218
    future of, 13
Organizational behavior, 36, 48, 80, 123, 125-126, 153, 265, 299, 301, 307, 311
    focus of, 265
Organizational change, 127, 287-288, 299, 303
Organizational commitment, 77
Organizational culture, 5, 11-12, 25, 30-32, 36, 38, 44-45, 47, 84, 186, 196-197, 200, 234, 245, 255, 285, 291, 294, 298, 302-304
    learning, 291, 298, 303
    strong, 32, 36, 38, 84, 245, 255, 298
Organizational politics, 85, 280
Organizational processes, 36, 46, 115, 287
Organizational structure, 111, 194, 196, 203, 245, 253
Organizations, 2-4, 7-11, 14-22, 25, 29, 31-32, 34-44, 46-48, 51, 65-67, 75, 81, 88, 104-106, 110, 114-117, 119-122, 127, 135, 138, 140, 143-145, 147, 154-157, 160, 166-167, 171, 182-186, 190, 192-194, 196-198, 200-206, 208, 212, 217-219, 222-224, 227-228, 231-235, 237-242, 246, 249, 253-254, 258, 261-264, 266, 268, 271, 283-292, 294-296, 299-303, 311
Orientation, 8, 33-35, 37-39, 48, 61, 73, 81, 87, 114, 147, 150, 226, 256, 286
    future, 34, 37, 286
    humane, 37, 256
    performance, 8, 34-35, 37-38, 48, 87, 286
Other not-for-profit organizations, 17
outlines, 64, 262
Output, 268
Outsourcing, 81
overhead, 230
Ownership, 184, 256, 301

P
PACE, 10, 17, 158, 282, 283, 286, 288
Pakistan, 239
Parmalat case, 195
participative management, 77, 186, 251-282
Partnership, 224
Part-time workers, 178
Paternalistic, 38, 187
Path-goal theory, 3, 67, 77-78, 87-88, 115
Peer pressure, 302
percentages, 46
Perception, 43, 83, 110, 124, 133, 160-161, 202, 285-286, 292, 297, 303, 310
Performance, 3-4, 8, 10, 12, 14-15, 21, 31-32, 34-38, 48, 67, 70, 72, 78, 80, 82-84, 86-88, 96-98, 100, 109-111, 116-117, 119, 127-128, 142, 151, 153-155, 157, 159-160, 163-164, 170,

185, 189, 191, 197, 199-201, 203-206, 213-214, 218-219, 221, 223, 231, 236-237, 242-243, 246, 248, 254, 257-260, 262-263, 265-266, 268-269, 273, 281-282, 284-286, 289-290, 295, 297, 311
    firm performance, 14, 221
Performance evaluation, 48
Performance expectations, 100, 109, 204, 213, 265
Performance measures, 200, 219, 286
Performance orientation, 37-38
Perils, 282
Personal relationship, 82, 84, 118
Personality, 11, 21, 53, 65-67, 81, 84, 106, 114, 119, 137-141, 153-156, 159, 161-165, 174, 196, 219, 223, 225, 261, 266, 309
    cultural differences in, 137
Personality traits, 53, 66, 119, 137-141, 153, 155, 159, 163, 165, 196, 225
Person-organization fit, 307, 311
Persuasion, 3, 114, 189, 199, 211
    defined, 3
    formal, 3
    leadership and, 3
    personal, 114, 189, 211
Philanthropy, 239
Philippines, 37-38
PHP, 79, 121, 179, 249, 311
Physical environment, 139
PILOTs, 256
Place, 13, 29, 38, 45, 47-48, 51, 54, 64, 73, 81, 83-84, 102, 106, 115, 126, 144, 149, 176, 186, 194, 197, 200, 221, 235, 248, 254, 269, 281, 283, 287-288, 290, 294, 298-299, 310
plagiarism, 5
Plans, 8, 27, 43, 52, 153, 179, 192, 254, 269, 304
    business, 8, 27, 52, 179, 192, 254
Poland, 37
Policies, 9, 20, 31, 39, 47, 84, 187, 203, 205, 288
    limited, 187, 205
politeness, 51
Political systems, 51, 185
Politics, 5, 85, 187, 239, 280, 285
    in China, 239
Poor countries, 193
Population, 19-20, 45, 51, 143
Portugal, 285-286
positive approach, 134, 301-302
posture, 32
Poverty, 240-241
Power, 5, 7, 9, 12-16, 18, 31, 33-34, 36-38, 40-41, 48, 51, 65, 69-73, 80, 85, 88, 96, 98, 106-107, 109-111, 113-114, 121, 142-143, 145, 147, 149, 154-155, 161-165, 172, 176, 181-215, 219, 221-224, 232-233, 235-238, 240-242, 247-248, 256-258, 261, 263-264, 281, 291, 293, 296, 311
Power distance, 33-34, 37-38, 48, 145, 147, 161, 183, 186-187, 232, 256-257
presentations, 124
Price, 7, 14, 79, 119, 203, 264
    economic factors, 14
Prices, 4, 27, 91, 142, 159, 218-219, 281, 288
    controls on, 288
Principal, 4, 15, 178, 207, 237, 243
Principle-Centered Leadership, 121
Principles, 17-18, 27, 64, 74, 86, 91, 133, 139, 147, 194, 238-240, 252, 257-258, 283, 296
Principles of management, 257
privacy, 147, 192
Private sector, 18, 194
Probability, 75-76
problem solving, 78, 152
Problem-solving skills, 152
Product development, 228
Product or service, 97, 191
Production, 17, 90, 192, 202, 224, 258, 263-264, 268, 284
Productivity, 77, 90, 115-116, 178, 201, 203, 218-219, 311
    labor, 201
Products, 5, 18, 81, 136, 143, 184, 191, 204, 206, 219, 223, 230, 235, 248, 254, 281-282, 283-284, 287-288, 290-291, 298
professionalism, 80
Professionals, 35-36, 83
Profit, 17, 27-28, 77, 101, 155, 193, 200-201, 204, 236, 238, 240, 254, 262, 282
Profit center, 262
Profits, 79, 120, 204, 231

Promotion, 4, 98, 162, 165, 201, 235, 246, 256, 272, 282, 291
prompting, 288
Property, 56, 175
proposals, 194
Protection, 116, 232
Psychology, 123, 125-126, 150, 153, 172, 174, 196, 309
Public relations, 92, 164, 273
Publicity, 27, 185
Purchasing, 91, 310
purpose, 9, 122, 143, 164, 207, 238, 263, 270, 281
    general, 143, 263

Q
Quality, 5, 11, 18, 46, 66, 70, 74-77, 79, 82-84, 87-88, 90-92, 94, 157, 159, 178, 184, 202, 204, 206, 218-219, 255-256, 262-263, 290
Quotas, 46

R
Race, 19, 31, 39, 46, 135, 138-139, 143, 228
Rates, 254
Rating, 14, 68, 96-99, 128-129, 133-134, 201, 210, 245, 247, 308
Rational decision making, 151
Rational persuasion, 189, 211
Rationalization, 269
Reach, 7, 45, 60, 77, 134, 143, 152, 161, 190, 203, 263-264, 270, 282, 298
Readiness, 213, 288
Recession, 146, 195, 291
recommendations, 73, 84, 120, 188, 192, 268
    focusing on, 73
Reconciliation, 72
Records, 195, 243
Recruiting, 120, 192, 255
Recruitment, 241
Reform, 108
Regulation, 149, 170-171
Regulations, 48, 222
    global, 48
Relationships, 7, 23, 32-33, 36, 58, 68-69, 71, 77, 79, 82-85, 105, 115, 117, 120, 122, 124-125, 134, 144-145, 149, 152, 162-164, 171, 190, 192, 196, 210, 232, 241-242, 257, 265, 267, 281
    preferences, 242
Religion, 31, 39, 138, 143
Repetition, 130-132, 287
reports, 45, 143, 161, 192-193, 249
    online, 249
research, 4, 8, 10-12, 14-16, 21, 32, 35-37, 39, 41-44, 47, 64-69, 72, 74, 77-78, 81-84, 86, 88, 105, 110, 112, 115-116, 119-124, 126, 135, 137-138, 141, 143-150, 152-153, 155-156, 159, 161-166, 183, 185-187, 189, 191, 195-196, 200, 202, 205, 218-219, 221, 224-226, 231-233, 237, 241-242, 254-256, 258, 262, 264, 266, 296, 300
    planning, 10, 43, 81, 163, 254, 258
    primary, 4, 11, 36, 39, 41, 44, 66-67, 69, 84, 88, 116, 119, 121, 145, 159, 218-219, 264
    secondary, 39, 84, 120
Research and development, 135, 226
Resources, 10, 17, 35, 37, 43, 47, 52, 68, 70, 72, 77-78, 85-87, 105, 107, 115-116, 161, 166, 178-179, 187, 190, 192-194, 197-198, 203, 206, 210, 212-213, 220, 234-235, 239-243, 246, 255, 257, 259-260, 264, 267, 272, 280, 284, 289-290, 302-303, 306
Responsibility, 12, 16-17, 21, 35-36, 51, 69, 83, 183, 186, 203, 205, 210, 214, 219, 230, 237-238, 242, 256, 258-260, 263, 265-266, 282, 283, 294, 302
Restricted, 44, 255
Restrictions, 255-256
Retail stores, 6
Retailers, 135, 204
Retailing, 6, 282
Retention, 46, 241, 262
Retirement, 142, 190, 241
Return on investment, 219
Reuters, 215
Revenue, 192, 224, 238
Revenues, 28, 101
revision, 174
Reward power, 187-188, 207, 212

Reward systems, 22, 234-235, 288
    organizational culture and, 234
Rewards, 8, 12, 80, 98, 104, 111, 116, 119, 144,
    187-188, 197, 203, 206-207, 213, 235,
    241-242, 257, 265, 277, 292, 302
Risk, 13, 34, 89, 112-113, 116, 156, 225-226, 228-230,
    233, 241, 245, 247, 269, 285, 290, 293, 297
    business, 89, 228, 230, 233, 241, 285, 293, 297
    clean, 116
    market, 226
    personal, 113, 226
    political, 112, 285
    strategic, 225-226, 228, 230, 233, 241, 245, 247,
        290
    tolerance for, 34, 226, 230
Risk taking, 13, 112-113, 226, 245
Risks, 8, 122, 151-152, 155, 170, 200, 203, 214, 226,
    245, 284, 298-299
Risk-taking, 116, 297
Role, 2-3, 9, 11-12, 15, 17-18, 22, 24-26, 28, 29,
    34-36, 42-43, 46-49, 51-52, 58, 61, 65-66,
    69, 74, 77-78, 82-84, 86, 104-109, 111-112,
    114-115, 117, 126-128, 134-135, 137-139,
    141, 143, 149-150, 152-153, 155, 160, 163,
    165, 167, 182, 185, 189, 193, 195, 197, 199,
    202-203, 217-225, 227-228, 234-235,
    240-243, 246, 252, 256, 263-264, 266-273,
    284, 287-288, 291-292, 294-297, 301-304,
    311
    in groups, 3, 22, 24-25, 270
    interpersonal, 3, 29, 46, 149, 152, 155, 165, 264
    managerial, 15, 22, 43, 155, 193, 221, 227, 246,
        263
Russia, 37-38

S

Salaries, 40, 183, 199, 201, 206, 236-237, 241-242
Salary, 40, 80, 108-109, 147, 185-186, 201, 236,
    281-282, 296
Sales, 11-12, 60, 79, 135-136, 154, 178, 219, 248,
    254, 258, 273, 281, 291, 294, 305, 310
Sales force, 135, 310
    high-pressure sales, 310
    training, 135
Salespeople, 6, 78-79
    Motivation, 78
    Outside, 6
SAP, 125
Saudi Arabia, 32, 49
Saving, 159, 232
Scandinavia, 33
Schema, 21
scope, 6, 218-219
Securities, 199
Security, 7, 142, 285, 292
Selection, 14, 81, 85, 164-166, 194, 203-204, 227,
    234-235, 241-242, 246, 303
Self-actualization, 123, 125
Self-concept, 115
Self-efficacy, 110, 125, 202
Self-esteem, 68, 70, 72, 110, 123-124, 162, 177
Self-interest, 127
Self-managed teams, 81, 259, 263, 272
Self-monitoring, 159-160, 165, 174
Self-promotion, 162
Self-reliance, 145-146
Sellers, 40, 61, 108, 135-136, 157, 233, 248-249
Sensitivity, 60, 183
sentences, 173
SEP, 204, 239
September 11, 2001, 135
Servant leadership, 121
Services, 5, 18, 142, 206, 214, 219, 230, 238, 254,
    257, 283, 285, 288, 290-291, 294
Sexual harassment, 43-44, 48, 54-56, 163, 195
Sexual orientation, 39, 61
Shared values, 9, 114
Shareholder, 85-86
Shareholders, 224, 242, 297
Silence, 196-197, 239
SIMPLE, 2, 8, 14, 27, 46, 61, 79, 87, 106, 108-109,
    115, 119, 141, 185, 198, 201, 219, 234, 248,
    258, 295, 302, 309
Singapore, 19, 29, 36-37, 119, 147
SIR, 120-121
Six Sigma, 287, 301
Size, 14, 214, 222-223, 237, 270, 301
Skills, 3, 7-8, 17, 19, 21, 43, 46-49, 52, 61, 66, 71,
    83-84, 86, 107-108, 111, 114, 118, 120, 130,

138-141, 147-153, 155, 160-161, 164,
    170-171, 188, 190, 211, 231-232, 241, 243,
    258-260, 264, 266-268, 273, 279-280, 284,
    288-289, 294, 296-297, 299-301, 308
Small business, 142-143
Small business owners, 142-143
Social class, 84, 143
Social entrepreneurs, 120
Social factors, 45
Social networking, 285
social networks, 83
Social norms, 37, 139
Social responsibility, 12, 219
Societies, 7, 154
Society, 51-52, 105, 172, 207, 238
software, 79, 85, 246, 257
South Africa, 119
South Korea, 36-37
Soviet Union, 18
Spain, 37
Span of control, 13, 167, 220
Specialization, 13, 167
speeches, 131-132
Stakeholders, 14, 17, 115, 135, 183, 194-195, 224,
    240, 281, 284, 290-291, 297
Stamina, 141
Standardization, 80, 301
Status, 9, 11-12, 32-33, 35-36, 39, 45, 82, 110, 145,
    171, 190, 194, 212, 225, 227-228, 232,
    236-238, 287, 291, 294-296
    culture and, 11, 35, 45, 227, 291
Status quo, 9, 171, 194, 225, 227-228, 287, 291,
    295-296
Status symbols, 11, 145, 190, 212
Stereotyping, 269
Stock, 4, 14, 108, 142, 159, 218-219, 236, 254,
    281-282, 288
Stockholders, 4, 159, 162, 219
Stories, 130-132, 176, 179, 214, 294-295
storytelling, 294
Strategic issues, 260
Strategic management, 220-221, 227, 243
Strategic planning, 10, 81
Strategies, 9, 21, 31, 45, 134-135, 156-157, 165, 178,
    183, 200, 219, 221, 223, 226, 228, 230, 233,
    266, 271-272, 275, 286, 291, 293, 296
    competitive, 31, 157
    corporate, 21, 135, 157, 178, 219, 228, 230
    functional, 293
Strategy, 12-15, 21, 27-28, 69, 81, 135, 156-157, 163,
    193, 204, 218, 220-221, 223, 226-227,
    230-231, 233-234, 241-243, 245
    combination, 163, 241
    defined, 220
    focus, 21, 27, 69, 81, 157, 218, 226-227, 230, 233,
        241, 243
    global, 21, 69, 135, 231
    push, 81, 230-231
    retrenchment, 13
Stress, 82-83, 155-156, 161, 178, 237, 258, 286, 291,
    304
    environmental, 237
Students, 4, 12, 15, 41, 45, 123, 154, 163, 192, 232,
    243, 296-297
Subgroups, 245
Success, 5-6, 14-16, 21, 31, 42-44, 48, 60-61, 67, 72,
    77, 79, 102, 107, 114, 117, 122-123, 136,
    146-148, 150-151, 154-155, 157-158, 162,
    164, 170, 178-179, 183-184, 188, 199, 204,
    206, 214, 219, 223-227, 230, 243, 246,
    248-249, 252, 254-258, 261-265, 268,
    271-272, 281-282, 284-285, 290, 295-296,
    299, 302, 306, 310
Sudan, 112, 146
Supermarkets, 235
Supply, 241
Support, 8-9, 14, 16-17, 22, 43-44, 47, 67, 69-70, 72,
    75, 77-82, 92, 96, 108, 111, 115, 118, 122,
    125, 130, 134, 137, 143, 160-161, 185, 187,
    211, 224-225, 232, 234, 238-239, 253, 259,
    263-266, 270-271, 285, 287, 289-293, 295,
    299, 301-304
surveys, 21, 33, 41, 44, 142, 144, 165, 204, 256, 284,
    286
Sustainability, 61, 284, 297
Sweden, 19, 29, 34-35, 37, 119, 145, 147, 257, 285
Switzerland, 33
Synergy, 262-263, 271, 300
system, 12, 38, 51, 91, 138, 144-146, 153, 165, 196,

204, 223, 234, 246, 262, 299-300, 304, 311
Systems approach, 149

T

Taiwan, 37
taxonomy, 153
Team building, 152, 271, 297
teams, 12, 16-17, 21, 36, 81, 83, 85-86, 113, 149, 157,
    159, 171, 182, 185-186, 190-192, 201-202,
    206, 219, 230, 234, 241, 251-282, 289-290,
    300, 305, 310
    disadvantages of, 272
    effective, 16-17, 81, 149, 157, 159, 182, 186, 190,
        192, 201-202, 219, 241, 252, 257,
        259-260, 264-265, 267, 270-272, 280,
        282
    evolution of, 262, 272
    roles in, 266
    types of, 83, 149, 159, 185, 252, 257, 289, 310
Teamwork, 17, 27, 80, 151, 254, 262, 294
Technical skills, 150, 152, 264
Technological advances, 284
Technology, 4, 35, 56, 81, 122, 136, 145, 192,
    220-222, 229-230, 234, 236, 243, 246, 254,
    257, 261-262, 265, 283-285, 288, 290, 304,
    310
    culture and, 35, 136, 230, 234, 285, 288
    information technology, 81, 192, 220, 246
Telecommuting, 81, 301
templates, 311
Tenure, 85, 101, 178, 236, 243, 272
Territory, 91, 110
Thailand, 34, 37-38, 147, 285
The New Yorker, 282
Theory X, 252-253
Theory Y, 252
Threats, 157, 212, 243
three-step process, 303
Time management, 102
Timing, 198, 292
    of change, 292
tone, 12, 32, 112, 136, 225
    controlling, 12
Top managers, 13, 193-194, 221-224, 234-235, 237
Tourism, 121
Trade, 146, 222, 263, 285
Trade barriers, 222
Trade secrets, 263
Training, 4, 6, 8, 12, 17, 20-23, 27, 35, 39, 47-48, 66,
    69, 73-74, 78, 80-81, 87, 97, 101-102, 116,
    120, 127, 135, 140-141, 147, 154, 184, 194,
    200-201, 203-204, 234, 248-249, 255,
    259-260, 264, 267, 271-272, 279, 285, 288,
    290, 292, 300, 304, 306, 311
    for leaders, 12, 17, 120, 200, 204, 259, 267
    for teams, 300
    methods for, 292
Training programs, 73
Transactions, 52, 117, 195, 214
Transfers, 47, 235
Transformational leaders, 119, 126-127, 287
Transparency, 18, 122, 124, 133, 142, 146-147, 201
Transparency International, 146-147
Trends, 19-20, 40, 146, 227-228, 284
TRIPS, 120
Trust, 27, 33, 51, 67, 82-85, 100, 117, 142, 150, 164,
    185, 193, 201-202, 207, 240-242, 255,
    262-264, 266, 269-273, 294-295, 308
Trusts, 175
Turnover, 6, 79, 101, 143, 178, 194, 218-219, 254,
    288, 310-311
Type A personality, 156, 159

U

Uncertainty avoidance, 33-34, 37, 48
Unions, 198, 290
United Kingdom, 281
United States, 5, 14, 18-21, 27, 30, 32-35, 37-38,
    40-41, 45, 47, 49-50, 60, 66-67, 81, 84-85,
    109, 111-112, 121, 126, 131, 139, 143-147,
    150, 153-154, 163, 178, 183-187, 191, 193,
    195, 205-206, 223-224, 230-232, 236-239,
    254, 257, 268-269, 284-285
Universities, 45, 92, 143, 191, 232, 238
U.S., 4-5, 12, 16-17, 19-20, 32, 34, 36-37, 41, 44, 47,
    52, 60, 72, 81, 86, 106, 108, 111, 121, 136,
    142-143, 147, 159, 161-162, 164, 171,
    183-184, 186-187, 190, 195, 198, 214, 223,

232, 236-237, 248-249, 261-262, 281,
285-286, 310
U.S., 4-5, 12, 16-17, 19-20, 32, 34, 36-37, 41, 44, 52,
60, 72, 81, 86, 106, 108, 111, 121, 136,
142-143, 147, 159, 161-162, 164, 171,
183-184, 186-187, 190, 195, 198, 214, 223,
232, 236-237, 248-249, 261-262, 281,
285-286, 310
U.S. Census Bureau, 19-20
U.S. economy, 187
U.S. Federal Reserve, 164, 187
U.S. Postal Service, 223
Utility, 222
Utility companies, 222

V
Validity, 69, 72, 119, 141, 164, 166, 296
Value, 30, 34, 38, 46-47, 51, 72, 77-80, 104, 112,
121-122, 125-127, 133, 139, 142, 144-147,
151, 165, 169, 186, 198, 200, 214, 225, 232,
249, 257, 268, 288, 295
building, 46, 79, 125, 214
defined, 30, 34, 77
Variability, 287
Variables, 87, 118-119, 140, 153, 221, 266
Venezuela, 5, 37
Vietnam, 32, 108, 146
Violence, 135, 214
Vision, 3, 9-10, 15, 17, 22, 27, 69, 83, 85, 105-108,
110-114, 117-118, 120-121, 124-125,
127-128, 130, 135, 171, 184, 189, 221,
232-235, 263-264, 283, 287-288, 294-296,
299-303
Visionary leadership, 3, 10, 67, 294-296, 298, 304,
308
voice mail, 234
Volume, 121
Volumes, 171

W
Wages, 6
Wall Street Journal, 8, 21, 179, 215, 249, 282, 297
War, 32, 66, 86, 108, 145-146, 239
Warrants, 195
Water, 61, 283
Weaknesses, 13, 73, 124-125, 133, 138, 170
Wealth, 35, 51, 161, 239
Web, 6, 11, 27, 39, 79, 107, 161, 194, 233, 262, 285,
304
Web site, 6, 79, 107
Web sites, 161
wireless access, 310
Women, 10, 19-20, 31, 39-49, 52, 58, 60-61, 119,
135-136, 143-144, 160, 166, 179, 232-233,
239-240, 248, 261, 284, 310
Won, 5, 31, 52, 89, 110, 175, 193, 204, 222, 246, 262
Work, 2, 6, 9-11, 16, 19-20, 23, 26-27, 31-32, 35-36,
41-43, 45-47, 51-52, 54-56, 58-61, 66-67,
69, 72-73, 77-79, 81-85, 89, 92, 95-96,
100-102, 107, 109, 116, 121-123, 126-128,
133-134, 136, 138, 142, 145-148, 150-151,
153-159, 161, 163, 165-166, 168-169,
171-173, 175, 178-179, 184, 186, 189, 191,
193, 195-196, 198-199, 201-204, 207, 210,
214, 224, 226, 230, 235-236, 239, 242, 246,
254, 257-258, 260, 262-267, 270-271, 273,
276, 279, 281-282, 284, 286, 290-293,
295-297, 299-300, 302-303, 305, 310-311
attitudes toward, 147
Work schedules, 168
Work teams, 81
Workers, 56, 80, 145, 147, 157, 159, 178, 185-187,
265, 282, 290
workforce, 19-20, 45, 48, 79, 120-121, 179, 288, 311
diversity in, 19, 45
women in, 19, 45, 48
Workforce diversity, 20
managing, 20
Workforce Management, 179, 311
Work-life balance, 6, 20, 32, 311
workplace, 20, 41, 43, 47, 55, 58, 61, 121, 178, 203,
281, 310
changing, 47, 203, 281, 310
Workplace discrimination, 43
Workplace spirituality, 121
World, 4-7, 9, 18-19, 21-22, 30, 32-33, 40, 46-48, 51,
59-60, 64, 66, 69, 74, 79, 101, 106, 108,
120, 122-123, 131, 135-136, 142-147, 150,

154, 162, 172, 176, 183-187, 195-196, 207,
219, 231, 236, 238-240, 248-249, 257, 261,
266, 272, 281, 283-284, 297, 301
world economies, 187
World War, 66
WWW, 6, 19-20, 27-28, 45, 61, 79, 121, 131, 136,
158, 179, 204, 215, 239, 249, 261, 282, 297,
311

X
Xers, 20, 145-146
Generation Xers, 20, 145-146

Y
YouTube, 131